To my children, Adriana and Alexander,
who make the world a better place.

`mapt.io`

Mapt is an online digital library that gives you full access to over 5,000 books and videos, as well as industry leading tools to help you plan your personal development and advance your career. For more information, please visit our website.

Why subscribe?

- Spend less time learning and more time coding with practical eBooks and Videos from over 4,000 industry professionals

- Improve your learning with Skill Plans built especially for you

- Get a free eBook or video every month

- Mapt is fully searchable

- Copy and paste, print, and bookmark content

PacktPub.com

Did you know that Packt offers eBook versions of every book published, with PDF and ePub files available? You can upgrade to the eBook version at `www.PacktPub.com` and as a print book customer, you are entitled to a discount on the eBook copy. Get in touch with us at `service@packtpub.com` for more details.

At `www.PacktPub.com`, you can also read a collection of free technical articles, sign up for a range of free newsletters, and receive exclusive discounts and offers on Packt books and eBooks.

Contributors

About the author

Joseph Ingeno is a software architect who oversees a number of enterprise software applications. During his career, he has designed and developed software for a variety of different industries. He has extensive experience working on web, mobile, and desktop applications using different technologies and frameworks.

Joseph graduated from the University of Miami a with Master of Science and a Bachelor of Business Administration degrees in Computer Information Systems, and followed that with a Master of Software Engineering degree from Brandeis University.

He holds several certifications, including the Microsoft Certified Solutions Developer and the Professional Software Engineering Master Certification from the IEEE Computer Society.

A special thanks to my wife, Sally, and the rest of my family for their understanding and patience while I devoted the time necessary to write this book.

I would like to thank Priyanka Sawant, Ketan Kamble, Ruvika Rao, Gaurav Aroraa, Anand Pillai, Denim Pinto, and everyone at Packt Publishing who provided input and support during the writing of this book.

About the reviewers

Gaurav Aroraa has done an MPhil in computer science. He is a Microsoft MVP, a lifetime member of **Computer Society of India (CSI)**, an advisory member of IndiaMentor, certified as a Scrum trainer/coach, XEN for ITIL-F, and APMG for PRINCE-F and PRINCE-P. He is an open source developer, a contributor to TechNet Wiki, and the founder of Ovatic Systems Private Limited. In his career of over 20 years, he has mentored thousands of students and industry professionals. Apart from that, he's written over 100 white papers for research scholars and various universities across the globe.

> *I'd like to thank my wife, Shuby Arora, and my angel daughter, Aarchi Arora, as well as the team at PACKT.*

Anand B Pillai is a technophile by profession with 20 years' of experience in software development, design, and architecture. Over the years, he has worked with numerous companies in fields ranging from security, search engines, large-scale web portals and big data. He is a founder of the Bangalore Python Users' Group and is the author of *Software Architecture with Python* (PacktPub, April 2017). Anand is currently a VP of an engineering at the early-stage legal technology startup, Klarity Law. He happily resides with his family in Bangalore, India.

Packt is searching for authors like you

If you're interested in becoming an author for Packt, please visit `authors.packtpub.com` and apply today. We have worked with thousands of developers and tech professionals, just like you, to help them share their insight with the global tech community. You can make a general application, apply for a specific hot topic that we are recruiting an author for, or submit your own idea.

Table of Contents

Preface

Modern software systems are complex, and the software architect role is a challenging one. This book was written to help software developers transition into the role of a software architect, and to assist existing software architects to be successful in their role. It helps readers understand how being a software architect is different than being a developer and what it takes to be an effective software architect.

This comprehensive guide to software architecture begins by explaining what software architecture entails, the responsibilities of the software architect position, and what you will be expected to know. Software architects must have technical and non-technical skills, and they must have both breadth and depth of knowledge.

The book progress to covering non-technical topics such as the importance of understanding your organization's business, working in the context of an organization, and gathering requirements for software systems. It then takes a deep dive into technical topics such as software quality attributes, software architecture design, software development best practices, architecture patterns, how to improve performance, and security considerations.

After reading this book, you should have a familiarity with the many topics related to software architecture and understand how to be a software architect. Technologies and practices may change over time, but the book lays a strong foundation on which you can build a successful career as a software architect.

Who this book is for

This book is aimed at senior developers and software architects who want to learn how to be a successful software architect. Readers should be experienced software development professionals who want to advance in their career and become a software architect. It covers a wide range of topics that will help readers learn what it takes to be effective in the software architect role.

What this book covers

Chapter 1, *The Meaning of Software Architecture*, begins the book by providing a definition of software architecture. The book establishes what makes up a software architecture and the reasons why it is important to a software system. It also details the software architect role, including the responsibilities of software architects and what they are expected to know.

Chapter 2, *Software Architecture in an Organization*, focuses on software architecture in the context of an organization. It covers the different types of software architect roles and software development methodologies that you may encounter. Non-technical topics such as project management, office politics, and risk management are explained. The development of software product lines and the creation of architectural core assets are also covered.

Chapter 3, *Understanding the Domain*, discusses the business aspects of being a software architect. It covers topics such as familiarizing yourself with your organization's business, **domain-driven design (DDD)**, and how to effectively elicit requirements for the software system from stakeholders.

Chapter 4, *Software Quality Attributes*, covers software quality attributes and their importance to a software architecture. Some common software quality attributes are presented, including maintainability, usability, availability, portability, interoperability, and testability.

Chapter 5, *Designing Software Architectures*, concentrates on the important topic of software architecture design. It details what is involved with architecture design and its importance to a software system. The chapter discusses different approaches to architecture design, the drivers for it, and the design principles that can be leveraged during the process.

The chapter presents the use of various systematic approaches to software architecture design, including **attribute-driven design (ADD)**, Microsoft's technique for architecture and design, the **architecture-centric design method (ACDM)**, and the **architecture development method (ADM)**.

Chapter 6, *Software Development Principles and Practices*, describes proven software development principles and practices that can be used to build high-quality software systems. Concepts such as loose coupling and high cohesion are covered, as well as principles such as KISS, DRY, information hiding, YAGNI, and the **Separation of Concerns (SoC)**.

The chapter includes a discussion of the SOLID principles, which include the single responsibility, open/closed, Liskov substitution, interface segregation, and dependency inversion principles. The chapter closes with topics related to helping your team succeed, including unit testing, setting up development environments, pair programming, and reviewing deliverables.

Chapter 7, *Software Architecture Patterns*, discusses one of the most useful software architecture design concepts. Learning the architecture patterns that are available to you and when to properly apply them is a key skill for software architects. The chapter details a number of software architecture patterns, including layered architecture, **event-driven architecture (EDA)**, **Model-View-Controller (MVC)**, **Model-View-Presenter (MVP)**, **Model-View-ViewModel (MVVM)**, **Command Query Responsibility Segregation (CQRS)**, and **Service-Oriented Architecture (SOA)**.

Chapter 8, *Architecting Modern Applications*, explains the software architecture patterns and paradigms that are used with modern applications deployed to the cloud. After describing a monolithic architecture, the chapter details microservices architecture, serverless architecture, and cloud-native applications.

Chapter 9, *Cross-Cutting Concerns*, places its focus on functionality that is used in multiple areas of the system. It explains how to handle cross-cutting concerns in your applications. Topics covered include using **Dependency Injection (DI)**, the decorator pattern, and **aspect-oriented programming (AOP)** to implement cross-cutting concerns. The chapter also provides a look at different cross-cutting concerns, including caching, configuration management, auditing, security, exception management, and logging.

Chapter 10, *Performance Considerations*, takes a close look at performance. It describes the importance of performance and techniques to improve it. Topics such as server-side caching and database performance are discussed. An examination of web application performance is included in the chapter, including coverage of HTTP caching, compression, minimizing and bundling of resources, HTTP/2, **content delivery networks (CDNs)**, optimizing web fonts, and the critical rendering path.

Chapter 11, *Security Considerations*, covers the critical topic of software application security. Security concepts such as the **confidentiality**, **integrity**, and **availability** (**CIA**) triad and threat modeling are presented. The chapter provides readers with various principles and practices for creating software that is secure by design.

Chapter 12, *Documenting and Reviewing Software Architectures*, places its focus on software architecture documentation and reviewing software architectures. It describes the various uses for software architecture documentation and explains how to use UML to document a software architecture. The chapter discusses various software architecture review methods, including the **software architecture analysis method (SAAM)**, **architecture tradeoff analysis method (ATAM)**, **active design review (ADM)**, and **active reviews of intermediate designs (ARID)**.

Chapter 13, *DevOps and Software Architecture*, provides coverage of the culture, practices, tools, and culture of DevOps. The chapter explains key DevOps practices such as **continuous integration (CI)**, **continuous delivery (CD)**, and **continuous deployment**.

Chapter 14, *Architecting Legacy Applications*, provides readers with an understanding of how to work with legacy applications. The widespread use of legacy applications makes this topic important for software architects. The chapter covers refactoring legacy applications and how to migrate them to the cloud. It discusses modernizing build and deployment processes for legacy applications as well as how to integrate with them.

Chapter 15, *The Soft Skills of Software Architects*, is all about the soft skills that software architects should possess to be an effective software architect. After describing what soft skills are, the chapter proceeds to topics such as communication, leadership, negotiation, and working with remote resources.

Chapter 16, *Evolutionary Architecture*, teaches how to design software systems so that they have the ability to adapt to change. It explains that change is inevitable, so software architects should design software architectures that can evolve over time. The chapter explains some of the ways that change can be handled and it introduces the use of fitness functions to ensure that an architecture continues to meet its desired architectural characteristics as it undergoes change.

Chapter 17, *Becoming a Better Software Architect*, stresses to readers that the process of career development is an ongoing one. After becoming a software architect, one must seek to continuously gain new knowledge and improve their skills. The chapter details ways that a software architect can practice self-improvement, including continuous learning, participating in open source projects, writing your own blog, spending time teaching others, trying new technologies, continuing to write code, attending user groups and conferences, taking responsibility for your work, and attending to your general well-being.

To get the most out of this book

Although readers should have experience of software development, no specific prerequisites are required to begin reading this book. All of the information that you need is contained in the various chapters. The book does not require knowledge of any particular programming language, framework, or tool. The code snippets in the book that illustrate various concepts are written in C#, but they are simple enough that prior C# experience is not necessary.

Download the color images

We also provide a PDF file that has color images of the screenshots/diagrams used in this book. You can download it here: https://www.packtpub.com/sites/default/files/downloads/SoftwareArchitectsHandbook_ColorImages.pdf.

Conventions used

There are a number of text conventions used throughout this book.

CodeInText: Indicates code words in text, database table names, folder names, filenames, file extensions, pathnames, dummy URLs, user input, and Twitter handles. Here is an example: "Now we can use that constant in our GetFilePath method."

A block of code is set as follows:

```
public string GetFilePath()
{
    string result = _cache.Get(FilePathCacheKey);

    if (string.IsNullOrEmpty(result))
    {
        _cache.Put(FilePathCacheKey, DetermineFilePath());
        result = _cache.Get(FilePathCacheKey);
    }

    return result;
}
```

When we wish to draw your attention to a particular part of a code block, the relevant lines or items are set in bold:

```
public string GetFilePath()
{
    string result = _cache.Get(FilePathCacheKey);

    if (string.IsNullOrEmpty(result))
    {
        _cache.Put(FilePathCacheKey, DetermineFilePath());
        result = _cache.Get(FilePathCacheKey);
    }

    return result;
}
```

Bold: Indicates a new term, an important word, or words that you see onscreen. For example, words in menus or dialog boxes appear in the text like this. Here is an example: "In a direct dependency graph, at compile-time, **Class A** references **Class B**, which references **Class C**"

Warnings or important notes appear like this.

Tips and tricks appear like this.

Get in touch

Feedback from our readers is always welcome.

General feedback: Email `feedback@packtpub.com` and mention the book title in the subject of your message. If you have questions about any aspect of this book, please email us at `questions@packtpub.com`.

Errata: Although we have taken every care to ensure the accuracy of our content, mistakes do happen. If you have found a mistake in this book, we would be grateful if you would report this to us. Please visit `www.packtpub.com/submit-errata`, selecting your book, clicking on the Errata Submission Form link, and entering the details.

Piracy: If you come across any illegal copies of our works in any form on the Internet, we would be grateful if you would provide us with the location address or website name. Please contact us at copyright@packtpub.com with a link to the material.

If you are interested in becoming an author: If there is a topic that you have expertise in and you are interested in either writing or contributing to a book, please visit authors.packtpub.com.

Reviews

Please leave a review. Once you have read and used this book, why not leave a review on the site that you purchased it from? Potential readers can then see and use your unbiased opinion to make purchase decisions, we at Packt can understand what you think about our products, and our authors can see your feedback on their book. Thank you!

For more information about Packt, please visit packtpub.com.

The Meaning of Software Architecture

1

A comprehensive look at software architecture must first begin with its definition. This chapter provides reasons as to why software architecture plays an important role in a software project, and the benefits of having a good architectural design.

It is also important to understand the stakeholders and team members who are affected by the software architecture of a system. The chapter will go into detail about the software architect's role, what software architects are supposed to know, and whether the role is right for you.

In this chapter, we will cover the following topics:

- What is software architecture?
- Why is software architecture important?
- Who are the consumers of software architectures?
- What is the software architect role?

What is software architecture?

What exactly is software architecture? You probably have your own ideas about what it is, based on your knowledge and experiences. Certainly, there are plenty of definitions out there. If you do an online search or ask various friends and colleagues, you will get varying answers. The definition is somewhat subjective and influenced by the viewpoints and perceptions of the individual who is providing the definition. However, there are some core concepts that are essential to software architecture, and before we delve into deeper topics, establishing a common understanding of what software architecture entails is imperative.

Using the word *architecture* for software originated from similarities with the construction industry. When the term was first used, the Waterfall software development methodology was common and it dictated that large, up-front designs needed to be completed before any code was written. Similar to the architecture of a building, which necessitates a lot of planning before construction takes place, so it was with software as well.

In modern software design, the relationship between the construction and software industries is no longer as close. Software methodologies now focus on developing software applications that are highly adaptable and can be changed easily over time, resulting in less of a need for rigid, upfront planning. However, software architecture still consists of early design decisions that can be difficult to change later.

ISO/IEC/IEEE 42010 standard definition

There is a standard definition for software architecture, which resulted from a joint effort between the **International Organization for Standardization (ISO)** and the **Institute of Electrical and Electronics Engineers (IEEE)**. ISO/IEC/IEEE 42010 systems and software engineering's architecture description is an international standard that defines software architecture as:

> *"Fundamental concepts or properties of a system in its environment embodied in its elements, relationships, and in the principles of its design and evolution."*

The standard makes the following main points:

- A software architecture is a fundamental part of a software system
- A software system is situated in an environment, and its software architecture takes into consideration the environment in which it must operate
- An architecture description documents the architecture and communicates to stakeholders how the architecture meets the system's needs
- Architecture views are created from the architecture description, and each view covers one or more architecture concerns of the stakeholders

What makes up a software architecture?

In the book, *Software Architecture in Practice, 2nd Edition*, a definition of software architecture is given as:

> *"The software architecture of a program or computing system is the structure or structures of the system, which comprise software elements, the externally visible properties of those elements, and the relationships among them."*

A software system contains structures, and this definition notes that a software system is made up of one or more of them. It is the combination of these that forms the overall software architecture. A large software project may have multiple teams working on it, each responsible for a particular structure.

Software architecture is an abstraction

Software architecture is an abstraction of a software system. The structures of a software system consist of its elements. Software architecture concerns itself with defining and detailing the structures, their elements, and the relationships of those elements with each other.

Software architecture focuses on the public aspects of the elements, and how they interact with each other. For elements, this may take the form of their public interfaces. It does not deal with the private implementation details of the elements. While the behavior of the elements does not have to be exhaustively documented, care should be taken in understanding how elements have to be designed and written so that they can properly interact with each other.

Software architecture is about the important stuff

Computer scientist Ralph Johnson, who co-authored *Design Patterns: Elements of Reusable Object-Oriented Software*, once said:

> *"Architecture is about the important stuff. Whatever that is."*

Software projects vary, and the amount of design effort, time, focus, and documentation devoted to particular aspects of a software architecture differ. Ultimately, software architecture consists of important design decisions that shape the system. It is made up of the structures and components that are significant to the quality, longevity, and usefulness of the system.

Software architecture consists of some of the earliest decisions that are made for a software system and some of the hardest to change. In modern software development, the architecture should anticipate change, and be designed in such a way as to maximize the potential of adapting and evolving to this change. We will be discussing evolutionary architecture in Chapter 16, *Evolutionary Architecture*.

Why is software architecture important?

Why should we care about software architecture anyway? Sometimes a developer just wants to jump right in and start coding.

Software architecture is the foundation of a software system. Like other types of engineering, the foundation has a profound effect on the quality of what is built on top of it. As such, it holds a great deal of importance in terms of the successful development, and eventual maintenance, of the system.

Software architecture is a series of decisions. Some of the earliest decisions come from designing the architecture, and these carry a high degree of importance because they affect the decisions that come after it.

Another reason software architecture is important is because all software systems have an architecture. Even if it comprised just one structure with one element, there is an architecture. There are software systems that don't have a formal design and others that don't formally document the architecture, but even these systems still have an architecture.

The greater the size and complexity of a software system, the more you will need a well thought-out architecture in order to succeed. Software architecture provides a number of benefits when done properly, which greatly increase the chances that the software system will succeed.

A proper foundation laid down by a software system's architecture yields a number of benefits. Let's take a deeper look at those benefits.

Defining a solution to meet requirements

Software strives to meet all functional, non-functional, technical, and operational requirements. Working closely with stakeholders, such as domain experts, business analysts, product owners, and end users, allows requirements to be identified and understood. A software architecture defines a solution that will meet those requirements.

Software architecture is the foundation for software, so software systems that lack a solid architecture make it more difficult to meet all of the requirements. Poor architectures will lead to implementations that fail to meet the measurable goals of quality attributes, and they are typically difficult to maintain, deploy, and manage.

Enabling and inhibiting quality attributes

Software architecture either enables quality attributes or inhibits them. Quality attributes are measurable and testable properties of a system. Some examples of quality attributes include maintainability, interoperability, security, and performance.

They are *non-functional* requirements of a software system as opposed to its features, which are *functional* requirements. Quality attributes and how they satisfy the stakeholders of the system are critical, and software architecture plays a large role in ensuring that quality attributes are satisfied. The design of a software architecture can be made to focus on certain quality attributes at the cost of others. Quality attributes may be in conflict with each other. A software architecture, when designed properly, sets out to achieve agreed-upon and validated requirements related to quality attributes.

Giving you the ability to predict software system qualities

When you look at a software architecture and its documentation, you can predict the software system's qualities. Making architecture decisions based on quality attributes makes it easier to fulfill those requirements. You want to start thinking about quality attributes as early as possible in the software development process as it is much more difficult (and costly) to make changes to fulfill them later. By thinking about them up front, and using modeling and analysis techniques, we can ensure that the software architecture can meet its non-functional requirements.

If you are not able to predict if a software system will fulfill quality attributes until it is implemented and tested, then costly and time-consuming rework may be necessary. A software architecture allows you to predict a software system's qualities and avoid costly rework.

Easing communication among stakeholders

Software architecture and its documentation allow you to communicate the software architecture and explain it to others. It can form the basis for discussions related to aspects of the project, such as costs and duration. We will discuss this topic further when we go into detail about software architecture in an organization.

A software architecture is abstract enough that many stakeholders, with little or no guidance, should be able to reason about the software system. Although different stakeholders will have different concerns and priorities in terms of what they want to know about the architecture, providing a common language and architecture design artifacts allows them to understand the software system. It is particularly useful for large, complex systems that would otherwise be too difficult to fully understand. As requirements and other early decisions are made for the software system, a formal software architecture plays an important role and facilitates negotiations and discussions.

Managing change

Changes to a software system are inevitable. The catalyst for change can come from the market, new requirements, changes to business processes, technology advances, and bug fixes, among other things.

Some view software architecture as inhibiting agility and would prefer to just let it emerge without up-front design. However, a good software architecture helps with both implementing and managing changes. Changes fall into one of the following categories:

- Limited to a single element
- Involve a combination of elements, but do not require any architectural changes
- Require an architectural change

Software architecture allows you to manage and understand what it would take to make a particular change. Furthermore, a good architecture reduces complexity so that most of the changes that need to be made can be limited to a single element or just a few elements, without having to make architectural changes.

Providing a reusable model

An established architecture might be used again within an organization for other products in a product line, particularly if the products have similar requirements. We'll discuss an organization's product lines, reuse of architecture, and the benefits in the next chapter. For now, simply recognize that, once a software architecture is completed, documented, understood, and used in a successful implementation, it can be reused.

When code is reused, resources, such as time and money, are saved. More importantly, the quality of software that takes advantage of reuse is increased because the code has already been tested and proven. The increase in quality alone translates to savings in resources.

When a software architecture is reused, it is not just code that is reused. All of the early decisions that shaped the original architecture are leveraged as well. The thought and effort that went into the requirements necessary for the architecture, particularly non-functional requirements, may be applicable to other products. The effort that went into making those decisions does not necessarily have to be repeated. The experience gained from the original architectural design can be leveraged for other software systems.

When a software architecture is reused, it is the architecture itself, and not just the software product, that becomes an asset to the organization.

Imposing implementation constraints

A software architecture introduces constraints on implementation and restricts design choices. This reduces the complexity of a software system and prevents developers from making incorrect decisions.

If the implementation of an element conforms to the designed architecture, then it is abiding by the design decisions made by the architecture. Software architecture, when done properly, enables developers to accomplish their objectives and prevents them from implementing things incorrectly.

Improving cost and effort estimates

Project managers ask questions such as: When is it going to be done? How long is it going to take? How much is it going to cost? They need this type of information to properly plan resources and monitor progress. One of the many duties of a software architect is to assist project management by providing this type of information and assisting with determining the necessary tasks and estimates for those tasks.

The design of the software architecture itself affects what types of task will be necessary for implementation. As a result, work-breakdown of tasks is dependent on the software architecture and the software architect can assist project management with the creation of the tasks.

Two major approaches to project management estimation are as follows:

- **Top-down approach**: This starts with the final deliverables and goals and breaks them down into smaller packages of work
- **Bottom-up approach**: This starts with specific tasks first, and groups them together into packages of work

For some projects, a project manager may take a more top-down approach, while developers who are going to be working on specific tasks may take a bottom-up perspective. With the experience and knowledge that most software architects possess, they can potentially assist with either approach. A combination of these approaches, where tasks are looked at from both viewpoints, can lead to the best estimates.

It can be helpful when project managers, the software architect, and the developers work together to provide estimates. The most accurate estimates can be obtained by mutual discussions between team members until a consensus is achieved. Sometimes during the consensus building, someone on the team will provide an insight that others had not previously considered, allowing everyone to rethink their position and possibly revise their estimates.

A software system with accurate requirements that are reflected in the software architecture can avoid costly rework that would be necessary if key requirements were missed. In addition, a well-thought-out architecture reduces complexity, allowing it to be easily reasoned about and understood. Reduced complexity can result in more accurate cost and effort estimates.

Serves as training for team members

The system's architecture and its documentation serve as training for the developers on the team. By learning the various structures and elements of the system, and how they are supposed to interact, they learn the proper way in which the functionality is to be implemented.

A software development team may experience change, such as having new team members join or existing ones leave. The introduction and orientation of new members to a team often takes time. A well-thought-out architecture can make it easier for developers to transition to the team.

The maintenance phase of a software system can be one of the longest and costliest phases of a software project. Like new team members introduced during development, it is common for different developers to work on the system over time, including those introduced to maintain it. Having a solid architecture available to teach and bring aboard new developers can provide an important advantage.

Software architecture is not a silver bullet

The Mythical Man-Month by Frederick P. Brooks is one of the seminal texts in software project management. It contains various essays on software engineering. Although this book was written some time ago, and some of the references are now outdated, it provides thought-provoking advice about software development that is timeless and still applicable today:

> *"There is no single development, in either technology or management technique, which by itself promises even one order-of-magnitude improvement within a decade in productivity, in reliability, in simplicity."*

Fred Brooks 1986 essay, *No Silver Bullet – Essence and Accident in Software Engineering*, which is included in the twentieth anniversary edition of the book, begins with this quote. It essentially conveys the idea that there is no silver bullet in software development.

Software architecture, as well, is not a silver bullet. Although we have covered a number of reasons why software architecture is important, there is no specific architecture or combination of components that will serve as a silver bullet. It can't be thought of as a magical solution that will solve all problems. As we will learn in more detail later, software architectures are about compromises between different and sometimes conflicting requirements. Each architectural approach has pros and cons that must be weighed and evaluated. No one approach should be viewed as a silver bullet.

Who are the consumers of software architectures?

When we create a software architecture, who is it for? There are a variety of stakeholders in a software system, such as the end users of the system, business analysts, domain experts, quality assurance personnel, managers, those who may integrate with the system, and operations staff members. Each of these stakeholders is affected by the software architecture to some degree. While certain stakeholders will have access to, and be interested in, examining the software architecture and its documentation, others will not.

Some of these stakeholders are indirect consumers of the architecture in that they care about the software, and because the software architecture is the foundation of the system, they become indirect consumers of the architecture. As a software architect, you are serving these types of consumers in addition to the direct consumers. For example, end users are perhaps one of the most important stakeholders and should be a major focus. The software architecture must allow the implementation to satisfy the requirements of the end users.

When we discuss the consumers of a software architecture, we can't omit the developers who work on that software. As a software architect, you need to be thinking about your developers, whose work is directly affected by the software architecture. They are the ones who will be working on the software on a daily basis.

What is the software architect role?

Now that we know what software architecture is, the importance and benefits of it, and have an understanding that there are a variety of stakeholders who are affected by it, let's examine the software architect role. What makes someone a software architect? What does it mean to be a software architect?

Certainly, software systems can be developed without a software architect. You may have worked on a project in which no one was playing the software architect role. In some of those cases, the project may have succeeded despite that, or it may have failed because of it.

When no one is specifically given the software architect title, someone on the team may end up making architectural decisions. Such an individual is sometimes called an **accidental architect**. They haven't been given the title of software architect, but they are performing some of the same duties and making the same types of decision. Occasionally, when there is no software architect, the architectural design results from a collaboration between multiple developers.

The smaller and less complex the software system is, the more you may be able to succeed without a software architect. However, if a project is large in size and/or complexity, you are more likely to need someone to play the formal role of software architect.

Software architects are technical leaders

Software architects are technical leaders of a software project and should be committed to the project no matter what challenges arise. They provide technical guidance to management, customers, and developers. As such, they are often a liaison between technical and non-technical resources.

Although software architects have many responsibilities, foremost among them is being responsible for the technical aspects of software systems. While the software architect collaborates with others, as the technical leader the software architect is ultimately responsible for the software architecture, its design, and the architecture documentation for a software system.

Software architects perform a number of duties

Software architects are required to undertake different types of duties, not all of which are technical. Software architects combine their experience, knowledge, and skills, both technical and non-technical, to fulfill such duties. Software architects will be expected to have a firm grasp of designing software architectures, architecture patterns, and best practices.

Software architects should have the ability to foresee possible issues and design architectures to overcome them. They should be able to mitigate risks and evaluate solutions such that they can select the proper one to resolve a particular problem. While some of the skills and duties of a software architect are similar to what a senior developer might do, it is a very different role. Software architects shoulder a greater amount of responsibility, and there is a larger expectation of what a software architect brings to a project.

Senior developers have a great *depth* of knowledge regarding the technologies that they use on a project. They are highly proficient in the languages, tools, frameworks, and databases that are used in their software systems. While software architects are expected to have this depth of knowledge as well, they must also possess a wide *breadth* of knowledge. They need to be familiar with technologies that are not currently being used in the organization so that they can make informed decisions about the design of the architecture.

Ideally, software architects have the breadth of knowledge to be aware of multiple solutions to a problem and understand the trade-offs between them. It can be just as important for a software architect to understand why a particular solution will *not* work as it is to understand why one will.

Ivory tower software architects

If you find yourself in the role of a software architect, you are going to want to avoid being an **ivory tower architect**. A software architect who is in an *ivory tower* refers to one who, either by how they approach their position or because of how an organization works, is isolated from others.

If a software architect is working from an ivory tower, they may be creating an architecture based on a *perfect-world* environment that really doesn't reflect real scenarios. In addition, they may not be working closely with the developers who will be creating implementations based on the architecture.

The more that a software architect works on their own, isolated from stakeholders and other developers, the more likely they are to be out of touch with the needs of those individuals. As a result, they may be designing software architectures that do not meet the varying needs and requirements of a diverse group of stakeholders.

Software architects should take a more hands-on approach. A software architect's duties should already include involvement in a number of phases in a software life cycle, but being hands-on helps avoid being out of touch. For example, a software architect may do some of the coding with the team in order to stay more involved. Leading by example, such as using your own code to serve as references for others, is one way to take a hands-on approach while also keeping your skills sharpened.

An involved approach will help you keep abreast of what issues and difficulties developers may be facing, and what the architecture may be lacking. Leading from the trenches can be much more effective than leading from an ivory tower, and you are more likely to gain the trust and respect of your teammates. If a software architect is out of touch or misinformed, even if the perception is inaccurate, their effectiveness as a leader will be diminished.

An ivory tower architect might be someone who is viewed as commanding from above. A software architect should use their experience and knowledge to teach others, and not preach. Take opportunities to make your teammates better by teaching, but also look forward to learning from others. Teammates can and will provide valuable and insightful feedback regarding your designs.

An organization should not have processes and/or an organizational hierarchy in place that separate the architect from stakeholders. They should not be separated from the technical implementation because doing so will take the architect away from the technology and skills that made them a good candidate for being a software architect in the first place.

What are software architects expected to know?

Software architects are expected to have skills and knowledge on a variety of topics. This book focuses on many of those topics. They include non-technical duties, such as:

- Providing leadership
- Assisting project management, including cost and effort estimation
- Mentoring team members

- Helping to select team members
- Understanding the business domain
- Participating in gathering and analyzing requirements
- Communicating with a variety of technical and non-technical stakeholders
- Having a vision for future products

Technical topics that software architects should be familiar with include:

- Understanding non-functional requirements and quality attributes
- Being able to effectively design software architectures
- Understanding patterns and best practices for software development
- Having a deep knowledge of software architecture patterns, their pros and cons, and knowing when to choose one over another
- Knowing how to handle cross-cutting concerns
- Ensuring performance and security requirements are met
- Being able to document and review software architectures
- Having an understanding of DevOps and the deployment process
- Knowing how to integrate and work with legacy applications
- Being able to design software architectures that adapt to change and evolve over time

Don't be overwhelmed

If you find yourself in the software architect role for the first time, or if you are joining a team that has been working on an existing software system for some time, it can be natural to feel overwhelmed by all that you do not know. It will take time to wrap your head around everything that you will eventually need to know.

As your experience grows, you'll feel more comfortable when you start on a new project. Just like anything, experience in different situations will make you more comfortable with taking on new challenges. You'll also understand that it will take some time to become acquainted with the business domain, people, processes, technology, details, and intricacies that come with each software system.

Is the software architect role right for you?

If you care about the software that you are working on and all of its stakeholders, including the software's end users and developers, then you care about the important design decisions that go into building the software. Ultimately, that means you care about its architecture. Concerning yourself with the most important decisions can be challenging, but it can be enjoyable and rewarding for that very reason.

Software architects need to communicate with a variety of stakeholders and sometimes serve as a bridge between management, technical staff, and non-technical staff. If this is not something you want to get involved with, being a software architect may not be the best fit for you.

Software architects are passionate about technology. They have a deep understanding of the technologies they are working with and keep those skills fresh by practicing their craft and being involved with projects. They must have a large breadth of knowledge and have a familiarity with technologies that they may not be currently using on a project. It is necessary to keep up with the fast pace of change in areas such as languages, tools, and frameworks. Being aware of a range of technologies will allow you to recommend the best solution to a particular problem.

Software architects should love to learn and play with new technologies because being a software architect requires continuous learning. As someone with a lot of wisdom to share, and who will be a leader on a team, you should enjoy mentoring and teaching others. Making those who work around you better at their jobs is a part of your job.

All software applications have a purpose. Good software architects make every effort to ensure that the software applications they work on serve their purpose as best that they can. If this is something you care about, the software architect role may be right for you.

Summary

Software architecture is the structure or structures of a system, their elements, and the relationships between those elements. It is an abstraction of a software system. Software architecture is important because all software systems have an architecture, and that architecture is the foundation for the software system.

Software architecture provides a number of benefits, such as enabling and inhibiting quality attributes, allowing you to predict software system qualities, easing communication with stakeholders, and allowing you to more easily make changes. It also provides a reusable model that could be used in multiple software products, imposes implementation constraints that reduce complexity and minimizes developer errors, improves cost/effort estimates, and serves as training for new team members.

Software architects are technical leaders who are ultimately responsible for technical decisions, the architecture, and its documentation. They perform a number of duties and are expected to have knowledge of a variety of topics, both technical and non-technical. Although the role can be challenging, if you care about the software that you are working on and all of its stakeholders, then the software architect role can be extremely rewarding.

In the next chapter, we'll explore software architecture in an organization. Most software architects operate within the context of an organization, so it is important to understand the dynamics of developing software within one. The chapter will detail topics such as the various software architect roles you will typically find in an organization, software development methodologies that are used, working with project and configuration management, navigating office politics, and creating software product lines that leverage architectural reuse.

Software Architecture in an Organization

2

In the previous chapter, we discussed software architecture and the role of the software architect. In this chapter, we will explore those topics further, but in the context of an organization.

Software systems are developed to satisfy the business goals of an organization. Many software architects work as part of an organization. As a result, the organization's business goals, objectives, stakeholders, project management, and processes greatly affect the software architect and their work.

This chapter focuses on topics a software architect should be familiar with when working within an organization. We will take a look at the various types of software architecture roles that are commonly found in organizations, and the software development methodologies they adopt. You'll gain a good understanding of how you might be expected to work with project management and the dynamics of office politics.

Risk management and configuration management are two other aspects of working on software projects within an organization. Finally, we'll take a look at software product lines, and how architectural reuse can create core assets that can make building software products faster, more efficient, and of a higher quality.

In this chapter, we will cover the following topics:

- Types of software architects
- Software development methodologies
- Project management
- Office politics
- Software risk management
- Configuration management
- Software product lines

Types of software architects

The role of a software architect can vary from organization to organization. You may have also heard of a variety of job titles related to software architects, such as the following:

- Enterprise architect
- Solution architect
- Application architect
- Data architect/Information architect
- Solution architect
- Security architect
- Cloud architect

Some organizations have one or more architects who perform a combination of these roles. They may go by the title of software architect or by the title of one of these roles. In other organizations, different individuals play different architectural roles. Some companies organize their software architects so that they are in an architecture team. They collaborate with the team on architecture tasks but also work on other teams to design and implement software products.

This book does not focus on any one type of software architect. It deals with mostly technical topics, and so is geared toward a number of technical architect roles. Many of the technical, non-technical, and soft skills described in this book are required by more than one type of software architect. Even in organizations that have different types of architects, there is an overlap in their responsibilities and duties. Let's take a closer look at the different types of software architect roles and what they typically mean.

Enterprise architect

Enterprise architects are responsible for the technical solutions and strategic direction of an organization. They must work with a variety of stakeholders to understand an organization's market, customers, products, business domain, requirements, and technology.

The enterprise architect ensures that an organization's business and strategic goals are in sync with the technical solutions. They need to take a holistic view to ensure that their architecture designs, and the designs of other architects, are in line with the overall organization.

They should have both a deep and broad understanding of technology so that they can make the proper recommendations and architecture designs. They must also look to the future to ensure that solutions are in line with both existing needs as well as anticipated ones.

In addition to high-level architecture design documents, enterprise architects work with other architects, such as application architects, to ensure that solutions meet all of the defined requirements. Enterprise architects come up with and maintain best practices for things such as designs, implementations, and policies. For organizations that have multiple software products, they will analyze them to identify areas for architectural reuse.

Enterprise architects provide guidance, mentorship, advice, and technical leadership for other architects and developers.

Solution architect

A **solution architect** converts requirements into an architecture for a solution. They work closely with business analysts and product owners to understand the requirements so that they can design a solution that will satisfy those requirements.

Solution architects select the most appropriate technologies for the problem that needs to be solved. They may work with enterprise architects, or if such a role does not exist in the organization, take on the responsibilities of an enterprise architect, to consider an organization's overall strategic goals and enterprise architecture principles when designing their solution.

The designs created by solution architects may be reused in multiple projects. It is common in an organization to reuse architectural components and to reuse patterns across architectures in different solution areas. In large organizations that have architects playing different roles, solution architects bridge a gap between enterprise architects and application architects.

Application architect

Application architects focus on one or more applications and their architecture. They ensure that the requirements for their application are satisfied by the design of that application. They may serve as a liaison between the technical and non-technical staff working on an application.

Most of the time, application architects are involved in all the steps in the software development process. They may recommend solutions or technologies for an application, and evaluate alternative approaches to problems. Individuals in this role need to keep up with trends and new technologies. They know when to use them in order to solve a problem or take advantage of an opportunity. When appropriate, they are involved with how applications within an organization will work and integrate with each other.

Application architects ensure that the development team is following best practices and standards during implementation. They provide guidance and leadership for team members. They may be involved in reviewing designs and code. Application architects work with enterprise architects to ensure that the solutions designed for an individual application align with the overall strategy of the organization.

Data architect/information architect

Data architects are responsible for designing, deploying, and managing an organization's data architecture. They focus on data management systems, and their goal is to ensure that the appropriate consumers of an organization's data have access to the data in the right place at the right time.

Data architects are responsible for all of an organization's data sources, both internal and external. They ensure that an organization's strategic data requirements are met. They create designs and models and decide how data will be stored, consumed, and integrated into the organization's various software systems. Data architects also ensure the security of the organization's data, and define processes for data backup, data archiving, and database recovery.

They maintain database performance by monitoring environments and may be tasked with identifying and resolving various issues, including problems in production environments. Data architects may support developers by assisting with their database design and coding work.

Some organizations have the role of an **information architect**. Although the data architect and information architect roles are related, and may even be fulfilled by the same person, there is a difference between the two roles.

While data architects focus their attention on databases and data structures, information architects place their focus on users. They are concerned with user intent related to data and how data affects the user experience. They are primarily interested in how the data is going to be used and what is going to be done with it.

Information architects want to provide a positive user experience and ensure that users can easily interact with the data. They want to design solutions so that users have the ability to intuitively find the information that they need. They may conduct usability testing to gather feedback so that they can determine what changes, if any, should be made to a system. They work with UX designers and others to develop strategies that will improve the user experience.

Infrastructure architect

Infrastructure architects focus on the design and implementation of an organization's enterprise infrastructure. This type of architect is responsible for the infrastructure environment meeting the organization's business goals, and provide hardware, networking, operating system, and software solutions to satisfy them.

The infrastructure must support the business processes and software applications of the organization. These architects are involved with infrastructure components such as the following:

- **Servers**: Physical or virtual servers for either cloud or on-premises environments
- **Network elements**: Elements such as routers, switches, firewalls, cabling, and load balancers
- **Storage systems**: Data storage systems such as **storage area networks** (**SAN**) and **network-attached storage** (**NAS**)
- **Facilities**: The physical location of the infrastructure equipment, and ensuring power, cooling, and security needs are met

Infrastructure architects support the delivery of an enterprise's software applications. This includes designing and implementing infrastructure solutions and integrating new software systems with an existing or new infrastructure. Once in production, they also ensure that existing software systems continue to fulfill requirements affected by infrastructure, and run at optimal levels. Infrastructure architects may make recommendations, such as using new technologies or hardware, which will improve an organization's infrastructure.

To fulfill the demands of the enterprise, they monitor and analyze characteristics such as workload, throughput, latency, capacity, and redundancy so that a proper balance is achieved and desired performance levels are met. They use infrastructure management tools and services to assist them with the management of the infrastructure.

Information security architect

A **security architect** is responsible for an organization's computer and network security. They build, oversee, and maintain an organization's security implementations. Security architects must have a full understanding of an organization's systems and infrastructure so that they can design secure systems.

Security architects conduct security assessments and vulnerability testing to identify and evaluate potential threats. Security architects should be familiar with security standards, best practices, and techniques that can be used to combat any identified threats. They recognize security gaps in existing and proposed software architectures and recommend solutions to close those gaps.

Once security components are put into place, security architects are involved in testing them to ensure that they work as expected. When a security incident does occur, security architects are involved in their resolution and conduct a post-incident analysis. The results of the analysis are used to take proper action so that a similar incident will not occur again.

A security architect may oversee an organization's security awareness program and help to implement an organization's corporate security policies and procedures.

Cloud architect

Now that cloud deployments are the norm, having someone in an organization dedicated to cloud adoption, with the relevant expertise, has become increasingly common and necessary. A **cloud architect** is someone who is responsible for an organization's cloud computing strategy and initiatives. They are responsible for the cloud architecture used for the deployment of software systems. An organization that has someone who is focused on cloud architecture leads to increased levels of success with cloud adoption.

The responsibilities of cloud architects include selecting a cloud provider and selecting the model (for example, SaaS, PaaS, or IaaS) that is most appropriate for the organization's needs. They create cloud migration plans for existing applications not already in the cloud, including the coordination of the adoption process. They may also be involved in designing new cloud-native applications that are built from the ground up for the cloud.

Cloud architects oversee cloud management, and create policies and procedures for governance. They use tools and services to monitor and manage cloud deployments. The expertise that cloud architects possess typically means they are involved in negotiating contracts with cloud service providers and ensuring that **service-level agreements (SLAs)** are satisfied.

Cloud architects should have a firm understanding of security concerns, such as protecting data deployed into different types of cloud and cloud/hybrid systems. They work with security architects, or if such a role does not exist in the organization, take on the responsibilities of a security architect, to ensure that systems deployed to the cloud are secure.

For organizations that have not fully migrated to the cloud, one of the tasks for a cloud architect is to lead a cultural change within the organization for cloud adoption. Cloud strategies can fail if the organization's culture does not fully embrace them. Part of the cloud architect's job is to evangelize cloud adoption by communicating the many benefits, and influence behavior changes toward cloud adoption that will ultimately lead to cultural changes.

Software development methodologies

As a software architect working in an organization, you will typically be required to use the software development methodology that has been adopted by the organization. However, in some cases, the software architect may play a role in deciding which software development methodology is used. Either way, software architects may be able to provide input to an organization's processes, giving them the ability to make suggestions that may improve these processes.

For these reasons, it is good to have an understanding of the more common software development methodologies. There are a variety of different types that can be employed for a software project, each of which has its own strengths and weaknesses. Today, Agile methodologies are much more widely used than traditional ones, but even among the methodologies that are considered Agile, there are numerous variations.

Unfortunately, sometimes, a software project moves forward with a software development methodology that is not appropriate for the project. Prior to choosing one, you should consider which one would be the most appropriate to use. In the following sections, we'll take a look at two types of software development methodologies: the Waterfall model and Agile.

The Waterfall model

The Waterfall software development methodology is a sequential one, in which each stage of the life cycle has to be completed in its entirety before moving on to the next stage. Some advantages of this model include the following:

- The model is simple and easy to understand.
- Stakeholders will know what to expect in terms of timeline, functionality, and cost.
- Due to the artifacts that are required to be produced out of each phase, different types of documentation about the system will be available. The documentation is beneficial for those who will be maintaining the software going forward. It can also facilitate bringing new employees onboard and minimize the impact of any employee turnover.

In the following diagram of the Waterfall model, you can see how the flow of steps resembles a waterfall:

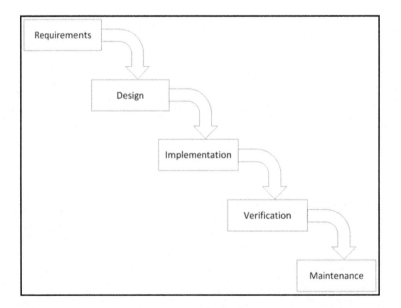

Waterfall model

Phases of the Waterfall methodology

The following are the most common steps in the Waterfall model:

- **Requirements**: During this initial phase, requirements are elicited from stakeholders and analyzed. The results are placed in a requirements document.
- **Design**: In the design phase, technical design specifications are created. The specifications detail how the requirements will be fulfilled by the technical solution.
- **Implementation**: This phase represents the actual work of coding. The design specifications are implemented in code.
- **Verification**: During this phase, testing is conducted to ensure that the implementation works correctly and that the requirements are fulfilled.
- **Maintenance**: Once the software has been deployed, the life cycle enters this phase for bug fixes and other enhancements.

There is also a variation in the Waterfall model wherein the names of the individual steps differ. For example, *coding* may be used instead of *implementation*, or *testing* may be used instead of *verification*. Some organizations add more steps to the process. There may be a separate step for analysis that occurs before the design phase, or one for deployment that occurs after the verification phase.

The Waterfall model has gone out of favor, but if the following is true (which is often not the case), the project may be a candidate for this model:

- The team is already very knowledgeable regarding the project's business domain, business rules, and functionality
- The requirements are well understood and unlikely to change
- The scope of the project is set and stable
- The team understands the technology and the architecture well, and those are unlikely to change
- The project is not large in size and does not have a high degree of complexity
- It is acceptable that a working version of the software will not be available to internal or external stakeholders until later phases
- The project is constrained by a time frame/deadline that has already been decided

Issues with the Waterfall methodology

There are a number of issues with the Waterfall approach. Testing does not begin until after all implementation is complete, so there is no testing feedback until later in the life cycle. Users do not receive a working version of the software until the very end, so valuable feedback can't be provided until that time. Users can have difficulty visualizing the final product from just the requirements documentation and may miss important requirements. Although mock-ups and wireframes can minimize this issue, it's not the same as having a working version of the software throughout an iterative approach.

If requirements are missed or incorrect, making changes late in the development process can be a large effort, resulting in cost and/or time overruns. If time is running out on a software development project, and testing occurs at the end, testing may be cut short, lowering the quality of the software.

The rigidity of the Waterfall model can be a major problem if the requirements are subject to change or are poorly understood. Even with projects that are thought to be predictable, the nature of software development is that change is almost inevitable in one form or another. As such, a process that is too rigid may put the project at a disadvantage.

For projects that are not suitable for a traditional Waterfall model, a more flexible life cycle model may be needed. Agile development processes can provide this type of flexibility. Due to the limitations of traditional models and the benefits that Agile methodologies provide, they have become more popular in modern software development.

Agile software development methodologies

Agile software development methodologies were created by leading software professionals based on their real-world experiences developing software. They address many of the limitations of traditional development methodologies, and as a result, have become much more popular.

There are a variety of different types of Agile processes available, such as **Scrum, Kanban, Extreme Programming (XP)**, and **Crystal**. They each have their differences, but in essence, they all focus on being adaptable to change. They attempt to find a balance between not having enough processes and having too much of them.

Agile values and principles

Agile methodologies have certain values and follow certain principles of software development. These were documented in the **Agile Manifesto** and the **12 principles of Agile software**, written by the thought leaders who created the Agile software development approach. The following are the four core values of the Agile Manifesto:

- Individuals and interactions are valued more than processes and tools. Valuing people is more important than processes and tools. The people are the ones who understand the business and drive the development of the software. Teams will be less responsive to business needs if it is the processes and tools that are more important than the people.
- Working software is more important than documentation. Traditional methods may have focused on a large amount of documentation, but software that works and meets requirements is more important. There need only be enough documentation as is necessary, and it shouldn't take precedence over working software.
- Customer interaction and continuous engagement are valued over contract negotiation. Agile stresses the importance of customer interaction and engagement throughout the software development process. This increases the likelihood that software will meet the needs of customers.
- Responding to change is more important than following a plan. Traditional software development methodologies place a high importance on up-front planning and a desire to avoid deviations from that plan. Agile embraces change, including requirement changes throughout the development process. Short iterations provide an opportunity to add and change requirements at any time, as long as it adds value and satisfies customers.

An iterative methodology

Unlike the Waterfall approach, which is sequential, Agile methodologies are iterative:

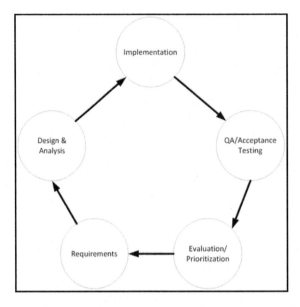

Iterative methodology

Software is built incrementally, with each iteration satisfying a portion of the total requirements. At the end of each iteration is a working version of the software, rather than attempting to deliver all of the software at once. Testing takes place in the same iteration as the coding. There is continuous feedback, and if something needs to be changed, it becomes apparent sooner.

Adaptive rather than predictive

Agile methodologies are *adaptive* rather than *predictive*. While methodologies such as Waterfall focus on a large amount of upfront planning to detail and predict outcomes in the future, Agile methodologies focus on adapting to changes as they occur.

Although it becomes difficult to know what the state of the software will be in the future, and increasingly so the further into the future you want to examine, Agile methodologies allow you to make changes after the initial planning takes place. Feedback from users and testers can be taken into consideration immediately, and incorporated into the work of subsequent iterations.

Daily stand-up meetings

If you are going to adopt an Agile software-development methodology, a common practice that you should consider implementing on your team is the daily stand-up meeting. If you are following the Scrum framework, this meeting is known as the **daily scrum**. It is a brief meeting, typically held toward the beginning of the day, in which everyone on the team provides a status update.

A **facilitator** typically runs the meeting, and this role should be rotated on a regular basis. There shouldn't be a reliance on any single facilitator. This also keeps the team talking with each other, which is the purpose of the meeting, and not just to a single facilitator.

During the stand-up, each person provides their daily status by answering three questions:

- What did I work on yesterday?
- What am I going to work on today?
- Are there any impediments that I am facing?

The meeting should be kept brief, so if anyone's status begins to expand into a larger discussion, the facilitator should ask that any such discussions be taken offline, to be discussed at another time.

There are several benefits to having this meeting:

- Everyone stays informed as to the current tasks that are being worked on by others on the team.
- When a team member states an impediment, it makes the impediment known to the team. It provides an opportunity for team members to help each other. Someone on the team may have ideas as to how to resolve the issue. Also, other team members may have the same issue. Even if they don't, they will become aware of the problem and the possible solution, and could help themselves or someone else in the future should they face the same issue.
- It keeps team members identifying as a team. Rather than working in isolation, having everyone interact with each other regularly will help everyone to identify with the team.

Project management

Software architects typically assist project management throughout the life cycle of a software system. One of the ways in which you will be asked to do so is in estimating the level of effort for technical tasks. How estimates are derived and who participates in estimation varies from organization to organization, but typically, software architects, with their expertise and experience, will be expected to provide some level of input during the process of estimating tasks.

The importance of software project estimation

The importance of estimation cannot be understated. Estimates and project planning are major factors in the success of a project.

Estimation can be difficult and must take into account a number of factors. However, the team should work together to come up with accurate estimates as project management relies on them. Estimates are used to organize work and plan releases. Inaccurate estimates and poor project planning are among the main reasons software projects fail.

Putting effort into the estimates

Sometimes, estimation is done informally. You may be asked to provide an estimate or an opinion on the spot without an opportunity to analyze the work further. You want to establish a culture within the organization that values putting effort into the estimates, rather than off-the-cuff estimates that amount to little more than guesswork.

If you are asked by someone to provide an estimate for a task extemporaneously, and you are not comfortable doing so, ask whether it's acceptable to get back to them. This will slow the process down, and provide you with an opportunity to conduct a proper analysis before providing an estimate. Sometimes, if you are on the spot to provide an estimate, it is easy to be inaccurate and later regret it.

When estimating tasks, some will involve work that is understood, making it easier to provide estimates. It is the work that involves unknowns that can be challenging. If you are put in that position, see whether you can afford some time to perform some analysis, or, if appropriate, even create a **proof of concept** (**POC**). A POC will allow you to prototype a solution to gain a better understanding of the effort involved, or whether the solution is even feasible.

Being a realist (or even a pessimist)

People who provide estimates are optimists, realists, or pessimists. If you are generally an optimist, or the other individuals who are working with you to come up with the estimates are generally optimists, consider making a conscious effort to be more of a realist or pessimist. Think about what could become challenging about the work, and make sure you are not leaving anything out when considering your estimate. Your knowledge and experience as a software architect, along with the proper approach, is what is necessary to produce a useful estimate.

Team and situational factors to consider

If you are involved with project planning, also consider situational factors such as the existing infrastructure of the organization (facilities, equipment), the organization's culture, the maturity of the organization's processes, and the tools that are made available for the project to use.

Make sure you also take into consideration the skill level and experience of your team. This includes not just the developers, but everyone on the team, such as the business analysts and QA testers. There can be quite a bit of variance depending on this factor. You may not know who will be assigned a particular task yet, but consider the overall skill levels of the team, along with their strengths and weaknesses, during project planning.

Whatever method your organization chooses to adopt, use it consistently and then analyze the results. Depending on how well it works, you can refine your methods over time based on the results you collect, which should yield even better results going forward.

Project schedule changes

It would be great if projects always stayed on schedule, but as we all know, a variety of factors can cause a project to fall behind schedule. For these types of situations, you will have to work with project management to discuss what could be done to bring the project back on schedule, or if the project timelines can be adjusted.

You may also find yourself in a situation where deadlines have been moved up. This might be initiated by internal management, but external forces may also dictate a change in the project schedule. A new business opportunity may present itself, such as the possibility of a new client, or your organization may be invited to an important trade show and want to demo the software application. When situations such as these arise, depending on the importance and the direction given by management, the team may need to make every attempt to conform to the new time frame.

Even if you have adopted an Agile software development methodology, which anticipates change and helps the team adapt to it, you will need to meet certain project deadlines.

Getting a project back on schedule

In order to get a project back on schedule, or to adjust to a new deadline, there are a number of approaches. Let's have a look at them.

Working overtime

One approach is to have the team work longer hours, allowing them to accomplish more in the same amount of time. However, you run the risk of lowering morale and productivity as hours increase.

One way to motivate your team with this approach is to pay extra for overtime work, or issue compensatory time that can be used later. Of course, this requires management's approval. If extra pay is involved, the budget of the project must be taken into consideration. Overtime pay, particularly if there are contractors on the project, can add up quickly.

Reducing scope

The team could choose to revisit the scope of the project. If you can identify anything superfluous on the project schedule, you could notify project management to have it removed. In addition, any *gold plating*, which refers to adding extra features that are not necessary, should be eliminated, pushed to a later time, or reduced in scope.

If nothing obvious can be found, you could work with the appropriate stakeholders, such as domain experts, business analysts, end users, and product owners, to consider changing requirements. Lower-priority functionality could potentially be dropped or delayed until a future release.

Adding resources

Another common way organizations may try to get a project back on schedule is to add more resources. However, this approach doesn't necessarily allow a project to be completed faster, and it may cause the project to take even longer. Brooks' Law, from *The Mythical Man-Month*, states that *...adding human resources to a late software project makes it later*.

As you add more people to a project, the communication paths increase in a multiplicative way. In addition to taking more time to communicate, many more opportunities for miscommunication are created. Productivity and the number of defects (both in requirements as well as design and implementation) are known to increase as projects get larger.

If the team is going to add more resources, make sure that it is prepared to support them. New team members will require guidance and mentorship in the early stages, but that effort is necessary so that they can become as productive as possible in the shortest amount of time.

Reallocating resources

Sometimes, it isn't so much about adding resources as it is about making sure that the ones you have are assigned to the right tasks. Some resources may be more knowledgeable or efficient at certain tasks. A software architect who is working closely with the team may be able to provide valuable input to project management to reallocate resources.

If you see resources who are not working on critical items, you can suggest that they be reassigned to more important tasks. If a project is behind schedule, everyone needs to be working on the critical path to complete the most important tasks first.

If there are tasks being worked on in a serial manner, which may cause a delay, think about how the tasks could potentially be reassigned so that they can be worked on in a more parallel fashion.

Identifying problem areas

Try to understand why the project is late. The first step in coming up with a solution is to figure out the problem. If you are going to make suggestions to project management about how to get back on schedule, make every attempt to identify the main problems.

Consider getting thoughts from the team as to what improvements could be done. You don't want to turn it into a finger-pointing exercise, but the team can provide good insight.

There could be some process that is causing a delay, which could be adjusted or eliminated. For example, maybe there is a regular meeting that is not adding much value but taking up valuable time, and the meeting could be eliminated or made to happen less frequently.

If there are any delays caused by external forces, examine whether anything can be done to alleviate those types of issues.

Acting as early as possible

Whatever approach you take, one thing you do not want to do is to cut testing time short. Not performing the adequate amount of testing can have serious implications for the success of the project. Software that does not meet requirements and/or contains defects can put the whole project in jeopardy. The cost of inadequate testing may be far greater than whatever time or cost saving it offers.

The absolute best thing you can do is act as early as possible. Communicate with project management so that they have a detailed understanding of the current state of the project. Use your experience to recognize warning signs and potential pitfalls for the team. Don't put off acting on potential problems, because the earlier in the project you realize there is an issue, the more options you have to resolve it.

Office politics

Almost everyone in an organization has to deal with office politics to some degree. As you can see from the following pie chart, the majority of people think it is best to have an awareness of the office politics in your own organization:

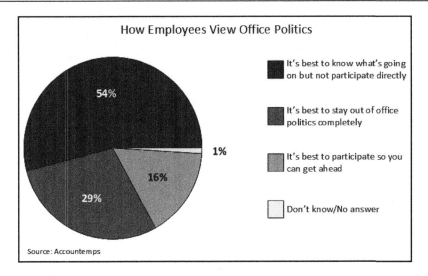

Pie chart displaying How Employees View Office Politics

As a software architect, you may find yourself engaging in office politics more than you have in the past, such as when you were a senior developer. This is because you will be interacting and communicating with a larger variety of stakeholders, and you may be doing so more frequently.

In an organization, individuals from diverse backgrounds, with their own unique goals and viewpoints, come together to work toward the goals of an organization. A variety of factors can shape people's motivations, which may lead to office politics.

When you want to achieve something, you may need the help of others in the organization. Different actions you undertake may cause you to spend, receive, or borrow political capital. It can be useful to have political skills when working within an organization.

I would rather focus on building great software and not deal with office politics, but sometimes it is unavoidable. The following are some things that you can do as a software architect to be successful in office politics.

Understanding your organization's goals

Be aware of your organization's strategic goals and direction. As much as possible, align your goals with the goals of the organization. There will be less friction with others, and those who are in conflict with such goals will be in conflict with the organization.

Having an understanding of how your organization makes money, and how that money is typically invested, can be useful. If you are seeking resources for your project, such as additional team members, equipment, and licenses for tools, it requires an investment by the organization. The organization is going to want a return on that investment, so be prepared to explain how it aligns with the organization's goals and objectives.

Addressing the concerns of others

In an organization, many stakeholders may come to the software architect with concerns over a software product or process. Although the priority and legitimacy of these concerns will vary, look to address these concerns as promptly as possible.

If an issue is left unresolved, it could be escalated to others in the organization. It may appear to be a bigger issue than it really is. When someone brings a concern to you, you want to make sure that person knows that you have listened to their concern, understand it, and will take appropriate action for it. If no action is going to be taken, explain the reasons behind that decision, and make sure the person knows that at least their concern has been noted.

Assisting people with their goals

When you have the opportunity, help others in your organization meet their goals or solve their problems. You are all working for the same organization. As long as what they are trying to accomplish does not conflict with your own values or the goals of the company, assist people when you can.

Do this without any expectation of getting anything in return. You don't want a reputation as someone who only does favors expecting some personal benefit. If you help your fellow employees, you will be looked upon kindly. At some point, you may need someone else's help, and even though you are not owed anything, you will be more likely to receive that help.

Knowing when to compromise

As a software architect, you will find yourself in discussions with others over a variety of topics. You may be negotiating something, or in conflict with someone, or you could be making a request for something. Whatever the reason, when it becomes apparent that you may not get what you want, be willing to compromise and know when to do so.

One reason to compromise is when you are simply lacking leverage, and if you fail to compromise, you may not accomplish any part of your request or goal. A compromise can make sense in that situation because you may still get something suitable out of the exchange. A compromise also makes sense if you think it will be beneficial in the long run. Giving up something now may pay off at some point in the future.

Be prepared to compromise from the onset by proactively thinking about how important the issue is to you as well as what would and would not make an acceptable compromise. Listen to the person or group you are dealing with regarding the issue and try to understand their viewpoints and reasoning. Understanding the other side may provide you with additional points you can make, or at the very least, give you an idea as to what might be an acceptable middle ground.

Being aware of cultural differences

Many organizations have offices and customers around the world, and they may outsource work to resources in other countries. Keep cultural differences in mind when communicating with individuals from other countries. Different cultures may prefer different phrases or approaches. Take the time to learn about the cultures of the people you will be dealing with to maximize the clarity of your communications and to avoid misunderstandings.

Software risk management

Risks are potential problems, and there are many risks involved in designing and developing software. Organizations, and the people working for them, have different levels of risk tolerance. Whatever that level is, an organization should have a plan for **risk management**.

As a software architect, you will need to assist project managers in managing those risks. If left unmanaged, risks can lead to cost/time overruns, rework, operational failures, and possibly total project failure.

The first step in assisting with risk management is being able to identify risks. The team should come up with and document potential risks. Using your knowledge and experience as a software architect, you may be able to help identify risks that stakeholders, project management, and other team members cannot.

Some examples of potential types of risks include the following:

- **Functional risks**: Incorrect requirements, lack of participation from end users and business analysts, conflicting business goals
- **Technical risks**: Degree of complexity, size of the project, new languages/tools/frameworks that the team is not familiar with, dependencies on vendors and subcontractors outside of the organization
- **Personnel risks**: Team members without the proper experience or skillset, inability to staff the project, productivity issues with team members
- **Financial risks**: Lack of sufficient funding for the project, **return on investment (ROI)** constraints that will be difficult to meet
- **Legal risks**: Needing to abide by government regulations, changing legal requirements, contractual changes
- **Management risks**: Lack of the appropriate experience and skillset, incorrect planning, lack of communication, organizational issues

Once a risk is identified, it should be evaluated for its potential impact and the probability that it will occur. Risks that have both a high impact as well as a high likelihood of occurring are the most critical to a project:

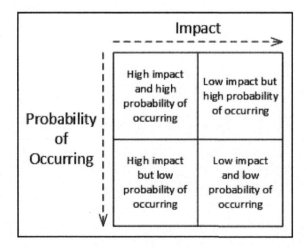

Risk Analysis

After risks are evaluated, software architects may be asked by the organization to assist with a plan on how to manage the risks. There are four main techniques that can be used to handle risks: risk avoidance, transferring the risk to another party, risk mitigation, and risk acceptance.

Risk avoidance

One technique for handling risk is **risk avoidance**, which involves changing the project in some way so as to eliminate the risk altogether. An example of a risk that could be dealt with in this way would be a project team that is considering using a programming language and/or technology that the team is not familiar with. Moving forward with such a choice brings with it some potentially significant risks.

The project may take longer than anticipated due to the learning curve, or it may be discovered that features the team wants to implement are not well suited to the chosen technology. One way to handle this risk would be to select a technology that the team is already familiar with, as long as it can satisfy the needs of the project. This would allow the team to effectively avoid the risk.

Keep in mind that not all risks can be avoided, and avoiding a risk could lead to other risks. In addition, taking risks is sometimes necessary in order to take advantage of an opportunity. These should be some of your thoughts when considering whether or not to avoid a risk.

Transferring the risk to another party

Another technique in risk management is to **transfer the risk to another party**. An example of this might be a project team that hires a subcontractor to implement parts of a project, such as the design and development of a user interface for a web application. There is a risk that the subcontractor may not complete their deliverables on time or that their deliverables may not meet certain quality standards. One way to handle this risk would be to transfer it to the subcontractor by building penalties into the contract that will be incurred if the deliverables are late or do not meet the level of quality desired.

Risk mitigation

One can also employ **risk mitigation** to handle a risk, which is reducing the likelihood that a risk will occur. Let's say a software project recently hired a new team member. This person is not as experienced as some of the other team members, so there is a risk that the work of the new team member could be delayed due to a learning curve or the work produced may not be correct because of a lack of knowledge regarding technical standards or the business domain. One way to mitigate, or lessen, this risk would be to assign the new employee a mentor. This mentor could devote some time to teaching, answering questions, and reviewing the work of the new team member.

Risk acceptance

Risk acceptance is another way deal with a risk. This approach is to simply accept the risk and any possible consequences. For example, perhaps your company and another company are both developing a new software product to serve a new market. Ideally, your product would be the first to the market, but since you started later, there is a risk that you may not be. Not being the first to the market could result in a loss of market shares. After analyzing the risk, you may decide to accept any consequences of not being the first to the market in exchange for developing a better product by not rushing it.

One point to keep in mind is that actions taken to resolve a risk by mitigating or transferring it may have their own set of risks. This must be taken into consideration as part of the analysis of that risk. If, in the last example, the company decided to mitigate the risk by attempting to complete the product sooner, additional risks might have been created, such as a greater probability that requirements could be missed or that the quality might suffer.

Configuration management

As a software architect in an organization, you will be expected to be involved with configuration management. In many organizations, there is a **software configuration management (SCM)** team. In addition, there may be an SCM team at the project level. For small projects, this may be a single person, or it may even be taken on by someone who isn't even dedicated to the role, such as a team member who performs other duties.

Some of the responsibilities for a software configuration management team include identifying configuration items (software, documents, models, plans), implementing a change control process, and managing the process and tools used for builds. We will examine automated builds and **continuous integration** (**CI**) in `Chapter 14`, *Architecting Legacy Applications*.

Changing management

Organizations will implement a formal change control process to handle changes to a software product. This includes all aspects of a software system, such as requirements, source code, and documentation. There are many reasons a change might be proposed, including correcting a problem (a bug in the software), implementing a functional change (a change to a business rule), or adding new functionality to the software.

The goal of the process is to ensure that if changes are made, it is appropriate to do so, and to minimize the effort, difficulty, and disruption when implementing the change.

Some change control processes involve a **change control board** (**CCB**). This is a group of project stakeholders who are designated to analyze proposed changes and decide whether they should be implemented. As a software architect, you may be part of a formal or informal CCB. Your knowledge and experience might be leveraged by the board to help with:

- Evaluating a proposed change to decide whether the change is something that should be implemented in the project
- Prioritizing the proposed change based on its importance and severity (if it's a defect)
- Providing an estimate as to the effort involved to implement the change

There are several approaches to change management that an organization might use. A software architect should be familiar with their organization's process. As a software architect, you may offer input to change an existing process or you may need to help formulate the process for the first time.

One approach to change management, which is the most formal, requires that a CCB review all changes, regardless of how large or complex the change may be. It does have the advantage of allowing multiple people to consider the change. Having more people aware of the proposed change and giving them the opportunity to discuss it will increase the chances of making the right decision. Especially with large, complex systems, it can be very difficult or even impossible for a single person to be aware of all of the technical and functional ramifications of a particular change. Having multiple sets of eyes looking at it can certainly help. Unfortunately, this process is going to take more time. The CCB could easily become a bottleneck. Not only will more time be spent making decisions, sometimes, time will pass just setting up the meetings to get everyone together. For situations where many changes or decisions need to be made in a timely manner, having a CCB review all changes may not be practical.

The second approach to change management is the opposite of the first method. Rather than have a CCB review every change, in this approach to change control, there is no CCB. Individual developers make their own decisions for all changes. The advantage of this approach is that changes can move through the process much more quickly than either of the other two approaches. Also, empowering developers can give them a certain level of confidence and satisfaction. However, only one person is thinking about each change, and as mentioned earlier, this can have a detrimental effect. The quality achieved for a given change will solely depend on the developer making the change. Some developers may be new to the software or inexperienced in general, or they may simply not be very good. Whatever the reason, the change they decide to make could end up causing even more problems than what it is attempting to solve. As was mentioned earlier, even with an experienced and quality developer, it can be difficult with large systems to be aware of all of the ramifications of a particular change. For minor defects, this isn't much of an issue, but it can be for large changes.

The third approach to change management seeks a balance between the first and second. In this approach, a CCB only reviews some of the changes. Typically, this means reviewing the most important or most complex changes. While changes won't be completed as fast as the second approach, and the changes won't be under as much scrutiny as the first approach, at least the changes that could potentially cause the most problems are reviewed, and the CCB is not a bottleneck for the other changes. It simply may not be practical to have a CCB review everything, but you also don't want to sacrifice all reviews. For example, the CCB might review the majority of enhancements and high-priority/severity defects, but not the lower-priority/severity defects (although an analyst, developer, and tester will still have an opportunity to think about all fixes while they are working on a defect). It really depends more on how large and complex the change is, and how important the functionality is that will be affected, and not so much on whether it is a defect or an enhancement. Sometimes, a defect fix is more complicated than an enhancement, so those factors are always taken into consideration.

Perhaps the best approach to change management, and the most pragmatic, is to always use a CCB, but create multiple levels of it. The organization may designate different levels of authority, and changes with limited impact and scope can be approved at lower levels of authority, while changes that have a larger impact are escalated to higher levels of authority within a CCB. When there are multiple levels of a CCB, the project's stage (that is, how close the team is to releasing) is sometimes considered when determining what CCB level is appropriate. A shift typically occurs as a project gets closer to release, with the focus going from wanting flexibility to wanting more stability and control over the changes.

Software product lines

Growing competitive pressures combined with the complexity of developing software systems makes it a necessity for organizations to increase efficiencies wherever possible. One way to accomplish this is to create **software product lines**. A variety of industries, including the software industry, have used **product line engineering** (**PLE**) successfully.

Product lines are multiple products from a single company that address a particular need or market. These products could be sold under the same brand, with the idea that customers who use one product from the brand are more likely to purchase another product from the same brand.

Organizations that develop software may have multiple existing software products and/or other software products in development. These software products may work in a similar way, have similar functional and/or non-functional requirements, and have a similar look/feel.

Without any type of reuse, the same functionality may be written multiple times. When working as a software architect in an organization, you should seek to reuse architecture by building software systems from core assets. A software architecture that provides a solution for one software product may also be useful for another one. Architectural components can be reused, allowing a generic solution to address the same problem in multiple products.

In addition to building software, organizations may acquire software, or other organizations that have existing software products, and this software may become a new software line for the acquiring organization. The acquired software may also be merged with an existing product line.

Benefits of a software product line

Some of the benefits of strategic, planned architectural reuse across a software product line include the following:

- Reduced development effort
- Lower costs
- Increased productivity
- Increased quality
- Decreased time to market

Core assets of an organization

The goal of a software product line is to have reusable components, known as **core assets**, that share a common architecture. Some of the components that can be reused and designated as core assets include the following:

- Requirements analysis
- Domain models and analysis
- Software architecture design
- Test plans and test cases
- Work plans, schedules, budgets
- Processes, methods, tools
- The knowledge, skills, and experience of the employees
- User guides and technical documentation

The core assets need to be built while keeping in mind that they will be used across multiple products in a product line. Each product will have variation, so to account for this, core assets should be built with **variation points**, places that provide an opportunity to take into consideration this variation and allow the team to tailor the asset for use in a specific product.

Once these assets have been compiled, it will require less effort, time, and cost to reuse the assets than to create them each time they are needed. Building a software system then requires the team to reuse the appropriate assets, using the variation points as appropriate, and building the system from there.

Risks of product line engineering

Although product line engineering for software may result in benefits, be aware that there are risks related to its successful implementation. Moving to this type of approach requires adopting a new technical strategy for the organization as a whole. It requires coordination and managerial support.

It needs to be clear to development teams what core assets are available to them, and what the variation points are so that they can utilize them properly. The scope of the product line needs to be set appropriately so that it is neither too broad nor too narrow.

If the organization is creating all of the products in the same product line, it requires successful execution by the software architects and development teams, as well as the proper organizational management. If the organization is acquiring software products to be included in a software product line, then the proper resources, both technical and managerial, must be available and prepared to put forth the effort required to identify and utilize the common components of those products.

Organizations that are not prepared to fully adopt this approach may experience failure.

Summary

When working as an architect in an organization, you should be aware of the various types of software architect roles. The various roles have similarities and differences in terms of their responsibilities and duties. If you are required to use a software development methodology that has already been selected for your organization, it is important to become familiar with it and its practices. If you are in a position to select the software development methodology, be sure to be knowledgeable about the choices so that an appropriate one can be selected for the project's needs.

Software architects use their expertise and experience to work with project management on estimates for tasks, project planning, and controlling and monitoring the project during its life cycle.

Due to communicating with a larger number of stakeholders and management, office politics is a reality that a software architect will have to deal with more than those in other development roles.

Organizations will want involvement from software architects for risk management. Software architects can identify risks and come up with approaches to handle them. Software architects work with the SCM team to coordinate builds, development environments, and to provide input for change management.

Software architects should consider introducing software products lines for the many benefits that they provide. Reusing architectural components to create software products allows them to be created faster and with a higher degree of quality.

In the next chapter, we will examine software requirements and how they affect the software architecture. Software architects should have an understanding of the business domain and requirements in order to design an appropriate solution. We will learn about requirements engineering, how to extract and summarize requirements from stakeholders, and architectural quality attributes.

Understanding the Domain

3

Moving from other roles, such as a software developer role, to being a software architect requires one to expand and broaden their sphere of knowledge to include a deep understanding of their domain. Effectively designing a solution for a problem space requires knowledge about the domain and the requirements for the software.

This chapter begins by describing the foundation of understanding a domain, which includes general business knowledge and a keen understanding of your organization's business. We will go over the important concepts of **domain-driven design** (DDD), and how it can help your software project team handle complexity and model a solution around real-world concepts. The chapter also details the different types of software requirements and the techniques to elicit them from key stakeholders.

In this chapter, we will cover the following topics:

- Developing business acumen
- Domain-driven design
- Requirements engineering
- Requirements elicitation

Developing business acumen

While being a software architect requires in-depth technical knowledge, to be successful in the role also requires a thorough understanding of your organization's business. In order to design an appropriate architecture, you need to have knowledge of the business problems you are trying to solve and the business opportunities your organization is seeking to exploit. A technically advanced software system is of no use if it does not meet its goals.

When designing a software architecture, in order to ensure that the solution is an appropriate one, you must consider the goals of the **business**, the **users**, and the **software system**:

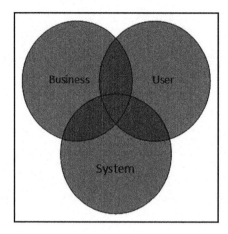

Each of these focus areas has its own goals, which can significantly overlap and impact each other. For example, a business goal of a specific, aggressive time to market could mean that there is not enough time for things such as proper requirements analysis or quality assurance testing, which could significantly impact user goals. When goals are in conflict with each other, it requires you to find an acceptable balance among them when designing your software architecture.

Familiarity with general business topics

Having a competent and practical understanding of business and its terminology will be useful to you in becoming a complete architect. While your passion may be for technology, as a software architect you will benefit from business knowledge more than other roles, such as a software developer. Software architects need to interact with a variety of stakeholders, and understanding the language of business will ensure that you have a common understanding with them.

Ultimately, you are designing a software architecture that will fulfill business goals, and your understanding of business will guide you in that task. Having general business knowledge of topics such as finance, operations, management, and marketing will help you to understand the value your software is supposed to bring to an organization. Business decisions will be made based on things like **return on investment (ROI)** calculations for the software project and cost-effectiveness analysis of different approaches. A good grasp of these concepts will help you to add value to such discussions.

One way to gain this knowledge is through formal education. If that is not feasible, there are other ways to get at least a rudimentary understanding of business topics. There are online classes available, some of which you can attend for free. Another option is to obtain and read one or more books on the relevant topics.

Understanding your organization's business

Once you have some general business knowledge, you will want to gain a good understanding of your organization's business. It is a crucial aspect of being a successful software architect and separates a good architect, who only has technical knowledge, from a great one.

A good starting point is to gain an understanding of your organization's products and services, and the value they provide to their customers. How does your organization make money? If you are the software architect for a specific product, pay particular attention to that product. Invest the time to understand the various business processes of your organization.

You should learn about the market that your organization operates in and its trends. It is prudent to become familiar with your organization's competitors. You should seek out answers to questions such as:

- What do your competitors do differently?
- What do they do that is similar?
- What are the strengths and weaknesses of your competitors?

Most importantly, spend the time to understand your organization's customers. The software products you help design are for your customers, and they are perhaps the most important aspect of your organization's business. What does their business do? How do they use your products and services? Why did they choose your products and services over those of a competitor?

Once you become familiar with your organization's business, the market in which it operates, its products/services, and its customers, you are on the path to fully understanding your organization's domain.

Domain-driven design

Understanding the domain of your software application is part of what is necessary to discover the appropriate architecture for any solutions you need to develop. The domain is the subject and body of knowledge on which the software will be applied.

The term **domain-driven design** (**DDD**) was coined by Eric Evans in his book, *Domain-Driven Design: Tackling Complexity in the Heart of Software*. DDD is an approach to developing software that aims to make the software better by focusing on the domain. It has a set of concepts and patterns that have successfully been used to solve problems and build great software.

DDD is particularly useful for large software applications that have complex and sizable models. DDD helps you to solve complex problems. Even if you decide not to follow DDD fully while architecting your applications, some DDD concepts may be helpful to you. It is beneficial to become familiar with these concepts as some of them are referenced in other areas of this book, and in the event that you encounter them in your work.

Encourages and improves communication

One of the benefits of DDD is the fact that it encourages and improves communication. Communication among all team members is encouraged. In particular, DDD stresses the importance of interacting with domain experts.

A **domain expert**, or **subject matter expert** (**SME**), is someone who possesses expertise about, and is an authority in, a particular area. Understanding the domain of your software application is highly beneficial and domain experts will help the entire team gain this understanding.

In addition to encouraging communication with domain experts, DDD improves communication among all team members and stakeholders by introducing the concept of a ubiquitous language.

What is a ubiquitous language?

The development team may not have a strong understanding of the domain, and may not be familiar with terms and concepts used by stakeholders, including the domain experts. They may use their own language when discussing the functionality and discuss the domain in terms of their technical design. The stakeholders, including the domain experts, will use their own jargon when discussing their domain, and may not have a good understanding of technical terms. Because different people may use different language to describe the same concepts in a particular domain, it can take longer to communicate ideas, and it can lead to misunderstandings.

In *Domain-Driven Design: Tackling Complexity in the Heart of Software*, Eric Evans described this problem:

> *"The terminology of day-to-day discussions is disconnected from the terminology embedded in the code (ultimately the most important product of a software project). And even the same person uses different language in speech and in writing, so that the most incisive expressions of the domain often emerge in a transient form that is never captured in the code or even in the writing.*
>
> *Translation blunts communication and makes knowledge crunching anemic.*
>
> *Yet none of these dialects can be a common language because none serves all needs."*

Some team members may become familiar with the domain terminology and act as *translators* for the rest of the team, but they can become bottlenecks.

In order to mitigate these types of risks, Eric Evans created the concept of a **ubiquitous language**. It is a common language among all team members and stakeholders based on the domain model:

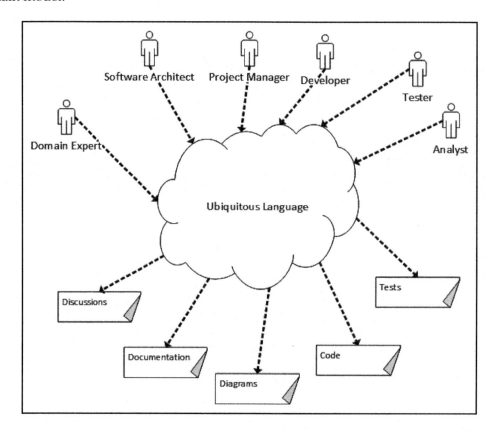

Developing a ubiquitous language can take time, and can evolve and grow as the team's understanding of the domain changes. Domain experts should use their understanding of the domain to point out terms that don't correctly express an idea, and everyone can look for inconsistencies and ambiguities in an effort to improve the ubiquitous language.

Although it takes effort, once you have a ubiquitous language, it simplifies communication and leads to a greater understanding among everyone involved with the project. No translation will be needed because everyone has agreed on and understands the various terms. The important thing is to use it consistently and throughout the project. The ubiquitous language should be used during **discussions** and in all of the project artifacts such as **documentation**, **diagrams**, **code**, and **tests**.

Entities, value objects, and aggregates

Some of the basic building blocks of DDD are entities, value objects, and aggregates. When modeling them, the ubiquitous language should be used.

Entities

Entities are objects that are defined by their identity and not their attributes. They are mutable because the values of their attributes can change without changing their identity. If two objects have the same values for their attributes, other than their unique identifier, they are not considered equal.

For example, if you had two `Person` objects with the same first and last name values for those corresponding attributes, they are still two different objects because they have different identities. This also means that a value for an attribute such as last name can be changed on a `Person` object and it still represents the same person.

Value objects

Unlike entities, value objects are objects that describe some characteristic or attribute, but have no concept of identity. They are defined by the values of their attributes and are immutable. If two objects have the same values assigned to their properties, they can be considered equal.

For example, if two objects that represent points on a graph using Cartesian coordinates have the same x and y values, they can be considered equal and would be modeled as a value object.

Aggregates and root entities

Aggregates are groupings of entities and value objects that are treated as a single unit. A boundary is defined that groups them together. Without aggregates, complicated domain models can become unwieldy to manage, as the many entities and their dependencies grow large in number. Retrieving and saving an entity and all of its dependent objects can become difficult and error-prone.

An example of an aggregate is an order object that contains an address object and a collection of line item objects. The address object and the collection of line item objects are all separate objects, but they are treated as a single unit for data retrieval and changes.

Separating the domain into subdomains

One practice of DDD is to separate the domain model into multiple subdomains. While a domain is the entire problem space that the software solution is being developed for, a subdomain is a partitioned piece of the overall domain. This is particularly useful for large domains, where it is not feasible to have one large and unwieldy domain model.

By focusing on one subdomain at a time, it reduces complexity and makes the overall work more digestible. Rather than attempting to address too many issues at once, dividing your domain into subdomains provides more of a *divide and conquer* approach.

For example, in a student information system, you may have subdomains for contact management, admissions, financial aid, student accounts, and academics, among others.

One or more of the subdomains may be designated as a **core domain**, which is typically the part of the domain that is fundamental to the organization. If there is a part of the domain that differentiates the organization from competitors, it is probably one of the core domains. Core domains are the reason that the software is worth writing, rather than buying existing software off the shelf or outsourcing the work.

The domain experts on the project can help with identifying the core domains, as well as the division of domains into subdomains.

What are bounded contexts?

A domain model is a conceptual model based on the domain and includes both behaviors and data. It represents a part of the overall solution that fulfills the goals of the business. **Bounded contexts** are a pattern in DDD that represent partitions in the domain model. Similar to subdomains, which are partitions in the *domain*, bounded contexts are partitions in the *domain model*. As is the case with subdomains, creating partitions and boundaries reduces the overall complexity.

A bounded context may map to a single subdomain, but keep in mind that is not always the case. The domain model for a subdomain may require multiple bounded contexts for the overall solution of that subdomain.

For example, if we were creating a software system for a business that sells clothing online, we might allow customers to sign up for a newsletter that contains deals and discounts. Another part of the application would allow customers to place orders and provide payment information.

With these two pieces of functionality, some concepts are shared, while some are not. If different development teams, or different developers on a single team, are working on these two sets of functionality, it is not clear what overlap, if any, exists. If there is overlap, what should or should not be shared between these two pieces of functionality? This is where the concept of bounded contexts is applicable. A domain model applies to a particular context, so we can define the various contexts to clear up some of the ambiguities that exist.

In this example, we could create one bounded context for marketing (**Marketing Context**), and one for order processing (**Order Processing Context**). Each bounded context may have entities that are unique to itself. For example, the **Order Processing Context** has the concept of an order line item, whereas the **Contact Management Context** does not. However, both bounded contexts have the concept of a **Customer**. Is **Customer** referring to the same concept in both bounded contexts? By separating them out, we can begin to answer this question:

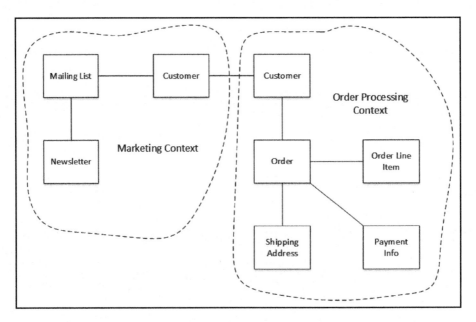

In the context of marketing, all that may be required for a **Customer** entity is an identity (unique identifier), first name, last name, and email address. However, in the context of placing an order, the **Customer** entity would require additional information, such as a shipping address and payment information.

You could create one **Customer** entity, but using it for different contexts adds complexity and can lead to inconsistencies. Validation that requires payment information only applies in the **Order Processing Context**, and not the **Marketing Context**. The behavior required for a **Customer** in the **Order Processing Context** should not prevent a **Customer** from being created in the **Marketing Context**, where only the first name, last name, and email address are required.

We will discuss the **single responsibility principle (SRP)** later in this book, but the basic idea is that each class should be responsible for a single aspect of the functionality. The **Customer** entity is still small now, but you can begin to see how it could grow quickly. If it were to be used in multiple contexts, it would attempt to fulfill too many disparate responsibilities and break the SRP.

The context for each model should be clearly defined and there should be an explicit boundary between bounded contexts. They are created so that everyone on the team, or across multiple teams, can have the same understanding of what belongs in each context. While the example used is a simplistic one, a large domain model will have many entities and contexts, and it usually isn't immediately clear what is unique or common across different contexts, and how each context should interact with each other.

DDD and the concept of bounded contexts work well with microservices, which we will be discussing in further detail later in this book. Now that we have a better understanding of DDD concepts, let's go into detail about requirements. Working with domain experts and other stakeholders, we need to have an understanding of the requirements prior to design.

Requirements engineering

In order to model your domain and design an appropriate architecture, you will need to know the requirements for the software you are building. **Requirements engineering** involves establishing the functionality that is required by the stakeholders, along with the constraints under which the software must be developed and operate. It encompasses all of the tasks involved in eliciting, analyzing, documenting, validating, and maintaining the requirements of the software system. As a software architect, you will be participating in these tasks so it is helpful to be familiar with them.

Types of software requirements

There are different types of software requirements, and software architects should be knowledgeable about them. The main types of software requirements include:

- Business requirements
- Functional requirements
- Non-functional requirements
- Constraints

Let's take a closer look at each of these types.

Business requirements

Business requirements represent the high-level business goals of the organization building the software. This type of requirement defines the business problems that the software will solve or the business opportunities that will be addressed by the software.

Business requirements may include requirements that come from the market. An organization may want to ensure that they are not excluding some functionality that a competitor is providing. They may also want to differentiate themselves from a competitor by providing functionality that a competitor is not, or provide the same functionality but in some improved form (for example, faster response times). As a result, business requirements often influence the quality attributes of a software system.

Functional requirements

Functional requirements describe the functionality of the software., In other words, what the software system must do. They detail the capabilities of the software system in terms of behavior. The functionality and capabilities described by the functional requirements enable stakeholders to perform their tasks.

Functional requirements include the interaction of the software with its environment. They consist of the inputs, outputs, services, and external interfaces that should be included with the software.

Keep in mind that requirements can come from a variety of sources, such as the following:

- **Organizational requirements**: Requirements that are based on organizational policies and procedures
- **Legislative requirements**: Non-functional requirements that detail any laws and regulations that the software must follow
- **Ethical requirements**: Any requirements for the ethical operation of the software, such as concerns related to privacy or safety
- **Delivery requirements**: Requirements that are related to the delivery and deployment of the software
- **Standards requirements**: Requirements for any standards that must be followed for the development of the software or how the software must operate

- **External requirements**: Requirements that originate externally, such as requirements from external systems that must integrate with the software system being designed

Non-functional requirements

Non-functional requirements are conditions that must be met in order for the solution to be effective, or constraints that must be taken into consideration. Business analysts and other stakeholders tend to do a good job at capturing functional requirements, but they don't always focus as much on non-functional requirements. However, non-functional requirements are an important part of requirements engineering. The success of the project is dependent on the non-functional requirements and whether or not they are met.

When a software architecture is designed, the software architect must ensure that the non-functional requirements can be satisfied. Non-functional requirements can have a significant impact on the design of the architecture. For that reason, they are of great importance to software architects. Software architects need to play an active role in eliciting non-functional requirements from stakeholders and ensuring that they are captured.

Quality attributes are a subset of non-functional requirements and include the *ilities*, such as maintainability, usability, testability, and interoperability. We'll go into more detail on some of the different quality attributes in the next chapter.

Constraints

Constraints are some type of restriction on the solution and may be technical or non-technical in nature. Some constraints on a project might be captured and classified as a functional or non-functional requirement, or they might be explicitly categorized as a constraint. Either way, the important thing is that they are decisions that have already been made and must be honored. Typically, a constraint cannot be changed, and the software architect does not have any control over it. However, if you have reasons why you believe a constraint should be changed or removed, there may be situations in which you could provide your input.

Constraints can pertain to a number of aspects of a software project. The following are some examples of constraints:

- An organization might have an existing agreement with a particular vendor or has already purchased a certain technology or tool that you will be required to use
- There may be a law or regulation that the software must follow

- There may be a particular deadline for a milestone or the final delivery of the software that cannot be altered
- Management might dictate that a certain number of resources be assigned to the project, or that the project must utilize outsourced resources
- If the development team already exists and they are skilled in a particular programming language, the organization may require that programming language be used

Constraints should be considered while designing the solution, just like other types of requirements.

The importance of requirements engineering

The importance of requirements analysis cannot be overstated. Proper requirements analysis is crucial for a successful project since it affects all of the subsequent phases. If it isn't done properly, additional work will be required, resulting in time and cost overruns.

The later in the life cycle such problems are encountered, the more it will cost and the longer it will take to correct those mistakes. When a problem with requirements is discovered later in the life cycle, the deliverables that have already been produced in subsequent phases, such as design and development, may require refactoring. In *Code Complete (Second Edition)*, Steve McConnell explains that *the principle is to find an error as close as possible to the time at which it was introduced. The longer the defect stays in the software food chain, the more damage it causes further down the chain.*

Some of the many benefits of proper requirements analysis include:

- Reduced rework
- Fewer unnecessary features
- Lower enhancement costs
- Faster development
- Reduced development costs
- Better communication
- More accurate system testing estimates
- Higher customer satisfaction levels

It is imperative that management understands the importance and benefits of proper requirements engineering. If they do not, an attempt must be made to communicate that to them so that proper time can be scheduled for requirements engineering.

Software requirements must be measurable and testable

When defining software requirements, they should be complete in that all of them are defined, and consistent in that they are clear and do not contradict each other. Each software requirement should be unambiguous, measurable, and testable. Testing should be considered when requirements are written. Requirements need to be specific enough that they can be verified.

Business analysts and other stakeholders who are defining the requirements must write them in a way so that they are measurable and testable. As a software architect, if you see requirements that do not satisfy these conditions, you need to point them out so that they can be modified.

If a requirement is to be considered measurable, it should provide specific values or limits. In order for a requirement to be testable, there must be a practical, cost-effective way to determine whether the requirement has been satisfied. It must be possible to write a test case that can verify whether or not the requirement has been met.

For example, consider a requirement that states that *the web page must load in a timely manner*. What exactly does that mean? Stakeholders and the development team may have a different understanding of what will satisfy such a requirement. It should be written with a specific limit in mind, such as *the web page must load within two seconds*.

A common understanding and mutually agreed upon expectations need to be set with stakeholders so that there are no surprises when the final product is delivered.

Software requirements that affect architecture

As a software architect who is designing an architecture that will satisfy the requirements, complete and validated requirements are crucial to your job. Requirements, particularly the quality attributes, can greatly affect the architectural design.

However, the degree to which a particular requirement has an effect on the architecture varies. Some do not have any effect, while others have a profound one. You must be able to recognize the requirements that may affect decisions you are making architecturally.

Many times, the requirements that affect a software architecture's design are quality attributes. Therefore, you should pay particular attention to those. Be aware though that it is common for the definition of quality attributes to be lacking when defining requirements. Stakeholders may focus on functional requirements, and may not define quality attributes, or if they do, they may do so in a way that is not measurable and testable.

Software architects may need to make an extra effort to understand the quality attributes that are important to the stakeholders, and the values expected to make them testable to get the quality attributes defined and documented. In the next section, let's examine ways in which you might elicit requirements, including quality attributes, from stakeholders.

Requirements elicitation

Perhaps you have heard of the terms *known knowns*, *known unknowns*, and *unknown unknowns*. They are used to describe that which we know about, that which we are aware of but do not know about, and that which we are not even considering because we do not know about them.

Ideally, the requirements and business domain of a software project are well understood. However, the development team may not have such an understanding from the onset of the project. Even for those who do have the knowledge, such as some of the stakeholders, they may not know exactly what they want from the software.

As a result, you will be dealing with both knowns and unknowns. Part of requirements engineering involves gaining as much knowledge as possible regarding the requirements of the system we want to build. We seek to eliminate the *unknown unknowns* and consider as many of the requirements as possible when designing the software.

The start of that process is to elicit requirements from stakeholders, which is known as **requirements gathering** or **requirements elicitation**. Requirements gathering seems to imply simply collecting requirements that are easy to discover, although it typically involves much more than that. Often, it is necessary to *elicit* the requirements from stakeholders because not all of them are at the forefront of the thoughts of stakeholders. It is more of a proactive, and not a reactive, process.

As Andrew Hunt and David Thomas point out in *The Pragmatic Programmer*:

> "*Requirements rarely lie on the surface. Normally, they are buried deep beneath layers of assumptions, misconceptions, and politics.*"

Techniques to elicit requirements

Obtaining information from stakeholders takes effort, but there are proven techniques that can assist you to draw them out. Each technique has its own advantages and disadvantages, so select the ones that are most likely to work given your situation. Don't forget that you can use more than one of these techniques. Using multiple techniques in conjunction with each other may yield the best results.

Interviews

One way to elicit requirements is to conduct **interviews** with stakeholders. Interviews for this purpose can either be conducted formally or informally. Each interview session should either be with a single person or a small group. If it is with more than one person, you don't want to have too many people in the session or you risk not getting the maximum amount of information from each individual stakeholder.

One or more people can ask questions, and at least one person should be designated to take notes. Ask open-ended questions to spur discussion and get information, and closed-ended questions can be used to confirm facts.

As with all of the techniques, the success of interviews depends on the knowledge of the interviewee, as well as their willingness to participate. It is good to interview different types of stakeholders in order to get different perspectives. You need to take into consideration their knowledge and experience when reviewing the results of the interviews. Interviews are not always a good way to reach consensus because not all of the stakeholders may be present, but they could be effective to obtain information.

Requirements workshops

Requirements workshops are one of the most common and effective elicitation methods. They are used to collect and prioritize requirements. A group of relevant stakeholders is invited to attend a session in which they will provide their feedback. An inevitable result of having such discussions will be a higher level of clarity on how the software should work, and what it is required to do.

A clear agenda should be set for each requirements workshop. The scope varies, but you might want to keep each session restricted to a certain part of the business process or software application. Someone should be designated as the facilitator who can run the meeting, and a different person should take notes.

The duration of a requirements workshop can vary and is dependent on the scope. It can last anywhere from an hour to several days. The length of the workshop should be appropriate for its scope.

You can acquire quite a bit of information from a requirements workshop. Just be sure to have an ideal number of people participate. If there are too many, the process could be slowed down, and some people may not have an opportunity to share their thoughts. On the other hand, if there are not enough attendees, then you may not gather enough information.

Sometimes it can be difficult to get all of the stakeholders in one place at the same time. If you can't arrange that, you could consider running multiple workshops on the same topic.

Brainstorming

Brainstorming sessions involve getting thoughts from a group spontaneously and documenting those thoughts. It can be a fun, productive way to get requirements for a system. If you are going to conduct such a session, make sure you invite the relevant stakeholders. If there are many stakeholders, you may want to consider holding multiple sessions and keeping the attendance of each one to between five and ten people.

When inviting the stakeholders, make sure you have a variety. Different types of stakeholder will have different perspectives and may provide ideas that others would not have considered.

The brainstorming session should have clear goals, and each session should not be too broad. You may conduct a brainstorming session to get requirements for a specific piece of functionality within the software system.

Try to hold the brainstorming session in a relaxed, comfortable environment so that the participants feel comfortable sharing their ideas. Someone should be designated as the facilitator. The facilitator may need to encourage participation, especially at the beginning of the session, since some participants may hold back their thoughts. As a software architect who wants the group to generate ideas, you can take it upon yourself to come up with the first idea to encourage others.

Criticism of ideas shouldn't be tolerated, as you don't want to discourage anyone from participating further. While there may not be any bad ideas, sometimes there will be thoughts that are not relevant to the goals of the meeting. If a discussion does get off topic, the facilitator should limit the discussion and steer it in another direction.

Either the facilitator or another person should take notes, preferably on a whiteboard so that everyone can see the ideas that have previously been given. For remote meetings where everyone is not in a room together, someone should share their screen so that the ideas are visible.

There should be a time limit so that everyone is aware when the session will end. If there is a clear ending where no more new ideas are being generated, the session could be called off early.

Observation

Observation is a technique where someone studies a stakeholder in their work environment, performing tasks related to the software project. It is particularly useful when you are attempting to understand a current process. It is effective because the observer may notice things that aren't mentioned through other elicitation techniques. Stakeholders may forget certain requirements or may not even be aware that what they are doing is a requirement that needs to be documented. By observing the actual work performed, you can sometimes gather important information.

This technique can either be performed in a passive way or in an active way, depending on what is agreed upon and what would be most effective. If the observer is passive, then he or she makes every attempt not to be disruptive. The observer does not ask many questions, nor do they interrupt the tasks that the stakeholder is performing. If the observer is active, then they can have an ongoing dialog with the stakeholder and ask questions while they are performing their tasks.

There are disadvantages to this technique. It can be time-consuming to observe someone performing his or her daily work. The person who is being observed may find it disruptive to their work, so you may only get limited time to perform the observation.

Even if a lot of time is spent observing, you may not witness all of the possible scenarios, and being aware of scenarios that do not happen as frequently is still important for the requirements of the software.

Although you shouldn't use this technique as the only one, it can be useful as a supplement to other techniques because it may draw out requirements that would not be revealed using other elicitation techniques.

Focus groups

Focus groups can be organized to elicit requirements. This technique is more formal than brainstorming and involves inviting a group of participants to provide feedback. This technique is commonly used for public applications that will have external users. In that case, the invited participants are users or outside experts who are external to the organization.

A moderator runs the session. The selected moderator is often skilled at running focus groups and is hired specifically to perform that role. The moderator asks the questions and encourages the participation of all the participants. Moderators should remain neutral during the session.

The questions asked during a focus group are typically open-ended and promote discussion. Responses in a focus group are typically spoken, as opposed to written. In that type of setting, things like nonverbal communication and group interaction can be observed. Focus group participants can foster new ideas from each other. This technique can be faster than conducting interviews individually.

Despite the advantages, there are some disadvantages to this technique. Focus groups run the risk of individuals following the crowd as they hear the feedback from others in the group. Some people are hesitant about sharing their ideas in a group setting, and the moderator may need to be paid to conduct the focus group.

Surveys

Surveys can be created and given to stakeholders to get information. Surveys should have a clear purpose. Rather than create a large survey that covers many topics, it may be more effective to create multiple surveys, each covering a portion of the business processes or software application. Some people will be averse to filling out extremely long surveys.

The questions in the survey should be well thought out, clear, and concise. Although surveys can have open-ended questions, typically the questions in a survey are closed-ended ones. This makes it easier for participants to provide answers, and, more importantly, the answers will be easier to analyze. If you do want to ask open-ended questions in a survey, keep in mind that it will require more effort to analyze the answers.

Document analysis

Document analysis utilizes existing documentation to obtain information and requirements. The documentation may cover the relevant business processes or existing software systems. If there is an existing system in use, it can serve as a starting point for the requirements of the new system. The documentation may come in the form of technical documentation, user manuals, contracts, statements of work, emails, training materials, and anything else that may be of use.

The documentation may even be **commercial off-the-shelf** (COTS) software package manuals. There may be existing software that provides part or all of the functionality you are seeking to implement, and by analyzing that documentation you can get the requirements for your software system.

Analyzing documents is particularly useful if stakeholders are not available for other requirements elicitation techniques.

Prototyping

Prototyping is a requirements elicitation technique that involves building a prototype that stakeholders can use to some degree, or at least see. Some people are more visually-oriented than others, and having a prototype can trigger ideas regarding requirements.

The disadvantage of prototyping is that it can take time to build a prototype. However, with most modern technologies a prototype can be built quickly. There is also the option of simply creating visual diagrams of the software, rather than a prototype. For web applications, this involves creating wireframes, which are visual representations of web pages that let a person see the layout and structure of web pages.

The scope of a prototype can be as broad or narrow as you want it to be. While it can demonstrate an entire application, it could be focused on a specific piece of functionality. Prototyping can be useful in conjunction with other techniques so that you can validate requirements and uncover things that had not already been discussed.

Prototyping can also be taken to a different level in which a working version of the software is produced. In a situation where the direction and purpose of the software have not been fully evaluated yet, perhaps because the stakeholders don't know where to begin, or they have many ideas but cannot agree among themselves, an initial prototype can be developed. If you are using an agile methodology, a few initial iterations can take place, each ending with a working version of the software that can be shared with the stakeholders.

Once they have something concrete to look at and use, it may inspire them with new ideas and approaches. Everyone will be able to see what works, and just as important, what does not work. If done properly, as refactoring occurs and further iterations take place, the requirements will become more apparent as the software takes shape.

Reverse engineering

Reverse engineering is a method in which existing code is analyzed to determine the requirements. It is similar to the document analysis technique in that it assumes that there are existing artifacts to analyze. This is not always the case when designing a new software system. It also requires access to the source code, and someone with the technical skill to analyze the code and extract requirements from it.

It is a time-consuming technique but might be used as a last resort if other techniques are not possible. For example, if stakeholders are not available to you, or the ones who are available to you are not knowledgeable, many of the other techniques may not be viable. If there is also a lack of documentation, then document analysis may also not be possible.

This method is not just a final course of action when others are not possible though. When appropriately used, it can be a powerful technique. Stakeholders may have limited perspectives, and may not think of everything that the software is required to do. If there is an existing system, looking at the code is a way to determine exactly what needs to happen.

Get access to the proper stakeholders

Even armed with techniques to elicit requirements, it can be difficult to get them from the proper stakeholders. You may find yourself in situations where certain stakeholders are not made available to you. You may also find yourself in a situation where certain stakeholders, for various reasons, are not being helpful or do not want to participate in the project.

Due to the importance of requirements analysis, you must make the effort to get access to the relevant stakeholders. This may involve speaking with management to get the proper access. Although this may be easier if you work for the same organization, many stakeholders will be external to the organization. The success of the project may depend on it, so you may need to escalate this need to your own management or to the management of the stakeholder's organization.

Summary

Being an effective software architect means understanding the domain of the software you are building. Gaining knowledge of general business topics and a deep understanding of the organization's business is the foundation for becoming an expert on the problem space for which you will be designing a solution.

DDD is a proven approach to modeling a domain. Creating a ubiquitous language that will simplify and facilitate communication between everyone involved in the software project, and working with domain experts, will facilitate learning a particular domain.

Other practices, such as separating your domain into subdomains and creating bounded contexts in your domain model, will minimize complexity and allow you and your team to firmly grasp even complex domains.

One of the keys to building software successfully is proper requirements engineering, including knowing how to effectively elicit requirements from stakeholders. Knowing the requirements for the software is crucial to designing an appropriate solution.

In the next chapter, we will further explore one of the most important types of software requirements: quality attributes. Building quality software requires the software architect to know and understand the details of the quality attributes that are important to the stakeholders.

Software Quality Attributes

4

Quality attributes are of the utmost importance to software architects because they affect architectural decisions. In this chapter, we will begin by explaining what quality attributes are, and why it is important to consider them throughout the software development life cycle. Some quality attributes can be difficult to test, so we'll explore what it takes to test them.

We will go into detail on some more common software quality attributes, such as maintainability, usability, availability, portability, interoperability, and testability. After reading this chapter, you will know the considerations that need to be taken into account for a software system to meet these quality attributes.

In this chapter, we will cover the following topics:

- Quality attributes
- Maintainability
- Usability
- Availability
- Portability
- Interoperability
- Testability

Quality attributes

Quality attributes are properties of a software system and a subset of its non-functional requirements. Like other requirements, they should be measurable and testable. Software quality attributes are benchmarks that describe the software system's quality and measure the fitness of the system. A software system is made up of a combination of quality attributes, and the degree to which they are fulfilled describes the overall quality of the software.

Quality attributes can have a significant impact on the design of the architecture, so they are of great interest to software architects. They affect multiple facets of a software system, such as its design, degree of maintainability, runtime behavior, and the overall user experience.

When designing your architecture, it is imperative to understand that software quality attributes can affect each other, and the degree to which one is met can affect the degree to which others can be met. It's important to identify potential conflicts between quality attributes. For example, a need for ultra-fast performance may conflict with the ability to achieve extreme scalability, and having a high level of security could decrease the level of usability.

Such trade-offs need to be analyzed to provide a balance so that an acceptable solution can be created. The priority of each quality attribute will be a factor in your overall design.

External or internal

Quality attributes can be internal or external. Internal quality attributes can be measured by the software system itself and are visible to the development team. Consequently, they are measurable both during and after development. Examples of internal quality attributes are aspects of the software system such as **lines of code** (**LOC**), level of cohesion, readability of the code, and the degree of coupling between modules.

These attributes reflect the complexity of the software system. Although internal quality attributes are not visible to users directly, they affect external quality attributes. A greater level of internal quality often leads to a greater level of external quality.

External quality attributes are properties that are externally visible; hence, they are noticeable to end users. These quality attributes are measured with respect to how the software system relates to its environment. Unlike internal quality attributes, a working version of the software must be deployed so that it can be tested. Examples of external quality attributes are the performance, reliability, availability, and usability of the system.

Quality attributes and the SDLC

Quality attributes should be considered throughout the **software development life cycle** (**SDLC**). The process begins during requirements engineering by ensuring that they are captured completely and correctly. In the previous chapter, we discussed the importance of measurable and testable requirements. This should be stressed further in relation to quality attributes, as some quality attributes can be difficult to measure. Quality attributes must be measurable and testable in order to determine if the software system satisfies the needs of stakeholders.

The software architecture design must ensure that it can meet the quality objectives. During testing, quality attributes must be verified to ensure that the software system satisfies the requirements.

Testing quality attributes

What kinds of testing techniques should be used to verify quality attributes? Beyond the simplest of software applications, it can be challenging to test software quality attributes and all of the possible scenarios that are affected by them. A variety of testing techniques must be employed in order to test different properties. For example, the following are some tests you may need to conduct:

- Manually testing the software for usability
- Creating benchmarks and using tools for performance testing
- Performing code reviews and calculating code metrics to test for maintainability
- Executing automated unit tests to ensure the system behaves as expected

Each testing technique comes with its own set of strengths and weaknesses. Some software quality attributes are difficult to assess, so you may need to combine multiple testing techniques in order to effectively test a quality attribute. Given unlimited resources, we might perform an exhaustive amount of testing, but projects are typically constrained by some combination of cost and time. As a result, a balance sometimes needs to be reached between the amount of testing and the time available.

Automating as much of the testing as possible is key to being able to execute tests in a short amount of time while maximizing test coverage. Automated tests can be executed on-demand or as part of a continuous delivery process (for example, as part of an automated build). Development teams can be assured that they still meet quality attribute objectives as they continue to make changes to the code.

Now that we know more about quality attributes, let's go into detail about some common ones (performance and security will be covered in `Chapter 10`, *Performance Considerations*, and `Chapter 11`, *Security Considerations*).

Maintainability

Maintainability focuses on the ease with which a software system can be maintained. Maintenance of a software system takes place as changes are made to it after the software is in operation. Maintenance is necessary to preserve the value of the software over time.

Change is constant in the real world. Sometimes it is expected and can be planned for, while other times it is not. Either way, it is inevitable that software systems will experience change. With the knowledge that change is unavoidable, it is important to build maintainable systems.

Decades ago, the greater part of a software project's costs went into software development. However, over the years there has been a shift in the cost ratio from development to maintenance. Today, the majority of a system's lifetime costs can typically be attributed to maintenance. Doing whatever is possible to keep those costs down can make a significant difference in the total money spent on the software over its lifetime.

Code that is easy to maintain allows maintenance work to be completed more quickly, and in turn will help to keep maintenance costs down. When a developer is writing code, he or she has to take into consideration not just the end user of the software, but also those who will be maintaining it.

Even if the original developer ends up also being responsible for the maintenance of a particular piece of code, consider the fact that the developer could leave the organization. Further, a developer may have a need to revisit their own code after some time passes, only to have forgotten the intricacies of it. In some cases, a developer may not even remember at first that they were the original developer of the code! Maintainable code benefits whoever needs to maintain it, even if it is the original developer.

Maintainability also affects how easily a software system can be reverse-engineered. There may be a need for a software system to be reverse-engineered, possibly so that it can be migrated to a newer technology. An architecture that exhibits a high level of modifiability will be easier to understand and reason about, making it easier to reverse-engineer.

Types of software maintenance

Software maintenance is performed for a variety of reasons, such as correcting defects, improving quality in some way, or meeting new requirements. As a result, software maintenance work can be categorized into the following different types of software maintenance:

- Corrective
- Perfective
- Adaptive
- Preventive maintenance

Corrective maintenance

Corrective maintenance is the work involved in analyzing and fixing defects in the software. Although it isn't the only kind of maintenance, it is the type that people associate most with maintenance work. Defects might be found internally, or by users in production. The severity and priority of defects vary depending on the nature of the bug.

Severity represents the level of impact the bug has on the operation of the software. Organizations have various classification systems for severity, but categories such as *critical*, *high*, *medium*, and *low* are common examples.

The priority of a defect is the order in which it will be fixed. Typically, the higher the priority, the quicker it will be fixed. Like severity, organizations may have different classification systems for priority, but categories such as *high*, *medium*, and *low* are common. Another common classification system is P0, P1, P2, P3, and P4, with P0 being the highest priority. P0 defects are critical and are considered *blockers*. A release will be put on hold until all P0 defects are fixed.

Maintainability can be measured by the time it takes to analyze and fix a particular defect. Higher levels of maintainability allow these tasks to be completed in a shorter amount of time.

Perfective maintenance

Perfective maintenance is necessary when the software needs to implement new or updated requirements. These types of changes are mostly focused on the functionality of the software. An example of perfective maintenance is a new enhancement to the software system.

Software that has a higher level of maintainability will allow for perfective changes to be made with less effort, and therefore at a lower total cost.

Adaptive maintenance

Adaptive maintenance is defined as the work required to adapt a software system to changes in the software environment. Examples of this may be to adapt the software system for a new **operating system (OS)**, a new version of the same OS, or to use a new **database management system (DBMS)**.

The duration of time it takes to adapt a software system to changes in the environment is a measure of the maintainability of the software.

Preventive maintenance

The goal of **preventive maintenance** tasks is to prevent problems in the future, by increasing quality. This may include improving quality attributes of the software system, such as increasing maintainability and reliability.

Preventive maintenance may take place to make maintenance easier in the future. An example of this is refactoring a software component to make it less complex.

Modifiability

Modifiability is one aspect of maintainability. Modifiability is the ease with which changes can be made to the software without introducing defects or reducing quality. It is an important quality attribute because there are a number of reasons why software needs to be changed.

Some software can remain useful in production for years, or even decades. Inevitably, that code will need to be modified for the different types of maintenance that were described previously. The time required from when a change is specified until it is deployed is an indication of the modifiability of the system.

In today's world, agile software development methodologies are the most common. These software projects embrace change. In addition to new functionality, each iteration of the project can involve changes to existing code. Improving modifiability is not just beneficial for maintenance but also for the entire development of the software.

Extensibility and flexibility

Extensibility and **flexibility** are additional characteristics related to maintainability. The level of extensibility reflects how easy it is to extend or enhance the software system. Software systems that are designed to be extensible take future growth into consideration by anticipating the need to add new functionality.

Flexibility is similar but mostly focuses on how easy it is to change a capability so that it can be used in a way that wasn't originally designed. Both extensibility and flexibility are characteristics that dictate the level of ease with which someone can perform perfective maintenance.

Scope of modifications

Not all changes to software are equal, and the scope of a particular modification is a factor in how difficult the change will be to implement. The larger and the more complex the modification, the greater the effort to complete it.

In addition to size, if the changes require architecture level changes, that will increase the level and scale of effort involved. Some components and their interactions may need to be refactored extensively for large changes.

Designing for maintainability

In order to design a software architecture that exhibits maintainability, you must reduce the difficulty in implementing changes. Making it easier to implement changes, in large part, means reducing the complexity of the architecture and its components.

Higher levels of complexity make software systems harder to understand, test, and maintain. For this reason, the level of complexity is a predictive measure of some quality attributes, including maintainability.

Evidence shows that modules with greater complexity are also more likely to contain errors. What makes this situation worse is that such modules are also more difficult to test, meaning that it may be more likely that an error will go undetected.

Although taking measurements and designing architectures to lower complexity may require more time (and therefore cost more money) during development, cost savings will be realized in the long term due to higher quality and a greater level of maintainability.

Some techniques used to reduce complexity and increase maintainability are to:

- Reduce size
- Increase cohesion
- Reduce coupling

Reducing size

Modules that are large tend to be more complex, and are responsible for a larger share of the logic. Therefore, the larger a module is, the more difficult it can be to change. Your design should seek to reduce the size of individual modules. One way to accomplish this would be to split up a module into multiple ones.

Increasing cohesion

Cohesion represents how interrelated the elements in a particular module are. Designs should seek to increase cohesion by not allowing a particular module to have too many disparate elements. Increasing cohesion reduces complexity and enables a number of different quality attributes, including maintainability. High cohesion often correlates to loose coupling.

Reducing coupling

Coupling refers to how dependent different modules are on each other. Designs should seek loose coupling, such that different modules are independent of each other or almost independent. If it becomes necessary to make changes to a highly coupled module, it will be more likely that other modules will be affected and therefore also require changes. Loose coupling reduces complexity and enables a number of different quality attributes, including maintainability. Loose coupling often correlates to high cohesion.

Measuring maintainability

A number of **software metrics** can help to measure the complexity of software, and therefore also the maintainability of software. Although measuring complexity and maintainability can be difficult, there are software metrics that can provide you with insights about the level of complexity and maintainability of your software.

Lines of code (LOC)

One such software metric is **lines of code (LOC)**, also known as **source lines of code (SLOC)**. This measurement simply represents the size of a software system by determining the number of lines in its source code.

Typically, software systems with more lines of code are greater in complexity and more difficult to maintain than those with fewer lines of code. However, comparisons of LOC between different software systems are really only useful if they involve an order of magnitude difference in lines of code. For example, if one software system has 50,000 lines of code, and another has 48,000 lines of code, you won't be able to make a determination on which software is more maintainable. However, if you were to compare a software system with 10,000 lines of code with one that has 100,000 lines of code, then you are more likely to make a useful determination.

Development tools and **integrated development environments (IDEs)** can count the number of lines of code for you. However, there are different ways that it can be calculated, and it is debatable which is the most useful. There is also a challenge if a software system uses multiple languages.

The two major ways that it can be calculated are the physical LOC and the logical LOC. The physical LOC typically is just a count of all of the source code lines, excluding comment lines. The logical LOC takes into consideration the actual number of program language statements in an attempt to only count *effective* lines of code. While the physical LOC is easier to calculate, it is more sensitive to being affected by such things as line spacing and other formatting.

Cyclomatic complexity

Cyclomatic complexity is a quantitative software metric that reflects the complexity of a software module. It was developed by Thomas J. McCabe and is sometimes referred to as McCabe's cyclomatic complexity. It measures the number of linearly independent paths through a module or detailed design element. Higher cyclomatic complexities indicate that the software is more complex.

Cyclomatic complexity can be calculated in a few different ways, but one of the most common is by using the following formula:

$$CC = E - N + 2P$$

An explanation for the preceding formula is as follows:

- *CC* = Cyclomatic complexity
- *E* = the number of edges of the graph
- *N* = the number of nodes of the graph
- *P* = the number of connected parts in the graph

Given a control flow graph created by examining the code or simply by eyeballing the code without creating a control flow graph, you must first count the number of nodes and edges. Nodes are a single block of code with statements executed in a sequence with no jumps. Edges represent control flow between nodes.

For example, assume we have the following pseudocode representing a simple if/then/else structure:

```
if (N1)
    then N2
    else N3
end if
    N4
```

The control flow graph for it would look like the following:

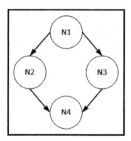

There is only one entry point (**N1**), and one exit point (**N2**) to this example, so there is only one path (P = 1). There are four edges and four nodes, so the cyclomatic complexity is 4 - 4 + (2 x 1) = 2.

Cyclomatic complexity values greater than 10 typically indicate modules that are complex, making them more error-prone and harder to test. Teams should seek to refactor complicated modules to lower their cyclomatic complexity.

Depth of inheritance tree (DIT)

The **depth of inheritance tree** (**DIT**) is a code metric that is specific to object-oriented programming. It measures the maximum length between a node and the root node in a class hierarchy. Take a look at the following diagram of a simple class hierarchy:

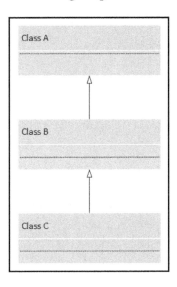

In this example, **Class C** inherits from **Class B**, which inherits from **Class A**. The DIT of **Class A** is 0, the DIT of **Class B** is 1, and the DIT of **Class C** is 2. A higher number for the DIT indicates a greater level of complexity. It also means there is a larger number of attributes and methods being inherited, which means there is code reuse through inheritance but it may make it more difficult to predict behavior. A lower number for the DIT indicates less complexity but it also may mean that there is less code reuse through inheritance.

Inheritance is a powerful concept in object-oriented programming and designs should strive for code reuse. Therefore, it is not that the DIT should always be kept to a minimum. A balance must be reached between code reuse and complexity. As a general rule, if the DIT is greater than 5, you may want to analyze the reasons for it and possibly reduce complexity by refactoring so that the tree is not as deep.

Usability

Usability describes how easy it is for users to perform the required tasks using the software system. User satisfaction is directly correlated to its level of usability. Users are much more likely to be satisfied with a software system if it is easy to use and provides a good user experience. The users' perception of the software system's overall quality will also be higher. Increasing usability can be one of the easiest and cheapest ways to improve the quality of a software system.

Usability is an important quality attribute because software that is not sufficiently usable will decrease the productivity of users. Even worse, users may not want to use the software at all. If the software is a website, and it is hard to use, difficult to navigate, slow to load, or difficult to read, users will simply start using an alternative.

Allowing users to complete their tasks efficiently

Software systems that exhibit usability allow users to complete their tasks efficiently. Once users have learned how to use the system, the speed at which they perform actions reflects the usability of the software system.

Learnability

Learnability is the degree to which new users can learn how to effectively use the software system. It is defined in ISO/IEC 25010, which is a series of standards that focus on a number of product quality characteristics. It reflects how easy it is for users to achieve their goals of learning how to use the software system. In addition to new users, learnability also includes how easy it is for experienced users to learn new functionality that is added to the system.

If a software system is usable, then its learnability level will be higher. The system should be intuitive, so that it does not take a lot of time or effort to learn a piece of functionality that is part of the software system.

Providing useful feedback

Usable software systems help users by preventing them from making mistakes, minimizing the impact of mistakes, and providing feedback. Examples of useful feedback include:

- Appropriate validation and helpful messages when validation fails
- Friendly and informative messages to the user
- Tooltips
- Feedback for long-running processes, such as a progress-bar or notifications when asynchronous operations complete successfully or fail for some reason

Accessibility

Accessibility is the aspect of usability which provides features that make it easier for people with disabilities or impairments to effectively use the software. This could potentially mean thinking about vision (partial or total blindness, color blindness), hearing (deaf or hard of hearing), and physical (not being able to type or use a mouse) impairments.

Designing for accessibility may include things such as:

- Making the software usable when only using a keyboard (no mouse)
- Providing support for assistive technologies, such as screen magnifiers, screen readers, text-to-speech software, alternative keyboards, and pointing devices
- Ensuring non-text content (for example, controls, time-based media, and CAPTCHAs) has a text alternative
- Designing the software so that there are ways to help users navigate the software
- Providing users with enough time to read and use the web page or screen (for example, allowing users to adjust or turn off time limits and provide users with the ability to pause, or stop content, such as auto-updating or scrolling content)
- Using colors that take into consideration color blindness
- Ensuring there is a logical tab order for controls and input fields

One key to success in this area is to include people with impairments in the requirement, design, and usability testing processes. Their feedback can be tremendously helpful in gauging how accessible your software system is for them.

Usability needs to be considered during requirements

During requirements engineering, use the requirement elicitation technique of observation that was previously mentioned to observe how users go about their work. This includes the process they go through as well as the current software that they use (if that software is relevant to the one being built). Through this technique, you can glean what works for the users, and just as importantly, what does not work.

Other requirement elicitation techniques, such as interviews where you can ask questions, can provide information regarding usability as well. The results of requirements elicitation can be used to create requirements related to usability.

Usability testing

Once a working version of the software is available for testing, **usability testing** should take place. Some of the same techniques used for requirements elicitation can also be used to get usability feedback. Arrange for users to operate the software and perform tasks with it while observing what works well and what pain points they may be having. Use interviews and focus groups to get feedback from users on what they liked and did not like about the software.

Appealing visual design

The aesthetics, or the visual appearance, of the software system, is a component of usability. The appearance of the application can have a great effect on users, so it is worth spending time ensuring that the application is designed to be visually appealing to users.

For web applications, there are a number of design choices that can be made to increase usability. When designing web applications, consider the following:

- Place emphasis on readability, including using headers, proper spacing, readable fonts, attractive colors, and appropriately formatted text
- Make sure the page layouts for all pages are well thought out
- Keep content concise by avoiding excessive text
- Ensure navigation and menus are not overly complicated to avoid making it difficult for users to find what they want
- Ensure that any links are not broken

- Provide tooltips, such as using the title attribute on hyperlinks so that helpful pop-up text will let users know more about a link
- Be consistent throughout the application with things such as colors, icons, fonts, and captions/terms
- Display progress indicators when the user has to wait for a response, such as a wait animation or a percentage complete indicator

The following are some things to consider when designing user interfaces for Windows desktop applications:

- Design with proper spacing of controls so that they are not too close or too far from each other
- Size windows and controls such as buttons, dropdowns, grids, and list views appropriately based on their expected content
- If a window is made to be resizable, and content is truncated, make sure that more content is shown as the window is made larger
- Consider setting a minimum window size if content is no longer usable at a particular size
- Label every control and every group of controls
- Make sure that the tab order of the controls on a window is correct
- Designate shortcut keys (a single key or key combination) that will allow users to quickly perform frequently executed commands
- Assign access keys (alphanumeric keys used with the *Alt* key) so that users can quickly activate a command
- Ensure proper capitalization in window headers, controls, labels, and content
- Provide helpful tooltips
- Be consistent throughout the application with things such as colors, icons, fonts, and captions/terms
- Provide the user with feedback on system status when it is busy with a long-running process, such as showing a progress bar
- The application should display informative messages to the user, such as confirmation, warning, and error messages, when appropriate

Providing a good help system

Designing a system that is highly usable also means that it should be designed to allow users to easily learn how to use it. A thorough and up-to-date help system makes an application easier to learn. Whether you are developing a desktop application or a web-based one, ensure that you have a help system that is extensive enough for the given application so that it will be of use to people. Depending on the software, who is using it, and how it is being used, an overall help system may include tooltips, online help, product manuals, tutorials, **frequently asked questions (FAQs)**, a knowledge base/discussion forum, training events, and ways to submit support cases.

This is not to say that a help system is the primary way of making an application usable. The application should be intuitive and easy to use based on other factors, but an appropriate help system does *supplement* the overall effort to increase learnability and usability.

Software must be useful, and not just usable

Keep in mind that, regardless of how usable the software is, it must have utility. For a system to have utility, it must provide the functionality that its users need. Being usable is great, but in order to be *useful*, it must also have utility. Users must be able to accomplish their goals and the software must serve its purpose.

Is the software system meeting the needs of the users? Is it useful to them? Even if the software system provides a nice visual experience, without usefulness it will not be a good user experience.

Availability

Availability describes the degree to which the software system will work as required when it is needed. It is the probability that the software system is operating properly when needed by a user and is not experiencing unplanned downtime due to failure and repair.

It is typically measured in terms of *nines*, as in how many *nines* represent the availability level (99.9%, 99.99%, or 99.999%).

Calculating availability based on time

Availability can be calculated with the following formula:

$$Availability = \frac{MTBF}{(MTBF + MTTR)}$$

MTBF is the mean time between failures, which is the average time between two failures of the system. MTTR is the mean time to repair, which is the average time to troubleshoot and repair the system back to its operational state. Only unplanned outages are considered when calculating system downtime.

To achieve high availability, which is considered *five nines*, or 99.999% availability, your software system can only be down for 5 minutes and 15 seconds or less during the course of a whole year! The following table shows some sample availability calculations:

Availability	Downtime per year	Downtime per month	Downtime per week
99.0%	3.65 days	7.2 hours	1.68 hours
99.9%	8.76 hours	43.2 minutes	10.1 minutes
99.99%	52.6 minutes	4.32 minutes	60.5 seconds
99.999%	5.26 minutes	25.9 seconds	6.05 seconds

Extreme levels of availability are not necessarily ideal because, at a certain point, you will experience diminishing returns. Consider that each additional *nine* requires a whole magnitude improvement of availability. This comes at a cost, in terms of time and money. This can have a negative effect on the software because it will limit how much time and effort can be spent on other things, such as releasing new features.

Also, consider the fact that a user won't be able to tell the difference between 99.99% and 99.999% availability. For example, in the case of a web or mobile application, there are other factors such as the user's device and the network that the user is on, which may not be as reliable as the software system.

The software architect and the stakeholders need to weigh the benefits of higher availability levels against the increased costs of providing them to determine which level suits them best.

Calculating availability based on request success rate

If your software is globally distributed, perhaps by taking advantage of cloud services provided by companies such as Amazon, Microsoft, or Google, you may be experiencing very high availability, such that at least some traffic is being served at any given time. As a result, calculating availability based on time as we did previously may not be very meaningful.

An alternate calculation would be to base availability on the request success rate. This can be calculated as follows:

$$Availability = \frac{Successful\ Requests}{Total\ Requests}$$

Your software system will have a variety of requests, some of which are more important than others, but looking at all requests should provide a good estimation of unplanned downtime.

Availability calculations based on time take into consideration the total failure duration, including the time to repair the software system. It doesn't distinguish between, for example, two failures of 30 minutes and one failure of an hour, but a calculation based on the request success rate does. Considering both of these metrics provides insights into different facets of your software's availability, which gives you a more complete picture.

Faults, errors, and failures

A part of availability involves how a software system can handle and overcome faults so that the duration of an unplanned outage does not exceed the specified value over a particular amount of time.

A system **fault** is a characteristic of a software system that can lead, either on its own or in conjunction with other faults, to a system failure. A system fault exists somewhere in the code. An **error** is an erroneous state of the software system caused by one or more faults. A system **failure** is an event experienced by a user in which the software system does not behave as expected. System failures are caused by one or more faults.

In order to handle and overcome faults and prevent failures, we can attempt to detect faults, recover from faults, or prevent faults.

Detecting faults

Before a software system can recover from a fault, it must first detect a fault. The following are some techniques that can be used to detect faults.

Ping/echo reply

In this method of detecting faults, a component, acting as a system monitor, sends an **Internet Control Message Protocol (ICMP)** echo request to another component (it pings the component) and waits for an ICMP echo reply. If the target does not respond to the ping in a predefined amount of time, the component acting as the system monitor reports that the other component has failed.

Heartbeat

This technique requires one component to periodically send a message (heartbeat) to indicate that it is operating normally. If the listening component does not receive the heartbeat message within the predefined amount of time, it determines that a system fault has occurred and takes the appropriate action.

Timestamp

This strategy of detecting faults focuses on catching an incorrect sequence of events. By using a timestamp, or even just a sequence of numbers, faults can be reported if the sequence is in the incorrect order.

Voting

A voting system can be used to report faults. One such approach is **triple modular redundancy (TMR)**, sometimes called triple-mode redundancy. It utilizes three components to perform the same process.

Voting logic will compare the results to produce a single output. If all three components produce the same output, then everything worked as expected. If two out of three components agree, they can correct the fault by outvoting the third component. A fault is then reported on the third component.

Sanity test/sanity checking

This fault detection technique uses a test to evaluate if a result from a process is reasonable and possible. If the test determines that the result is not, it can report a fault. Such a test is a simple one, and not intended to test for a wide variety of issues. It is used to detect obvious faults in a quick way.

Condition monitoring

Condition monitoring is a method whereby conditions are checked in a software system in order to detect a fault or a situation in which a fault may develop. When a problem is detected, the fault can be handled.

One benefit of condition monitoring is that it may detect a problem before a fault occurs, or at least before it becomes an even bigger issue.

Self-tests

Software systems can incorporate self-tests, allowing their components the ability to detect faults. Such a test is sometimes referred to as a **built-in self-test** (**BIST**) or a **built-in test** (**BIT**). If this technique is used, software components or combinations of components are developed with the logic that gives them the ability to test themselves for correct operation.

Self-tests can be initiated by the component they are testing or by a separate component acting as a system monitor. If a test fails, the fault is reported.

Recovering from faults

Once faults are detected, a strategy can be undertaken to recover from them. The following are some ways to recover from faults.

Exception handling

Once an exception is detected, the software system can utilize an exception handling mechanism. How an exception is handled is dependent on the language, framework, and type of exception, but it can involve anything from simply returning an error code to returning an instance of some error class that contains helpful information about the exception, such as an error code, a message, and a stack trace.

The software can use exception information to potentially recover from the fault, such as correcting the cause of the exception and retrying the operation, and/or showing the user a user-friendly message about the problem.

Retry strategy

Transient faults are errors that occur due to some temporary conditions, such as network connectivity issues, temporary unavailability of a service, timeout of a service, or infrastructure-level faults.

Retry strategies can be used to attempt to retry an operation when it encounters a transient fault. A retry policy can be tailored based on the nature of the component that caused the error, which can dictate things such as how many retry attempts are made, and the length of time to wait in between attempts.

Some common retry interval types include:

- **Regular intervals**: The software system waits the same amount of time in between each interval attempt.
- **Incremental intervals:** The software system waits a short amount of time before the first retry, and then incrementally increases the amount of time before each subsequent retry. For example, retry attempts may occur at 2 seconds, 6 seconds, 12 seconds, and so on.
- **Exponential backoff**: The software system waits a short amount of time before the first retry, and then exponentially increases the amount of time before each subsequent retry.
- **Immediate retry**: A retry can take place immediately. However, there should not be multiple immediate retry attempts. If a single immediate retry attempt fails, then any subsequent attempts should use one of the other interval types.
- **Randomization**: Any of the aforementioned interval types can be used in conjunction with randomization to prevent retry attempts from being sent at the same time from multiple instances of a client.

Varying levels of redundancy

One way to recover from faults and achieve availability is to have a failover mechanism. There are varying levels of redundancy that can be provided.

In *active/hot spare* environments, each component has another one that performs the same processes with the same inputs, so that, if one fails, the other component can take over at any time. Failover is generally transparent because the recovery time is nearly instantaneous.

A *passive/warm spare* environment is one in which only active components perform processes from inputs, but the active components provide the backup components with periodic state updates. A passive redundancy approach is not as highly available as an *active/hot spare*, but it is less expensive to operate. Depending on how frequent state updates are provided to the backup, recovery time can be in terms of seconds or minutes.

With a *cold spare* approach, redundant components are kept out of service until they are needed. The component that failed will be out of operation until it can be repaired or replaced. Using a cold spare takes more time to bring the redundant component into operation as compared with hot or warm spares. Recovery time could be a few hours.

Rollback

The rollback technique returns the system to a checkpoint in which the system is known to have been in a good state. This does require that checkpoints be persisted in some manner. Once the system is rolled back, regular operations can continue once again. This approach can be used with active or passive redundancy so that a failed component can be made active again after a rollback.

Graceful degradation

Graceful degradation is a fault recovery approach in which some functionality is made unavailable in order to prevent the entire system from becoming unusable. If failures are preventing the entire software system from being operational, then some functions can be dropped in favor of others. For example, if a system is running low on resources, the most critical functions can be kept working while others are shut down.

Ignoring faulty behavior

Another approach to fault handling is to simply ignore the fault. If a particular type of fault from a certain source is known to be one that can be ignored, then the system may simply disregard the fault and processing can continue.

Preventing faults

An alternative to detecting and recovering from faults is to prevent them from occurring in the first place. There are a number of strategies that can be employed to prevent faults.

Removal from service

One way to prevent faults is to remove the offending component from service. A software component can be removed from operation in anticipation of faults. It can then be restored when it is operational again.

Transactions

Transactions can be used to prevent faults. Multiple steps in a process can be bundled together in a transaction, so that if one step fails then the entire bundle can be undone. This approach can prevent data from being saved in an incorrect state, or prevent race conditions when more than one process attempts to access or change the same data.

Increasing competence sets

The *competence set* for a given component in a software system determines what states and conditions it can handle. A component's level of fault tolerance and the cases that it is designed to handle depend on the collection of logic that make up its competence set. A component can be modified so that it handles more cases, reducing the exceptions that are thrown.

For example, if a method does not handle a *null* value for a particular parameter, an exception may be thrown, leading to a system failure. The code could be modified to handle *null* values, increasing the competence set of the software and preventing a fault.

Exception prevention

This strategy involves writing the code in such a way that exceptions can be prevented. For example, methods could perform bounds checking on arguments and handle them gracefully, which would prevent exceptions from being thrown.

Portability

Portability describes how efficiently and effectively a software system can be transferred from one environment to another. Some factors that influence portability are adaptability, installability, and replaceability.

Adaptability

Adaptability is the degree to which a software system can be adapted for different environments, such as different hardware, operating systems, or other operational characteristics.

In order to test for adaptability, functional testing must be conducted to ensure that the software system can perform all of its tasks in all target environments.

Installability

Installability is the ease with which a software system can be installed or uninstalled in a specified environment. The installation process should be easy to understand, and may also provide configuration options as part of the installation. For example, the process may prompt the user to configure things such as the location for the installation, database connection information, and other configuration options for the software.

Another aspect of installability is how the software handles an update/upgrade process. The software system should provide a friendly and usable update process so that a user can upgrade the software to a newer version. The update process should clean up the older version, possibly by automatically uninstalling it first.

Installability also encompasses any functionality to uninstall the application. When a software system is uninstalled, it should remove the software system and any related components entirely from the machine. It may also delete any folders that are no longer needed.

A feature you may consider including that increases installability is providing users with the ability to cancel an install, update, or uninstall process once it has been initiated. Ideally, the process will clean-up after itself properly if the user aborts it or if it fails.

Installability testing should ensure that all of the functionality related to installing, updating, and uninstalling the software works properly and without error. It should test that any configuration options work properly, and check how the process handles situations such as when there is an insufficient amount of disk space available to install the software or an update.

Replaceability

Replaceability is the capability of a software system to replace another software system for the same purpose, in the same environment. This may entail only replacing one or more software components within a software system.

A good example of replaceability is when a software system is upgraded. Customers desire a system that is highly replaceable so that an upgrade to a newer version of the software from an older version goes smoothly.

Testing for replaceability should confirm that, after any replacement, the software system still works properly. All relevant functionality should be tested to verify that it works as expected.

Internationalization and localization

Internationalization and **localization** are part of portability and consist of adapting a software system for use with different languages, taking into consideration cultural differences, and meeting other requirements for various locales.

As a software architect, you will need to know if there are internationalization/localization requirements, so that you may consider them in the design. Even if there are no requirements currently, if your organization has business goals for international business expansion, the software may eventually be used in different areas around the world. If that is the case, you will want to consider that fact in your initial design, as it is more difficult to provide this capability later.

Internationalization is designing software in such a way as to enable localization and support for different languages, cultures, and regions. Internationalization in this context is often abbreviated to **i18n**, where 18 is the number of letters between *i* and *n* in the word internationalization. Sometimes the word **globalization** is used instead of internationalization. When that is the case, it is sometimes abbreviated as **g11n**.

As part of internationalization, the software should be designed so that adapting it to different locales later will not require modifications to the code. For example, all translatable strings, such as captions, messages, tooltips, and other content, should be placed in resource files. The code can then reference those resource files when it needs that content. Later, while localizing the application, these strings can be translated for different locales without having to change any code.

Unicode should be used as the character set for applications that require internationalization, as it supports all of the characters from any written language worldwide. If a development team were to use different character sets for different languages, localizing an application would be much more difficult. Unicode will facilitate displaying characters from any language that needs to be supported, and because there is a unique encoding for each character, data can be sorted, searched, and manipulated in the same way.

Once an application is ready to be localized, the following are some things which need to be considered:

- Translating captions, messages, tooltips, and other content for another language
- Ensuring the user interface can accommodate words properly after they are translated (for example, spacing and the wrapping of words could be different)
- Variation in the spelling of words, even for countries which use the same language, such as aeroplane/airplane, capitalise/capitalize, and organisations/organizations
- Language and cultural differences may require content to be rewritten to ensure that nothing will be misunderstood or taken the wrong way
- Whether text is read from left to right or right to left
- Differences in telephone numbers
- Differences in weights and measures
- Different date/time formats, such as whether 6/1/2019 should be interpreted as June 1st or January 6th
- Time zone differences (UTC)
- Formatting numbers, such as decimal mark symbols, digit group separators, and digit groupings
- Different currencies, such as currency symbols and whether the currency symbol should appear before or after the monetary value
- Any legal requirements

Maintaining portability

Once a software system is made portable for different environments, it is important that portability is maintained. As changes are made to the software as part of maintenance, it is possible those modifications could affect portability.

While making modifications, consideration must be given as to whether or not it will affect portability. During testing, it must be verified that any changes made did not adversely affect any requirements for portability.

Interoperability

Interoperability is the degree to which a software system can exchange and use information from another software system. In order for two systems to interoperate in a useful manner, they must be capable of communicating with each other (syntactic interoperability) as well as be able to interpret the information exchanged in a meaningful and correct way (semantic interoperability).

The term interoperability is related to, and sometimes used interchangeably with, the term integration.

Challenges with interoperability

There are a number of difficulties in providing interoperability between existing or new software systems. When dealing with requirements related to interoperability, keep in mind the following potential pitfalls:

- Even when a software system follows a particular standard when developing interoperability with another software system, the desired level of interoperability may not be met due to the two systems interpreting the standards specifications in different ways.
- Interoperability between two software systems is sometimes scaled back or put on hold because of the involvement of an existing legacy system, either directly or indirectly, when there is a desire to maintain compatibility with the legacy system. An organization may not want to make modifications to the legacy system.

- Tests for interoperability are sometimes insufficient and may miss certain interoperability issues.
- Software systems are sometimes released even when there are known interoperability issues.
- Even if interoperability is achieved between two software systems, it can be difficult to maintain as new versions of the two software systems get released. It is not uncommon for interoperability to be broken, requiring ongoing maintenance to maintain it.
- There can be legal issues for interoperability, so be aware of any that may affect your system when interoperating with another one. This may be particularly true if the two software systems are owned by different organizations, and even more so if they operate in different jurisdictions, such as two different countries. One example of this may be privacy and security laws related to healthcare information being exchanged.

Locating and exchanging information with another system

To achieve interoperability between two software systems, the consumer system must be able to locate the other and the two systems must be able to exchange information in a semantically meaningful way.

The consumer system may or may not need to discover the other system at runtime. If it does need to happen at runtime, a known directory service is searched by one or more attributes (for example, a URL) in order to locate the system. It should be noted that there can be *n* levels of indirection during the location process. For example, once one location is found, it may lead to another location, and so on, until the service is discovered.

Once the system is located, the response must be handled. The service will send back a response to the requester, forward a response on to another system, or broadcast a response to any interested services that may be listening.

In order for the two systems to exchange information, interoperability tactics, such as orchestration and the management of interfaces, are used. Orchestration involves directing and managing the services that are called and ensuring that the necessary steps take place in the correct sequence.

In order to manage interfaces to facilitate information exchange, capabilities may be added or removed for the purposes of interoperability. A capability may be added to an interface specifically to enable data exchange. An example of this may be functionality related to the buffering of data. In addition, capabilities may be removed from an interface if we do not want those capabilities to be exposed to other systems. For example, functionality to delete certain data may be removed from the interface if we do not want any external clients to have that capability.

Interoperability standards

When interoperability involves software systems from different organizations, one of the ways to achieve interoperability is to follow a common standard. The standard may be created by the two organizations working together as part of a partnership, or it may be an existing industry, national, international, or open standard.

In some cases, an entire industry will work together to come up with a standard. The standard may be one that is newly created by the industry, or some existing standard might be used as a starting point. The interoperability standard that is agreed upon can then be followed during the course of development and used during testing.

Another aspect of standards that may facilitate interoperability is using a common technology, such as agreeing on the data interchange format and the communication protocol. For example, it may be agreed upon that **JavaScript Object Notation (JSON)** is used as the data interchange format and that **Hypertext Transfer Protocol Secure (HTTPS)** is used as the web transfer protocol.

Interoperability testing

In addition to unit and system testing the two systems that must interoperate, it is critical to perform integration testing between the two systems. Tests must be conducted to ensure that the consumer system can locate the other system and that they can exchange information properly.

The testing environment should be as close to what will be experienced in production as possible. Keep in mind that, even if both systems follow a particular standard for interoperability, and even if both systems have passed their own conformance tests based on those standards, it is not uncommon for there to be issues with interoperability. Some issues may not be uncovered until both systems are tested together.

Testability

Testability is the degree to which a software system supports testing in its given context. The higher the level of testability, the easier the software system and its components are to test. If a component is not easy to test, it may indicate that the design is not ideal, leading to an implementation that is unnecessarily complex. A significant part of the development costs for software systems is related to testing, so if the software architecture can play a role in testability there can be noticeable cost benefits.

A software system that has a higher level of testability makes it easier to test, which results in an increase in both the efficiency as well as the effectiveness of testing. Testing efficiency increases because it takes less time and effort to create and execute tests. Testing effectiveness is increased because you are more likely to find existing defects in the software system, and you are more likely to find them sooner.

Finding defects sooner has a tremendous effect on the software system's overall level of quality. Not only is it more likely that defects won't make it into production, but the sooner a defect is found, the less costly it is to repair.

Some factors that influence testability are as follows:

- Controllability
- Observability
- Isolability
- Automatability
- Complexity of the software

Controllability

Controllability represents the level to which it is possible to control the state of the component being tested. The component being tested is sometimes referred to as the **system under test** (SUT) or the **component under test** (CUT). Controlling the state of a component involves being able to dictate the inputs of the component as well as the level to which those inputs exercise its capabilities.

When designing components, you should seek to increase their controllability, as this increases testability.

Observability

Observability represents the level to which it is possible to observe the state of the component being tested. This includes being able to observe inputs and outputs so that we can determine if the component is working correctly.

If it is not possible for the testing framework being used to see the inputs and outputs of a component, then the component is not observable, and it won't be possible to confirm if the results are correct.

When designing components, you should seek to increase their observability, as it is directly correlated to testability.

Isolability

Isolability is the degree to which a component can be isolated. The goal is to have tests that can focus on specific pieces of functionality (for example, unit tests) that do not have dependencies on other components. This allows us to create and execute tests on a completed component, even if other components are not complete.

We want to avoid a situation where we have to write a great deal of code before any of it can be tested since it is desirable to get feedback as quickly as possible. If a problem is found, it will be easier to determine its source and cause if components exhibit isolability.

An increase in isolability increases the testability of a component.

Automatability

Automatability is the level to which a process or action can be automated. If a system exhibits automatability, then automated tests can be created and executed for the system. Automated testing utilizes pre-scripted tests that can then be executed automatically. These tests can be run at any time, such as before a code check-in or prior to a build taking place. If automated builds are in place, automated tests can be executed as part of that process.

Automated tests give you quick feedback on whether a new defect was introduced into the system. As we just noted, discovering a defect as close to when it was introduced is highly beneficial. When designing a software system, you should seek to increase automatability, as the ability to have automated tests increases testability. Automated builds and automated testing will be covered further in `Chapter 13`, *DevOps and Software Architecture*.

Complexity of the software

As is the case with other quality attributes, the complexity of the software plays a role in testability. Reducing dependencies and isolating modules (isolability), decreases the complexity of the software.

When we discussed maintainability, we mentioned that minimizing the complexity of architectural elements can be accomplished by reducing the number of lines of code in modules, increasing cohesion and reducing coupling. Techniques that increase maintainability also increase the controllability of elements. This has a direct and positive impact on testability.

In addition to the *structural complexity* of components, there is *behavioral complexity*. Non-determinism is one type of behavioral complexity. If some algorithm we are testing is non-deterministic, then it means that given the same inputs, it can exhibit different behavior with each execution. This is in contrast with a deterministic algorithm, which, if given the same inputs, will behave in the same way each time it is executed.

Non-deterministic code is more difficult to test, so the first step would be to identify any areas in the software system that are non-deterministic. For such areas, the ideal approach, if possible, would be to refactor the logic to make it deterministic, or allow the logic to be mocked as deterministic.

A simple example often seen in practice involves tests and the current time. In most programming languages, there is a way to get the current date and time of day. Doing so can tightly couple your code to the host environment. It is non-deterministic because each time we make a call to get the current date and time, the result will be different. If there is logic that uses this value in a way that would affect a unit test, your test results will vary due to the non-deterministic nature of the result. This logic can be refactored to wrap the call to get the current date and time into some other class. Doing so will allow you to inject this dependency into the class that needs this logic. At that point, a testing framework can mock the dependency, specifying what the result will be when the call to get the current date and time is made.

However, there are cases where it will not be possible to refactor logic to make it deterministic, or to make it so that the logic can be mocked as deterministic. An example of this is if you had a multi-threaded system that is required to interact with an external component, and that external component raises events in a non-deterministic manner.

Importance of test documentation

An aspect of testability is the ease with which tests can be executed, including testers who did not originally write the test cases. The reusability and maintainability of tests, part of testability, are improved with the existence of quality test documentation. When dealing with a large system, it can be difficult to remember all of the business rules and alternative paths related to a particular scenario.

With agile software development methodologies, excessive documentation is viewed as a project risk rather than something that will reduce risk. Project teams aim to be efficient with documentation and produce only as much as is needed. In addition, automated tests should be fairly self-documenting through things such as the test method names, test class names, and comments.

However, there are many different types of testing beyond automated tests that need to be conducted, and some can be quite involved. There can be complexity in the business logic, in the inputs and outputs of tests, in the data that is needed to set up particular tests, and to ensure adequate coverage on a variety of business scenarios. Some form of test documentation can really be of benefit.

Resources can, and more than likely will, change over time. An employee may leave an organization, or testers simply get different assignments over time and a piece of functionality isn't necessarily *owned* by a single tester. Testing documentation allows different testers to use the test case over time and it facilitates such transitions so that quality is not sacrificed.

To add to that point, it is increasingly common for development departments to outsource development work, including testing. Not only may you have to deal with outsourced resources changing, but testing tasks may need to move from internal resources to outsourced resources, and vice versa.

Documentation of artifacts such as designs and tests is very useful so that new resources can get up to speed quickly. It's basically the concept of *tribal knowledge* and being able to pass on things that have been previously learned to others. Projects with good documentation typically demonstrate a higher level of organizational maturity and contribute to the project's overall success.

What makes a good tester?

While we are on the topic of testability, I wanted to touch upon the characteristics of a good tester. As a software architect, you may be providing guidance to testers. Good testers perform their tasks with a greater level of efficiency, effectiveness, and thoroughness.

Testers that operate efficiently do so in an organized way and their efficiency allows them to complete test cases faster, and find defects quicker. They are not just using the software and happening upon bugs, but using a systematic approach to finding defects.

Testers who achieve a greater level of effectiveness do so because they focus particular attention on problems that users will care about in the released version. Part of the process of finding defects involves documenting the problem and giving them to developers so that they can be fixed.

Exceptional testers are thorough in their work. They plan their testing activities and they document their test cases. Testers attempt to be as thorough as possible, exercising all aspects of a software's functionality and considering a variety of scenarios. They use a variety of inputs and test things such as edge cases, which are scenarios that involve extreme input values, such as those at the minimum or maximum of a range of possibilities.

Another characteristic of a good tester is the ability to understand the software's behavior, environments, and capabilities. Because a tester cannot test all possible inputs and scenarios, an effective software tester must understand the software's behavior. This includes what the software is doing, and what things could potentially cause it to fail.

Software operates in an environment that interacts with a variety of inputs and outputs. There is the **user interface** (**UI**) that people interact with, but there is also the kernel interface (operating system), software interfaces (for example, in things such as database systems), and file system interfaces (for example, errors related to accessing, reading, and writing to files). A good tester must consider the totality of the environment in which the software operates.

Finally, the tester must understand the software's capabilities. Although there may be a limited number of basic capabilities (for example, accepting input, producing output, storing data, and executing calculations), these capabilities can be combined into complex functionality. A suitable tester should consider all of these capabilities in order to maximize the probability that any defects that exist will be found.

Summary

Software architects should pay particular attention to quality attributes, as they influence the architecture of software. The software must meet the designated quality attributes, so identifying and specifying them in a way that they can be measured and tested is important.

Although some stakeholders might focus on functionality, non-functional requirements such as quality attributes are a principal factor in whether or not a software system will be a success. Some of the more important quality attributes include maintainability, usability, availability, portability, interoperability, and testability.

Now that we understand more about quality attributes and the fact that they influence software architecture, we are ready to explore software architecture design. Architecture design involves making decisions to create a solution for functional requirements, quality attributes, and constraints. You will learn what is involved with architecture design, about design principles that you can leverage in your designs, and about architecture design processes.

5
Designing Software Architectures

Software architecture design is a key step in building successful software systems, and this chapter begins by exploring what software architecture design is, and why it is important in a software project.

There are two main approaches to architecture design: the top-down and bottom-up approaches. Each approach has advantages and disadvantages, and in this chapter you will learn how to select the best approach for a given project. Designing a software and architecture can be challenging, but we will take a look at design principles and existing solutions that can be leveraged in a design.

Architecture design processes provide guidance to software architects to ensure that a design satisfies requirements, quality attribute scenarios, and constraints. This chapter covers the activities that are typically performed as part of an architecture design process and then provides an overview of four processes: **attribute-driven design (ADD)**, **Microsoft's technique for architecture and design**, the **architecture-centric design method (ACDM)**, and the **architecture development method (ADM)**.

The chapter will conclude by explaining how to use an architecture backlog to prioritize work and track the progress of architecture designs.

In this chapter, we will cover the following topics:

- Software architecture design
- The importance of software architecture design
- Top-down versus bottom-up design approaches
- Greenfield versus brownfield software systems
- Architectural drivers
- Leveraging design principles and existing solutions
- Documenting the software architecture design

- Using a systematic approach to software architecture design
- Attribute-driven design (ADD)
- Microsoft's technique for architecture and design
- Architecture-centric design method (ACDM)
- Architecture development method (ADM)
- Tracking the progress of the software architecture's design

Software architecture design

Software architecture design involves making decisions in order to satisfy functional requirements, quality attributes, and constraints. It is a problem-solving process that leads to the creation of an architecture design.

Software architecture design comprises defining the structures that will make up the solution and documenting them. The structures of a software system are made up of elements, and the relationships between the elements. The properties and behaviors of the elements that are publicly exposed, through an interface, should be identified as part of the design. The design allows you to understand how the elements behave and interact with each other. Private implementations of the elements are not architecturally significant and need not be considered as part of the design.

The software architecture design serves as technical guidance for development and typically occurs iteratively until the initial architecture is at a point where the development team can begin their work. Once an initial architecture is designed, it can continue to evolve as development is taking place. For example, additional design iterations may occur to refactor an architecture to fulfill new requirements or quality attributes.

Software architecture design is a creative process. Software architects have the privilege of coming up with solutions to complex problems and can use creativity to do it. It can be one of the most fun and rewarding parts of a software project.

Making design decisions

The set of software requirements consists of a series of design issues that must be solved. For each of these design issues, such as providing certain business functionality, respecting a particular constraint, meeting performance objectives, or providing a certain level of availability, there may be numerous ways to solve the problem. You will need to consider the strengths and weaknesses of these alternatives in order to select the most appropriate choice.

A large part of software architecture design is making design decisions to resolve issues so that a solution can be implemented. As the software architect, you will be leading the decision-making process.

It is a collaborative process, and usually the best designs incorporate knowledge and feedback from multiple people, such as other software architects and experienced developers. Joint designs and reviewing the architecture with others is beneficial in coming up with a solid software architecture design.

The result of the design is a set of decisions that shape your software architecture. The design is documented in artifacts that can be used for the implementation of a solution.

Software architects should keep in mind that a decision that is made for one design issue may affect another one. This is why software architecture design is an iterative process. Each decision for a design issue may not be optimal for another issue, but the overall solution must be acceptable by satisfying all of the requirements.

Perfect is the enemy of good, an aphorism that has its origins in the thoughts of the French philosopher, Voltaire, and others, is applicable to software architecture design. A completed design may not be perfect, as there will be conflicting requirements that need to be met, and trade-offs made in order to meet them. If the design satisfies all of the requirements, then it is a good one, even if it is not perfect.

Software architecture design terms

Before we go any further, let's define some of the terms that we will be using while detailing the process of software architecture design. These terms can vary, depending on the organization and the team. Regardless of the terms used, the important thing is that they are used consistently by the team members and that they are understood by all team members.

For the purposes of this book, we'll be using the terms structure, element, system, subsystem, module, and component.

Structure

Structures are groupings of, and relations between, elements. Anything that is complex and made up of elements can be referred to as a structure. We previously defined software architecture, in part, by saying it is made up of the structures, their elements, and the relationships of those elements with each other.

Element

An element is a generic term that can be used to represent any of the following terms: system, subsystem, module, or component. If we want to refer to pieces of a software application in a general way, we can refer to them as elements.

System

The software system represents the entire software project, including all of its subsystems. A system consists of one or more subsystems. It is the highest level of abstraction in a software architecture design.

Subsystem

Subsystems are logical groupings of elements that make up a larger system. The subsystems can be created in a variety of ways, including partitioning a system by functionality.

Although they do not have to be, subsystems can represent standalone software applications. An overall software system may be composed of multiple subsystems, and any number of them might be a standalone application. These standalone applications can be external applications that were not developed by the organization.

Organizing a larger software system into subsystems lowers complexity, and allows for software development to be better managed. In some cases, one or more development teams may be formed for each subsystem. Each subsystem is made up of one or more modules.

Module

Modules, like subsystems, are logical groupings of elements. Each module is contained within a subsystem and consists of other modules and/or components. They are typically focused on a single logical area of responsibility.

Development teams assigned to a particular subsystem will be responsible for the modules that make up that subsystem.

Component

Components are execution units that represent some well-defined functionality. They typically encapsulate their implementation and expose their properties and behaviors through an interface.

Components are the smallest level of abstraction and typically have a relatively small scope. Components can be grouped together to form more complex elements, such as modules.

The importance of software architecture design

A software architecture is the foundation of a software system. The design of the architecture is significant to the quality and long-term success of the software. A proper design determines whether the requirements and quality attributes can be satisfied.

There are a number of reasons why a good software architecture design is critical to building useful software. In this section, we will explore the following reasons:

- Software architecture design is when key decisions are made regarding the architecture.
- Avoiding design decisions can incur technical debt.
- A software architecture design communicates the architecture to others.
- The design provides guidance to the developers.
- The impact of the software architecture design is not limited to technical concerns. It also influences the non-technical parts of the project.

Making key decisions

It is during software architecture design that key decisions are made that will determine whether requirements, including quality attributes, can be satisfied. Software architecture enables or inhibits quality attributes, so design decisions play a large role in whether or not they can be met.

Some of the earliest decisions are made during design. If these decisions need to change, it is easier and less costly to change architectural decisions early, before coding has even begun, than to make changes later.

Avoiding design decisions can incur technical debt

Critical decisions are made during the design, and for that reason, there is a cost to either delaying a design decision or not making one at all. Delaying or avoiding certain design decisions can incur technical debt.

Technical debt is similar to financial debt. In the context of design, it is the cost and effort for the additional work that will be necessary later due to decisions that are made now, or because decisions have not been made.

In addition to delaying or avoiding decisions, a decision may be made knowing that it will cost some amount of technical debt. As a software architect, you may decide to take an easier route to a solution, incurring technical debt, even though there is a better solution. As is the case with financial debt, technical debt is not always a bad thing. Sometimes, you will want to pay a debt later in order to get something now. For example, designing a better long-term solution may take more time and effort, and you may decide on a solution that takes less time in order to get the software in production to take advantage of a market opportunity.

It can be difficult to measure the impact of technical debt accurately. Keep in mind that in addition to the time and effort that might be required later to make up for a decision that is made or avoided now, technical debt can have other negative repercussions. For example, a design that is not optimal, leading to lower levels of modifiability and extensibility, can hinder the team's ability to deliver other functionality. This is an additional cost that should be added to the technical debt.

The software architect needs to take all of these factors into consideration when deciding whether or not to incur a technical debt.

Communicating the architecture to others

The results of the architecture design allows you to communicate the software architecture to others. There will be a variety of people who will potentially be interested in the design of the architecture.

The design will also improve cost and effort estimates since it influences what tasks will be required for implementation. Understanding the nature of the work that lies ahead and what types of tasks will be needed to complete the project will assist project managers with their planning. Being able to estimate cost, effort, and the quality attributes that will be met is also useful for project proposals.

Providing guidance to developers

A software architecture design provides guidance to the development team, by steering implementation choices as well as providing training on the technical details of the project.

The design imposes implementation constraints, making it important for coding tasks. Knowing the software architecture design helps developers be aware of the implementation choices available to them, and minimizes the possibility of making an incorrect implementation decision.

It can also be used as training for developers. At the start of the project, the development team will need to understand the design decisions that have been made, and the structures that have been designed. Creating detailed designs for components and implementing them requires an understanding of the architecture design. If new developers join the team later, they can also use the architecture design as part of their onboarding.

Influencing non-technical parts of the project

Another reason that software architecture design is important is the fact that design decisions affect aspects of the software project other than the architecture. For example, certain architecture design decisions could affect the purchasing of tools and licenses, the hiring of team members, the organization of the development environment, and how the software will eventually be deployed.

Top-down versus bottom-up design approaches

There are two fundamental approaches to the design of software architecture. One is a top-down design approach, and the other is a bottom-up approach. These strategies apply to a variety of disciplines, including software architecture design. Let's look at both of them in more detail.

Top-down approach

A **top-down approach** starts with the entire system at the highest level, and then a process of decomposition begins to work downward toward more detail. The starting point is the highest level of abstraction. As decomposition progresses, the design becomes more detailed, until the component level is reached.

While the detailed design and implementation details of the components are not part of the architecture design, the public interfaces of the components are part of the design. It is the public interfaces that allow us to reason about how components will interact with each other.

A design using the top-down approach is typically performed iteratively, with increasing levels of decomposition. It is particularly effective if the domain is well understood.

This systematic approach has been favored by enterprises since it can handle large and complex projects and because the method of design is planned. A systematic approach to architecture design is attractive to enterprises because it can help with time and budget estimates. However, a strict top-down approach, which requires a lot of upfront architecture design, has become less common in modern software architecture.

Advantages of the top-down approach

There are a number of benefits to using a top-down approach. It is a systematic approach to design and breaks the system down into smaller parts. As a system is decomposed, it lends itself well to the division of work. On larger projects with multiple teams, this work can be divided among the teams.

As further decomposition takes place, tasks can be created for individual team members. This supports project management in the assignment of tasks, scheduling, and budgeting. This type of ability to plan is attractive to enterprises. The management teams of organizations may prefer, or even insist on, a top-down approach. Earlier in the book, we discussed how, as a software architect, you may be asked to assist with project estimates, and a top-down approach will allow you to do that with more accuracy.

Although this approach works well on both small and large projects, it can be particularly useful for large projects. By decomposing a system into smaller components, a large project can become more manageable as the size and complexity of each component is reduced.

Disadvantages of the top-down approach

A strictly top-down approach runs the risk of a **big design up front** (BDUF), sometimes referred to as a **big up-front design** (BUFD). Software is complex and it can be difficult to create the entire architecture up front. Design flaws or missing functionality in the architecture may not be uncovered until later in the process, when components are designed or implemented. If architecture changes are required in higher levels of the architecture after some work is already completed, it will be more difficult to make the modifications.

A top-down approach works best when the domain is well understood, which is not always the case. Plenty of projects begin without the domain being fully understood. Even when it is understood, stakeholders and users can sometimes be unclear as to what the software should do, and how it should work.

If multiple teams are working on a project, each responsible for a particular subsystem or module, knowledge sharing and reuse can be difficult with this approach. Each team can work independently of the others, which has its advantages, but it does not facilitate the sharing of code or knowledge. The software architect may have to recognize areas of reuse, abstract them out, and communicate them to the teams. Another way to mitigate this issue is to provide opportunities and collaboration tools for teams to communicate with each other.

If you use the top-down approach, be careful not to become an ivory tower architect. If you design the higher levels of an architecture and then hand them off to developers to handle the lower-level detailed design, it is easy to become disengaged. As much as your organization and the project permits, make an effort to stay involved with the team. If architectural changes are required later, you will already be familiar with the ongoing implementation, which will help you to make the correct changes.

Bottom-up approach

In contrast with the top-down approach, the **bottom-up approach** begins with the components that are needed for the solution, and then the design works upward into higher levels of abstraction. Various components can then be used together, like building blocks, to create other components and eventually larger structures. The process continues until all the requirements have been met.

Unlike the top-down approach, which begins with the high-level structure, there is no up-front architecture design with the bottom-up approach. The architecture *emerges* as more work is completed. Hence, this is sometimes referred to as *emergent design* or *emergent architecture*.

The bottom-up approach does not require that the domain be well-understood, as the team only focuses on a small piece at a time. The system grows incrementally as the team learns more about the problem domain as well as the solution.

Advantages of the bottom-up approach

One advantage of a bottom-up approach is the greater level of simplicity. The team only has to focus on individual pieces and builds only what it needs for a particular iteration.

This approach works well with agile development methodologies. With an iterative approach that handles change, refactoring can take place to add new functionality or to change existing functionality. Each iteration ends with a working version of the software until eventually the entire system is built. Agile practices, such as automated unit testing and continuous integration, are encouraged and can lead to higher quality software.

A bottom-up approach avoids the possibility of a big design up front, which can lead to overdesigning a solution. Some in the agile community feel that a lot of design effort up front is wasted time and that an emergent design, or **no design up front** (**NDUF**), would be more effective.

The bottom-up approach allows the development team to begin coding very early in the process, which also means testing can occur earlier. This includes automated unit testing as well as manual testing by team members such as QA analysts and other users. Getting feedback earlier in the process allows the team to identify any necessary changes earlier.

This approach facilitates code reuse. As the team is focused on a limited number of components at any given time, recognizing opportunities for reuse becomes easier.

Disadvantages of the bottom-up approach

A bottom-up, or emergent, approach, assumes that change is cheap. Agile methodologies and practices provide an approach that anticipates change and can adapt to it. However, depending on the nature of the change, refactoring software architecture design can be very costly.

A bottom-up approach, with no initial architecture, can lead to lower levels of maintainability. With the refactoring that may be necessary with this approach, issues can arise. If the team is not diligent, this problem can become worse over time.

The entire scope of work may not be known when using this approach. This makes it more difficult to plan and estimate the entire project, which may be unacceptable for enterprise software.

One of the disadvantages of the top-down approach is that design flaws may not be detected until later, leading to costly refactoring. However, just because there is no initial design with the bottom-up approach does not make it immune to uncovering design flaws later in the project. It may not be until after the architecture *emerges* that certain design flaws become apparent.

Which approach should I use?

There are certain factors to consider when deciding whether the top-down or bottom-up approach is better for a software project. Software architects may find it advantageous to use a top-down approach if more than one of the following is true:

- The project is large in size
- The project is complex
- Enterprise software is being designed for an organization
- The team is large, or there are multiple teams that will be working on the project
- The domain is well-understood

It may be more appropriate to use a bottom-up approach if more than one of the following is true:

- The project is small in size
- The project is not very complex
- Enterprise software for an organization is not being designed
- The team is small, or there is only a single team
- The domain is not well-understood

Taking an extreme approach, such as doing a big upfront architecture design or no architecture design at all, is typically not ideal. Although some situations will lead you to select a top-down or bottom-up approach, software architects should also consider using a combination of the two approaches. In this way, you may be able to realize some of the benefits of both approaches, while minimizing the drawbacks.

In the beginning of the project, rather than starting to code immediately, a top-down approach will provide the opportunity to spend at least some time thinking about the overall structure of the design. The design of a high-level architecture provides some structure that can then be leveraged for further design and development.

A high-level architecture design can be used to define and organize the teams, and provides details to project management so that they can perform resource allocation, scheduling, and budget planning. As a software architect, you may be asked to provide input regarding these types of project management activities, and having at least a high-level architecture will assist you in such tasks.

Those who advocate for a strictly bottom-up approach, in which the architecture emerges from implementation, tend to think that software architecture inhibits agility and the ability to make changes to the software. However, as was mentioned in Chapter 1, *The Meaning of Software Architecture*, a good software architecture actually facilitates making changes as well as managing them. A good architecture allows you to understand what it would take to make a particular change.

Using a top-down approach for part of the design does not require a big upfront design. You can focus on architecturally significant design issues, and once a high-level architecture is established, you can employ a bottom-up approach. Components and modules based on the high-level architecture can then be designed and implemented.

The quality of the architecture design is not solely dependent on selecting the correct approach. The correct design decisions must be made during the design process, as both a top-down as well as a bottom-up approach can lead to poor architecture designs. A design created with a top-down approach can miss key requirements, which may lead to costly architectural refactoring. A design created with a bottom-up approach may require substantial refactoring while the team figures out how the software system should be structured.

No single approach is applicable to all situations. Each project, organization, and team is different, so the decision of which approach to take will vary. Even with a hybrid approach, the amount of upfront architecture design that is necessary will vary, so it is about determining how much design is needed. That is part of the challenge of being a software architect. Good architects eventually learn how much design is appropriate for a given situation.

Greenfield versus brownfield software systems

When you are starting the design process, one of the first considerations is whether you are designing a greenfield or a brownfield system. The terms **greenfield** and **brownfield** are used in a number of disciplines. It is an analogy to a construction project, and whether it will begin on *greenfield* land, as in land that is undeveloped, or *brownfield* land, referring to land that was previously developed but is not currently in use.

Greenfield systems

A **greenfield software system** is a completely new software application, one in which you can start with a clean slate. There are no constraints based on any prior work. A greenfield system can be designed for a well-understood domain or for a novel domain.

A well-understood domain is one that is mature, and the possibilities for innovation are very limited. Examples include Windows desktop applications, standard mobile applications, and enterprise web applications. There will be existing frameworks, tools, and sample architectures for the software that you need to build. The software architectures of existing applications can be used as a guide.

It will be more likely that you are developing software for a well-understood domain, and the benefit is that there will be a tremendous amount of knowledge that you can leverage from the experience of those who have built similar applications.

A greenfield system for a novel domain is also a new software application that does not need to take into consideration any prior work. The difference between a greenfield system for a mature domain and one for a new domain lies in the fact that a new domain is not as well understood, and requires a lot more innovation.

Unlike a well-understood domain, you will not find as much supporting information for a new domain. Rather than relying on a plethora of reference architectures or referring to a large knowledge base, you will find yourself spending time building prototypes to test out your solutions.

For novel domains, it may be beneficial to design a *throwaway prototype* initially. These are prototypes of some piece of a software system so that you can test it out, such as getting feedback from users or testing quality attributes. They will help you to gain an understanding of what will make a viable solution for a novel domain.

Throwaway prototypes are not built for long-term use, hence the term throwaway, so qualities such as maintainability and reusability are not the focus of such prototypes. If you are using new technologies, or technologies that are not already familiar to you, a prototype can be a good way to try out a solution.

Brownfield systems

A **brownfield software system** is an existing software system. If changes to an existing system require architectural changes, architecture design will be needed. Modifications may be necessary for purposes such as correcting defects, implementing new functionality, or changing existing functionality.

Architectural changes may also be performed on existing software to improve it in some way without changing any functionality. For example, an architecture for an existing software system might be refactored to improve a particular quality attribute. Most of the time, work on brownfield systems does not involve wholesale changes in the overall architecture unless major rework is required.

One of the crucial first steps for the software architecture design of brownfield systems is to gain an understanding of the existing architecture. You need to understand the overall structure, the elements, and the relationships between those elements. From there, the design is not so different from a greenfield system that has been through some iterations to establish an initial architecture.

We will explore the topic of architecture for legacy systems in `Chapter 14`, *Architecting Legacy Applications*.

Architectural drivers

Architectural drivers are considerations that need to be made for the software system that are architecturally significant. They *drive* and guide the design of the software architecture. Architectural drivers describe what you are doing and why you are doing it. Software architecture design satisfies architectural drivers.

Architectural drivers are inputs into the design process, and include:

- Design objectives
- Primary functional requirements

- Quality attribute scenarios
- Constraints
- Architectural concerns

Design objectives

Design objectives focus on the purpose of the specific architecture design. For the particular design in question, what are the reasons behind why the software is being designed?

The design objectives influence the design and are therefore one of the architectural drivers. A common design objective is to design an architecture for a solution, prior to development. The overall objective is to facilitate the implementation of a solution that will satisfy requirements.

This type of design objective might be for a greenfield or a brownfield type of system. As we already explored, the differences between these types of systems might lead you to focus on different design objectives.

Designing a software architecture for development is not the only type of design objective. As a software architect, you may find yourself involved with project proposals. For such pre-sales activity, the design objective may focus on coming up with the software's capabilities, the possible timeframe for delivery, a breakdown of work tasks, and the feasibility of the proposed project. If this is the purpose of the design, then this type of initial design will not be nearly as detailed as one that you are designing for development.

For the purposes of a project proposal, it will not be necessary to be as detailed as you would be in preparation for development. You may be required to produce a design for a project proposal in a short amount of time to meet a particular sales deadline. In addition, until the sale is complete, you will probably not be allocated the funds or time for a full-scale design.

Similarly, software architects may need to create a prototype. This may be for a project proposal, but it could also be to test out a new technology or framework, to create a **proof of concept** (POC) for some solution to a particular problem, or to explore how a certain quality attribute might be effectively met. As with project proposals, if the design objective is to build a prototype, the focus and scope of the software architecture design will be different from one that is being done for development.

It is important to keep the design objectives in mind as an architectural driver when software architecture design is about to begin.

Primary functional requirements

Another important type of input into the architecture design is the **primary functional requirements** that need to be satisfied. Primary functional requirements are those that are critical to the organization's business goals. In Chapter 3, *Understanding the Domain,* we discussed core domains, which refer to the part of the domain that makes the software worth writing. Some of the primary functionality will come from the core domain. It is what differentiates the organization from competitors.

Although satisfying functional requirements is a goal of software architecture design, keep in mind that not all functionality is affected by the architecture. While some functionality is highly affected by the architecture, other functionality can be delivered equally as well with different architectures.

Even in cases where functionality is not influenced by the architecture directly, functional requirements may be an architectural driver for other reasons. One example of this would be the need to make modifications to the functionality later. Maintainability and modifiability of the software are affected by the software architecture.

Quality attribute scenarios

Quality attributes are measurable properties of a software system. They are the *ilities,* such as maintainability, usability, testability, and interoperability. We have been stressing the importance of quality attributes since they play such an important part in the success of software systems, and because software architecture decisions will affect them.

This makes quality attributes one of the main architectural drivers for software architecture design. The design decisions that are made will determine what quality attributes will be met. As an architectural driver, quality attributes are typically described in the context of a particular scenario.

A **quality attribute scenario** is a short description of how the software system should respond to a particular stimulus. Scenarios make quality attributes measurable and testable. For example, a quality attribute of *performance* or a requirement that states a particular function should be fast is not measurable or testable. An actual example of a valid quality attribute related to performance would be as follows: *When the user selects the Login option, a Login page is displayed within two seconds.*

Prioritizing quality attribute scenarios

Prior to the start of the architecture design process, the quality attribute scenarios should be prioritized. It is helpful to be aware of the priority of each quality attribute scenario when designing the architecture. In addition to being able to plan accordingly, such as focusing on higher priority quality attributes first, there may be trade-offs involved when enabling certain quality attributes. Understanding the priorities will help you make better design decisions regarding the quality attributes and any trade-offs that need to be made.

Quality attribute scenarios can be prioritized by ranking them based on two criteria: their business importance and the technical risk associated with the scenario. A ranking scale of **High (H)**, **Medium (M)**, and **Low (L)** can be used.

Stakeholders can help to provide the ranking based on business importance, while the software architect typically provides the ranking based on technical risk. Once the rankings are complete, each quality attribute should have a combination of the two rankings.

If each quality attribute scenario were assigned a unique number, they could be placed in a table such as the following:

Business importance/technical risk	L	M	H
L	6, 21	7, 13	15
M	3, 10, 11	14, 16, 17	1, 5
H	4, 18, 19, 20	2, 12	8, 9

Quality attribute scenarios located toward the bottom-right side of the table will be of higher importance. The most important ones will be those with an *H, H* ranking, indicating they were ranked high on both criteria. Initial design iterations can focus on those scenarios first. Subsequent iterations can consider the most important quality attribute scenarios that remain, such as *H, M* and *M, H*, until all of the quality attribute scenarios have been considered.

Constraints

Constraints are decisions imposed on a software project that must be satisfied by the architecture. They typically cannot be changed. They can affect the software architecture design and are therefore an architectural driver.

Constraints are generally fixed from the beginning of the project and might be technical or non-technical. Examples of technical constraints include being required to use a specific technology, having the ability to deploy to a particular type of target environment, or using a specific programming language. Examples of non-technical constraints are being required to abide by a certain regulation, or that the project must meet a particular deadline.

Constraints may also be classified by whether they are internal or external. Internal constraints originate from within the organization and you may have some control over them. In contrast, external constraints come from outside of the business and you may not have any control over them.

Like the other architectural drivers, constraints need to be considered in the design as an input into the design process.

Architectural concerns

Architectural concerns are interests of the software architect that impact the software architecture. As a result, they are an architectural driver. Just as functional requirements and quality attributes are design issues important to stakeholders, architectural concerns are design issues important to the software architect.

Architectural concerns need to be considered part of the design, but are not captured as functional requirements. In some cases, they may be captured as quality attributes rather than architectural concerns, or an architectural concern may lead to new quality attribute scenarios that need to be met.

For example, a software architect may have concerns related to software instrumentation or logging. If not already recorded as part of a quality attribute, such as maintainability, the architectural concern may lead to a new quality attribute.

Good software architects will be able to recognize possible architectural concerns based on the type of software they are designing. Architectural concerns may also arise from previous architecture design iterations, so be aware that architecture changes may lead to new concerns being created from them.

Leveraging design principles and existing solutions

Designing a software architecture from scratch for a project with some level of complexity can be a challenging task. However, software architects have a number of tools at their disposal when designing an architecture.

The design issues facing a project may have already been solved by others, and rather than *reinventing the wheel*, those solutions can be leveraged in your architecture design. These architecture design principles and solutions, which are sometimes referred to as **design concepts**, are building blocks used to design a software architecture.

Selecting a design concept

There are many design concepts, so a software architect needs to know which ones are suitable for a particular problem, and then select the one that is most appropriate among the alternatives. You may also find cases where you need to combine multiple design concepts to create a solution.

Depending on the stage of the architecture design you are in and the nature of the problem, certain design concepts will make more sense than others. For example, a reference architecture would be useful when creating the initial structure of the architecture, but later in the design, when considering a specific quality attribute scenario, a tactic might be used.

Software architects generally determine which design concepts are available by using their knowledge and experience, leveraging the knowledge and experience of their teammates, and following best practices.

When choosing a specific design concept among multiple alternatives that have been identified, you'll want to weigh the pros and cons, as well as the cost of each alternative. Keep any project constraints in mind when selecting design concepts, as a constraint may prevent you from using certain alternatives.

Some of the design concepts available to you include software architecture patterns, reference architectures, tactics, and externally developed software.

Software architecture patterns

When designing a software architecture, some of the design issues that you will face have already been solved by others. **Software architecture patterns** provide solutions for recurring architecture design problems. Patterns are discovered while observing what people were doing successfully to solve a particular problem, and then documenting those patterns so that they can be reused. They can be leveraged in an architecture design if the software application has the same design issue.

Software architects should take advantage of the work and experience of others when they have a problem that can be solved by a pattern. The challenging part is to be aware of what patterns are available, and which ones are applicable to the problem you are trying to solve.

As with any design pattern though, you shouldn't try to force the use of one. You should only use an architecture pattern if it truly solves the design issue that you have and if it is the best solution given your context.

We will be exploring software architecture patterns in more detail in Chapter 7, *Software Architecture Patterns*.

Reference architectures

A **reference architecture** is a template for an architecture that is best suited to a particular domain. It is composed of design artifacts for a software architecture that provides recommended structures, elements, and the relationships between the elements.

Benefits of reference architectures

A reference architecture can answer many of the most common questions for systems that need a particular design. They can be very helpful to software architects because they provide a tested solution to a problem domain, and reduce some of the complexities involved in designing a software architecture. Reference architectures are proven, in both technical as well as business contexts, as viable solutions for certain problems.

Using a reference architecture allows the team to deliver a solution quicker, and with fewer errors. Re-using an architecture provides advantages such as quicker delivery of a solution, reduced design effort, reduced costs, and increased quality.

Leveraging the experiences of past software applications and learning from them can be of great value to software architects. They help us to avoid making certain mistakes and can prevent costly delays that may result from not using a previously proven approach.

Refactoring a reference architecture for your needs

Just as a design without using a reference architecture may require multiple iterations to achieve the final result, it is also the case when using a reference architecture. Design decisions will need to be made regarding the reference architecture.

During iterations for the architecture design, refactoring can take place on a reference architecture to meet the specific needs of the software application being designed. The amount of refactoring necessary depends on how closely the reference architecture meets the functional and quality attribute requirements.

Reference architectures may be created at different levels of abstraction. If you want to use one and it is not at the level of abstraction you need, you might still be able to learn from it, and use it as a guide when designing your own architecture.

For well-understood domains, there may be a number of reference architectures available to you. In contrast, if you are designing a solution for a greenfield system that is in a novel domain, there may be few, if any, available for you to use. Even for those types of projects though, you may find a reference architecture you can leverage, even if it is just for a portion of the design. It might just require more refinement and refactoring than when a more fitting reference architecture is available.

When you use a reference architecture, you adopt issues from that reference architecture that you will need to address. If a reference architecture deals with a particular design issue, you will need to make design decisions about that issue, even if you don't have a specific requirement related to it. The decision might very well be to exclude something from your architecture that is in the reference architecture.

For example, if a reference architecture includes instrumentation as a cross-cutting concern, you will need to make design decisions about instrumentation during your design.

Creating your own reference architecture

Once an organization has a completed software architecture, which may or may not have used a reference architecture, it can then become a reference architecture itself. When an organization needs to create new software applications, perhaps as part of a software product line, it can use the architecture of an existing product as a reference architecture.

Using a reference architecture from your own organization is just like using a reference architecture from somewhere else. You will reap benefits by doing so, but some amount of refactoring may be required to use it in a particular application. The added advantage is that the reference architecture would be likely to already be suited to your particular domain.

Tactics

Tactics are proven techniques to influence quality attribute scenarios. They focus on a single quality attribute, so they are simpler than other design concepts, such as architecture patterns and reference architectures, which aim to solve a greater number of design issues.

Tactics provide options to satisfy quality attributes, and the use of other design concepts, such as architecture patterns or an externally built framework, along with code, are required to fully complete the tactic.

We went over some tactics when we explored quality attributes, such as:

- Satisfying a maintainability quality attribute scenario by reducing complexity in a component by increasing cohesion and reducing coupling
- Increasing usability in a scenario by providing friendly and informative messages to the user
- Implementing a retry strategy in a process to handle a possible transient fault in order to improve an availability quality attribute scenario
- Satisfying a portability quality attribute scenario by increasing installability by ensuring that a software update process to a newer version properly cleans up the older version

Externally developed software

When designing a software architecture, you will be making design decisions for a number of design issues. Some of these design issues already have solutions in the form of concrete implementations that have been developed externally. Rather than build a solution in-house to solve a particular design issue, you can leverage software that has already been developed outside of the organization.

The **externally developed software** can come in different forms, such as a component, an application framework, a software product, or a platform. There are many examples of externally developed software, such as a logging library for logging functionality, a UI framework for creating user interfaces, or a development platform for server-side logic.

Buy or build?

One of the decisions that software architects need to make is the classic *buy or build* dilemma. When you are in need of a solution to a particular design issue, you will need to decide whether to buy or build it. When using the term *buy*, we are referring to using something built externally, and not necessarily the fact that it may have a monetary cost. Depending on what type of solution you are looking for, there may be a number of free solutions available to you, including those that are open source.

When deciding whether to use an externally developed solution or to build it in-house, you must first make sure that you understand the problem that you are trying to solve, and the scope of that problem. You will need to research whether externally developed software exists that will solve the design problem. If the problem is unique to your organization, there may not be any suitable software available.

You should also know whether or not the organization has, or can attain, resources to build, maintain, and support a solution. If the solution is to be built internally by the project team, there must be sufficient resources, including time, to build it.

Advantages/disadvantages of building

An advantage of building it internally is that the solution will be unique to your organization, and tailored to it. The organization will have complete control over the solution, including full ownership of the source code. This will allow the organization to modify it in any way that it wants. If a need arises to make changes or add functionality, the organization will be able to do so with full authority.

Another benefit of building it yourself is that there could be a competitive advantage. If the solution provides some feature that competitors do not currently have, building it and owning it could provide a strategic advantage to the organization.

The disadvantages of building it yourself are that it will require time and resources to do so. The end result may not have as robust a set of features as an externally developed solution. For example, if you are in need of a distributed, scalable, enterprise-level, full-text search engine as part of your application, it is probably impractical to build it yourself rather than use a proven solution that already exists.

Advantages/disadvantages of buying

Using an externally developed solution has its own set of advantages. It will save time, as no effort will need to be spent developing it. It may be of higher quality, assuming that it has already been tested and used in production. Feedback from other users of the software may have exposed problems that have already been fixed.

The external solution might be continually improved to achieve higher levels of quality and to introduce new features. Support and training may be available that your team will be able to leverage.

However, there are downsides to using an externally developed solution. There may be a cost to using such a solution. Depending on the license type, you may not have access to the source code and may be limited in how the solution can be used. If you can't modify the solution, then the solution's functionality will be controlled by someone else, and it may not exactly fit your needs. In addition, if there are issues with the solution, or you need it changed in some way, you will need to rely on an external organization.

Researching external software

In order to find out whether external software exists that will be a suitable solution for the problem being solved, or in order to select an external solution from multiple alternatives that might be available, some research will be required.

The software architect should consider the following:

- Does it solve the design problem?
- Is the cost of the software acceptable?
- Is the type of license that comes with the software compatible with the project's needs?
- Is the software easy to use? Does the team have resources that can use it?
- Can the software be integrated with the other technologies that are going to be used on the project?
- Is the software mature, providing stable releases?
- Does it provide the level of support that might be needed, whether that support is paid support or through a development community?
- Is the software widely known, such that the organization can easily hire resources familiar with it?

Creating one or more prototypes that use the possible candidate solutions is a good way to evaluate and compare them. A POC to ensure that it is a workable solution is a wise idea.

Should I use open source software (OSS)?

When searching for an externally developed solution that will solve a design problem, one possibility is to find **open source software** (**OSS**) that will fulfill your needs. OSS is written by the community and is intended for use by the community.

Given the wide availability and range of open source software, there are many solutions available for a variety of problems. It is much more common now to use open source solutions as part of a software application. Some organizations do not permit the use of open source software but if your organization does, then you should give it consideration as a viable alternative for a given task.

One consideration when selecting open source software is the license that is associated with it. The license dictates the terms and conditions under which the software can be used, modified, and shared. One set of open source licenses that are popular is a group of licenses that have been approved by the **Open Source Initiative** (**OSI**). Some of the OSI-approved licenses include (in alphabetical order):

- Apache License 2.0
- BSD 2-clause *Simplified* or *FreeBSD* license
- BSD 3-clause *New* or *Revised* license
- Common Development and Distribution License
- Eclipse Public License
- GNU General Public License (GPL)
- GNU Lesser General Public License (LGPL)
- MIT license
- Mozilla Public License 2.0

There are differences in the terms and conditions of the various licenses. For example, your application can incorporate open source software that uses the MIT license and you will be able to distribute your application without making it open source.

In contrast, if your application incorporates software that uses the GNU General Public License and you then distribute your application, your application would need to be made open source. This is true even if your application is free and you do not change the open source software you are using in any way. If your software is for internal use only and it is not distributed, then your application could remain proprietary and closed source.

Advantages of using open source software

There are benefits to using open source software, which explains its popularity. Using an open source solution for a design problem provides many of the same advantages as using one that has been purchased. You don't have to spend time building the solution, it may have a robust set of features, and it may already be a tested and proven solution with many other users.

Unlike software that must be purchased, open source software is freely available so there are cost savings. You just have to keep in mind the license that comes with the software.

If the open source software is a popular solution with an active community, it might be continuously improved with bug fixes and new features. You will be able to take advantage of this work. Bugs may be detected and fixed quickly because many people are using and working on the code. This is the idea behind *Linus's Law*, which is named after Linus Torvalds, the creator of the Linux kernel. Linus's Law basically states that given enough eyeballs, or people looking at the code, all bugs are shallow. In other words, with many people looking at the source code, problems will be detected sooner rather than later, and someone will be able to provide a fix.

Although some view open source software as less secure due to the availability of the code, some people see it as more secure because there are *many eyes* that are using, looking at, and fixing the code.

Another advantage of open source software is the fact that you have access to the source code. If necessary, your development team will be able to modify it just as you would with an in-house solution.

Disadvantages of using open source software

Despite its advantages, there are some disadvantages to using open source software that you should consider. Even though the software is free, there are still costs related to using it. Someone has to spend time integrating the solution into the software system, and there is an associated cost for that effort. If the open source software has to be modified in any way to suit the needs of the project, there is a cost related to that work as well.

If there is no one on the team who knows how to use the software, and it is complex enough that some training is required, learning how to use a piece of open source software may also take time.

Even for a popular open source project with an active community, there is no guarantee that the software will continue to experience support. There is always a risk of the software going out of favor. If the project is abandoned, you won't be able to rely on support for bug fixes or new features unless the development team performs that work for themselves.

One reason an open source software project may become less secure is if no one is actively working on it. Even if the project has not been abandoned, no one is necessarily reading the code. The average programmer writes much more code than they read. The existence of some prominent security bugs has shown that it is possible for critical security vulnerabilities to go undetected for some time.

Despite Linus's Law, the fact that the source code is readily available introduces a degree of security risk. Malicious individuals can analyze the source code to identify security vulnerabilities and attempt to take advantage of them.

Documenting the software architecture design

An important part of architecture design is documenting the design, including the many design decisions that are made during the process. This typically comes in the form of sketching architecture views and documenting the design rationale.

Sketching the architecture design

Software architectures are commonly documented through the creation of architecture views. Architecture views are representations of a software architecture that are used to document it and communicate it to various stakeholders. Multiple views of an architecture are typically required, as a software architecture is too complex to be represented in a single, comprehensive model.

Formal documentation of a software architecture through views will be covered `Chapter 12`, *Documenting and Reviewing Software Architectures*, and is not typically done as part of the design process. While that type of documentation comes afterward, informal documentation, in the form of sketches, should take place during the architecture design. Sketches can record the structures, elements, relationships between the elements, and the design concepts used.

The sketches do not necessarily need to use any formal notation, but they should be clear. While it's not necessary to sketch everything, at a minimum, you will want to sketch out important decisions and design elements. These sketches can be done on a whiteboard, on paper, or using a modeling tool.

Documenting the design by creating sketches during the design process will help you to create architecture views later. If you already have informal sketches, when the time comes to create formal documentation, you will find it to be an easier task.

Documenting the design as it occurs will also ensure that you do not forget any design details when it comes to creating the architecture views. Your architecture will be analyzed and validated later to ensure that it satisfies functional requirements and quality attribute scenarios, so it is helpful to record details during design that can then be used to explain how requirements and quality attributes were satisfied by the architecture design.

If you aren't able to sketch out a part of your design, you'll have to consider the possible reasons for that. Perhaps it is not well understood, too complex, you haven't put enough thought into how to communicate it, or there may be parts of it that are unclear to you. If that is the case, you should revisit the design until you are able to sketch it. If you can sketch the design created in an iteration effortlessly and clearly, your audience will be able to understand it.

Documenting the design rationale

Software architecture design involves making many design decisions, and software architects should document those decisions along with their design rationale. While design sketches may explain what was designed, they don't give any indication as to the design rationale.

A **design rationale** explains the reasons, and justification, behind the decisions that are made during the design of the software architecture. Design rationale can also include documentation on what decisions were *not* made, as well as alternatives that were considered for decisions that were made. Reasons for rejection can be recorded for each alternative that was not selected.

Recording design rationale can be useful during the design process, as well as once the design is complete. Software architects who document their design rationale are afforded an opportunity to clarify their thoughts and arguments as they capture the design rationale, which may even expose flaws in their thinking.

Once the design rationale is documented, anyone who wants to know why a particular design decision was made, even after some time has passed, can refer to it. Even individuals who were involved with a design decision, including the software architect, may forget the rationale behind a particular decision and will be able to refer to the documentation.

The design rationale should refer to the specific structures that were designed and the specific requirements that they intended to meet. Some software design tools provide functionality that can assist the software architect in capturing the design rationale.

A complete design rationale provides a history of the software architecture design process. There are a number of uses for design rationale, such as for design evaluation, verification, knowledge transfer, communication, maintenance, documentation, and reuse.

Design rationale for design evaluation

Design rationale can be used to evaluate different software architecture designs and their design choices. The various designs can be compared with each other, and an understanding can be gained as to the situations in which one design would be chosen over another.

Design rationale for design verification

The purpose of software architecture design verification is to ensure that the software system, as designed, is the software system that was intended. It verifies that the software architecture meets the requirements, including the quality attributes, and works as expected. The design rationale can be used as part of the verification.

Design rationale for design knowledge transfer

The design rationale can be used for knowledge transfer to team members, including those who may join the team later, either during development or after the software goes into its maintenance phase.

Team members can learn about the design decisions and the reasons behind them by reviewing the design rationale. It is particularly useful for knowledge transfer when the original software architect, and others who collaborated on the design of the software architecture, are no longer available to provide the information in other ways.

Design rationale for design communication

It will be necessary at different times to communicate the design of the software architecture to various stakeholders and other individuals. The information provided by the design rationale adds value to the overall communication.

In addition, the design rationale can be used by those who are reviewing the software architecture so that they can learn the reasons behind particular design decisions.

Design rationale for design maintenance

During the maintenance phase of a software project, it is helpful to know the design rationale for the decisions that went into the software architecture design. When a certain piece of the software needs to be changed for maintenance, the design rationale can assist in determining what areas of the software will require modifications.

It can also be used to identify weaknesses in the software, and areas of the software that could be improved. For example, based on certain design decisions, quality attributes may be enabled or inhibited, and if changes are being considered that would alter those decisions, team members could be aware of the reasons behind those decisions.

The design rationale will also point out design alternatives that were not chosen, allowing those considering modifications to either avoid previously rejected design alternatives or to at least be knowledgeable about the reasons those alternatives were rejected in order to make an educated decision.

Design rationale for design documentation

The software architecture must be documented, and the design rationale is an important part of that documentation. If the documentation only shows the design, those looking at it will know *what* was designed but won't know *why* it was designed that way. They also won't be aware of the alternatives that were considered, and why those alternatives were rejected.

Design rationale for design reuse

Software architecture reuse involves creating multiple software applications using *core assets*, allowing architectural components to be reused across multiple software products. Organizations seek to take advantage of efficiencies that can be gained when reusing architectural components to build multiple software products as part of a *software product line*.

Capturing design rationale can facilitate successful architectural reuse. It can help designers understand what parts of the application can be reused. It may also provide some insight into where modifications can be made to a component in order to reuse it in the application. Due to the variation between software products, reusable components are typically designed with *variation points*, or places where modifications can be made in order to adapt the component for use in a particular software product. Understanding the design rationale will help designers use the component properly, and prevent harmful modifications from being made.

Using a systematic approach to software architecture design

If you are going to dedicate some time to designing the architecture of a software system, and not just let it *emerge* after implementing features, you should do so in a systematic way.

Software architects need to ensure that the architecture they are designing will satisfy the architectural drivers, and a systematic approach can assist in accomplishing that goal. In *Designing Software Architectures, A Practical Approach*, the following is said about using an architecture design process:

> "The question is, how do you actually perform design? Performing design to ensure that the drivers are satisfied requires a principled method. By "principled", we refer to a method that takes into account all of the relevant aspects that are needed to produce an adequate design. Such a method provides guidance that is necessary to guarantee that your drivers are satisfied."

Using an established architecture design process will provide you, as the software architect, with guidance on how to go about designing an architecture that will satisfy functional requirements and quality attribute scenarios. There are a number of design processes that can be used for software architecture. Although they differ from each other, including differences in terminology, they also have some fundamental commonalities.

A general model of software architecture design

The paper, *A general model of software architecture design derived from five industrial approaches,* by Christine Hofmeister, Philippe Kruchten, Robert L. Nord, Henk Obbink, Alexander Ran, and Pierre America, compared five different architecture design methods to come up with a general model of architecture design based on the similarities. Having a general model helps us to understand the types of activities that are typically performed in a software architecture design process and allows us to compare the strengths and weaknesses of different processes.

It was found that most architecture design processes involve analyzing architectural drivers, designing candidate solutions that will satisfy the architectural drivers, and then evaluating the design decisions and candidate solutions to ensure that they are correct.

The three main design activities that were identified in *A general model of software architecture design derived from five industrial approaches* are **Architectural Analysis**, **Architectural Synthesis**, and **Architectural Evaluation**:

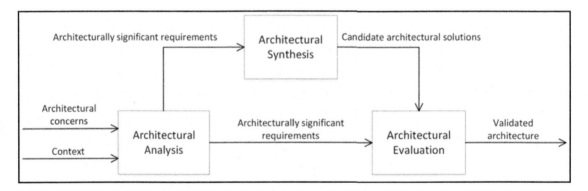

Architectural analysis

During **architectural analysis**, the problems that the architecture is trying to solve are identified. These are sometimes referred to as **architecturally significant requirements** (**ASRs**) because they will influence the design of the architecture. Not all of the design issues that must be considered are requirements though. We must address all of the architectural drivers, which include design objectives, primary functional requirements, quality attribute scenarios, constraints, and architectural concerns.

The output of this activity is a set of architectural drivers that will serve as the input to architectural synthesis.

Architectural synthesis

The **architectural synthesis** activity is where solutions are designed on the basis of the set of architectural drivers that were identified in the architectural analysis activity. It is during this activity that we leverage design concepts such as architecture patterns, reference architectures, tactics, and externally developed software, and combine them with the design of structures, elements, and relationships between the elements. This produces solutions for the set of architectural drivers.

The output of this activity is one or more candidate solutions for the problems selected.

Architectural evaluation

In the **architectural evaluation**, the candidate solutions that were designed during architectural synthesis are evaluated to ensure that they solve the problems that they were intended for, and that all of the design decisions that were made are correct.

At the conclusion of the architectural evaluation activity, each candidate solution has either been validated or invalidated. We will cover reviewing software architectures in `Chapter 12`, *Documenting and Reviewing Software Architectures*.

Architecture design is an iterative process

Another important similarity found in architecture design is the fact that it is an iterative process. Designing a software architecture is too complex to address all of the architectural drivers simultaneously.

The design of the architecture occurs over multiple iterations until all architectural drivers have been addressed. Each iteration starts by selecting the architectural drivers that will be considered for that iteration. If candidate solutions have been validated after they have been evaluated, those design decisions are integrated into the overall architecture.

If there are no more architectural drivers that need solutions, the validated architecture is complete. If outstanding architectural drivers exist, a new iteration will begin.

Selecting an architecture design process

Now that we understand the fundamental activities that occur during software architecture design, which one do we use? There are many different software architecture design processes. One way that we can compare design processes is to examine the activities and artifacts of the design process:

- What are the activities and artifacts of the design process?
- Are there any activities/artifacts that you think are not needed?
- Are there any activities/artifacts that you feel are lacking?
- What are the techniques and tools of the design process?

If it helps, you can compare the activities and artifacts of the design process with those that exist in the general model. Some of the activities and artifacts of the design process may have corresponding ones in the general model, although different names may be used. There may also be activities and artifacts in the design process that do not have any corresponding ones in the general model, as well as ones in the general model that do not exist in the design process.

After doing this type of comparison, you should have an understanding as to what each design process entails, along with their strengths and weaknesses. This knowledge can be used to select the one that is most suited to your project.

The software architect can modify a design process to make it more suitable for a project's needs, although such changes should only be done thoughtfully. If, after analyzing and selecting a design process, you feel that a particular activity or artifact is not needed, you could remove it.

Conversely, if you see that a design process lacks an activity and/or artifact, you can change the process to include it. You might be able to draw on a technique, tool, or even another design process to supplement what you feel is missing from the design process you want to use.

So far, we have been discussing architecture design processes in fairly general terms, so now let's explore several concrete ones at a high level. Three of the architecture design processes available to you are ADD, Microsoft's technique for architecture and design, and the ACDM.

Attribute-driven design (ADD)

Attribute-driven design (ADD) is one of the systematic approaches for designing software architectures. It is an iterative, organized, step-by-step method that can be followed during architectural design iterations.

This method pays particular attention to software quality attributes during the design process. As a result, one of the primary benefits of using ADD is that you begin to consider quality attributes early in the design process.

Enabling a quality attribute in a software architecture design may affect other quality attributes. Consequently, trade-offs between quality attributes may be necessary. By focusing on quality attributes using the ADD method, these types of trade-offs can be considered at an early stage during the process.

The ADD process is specifically focused on architecture design and, as such, doesn't cover the entire architectural life cycle. The process doesn't include the gathering of architectural drivers, documenting the architecture, or evaluating the architecture once it is designed. However, you can combine ADD with other methods to fill in these gaps.

ADD is a widely-used method for software architecture design, and has been used successfully on a variety of software applications. There are eight steps in the attribute-driven design process:

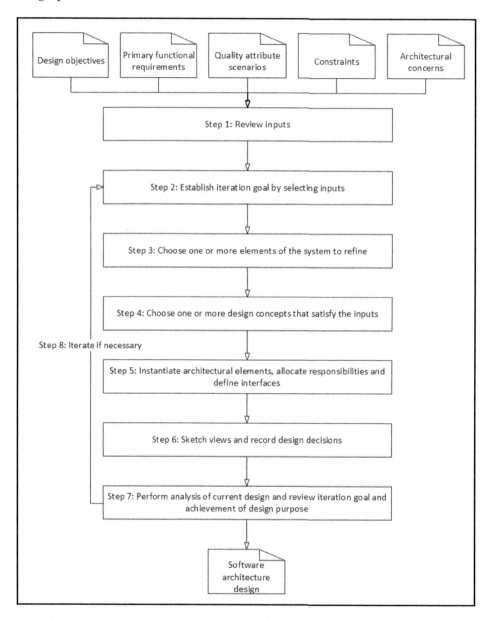

Step 1 – Reviewing inputs

The first step in the ADD process is to review the inputs into the attribute-driven design. Before the design starts, we want to ensure that we are clear on the overall design problem we are solving.

The inputs are the architectural drivers that we reviewed earlier:

- Design objectives
- Primary functional requirements
- Quality attribute scenarios
- Constraints
- Architectural concerns

If the software system is either a brownfield system or it is not the initial iteration for the architecture design of a greenfield system, there is at least some part of an architecture already in place. This existing architecture must be considered as part of the input into the iteration.

Step 2 – Establishing the iteration goal and selecting inputs to be considered in the iteration

Once inputs are reviewed, one or more design iterations will take place, with each iteration beginning with *Step 2*. If you are using an agile methodology, multiple iterations will take place until the architecture is complete and the design purpose has been accomplished. An agile methodology is preferred, and is more common, as attempting to provide solutions for all of the architectural drivers at once can be too difficult.

At the start of each iteration, we want to establish the design goal for that iteration. We should be able to answer the question, *What design issue are we trying to solve in the iteration?* Each goal will be associated with one or more inputs. The inputs, or architectural drivers, that are relevant to the goal are identified and will be the focus of the iteration.

Step 3 – Choosing one or more elements of the system to refine

Based on the iteration goal and the architectural drivers that we want to create a solution for, we must select the various elements that we want to decompose.

If your project is a greenfield system and this is the first iteration, you begin at the highest level and start by decomposing the system itself. For any other iteration, the system has already been decomposed to some degree. You would select one or more of the existing elements to focus on for this iteration.

Step 4 – Choosing one or more design concepts that satisfy the inputs considered in the iteration

Once elements have been selected for decomposition, we need to select one or more design concepts that can be used to meet the iteration goal and satisfy the inputs (architectural drivers). Design concepts refer to design principles and solutions such as architecture patterns, reference architectures, tactics, and externally developed software.

Step 5 – Instantiating architectural elements, allocating responsibilities, and defining interfaces

Based on the design concepts that can be leveraged for this iteration, analysis is performed so that details can be provided regarding the responsibilities for the elements being decomposed, along with the public interfaces of those elements that will be exposed.

Each element being decomposed (parent element) may yield one or more child elements. By considering the responsibilities of the parent element, we can assign responsibilities to the various child elements. All of the responsibilities of the parent element are considered, whether or not they are architecturally significant.

Step 6 – Sketching views and recording design decisions

Views should be sketched recording the solution designed so that it can be communicated. In this step, all of the design decisions that were made during this particular iteration are documented. This documentation should also include the design rationale.

The artifacts created in this step can simply be sketches and do not have to be the formal, detailed software architecture views. In the ADD process, the creation of the architecture views comes later, but the design decisions made in this iteration should be reflected in sketches that can then be used in the formal architecture views later.

We will explore documenting software architectures in Chapter 12, *Documenting and Reviewing Software Architectures*.

Step 7 – Performing analysis of current design and reviewing the iteration goal and design objectives

In this final step of a software architecture design iteration, the software architect and other team members should analyze the current design. The design decisions are analyzed to ensure that they are correct and satisfy the iteration goal and architectural drivers that were established for the iteration.

The result of this analysis should determine whether more architecture design iterations will be necessary.

Step 8 – Iterating if necessary

If it is decided that more iterations are needed, the process should go back to *Step 2* for another iteration. As a software architect, there will be times where you feel more iterations are necessary, but something will prevent you from conducting more iterations. For example, the project management team may decide that there is not enough time for more iterations and that the architecture design process is done.

If no further iterations will take place, the software architecture design is complete.

Microsoft's technique for architecture and design

Another example of a systematic approach for designing software architectures is **Microsoft's technique for architecture and design**. Like ADD, it is an iterative, step-by-step method. This process can be used to design the initial architecture as well as to refine it later, if necessary. There are five steps in the process:

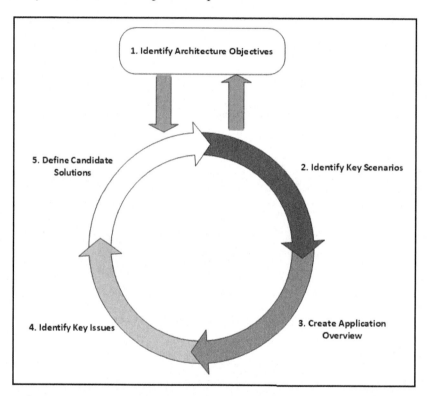

Step 1 – Identifying architecture objectives

The design process begins by identifying the objectives you want to achieve for the architecture. The purpose of this step is to ensure that the design process has clear objectives so that the solution focuses on the appropriate problems. Once design iterations start, we want to ensure that we are clear on the overall design problems that we are solving.

The various architectural drivers, such as design objectives, primary functional requirements, quality attribute scenarios, constraints, and architectural concerns all combine to form the architecture objectives. The software architect should also consider who will consume the architecture. The architecture design might be used by other architects, developers, testers, operations personnel, and management. Both the needs and the experience levels of the various people who will view and use the architecture design should be considered during the design process. As with ADD, if the software system has an existing architecture, either because it is a brownfield system or design iterations have already taken place, the existing architecture is another consideration.

Step 2 – Identifying key scenarios

Once the design objectives are identified and established, one or more design iterations will be necessary. *Step 1* will only occur once, and each design iteration will begin with *Step 2*. *Step 2* focuses on identifying key scenarios for the software application.

In this design process, a scenario is defined as a more encompassing user interaction with the software system, and not just a single use case. Key scenarios are the most important of these scenarios and are required for the success of the application. Scenarios could be an issue, an architecturally significant use case (one that is business critical and has a high impact), or involve an intersection between functional requirements and quality attributes. Once again, keep in mind that there may be trade-offs with quality attributes, so the scenarios should take those into consideration.

Step 3 – Creating application overview

In this step, armed with architecture objectives and key scenarios, an application overview is created. An application overview is what the architecture will look like when it is complete. An application overview is intended to connect an architecture design with real-world decisions.

Creating an application overview consists of determining your application type, identifying deployment constraints, identifying architecture design styles, and determining relevant technologies.

Determining your application type

The software architect must determine what type of application is appropriate based on the objectives and key scenarios. Examples of application types include web, mobile, service, and Windows desktop applications.

It is possible that a software application may be a combination of more than one type.

Identifying your deployment constraints

When designing a software architecture, among the many constraints that you may have to consider are constraints related to deployment. You may be required to follow particular policies of the organization. The infrastructure and target environment of the software application may be dictated by the organization, and such constraints may be something that you will have to work around.

The earlier that any conflicts and issues related to constraints can be identified regarding the software application and the target infrastructure, the easier those issues can be resolved.

Identifying important architecture design styles

Architecture design styles, also known as architecture patterns, are general solutions to common problems. Using an architecture style promotes reuse by leveraging a known solution to a recurring problem.

Identifying the appropriate architecture design style, or a combination of styles, that will be used in the software application is an important part of creating an application overview. We will go into detail about various architecture patterns in Chapter 7, *Software Architecture Patterns*, and Chapter 8, *Architecting Modern Applications*.

Determining relevant technologies

At this point, you are ready to select relevant technologies for your project. The decisions are based on the type of application, which was determined earlier, the architectural styles, and the key quality attributes.

In addition to technologies specific to the application type (for example, selection of a web server for a web application), technologies will be needed for categories such as application infrastructure, workflow, data access, database server, development tools, and integration.

Step 4 – Identifying key issues

This step of the process involves identifying the important issues you may be facing in the architecture. These issues may require additional focus because they are areas where mistakes are most likely to be made.

Key issues typically map in one form or another to either quality attributes or cross-cutting concerns. We took a look at quality attributes in Chapter 4, *Software Quality Attributes*, and will be exploring cross-cutting concerns in Chapter 9, *Cross-Cutting Concerns*.

Analyzing quality attributes and cross-cutting concerns closely based on the issues you identify will allow you to know which areas to give extra attention to in your design. The design decisions that are made as a result should be documented as part of the architecture.

Step 5 – Defining candidate solutions

Once key issues are identified, candidate solutions can be created. Depending on whether or not this is the first iteration, either an initial architecture is created, or the existing architecture is refined to include the solutions that were designed in the current iteration.

Once candidate solutions are integrated into the architecture design for the current iteration, the architecture can be reviewed and evaluated. We will go into further detail on reviewing software architectures in Chapter 12, *Documenting and Reviewing Software Architectures*.

If it is determined that more work is necessary for the architecture design, a new iteration can begin. The process goes back to *Step 2* so that key scenarios can be identified for the next sprint.

Architecture-centric design method (ACDM)

The **architecture-centric design method (ACDM)** is an iterative process used to design software architectures. It is a lightweight method with a product focus and seeks to ensure that the software architecture maintains a balance between business and technical concerns. It attempts to make the software architecture the intersection between requirements and the solution.

Like all architecture design processes, the ACDM provides guidance to software architects as they design an architecture. While it covers the complete life cycle of software architecture, it is not a complete development process. It is designed to fit in with existing process frameworks though so that it can be used in conjunction with other methods to cover activities outside of architecture. It does not have to replace an existing process framework and can complement it instead.

There are some minor variations in the number and naming of the steps involved with the ACDM, but the process is essentially the same. Let's go over the ACDM, which is a seven-step process:

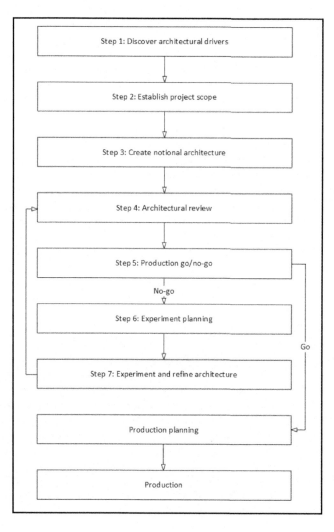

Step 1 – Discovering architectural drivers

The first step in the ACDM is to meet with stakeholders to determine the architectural drivers, which include design objectives, primary functional requirements, quality attribute scenarios, constraints, and architectural concerns. The prioritization of quality attribute scenarios also takes place in this step.

Step 2 – Establishing project scope

In this step, the architectural drivers established in *Step 1* are reviewed. First, consolidation of the information gathered takes place to remove duplicate architectural drivers.

Next, if any of the architectural drivers gathered are unclear, missing, or incomplete, additional information will be needed. The same is true of any requirements or quality attribute scenarios that are not measurable or testable.

If any clarification or additional information is needed, it will be gathered in this step from the relevant stakeholders.

Step 3 – Creating notional architecture

Using the architectural drivers, a notional architecture is created. It is the first attempt at designing the architecture. The initial representations of the structures that make up the architecture are created and documented.

Not a lot of time is typically spent on the notional architecture. The idea is that the architecture will be refined through multiple iterations until it is complete.

Step 4 – Architectural review

During this step, a review is conducted on the architecture as it currently exists. Reviews may be conducted internally, externally with stakeholders, or there may even be multiple review sessions so that both internal and external ones can be conducted.

The purpose of the review is to ensure that all of the design decisions are correct and to uncover any potential issues or problems with the architecture. For a given design decision, alternative approaches can be discussed, along with the trade-offs and the rationale behind the decision, in order to determine whether the best alternative was taken.

Step 5 – Production go/no-go

Once the architectural review is complete, a decision is made as to whether the architecture is complete and ready for production, or if further refinement is needed. In the ACDM context, *production* refers to implementation, including using the architecture in the detailed design of elements, coding, integration, and testing.

Any risks identified during the architectural review are considered in the production go/no-go decision. The decision does not have to be an all-or-nothing one. It is possible that only parts of the design require further refinement, in which case a portion of the design can move on to production.

If the production decision is a go, and no further refinements are needed, the process can skip ahead to production planning, and eventually on to production. However, if the production decision is a no-go, then the process moves on to *Step 6*.

Step 6 – Experiment planning

In this step, any experiments that the team feels are necessary are planned. The purpose of an experiment may be to resolve an issue uncovered during the architectural review, to gain a greater understanding of one or more architectural drivers, or to improve elements and modules of the design before they are committed to the overall architecture.

Experiment planning includes solidifying the goals of the experiment, estimating the level of effort, and assigning the resources that will be needed.

Step 7 – Experimenting with and refining the architecture

Any experiments that were planned are executed during this step. The results of the experiments are recorded. Based on the results of the experiment, if the architecture needs to be refined, it is done during this step.

After the refinement is complete, the process goes back to *Step 4* so that another architectural review can take place.

Production planning and production

Once architecture design iterations are complete, and the architecture is ready to move into production, production planning is conducted. Once again, *production* in the ACDM context refers to using the architecture in implementation.

Given this context, production planning involves planning the design and development of elements, scheduling the work, and assigning tasks to resources. The project management team creates plans for the work, and bases them, in part, on the architecture.

Once the architecture can be moved to production, it can be used by development teams for the detailed design of elements, coding, integration, and testing.

Architecture development method (ADM)

The **architecture development method** (**ADM**) is a step-by-step software architecture design approach specifically made for enterprise architectures. The ADM was created from the contributions of many software architecture practitioners.

Like the other architecture design methods that we have covered, the ADM is an iterative process. The process as a whole is iterative, but it is also iterative between phases and within a single phase. Each iteration is an opportunity to revisit scope, the level of detail to be defined, schedules, and milestones.

The Open Group Architecture Framework (TOGAF)

The ADM is a core part of **The Open Group Architecture Framework** (**TOGAF**), which is a framework for enterprise architecture. TOGAF provides a detailed method, the ADM, along with a set of tools for developing enterprise architectures.

TOGAF is maintained by *The Open Group*, which is a global industry consortium that focuses on using open and vendor-neutral technology standards to help organizations achieve business objectives.

TOGAF architecture domains

Four standard architecture areas, or architecture domains, for enterprise architecture are defined by TOGAF. They are business, data, applications, and technology architectures. These domains are sometimes referred to as the BDAT domains.

All four of these architecture domains are considered during the ADM and we will explore them in more detail when we go over the various phases of the ADM.

TOGAF documentation

The TOGAF documentation is broken up into the following seven sections:

- **Part I – Introduction**: The first part is an introduction to the concepts of enterprise architecture, the TOGAF approach, and definitions of relevant terms used in TOGAF.
- **Part II – Architecture development method**: This section details the **architecture development method (ADM)**, which is the core of TOGAF. We will be focusing our attention on the ADM part of the TOGAF.
- **Part III – ADM guidelines and techniques**: This part of the documentation provides guidelines and techniques for applying TOGAF and the ADM.
- **Part IV – Architecture content framework**: In this part, information is provided on the TOGAF content framework, including the architectural artifacts and deliverables that are part of the process.
- **Part V – Enterprise continuum and tools**: This section covers the architecture repository for an enterprise, including the categorization and storage of architecture artifacts.
- **Part VI – TOGAF reference models**: In this section, various architectural reference models are provided, including the **TOGAF Foundation Architecture** and the **Integrated Information Infrastructure Reference Model (III-RM)**.
- **Part VII – Architecture capability framework**: The final part provides guidelines on establishing and operating an enterprise architecture capability within an enterprise, including processes, skills, roles, and responsibilities.

Phases of the ADM

The architecture development method consists of multiple phases. There is a preliminary phase in which the organization prepares for a successful software architecture implementation. After this preliminary phase, there are eight phases to the process:

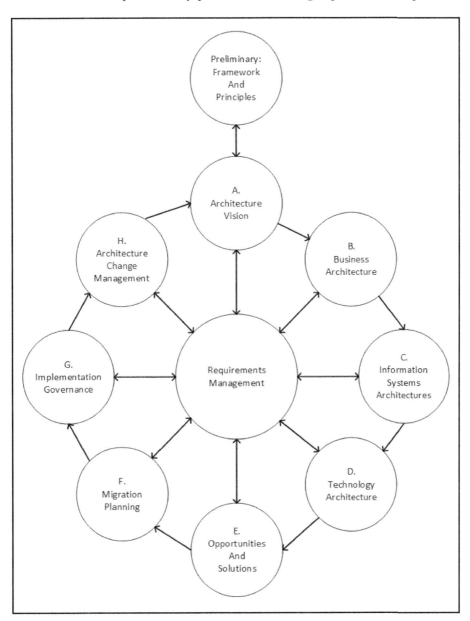

Each phase continuously checks with requirements to ensure that they are being met. Organizations can modify or extend the process to meet their needs, and it is usable with the deliverables of other frameworks if it is decided that those deliverables are more suitable.

Phase A – Architecture vision

In this step of the ADM, the team defines the overall vision for the enterprise architecture, including its capabilities and business value. The team agrees on items such as scope, business goals, business drivers, constraints, requirements, roles, responsibilities, and scheduling. These decisions are documented in the Statement of Architecture Work, which is a deliverable for this phase. The document typically contains the following:

- Architecture project request and background information
- Project description and scope of the architecture
- An overview of the architecture vision
- Change of scope procedures
- Roles, responsibilities, and deliverables for the project
- Details on the acceptance criteria and procedures
- Project plan and schedule

Phase B – Business architecture

Business architecture is one of the four architecture domains defined in TOGAF. The business architecture focuses on the business and/or service strategies of the organization, along with its business environment. An understanding of the business architecture is a prerequisite to perform architecture work on the other three domains defined in TOGAF (data, application, and technology).

The goal of this phase is to determine the target business architecture for how the enterprise achieves its business objectives and its strategic drivers. In order to create a roadmap on how to reach the target state, the following four steps are undertaken:

1. Gain an understanding of the current state of the architecture
2. Refine and validate the target state of the architecture
3. Determine the gap that exists between the current and target states of the architecture
4. Create a roadmap to transition between the current and target architecture states

Phase C – Information systems architectures

Data and application architecture are two of the other architecture domains defined in TOGAF. The data architecture focuses on an organization's data and how it is managed, while application architecture involves the enterprise's software applications.

The results from the architecture vision and business architecture phases are used to determine the architectural changes that will be necessary to an enterprise's data and application architectures.

As was the case with *Phase B*, the current and target states of the architecture are compared so as to determine the gap between the two. This allows for an architecture roadmap to be created for the candidate application and data components that will be needed to bridge the gap.

Phase D – Technology architecture

Technology architecture, one of the other architecture domains defined in TOGAF, involves the enterprise's infrastructure components. This includes the hardware and software necessary to support the enterprise's business, data, and application architectures.

The goal of this phase is to develop the target technology architecture that will support the enterprise's solutions. An assessment of the enterprise's current infrastructure capabilities is completed and compared with the desired target state so that the gap between them can be identified. From there, a roadmap of the target state for the technology architecture can be created along with the candidate components.

Phase E – Opportunities and solutions

This phase focuses on how to deliver the target architecture as we move from a conceptual view of the target architecture toward implementation. The roadmaps created in *Phase B*, *Phase C*, and *Phase D* are consolidated into an overall architecture roadmap. The candidate solutions that were created in the previous phases are organized into high-level candidate work packages.

The overall architecture roadmap, which includes all of the gaps between the current and target states of the architecture, is used to determine the best approach on how to deliver the target architecture.

If an incremental approach is to be taken, transition architectures are identified so that business value continues to be delivered.

Phase F – Migration planning

The overall architecture roadmap and the candidate work packages are used to plan the implementation of the architecture. The software architect works with the enterprise's project and program management teams to determine existing or new projects that can be used for the work.

An enterprise's existing processes for change and project management can be used to plan the necessary initiatives.

Phase G – Implementation governance

Implementation governance, along with the next phase, architecture change management, runs in parallel with the implementation of the architecture. The development of the architecture takes place using the enterprise's existing software development process.

This phase ensures that software architects stay engaged during implementation by assisting and reviewing the development work. Software architects must ensure that the architecture being implemented is achieving the architecture vision.

Phase H – Architecture change management

During implementation, issues may arise that require decisions to be made. It may be found that changes are necessary to the candidate solutions.

Software architects are involved with the enterprise's change management process to make decisions regarding proposed changes. Changes to the architecture must be managed and there must be a continuous focus on ensuring that the architecture meets requirements and stakeholder expectations.

Tracking the progress of the software architecture's design

During the software architecture design process, you will want to keep track of the design's progress. Keeping track of progress enables you to know how much of the design work is complete, and how much of it remains. The remaining work can be prioritized, assisting software architects in determining what should be worked on next. In addition to tracking progress, it serves as a reminder of design issues that are still outstanding, so that nothing is forgotten.

The technique that management will want to use to track progress really depends on your project, software development methodology, and the organization. If you are using an agile methodology such as Scrum, you may be using product and sprint backlogs to track progress.

Using a backlog to track the architecture design progress

A **product backlog** contains a complete list of the features and bugs of the product. You should consider creating a product backlog that is specific to the software architecture of the project, which is separate from the other product backlog. An architecture product backlog would contain items, design issues, design decisions that need to be made, and ideas that are specific to the architecture design.

Prior to each sprint, sprint planning takes place. The team selects items from the product backlog that they will work on and complete during the upcoming sprint. Once tasks can be created for the product backlog items, they can be assigned to a resource and then tracked for progress. Items from the product backlog that get selected for a sprint are then moved to the sprint backlog. Once an item is completed, it can be removed from the backlog.

Before sprint planning takes place though, the product backlog items should be prioritized, as the prioritization may affect what gets selected for a particular sprint.

Prioritizing the backlog

The list of features and bugs in the product backlog should be prioritized by the team, which assists with project planning so that teams know which items to focus on first.

Backlog prioritization is not something that occurs just once. As the architecture backlog changes, priorities may need to change as well. You can revisit the prioritization of architecture backlog items as many times as necessary.

Product backlog items should be linearly ordered based on criteria. One set of criteria that has been used in practice to prioritize backlog items is called the DIVE criteria.

DIVE criteria

DIVE is an acronym that stands for the types of criteria that are used to prioritize product backlog items. It focuses on **D**ependencies, to **I**nsure against risks, business **V**alue, and estimated **E**ffort as the factors used to determine priority.

Dependencies

Some product backlog items will be dependent on others, and therefore those dependencies will need to be completed first. For example, if item *A* depends on item *B*, *B* would be prioritized higher than item *A*.

Insure against risks

When prioritizing backlog items, you want to insure against risks, which include both business and technical risks. Taking potential risks into consideration may lead the team to prioritize a backlog item higher or lower when compared to other backlog items.

Business value

The business value of a product backlog item is an important criterion for prioritization. Product backlog items with greater levels of business value may be deemed a higher priority. The input of relevant stakeholders can help to determine the business value of a product backlog item.

Estimated effort

The estimated level of effort for a product backlog item may be a factor when prioritizing work. This may be due to factors such as scheduling or resource availability. There may be cases where a product backlog item has a large estimated effort, and the team wants to tackle the item sooner rather than later to ensure that it will be completed in time.

Active and dynamic architecture backlogs

As with any product backlog, the architecture backlog is not static and will evolve as the architecture design takes place. As architecture design iterations are completed, new architectural drivers may be uncovered, necessitating the need for new items to be added to the backlog.

Another reason that items may be added to the architecture backlog is when issues are discovered with the architecture. When the design is reviewed, a problem may become apparent, requiring further work to be done.

As architectural design decisions are made, it may cause the creation of new architecture backlog items. When a design decision is made, new concerns may arise from that decision. For example, if it is decided that the application will be a web application, backlog items related to security, session management, and performance that are specific to web applications may need to be added to the architecture backlog if they did not already exist. Changes to the architecture backlog may prompt you to revisit the priorities of the backlog items.

The architecture backlog should be made available to anyone who may need to be aware of the design's progress. If you do have separate backlogs for the architecture and the rest of the project, keep in mind that the audience for the two backlogs may be different. It really depends on the project and the level of involvement and transparency that exists between the project team and other stakeholders involved with the project.

In some cases, clients may have access to the product backlog to track functionality, but the team may want to keep the architecture backlog private.

Summary

Software architecture design plays a critical part in the creation and success of software architectures. At its core, architecture design involves making design decisions to produce solutions to design problems. The result is an architecture design that can be validated, formally documented, and eventually used by development teams.

There are two main approaches to architecture design, the top-down and bottom-up approaches. We examined situations in which one would be used over the other and learned how a combination of the two approaches often works best.

Architectural drivers, which are the inputs into the architecture design process, guide the architecture design. They include design objectives, primary functional requirements, quality attribute scenarios, constraints, and architectural concerns.

Designing a software architecture can be challenging, but we can leverage design concepts, such as software architecture patterns, reference architectures, tactics, and externally developed software, to assist with the design of solutions.

While formal documentation of an architecture does not need to occur during the design process, documenting, such as sketching the design and recording the design rationale, should take place.

Following an architecture design process helps to guide software architects with their design. There are a number of architecture design processes that are available to use, so you'll have to do some research in order to select a process that will work best for your project. Architecture design processes can be modified and supplemented with other techniques and processes to fill in any gaps with the process that you want to use.

A way of prioritizing and tracking the progress of architecture work should be put into place, such as having a backlog specific to architecture.

In the next chapter, we will explore some of the principles and best practices of software development. Some of them can be applied to software architecture, while others may be concepts that you will want to communicate to your team and encourage them to use in their implementations.

6
Software Development Principles and Practices

One of the main goals for software architects is to design high-quality software applications. There are a number of software design principles and best practices that can be applied to achieve that goal.

Software architects can apply these principles and practices when designing software architectures and encourage developers to use them in their implementations. These principles and practices are used to improve quality, simplify maintenance, increase reusability, find defects, and make software systems easier to test.

In this chapter, we will cover the following topics:

- Designing orthogonal software systems, including a focus on loose coupling and high cohesion
- Minimizing complexity in a software system by following principles such as KISS, DRY, information hiding, YAGNI, and Separation of Concerns (SoC)
- The SOLID design principles, which include the Single Responsibility Principle (SRP), Open/Closed Principle (OCP), Liskov Substitution Principle (LSP), Interface Segregation Principle (ISP), and the Dependency Inversion Principle (DIP)
- Using **Dependency Injection (DI)** to provide dependencies to a class
- Using unit testing to improve the quality of a software system
- Ensuring that development environments can be set up easily
- Practice of pair programming
- Reviewing deliverables, such as code reviews, formal inspections, and walkthroughs

Designing orthogonal software systems

In geometry, two Euclidean vectors are orthogonal if they are perpendicular (form a right angle of 90 degrees). The two vectors meet at the origin point, but do not intersect. The two vectors are independent of each other:

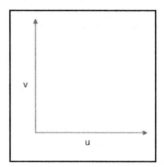

Software that is well designed is orthogonal in that its modules are independent of each other. Ideally, changes to one module in a software system should not require changes to another module. Software systems will undergo many changes during their lifetime and designing them with this in mind provides a number of benefits, including increased productivity for those who work on them and lowered risk of introducing defects when changes are made. Designing orthogonal systems may have higher upfront costs, but over time, a highly maintainable and extendable system will be worth it.

Orthogonal systems are designed so that their elements are loosely coupled and highly cohesive. Let's look at the concepts of coupling and cohesion in more detail.

Loose coupling

Coupling is the degree to which a software module depends on another software module. Coupling between modules is a measure of how closely connected they are, and it can either be loose, sometimes described as low or weak, or it can be tight, sometimes referred to as high or strong. The degree of coupling between modules reflects the quality of their design.

Software modules that are tightly coupled are more complex, which decreases their maintainability. Tight coupling makes modifying the code more difficult because a change in a tightly coupled module will likely require changes in other modules. This introduces a higher degree of risk as there is a greater likelihood that a new defect could be introduced if a software module is modified.

It is also easy to engage in parallel development if the code is loosely coupled. One developer can work on one part of the application independent of another developer who is working on a different part of the application.

Modules that are loosely coupled do not have as many dependencies with other modules. Changes to tightly coupled modules will take more time and effort due to the interdependencies with other modules. As the number of modules that are affected by a change increases, it will take longer for developers to make the modifications, and for testers to test the changes. Tight coupling also reduces reusability. It is harder to reuse a module when dependent modules must be included in the reuse.

Types of coupling

There are different types of coupling. The following are details regarding those types, in order of the tightest (least desirable) to loosest (most desirable) coupling. It should be noted that it is possible for two modules to be coupled in more than one way. In those situations, the coupling type is determined by the worst, or tightest, coupling type.

Content coupling

Content coupling is the highest type of coupling. It is considered so bad that it is also referred to as pathological coupling. It occurs when one module directly references the internal or private information in another module. For example, it exists when one module accesses or changes private data in another module.

Modules should never be designed to have this type of coupling. If modules have content coupling, they should be refactored so that there is a proper level of abstraction. The modules should not directly rely on the internal workings of each other.

Common coupling

Common coupling, also known as global coupling, is a high level of coupling. This type of coupling is highly undesirable. Although sometimes it is unavoidable, modules should be designed to minimize the existence of this type of coupling.

Modules exhibit common coupling when they share the same global data, such as a global variable. It is perfectly acceptable to share configuration data throughout an application. However, as a general rule, if you are going to use other types of global data, it is better to use something that has a fixed value, such as a constant, rather than a variable whose value can vary at runtime.

External coupling

External coupling is another type of high coupling. It exists when multiple modules share the same part of an environment that is external to the software. This could come in the form of having to use an external data format, interface, communication format, tool, or device.

Sometimes, external dependencies are imposed and unavoidable, but we should still seek to limit the number of modules that have those dependencies. Doing so will ensure that if the external dependency changes, only a limited number of modules are affected.

Control coupling

Control coupling is a moderate type of coupling. Two modules exhibit control coupling when one module controls the internal logic of the other by passing it information. An example of this is when a module passes a control flag to another module, which uses it to control its flow.

This type of coupling may be acceptable, but an effort should be made to make it known that the coupling exists so that the modules can be tested together. It is beneficial to detect any problems with either of the modules earlier rather than later.

Stamp coupling (data-structured coupling)

Stamp coupling is a fairly low type of coupling. It is also known as data-structure coupling because it occurs when modules share a composite data structure. By composite data structure, we mean that it is data that has some internal structure to it, such as a record.

When a composite data structure is shared between two modules, some of the fields in the data structure may not even be used. For example, a module passes a composite data structure to another module, which then just uses one field in it.

It is similar to data coupling, except that the data shared is a composite data type rather than primitive data values and that not all of the values shared may be used.

Data coupling

Data coupling occurs when two modules share some data which are just primitive data values. It is another low type of coupling. A common type of data coupling is when a module calls a method on another module, and inputs and outputs are shared in the form of method parameters and the return value.

When two modules need to interact, this is a common and acceptable type of coupling. Unlike stamp collecting, where some of the values in the shared composite data structure may not be used, all of the parameters in data coupling are used. If any parameters are not needed, they should be removed.

Message coupling

Modules exhibit message coupling when one module calls a method on another and does not send any parameters. The only coupling is on the name of the method, but nothing else. It is the lowest type of coupling.

No coupling

There are, of course, situations where there is no coupling between modules. This is when two modules have no direct communication at all. It is an ideal that allows the two modules to be implemented, tested, and maintained independently.

The Law of Demeter (LoD) / principle of least knowledge

The **Law of Demeter (LoD)**, or **principle of least knowledge**, is a design principle related to loose coupling. In order to minimize coupling between software modules, the principle can be followed when designing software.

The principle follows the *only talk to your friends* idiom, which keeps coupling loose by limiting a module's communication with other modules. Ideally, a method should only call other methods in the same object, in objects that were passed into it, in direct component objects, in objects that it created/instantiated, or in objects in a global variable that are accessible.

Another one of the tenets of LoD is that a software module should know as little as possible about other modules. This will ensure its independence from other modules, allowing coupling to remain loose. See the *Information hiding* section for a principle that helps to achieve this goal.

Designing for loose coupling

During designs and implementations, your goal as a software architect should be to minimize the amount of coupling that exists between modules. Modules should be designed to be as independent as possible.

Coupling can be reduced by eliminating or reducing the number of unnecessary dependencies. For any coupling that must exist, it should be the lowest type that is necessary. Loose coupling reduces complexity and increases maintainability and reusability.

Coupling typically affects the level of cohesion, so that loose coupling correlates with high cohesion and tight coupling correlates with low cohesion.

High cohesion

Cohesion is the degree to which the elements inside a module belong together. It is the strength of the relationships of elements within a module, and how united they are in their purpose. Cohesion is a qualitative measure of the consistency of purpose within a module.

There are different types of cohesion, and those that reflect a higher level of cohesion are preferable. Highly cohesive modules have a single, well-defined purpose, and reflect a better quality of design.

Software modules with low cohesion are harder to maintain. If a module contains multiple unrelated functions, changes to it are more likely to require changes in other modules. This will require extra time and effort, not just in development, but also testing. The extra complexity in modules with low cohesion make it more likely that defects may be introduced when they are modified. They may also be harder to understand, making them more difficult to modify.

Reusability is lessened for modules with low cohesion. Modules with low cohesion, performing many disparate functions, are less likely to be reused for other purposes. A module that works together as a logical unit with a clear purpose is more likely to be reused.

Types of cohesion

The level of cohesion in a module is represented by the type of cohesion. Let's examine the different types of cohesion, from lowest (least desirable) to highest (most desirable).

Coincidental cohesion

Coincidental cohesion occurs when elements in a module are grouped arbitrarily. There is no relationship among the different elements, making it the lowest (worst) type of cohesion. Sometimes, you will see this type of cohesion in a *utilities* or *helpers* class where a number of unrelated functions have been placed together.

Coincidental cohesion should be avoided and, if it is encountered in a module, the module should be refactored. Each part of the module should be moved to an existing or new module where it would make logical sense for it to exist.

Logical cohesion

Modules exhibit logical cohesion when elements are grouped together because they are related in some way logically. Even though the functionality of logically cohesive modules might be of the same general category, they may be different in other ways. For this reason, this type of cohesion is considered low. While better than coincidental cohesion, these types of modules are not very cohesive.

An example of logical cohesion would be a module that contains a set of functions that handles I/O for the application. While they are related logically, the nature of the various functions would be quite different. They would be more cohesive if each type of I/O was handled by a separate module.

Temporal cohesion

Temporal cohesion exists when the elements of a module are grouped together based on when they are processed. This can occur when different elements are grouped together simply because they need to be executed at a single moment in time. This is another type of low cohesion.

An example of temporal cohesion is grouping a bunch of elements together because they are all related to system startup, system shutdown, or the handling of a system error. Even though the elements are related temporally, they are only weakly related to each other. This makes the module harder to maintain and reuse.

The elements should be grouped into different modules, with each module designed for a single purpose.

Procedural cohesion

A module exhibits procedural cohesion when its elements have been grouped together because they always execute in a particular sequence. For example, payment processing for a customer placing an order might involve the following steps being executed in a particular sequence:

- Gathering payment information
- Validating payment method details
- Checking whether funds are available or whether there is enough available credit

- Persisting the order in a database
- Checking inventory levels
- Creating a back order or canceling an order based on inventory
- Sending the order for fulfillment
- Sending an email confirmation to the customer

Although the various parts are all related by the order of execution, some of the individual activities are quite distinct from each other.

This type of cohesion is considered moderate. Although it is an acceptable level of cohesion, it is not ideal. If possible, refactoring can be performed to improve the level of cohesion.

Communicational cohesion

Communicational cohesion occurs when parts of a module are grouped together because they use the same set of inputs and outputs. If a module has different elements that have been grouped together because they access and modify the same data structure, it would demonstrate communicational cohesion.

For example, a data structure that represents the contents of a customer's shopping basket might be used by a variety of elements in a single module. The elements might calculate discounts, shipping, and taxes based on the same data structure.

This level of cohesion is moderate and usually considered acceptable.

Sequential cohesion

Sequential cohesion exists when the different parts of a module are grouped together because the output of one part serves as the input for another part. Modules of this type have a moderate level of cohesion.

An example of a module that is sequentially cohesive would be one that is responsible for formatting and validating a file. The output of an activity that formats a raw record becomes the input for an activity that then validates the fields in that record.

Functional cohesion

Functional cohesion occurs when elements of a module are grouped together because they are united for a single, well-defined purpose. All of the elements in the module work together to fulfill that purpose. Functional cohesion in a module is ideal and is the highest type of cohesion.

Functional cohesion promotes the reusability of a module and makes it easier to maintain. Examples of functionally cohesive modules include one that is responsible for reading a particular file and one that is responsible for calculating shipping costs for an order.

Designing for high cohesion

Software architects should design modules to have high cohesion. Each module should have a single, well-defined purpose. The elements contained in the module should be related and contribute to that purpose.

If there are auxiliary elements contained in a module that are not directly related to the main purpose, consider moving them to either a new module or an existing module that has the same purpose of the element being moved.

Cohesion and coupling are related in that high cohesion correlates with loose coupling and low cohesion correlates with tight coupling.

Minimizing complexity

Building software is inherently complex and a number of problems result from complexity. Higher levels of complexity in software:

- Cause delays in schedules
- Lead to cost overruns
- May cause the software to behave in unintended ways or lead to an unanticipated application state
- May create security loopholes or prevent security issues from being discovered in a timely fashion
- Are a predictive measure of lower levels of some quality attributes, such as lower maintainability, extendibility, and reusability

In *The Mythical Man-Month*, Fred Brooks divides the problems facing software engineering into two categories, *essential* and *accidental*:

"All software construction involves essential tasks, the fashioning of the complex conceptual structures that compose the abstract software entity, and accidental tasks, the representation of these abstract entities in programming languages and the mapping of these onto machine languages within space and speed constraints."

Accidental difficulties are problems that are just inherent to the production of software in general. They are problems that software engineers can fix and may not even be directly related to the problem they are trying to solve. Improvements in programming languages, frameworks, design patterns, **integrated development environments (IDEs)**, and software development methodologies are just some examples of progress over the years in eliminating or reducing accidental difficulties.

Essential difficulties are the core problems that you are trying to solve and they can't simply be removed to reduce complexity. Software development teams spend more time on essential complexities than accidental ones.

We try to manage and minimize the complexity, whether it is accidental or essential. As it has probably become apparent by now, a recurring theme in this book is the importance of managing and minimizing complexity. It has a direct relationship with the quality of the software and is therefore a major focus for software architects.

Minimizing complexity in software helps to eliminate or manage both accidental and essential difficulties. Some of the principles related to minimizing complexity include KISS, DRY, information hiding, YAGNI, and SoC.

KISS principle – "Keep It Simple, Stupid"

The **KISS principle**, which is an acronym for *Keep It Simple, Stupid*, has been used in numerous contexts to convey the idea that systems generally work best if they are kept simple. The principle is applicable to the design of software systems. A development team should strive to not overcomplicate their solutions.

Variations of the acronym include *Keep It Short, Simple, Keep It Simple, Stupid, Keep It Simple, Straightforward*, and *Keep It Simple, Silly*. All of them have the same basic meaning, which is to express the value of simplicity in designs.

Origin of KISS

The creation of the principle is typically credited to the late Kelly Johnson, who was an aeronautical and systems engineer. Among other accomplishments, he contributed to aircraft designs for the Lockheed Corporation (now known as Lockheed Martin after its merger with Martin Marietta).

Though the principle is commonly communicated as *Keep It Simple, Stupid*, Kelly's original version didn't have a comma in it. The word *Stupid* wasn't intended to refer to a person.

Kelly introduced the principle by explaining to the engineers that the jet aircraft they were designing needed to be something that a man in the field could fix with basic training and common tools. The design needed to satisfy this requirement, which is understandable given that the aircraft might need to be repaired quickly in a combat situation.

Applying KISS to software

Simplicity is a highly desirable quality in software systems, and this includes their designs as well as their implementations. Making software more complicated than it needs to be lowers its overall quality. Greater complexity reduces maintainability, hinders reusability, and may lead to an increase in the number of defects.

Some ways to follow the KISS principle in software include:

- Eliminating duplication as much as possible (see the *DRY – "Don't Repeat Yourself"* section)
- Eliminating unnecessary features (see the *YAGNI – "You Aren't Gonna Need It"* section)
- Hiding complexity and design decisions (see the *Information hiding* section)
- Following known standards when possible and minimizing deviations and surprises

Even after a module is implemented, if you see a method or class that could be made simpler, consider refactoring it if you have the opportunity.

Don't make it overly simple

In a quest for simplicity, we cannot oversimplify a design or implementation, though. If we reach a point that it negatively affects the ability to deliver on required functionality or quality attributes, we have gone too far.

Keep the following quote, attributed to Albert Einstein, in mind when designing software: *Everything should be made as simple as possible, but not simpler.*

DRY – "Don't Repeat Yourself"

The **DRY principle** stands for *Don't Repeat Yourself* and strives to reduce duplication in a codebase. Duplication is wasteful and makes a codebase unnecessarily larger and more complex. This makes maintenance more difficult. When code that has been duplicated needs to be changed, modifications are required in multiple locations. If the changes applied everywhere are not consistent, defects may be introduced. Software architects and developers should avoid duplication whenever possible.

When a design violates the DRY principle, it is sometimes referred to as a WET (Write Everything Twice) solution (or *Waste Everyone's Time* or *We Enjoy Typing*).

Copy-and-paste programming

In poorly written codebases, code duplication often results from **copy-and-paste programming**. This happens when a developer needs the exact same or very similar logic, which exists somewhere else in the system, so they duplicate (copy and paste) the code. This violates the DRY principle and lowers the quality of the code.

Copy-and-paste programming can sometimes be acceptable and serve a useful purpose. Code snippets, which are small blocks of reusable code, may speed up development. Many IDEs and text editors provide snippet management to make the use of snippets easier for developers. However, beyond the appropriate application of snippets, it is usually not a good idea to copy and paste your application code in multiple places.

Magic strings

Magic strings are strings that appear directly in your code. Sometimes, these strings are needed in multiple places and are duplicated, violating the DRY principle. Maintenance of these strings can become a nightmare because if you want to change the value of the string, you have to change it in multiple places. The problem is exacerbated when the string is used, not just in multiple places within the same class, but within multiple classes.

There are many examples of magic strings, from exception messages, settings in configuration files, parts of a file path, or a web URL. Let's look at an example where the magic string value represents a cache key. This serves as a good example because this is a case where a magic string might be duplicated multiple times within the same class and even within the same method:

```
public string GetFilePath()
{
    string result = _cache.Get("FilePathCacheKey");
```

```
        if (string.IsNullOrEmpty(result))
        {
            _cache.Put("FilePathCacheKey", DetermineFilePath());
            result = _cache.Get("FilePathCacheKey");
        }

        return result;
    }
```

This key is repeated multiple times, increasing the possibility of a typo resulting in a defect. In addition, if we ever want to change the cache key, we will have to update it in multiple places.

To follow the DRY principle, let's refactor this code so that the cache key is not repeated. First, let's declare a constant at the class level for the magic string:

```
private const string FilePathCacheKey = "FilePathCacheKey";
```

Now, we can use that constant in our `GetFilePath` method:

```
public string GetFilePath()
{
    string result = _cache.Get(FilePathCacheKey);

    if (string.IsNullOrEmpty(result))
    {
        _cache.Put(FilePathCacheKey, DetermineFilePath());
        result = _cache.Get(FilePathCacheKey);
    }

    return result;
}
```

Now, the string is declared in just one location. If you are going to place a magic string in a constant, you should think about where the constant should be declared. One consideration is the scope of its use. It may be appropriate to declare it within the scope of a particular class, but in some cases, a broader or narrower scope will make more sense.

Although placing a magic string in a constant is a good technique for a variety of situations, it is not always ideal. This decision also depends on the type of string and its purpose. For example, if the string is a validation message, you might want to place it in a resource file. If there are any internationalization requirements, placing translatable strings, such as validation messages, in a resource file will facilitate translating the messages into different languages.

How to avoid duplication

DRYness can be achieved by being mindful and taking action when appropriate. If you find yourself copying and pasting code, or simply writing code that is identical or similar to existing code, think about what you are trying to accomplish and how it can be made reusable.

Duplication in logic can be eliminated by abstraction. This concept is referred to as the **abstraction principle** (or the **principle of abstraction**). The principle is consistent with the DRY principle and is a way to reduce duplication. The code that is needed in multiple places should be abstracted out, and the locations that need it can then be routed through the abstraction. Some refactoring may be necessary to make it generic enough to be reused, but it is worth the effort. Once the logic is centralized, if it needs to be modified in the future, perhaps to fix a defect or to enhance it in some way, you will be able to make the changes in a single location.

As we saw in the case of magic strings, duplication with values can be eliminated by placing the value in a central location, such as the declaration of a constant.

If there is duplication in a process, it may be possible to reduce it through automation. Manual unit testing, builds, and integration processes can be eliminated by automating those processes. The automation of tests and builds will be discussed further in `Chapter 13`, *DevOps and Software Architecture*.

Don't make things overly DRY

When attempting to follow the DRY principle, be careful not to consolidate disparate items that just happen to be duplicates in some way. If two or more things are duplicates, it may be that they are just *coincidentally repetitive*.

For example, if two constants have the same value, that does not mean they should be combined into one constant for the sake of eliminating duplication. If the constants represent distinct concepts, they should remain separate.

Information hiding

Information hiding is a principle that advocates for software modules to be designed such that they hide implementation details from the rest of the software system. The idea of information hiding was introduced by D.L. Parnas in *On the Criteria to Be Used in Decomposing Systems into Modules*, which was published in 1972.

Information hiding decouples the internal workings of a module from the places in the system that call it. The details of a module that do not need to be revealed should be made inaccessible. Information hiding defines constraints related to what properties and behaviors can be accessed. Callers interact with the module's public interface and are protected from the implementation details.

There are a number of reasons to abide by the principle of information hiding.

Reasons for information hiding

Information hiding is useful at all levels of design. Only exposing the details that need to be known reduces complexity, which improves maintainability. Unless you are specifically interested in the internal details, you do not need to concern yourself with them.

Another one of the key reasons for information hiding is to hide design decisions from the rest of the software system. This is particularly beneficial if the design decision might change. By hiding a design decision, if the decision needs to be changed, it minimizes the amount and extent of the modifications that will be necessary. It provides the flexibility to make changes later if it is necessary to do so.

Whether the design decision is to use a particular API, represent data in a certain way, or use a particular algorithm, the modifications necessary to change that design decision should be kept as localized as possible.

What needs to be exposed/hidden?

You and your team should really think about the properties and behaviors (methods) that need to be exposed for a module. Everything else can be hidden. Through the use of a public interface, we can define what we want to make available.

Information hiding assists with defining public interfaces. Rather than lazily exposing most of a class, it forces us to consider what really needs to be made public. The public interface defines a contract that the implementation must follow, and allows others to know *what* is available. It is up to the implementation to decide *how* it is accomplished.

YAGNI – "You Aren't Gonna Need It"

YAGNI, which stands for *You Aren't Gonna Need It*, or *You Ain't Gonna Need It*, is a principle from the software development methodology of **Extreme Programming** (**XP**). XP is one of the first agile methods and was the dominant one until the rise of the popularity of Scrum. YAGNI is similar to the KISS principle in that they both aim for simpler solutions, with YAGNI focusing on a specific aspect, which is the removal of unnecessary functionality and logic.

Avoid over-engineering a solution

The idea behind YAGNI is that you should only implement functionality when you need it and not just because you think you may need it some day. Ron Jeffries, one of the co-founders of XP, once said:

> *"Always implement things when you actually need them, never when you just foresee that you need them."*

Following the YAGNI principle helps you to avoid over-engineering a solution. You don't want to spend time on future scenarios that are unknown. The problem with implementing a feature that you think might eventually be needed is that quite often the feature ends up not being needed or the requirements for it change.

Code that is not written equates to time and money that is saved. Spending time and money on a feature you don't need takes away from time and money you could have spent on something that you do need. Resources are finite, and using them on something that is unnecessary is a waste. As was the case with code duplication, adding unnecessary logic to an application increases its size and complexity, which reduces maintainability.

Situations where YAGNI doesn't apply

YAGNI applies to presumptive features, as in functionality that is not currently needed. It does not apply to code that would make the software system easier to maintain and modify later. In fact, following YAGNI means you may be changing the system later to add a feature, so the system should be well designed for this purpose. If a software system is not maintainable, making changes later may be difficult.

You may come across times where, in hindsight, a change made sooner would have prevented more expensive changes later. This may be particularly true for software architects if the change is architecture related. Design decisions made for architecture are among the earliest decisions made, and having to change them later can be costly.

It can sometimes be difficult to foresee which changes should have been made before they were needed. However, for the most part, following YAGNI is beneficial. Even in the case of an architecture change, a good architecture design reduces complexity and makes it easier to make changes. It also makes it more likely that when a change is needed, it can be limited in scope and may not even require architectural changes.

As software architects gain more experience, they become more adept at spotting exceptions to the YAGNI principle where a particular change should be made before it is needed.

Separation of Concerns (SoC)

Concerns are the different aspects of functionality that the software system provides. **Separation of Concerns (SoC)** is a design principle that manages complexity by partitioning the software system so that each partition is responsible for a separate concern, minimizing the overlap of concerns as much as possible.

Following the principle involves decomposing a larger problem into smaller, more manageable concerns. SoC reduces complexity in a software system, which reduces the effort needed to make changes and improves the overall quality of the software.

When the DRY principle is followed, and logic is not repeated, a SoC is usually a natural result as long as the logic is organized properly.

SoC is a principle that can be applied to multiple levels in a software application. At the architecture level, software applications can follow a SoC by separating different logic such as user-interface functionality, business logic, and infrastructure logic. An example of an architecture pattern that separates concerns at this level is the **Model-View-Controller (MVC)** pattern, which we will cover in the next chapter.

We can apply SoC at a lower level, such as with classes. If we were providing order processing functionality in a software system, the concern of validating credit card information shouldn't exist in the same place as the concern for updating inventory. They are distinct concerns that should not be placed together. At this level, it is related to the Single Responsibility Principle, which we will discuss shortly.

An example of separating concerns by language in web programming is **Hypertext Markup Language (HTML)**, **Cascading Style Sheets (CSS)**, and **JavaScript**. They complement each other with one being focused on the content of web pages, one for the presentation, and one for the behavior.

Following SOLID design principles

SOLID design principles focus on creating code that is more understandable, maintainable, reusable, testable, and flexible. SOLID is an acronym that represents five separate software design principles:

- Single Responsibility Principle (SRP)
- Open/Closed Principle (OCP)
- Liskov Substitution Principle (LSP)
- Interface Segregation Principle (ISP)
- Dependency Inversion Principle (DIP)

Software architects should be familiar with SOLID principles and apply them in their designs and implementations. They should realize, though, that the principles are guidelines, and while you should strive to follow them, you may not always be able to accomplish that fully. Use your judgement as to when, and to what degree, these principles should be followed.

Now, let's explore the five design principles that make up SOLID in more detail.

Single Responsibility Principle (SRP)

The **Single Responsibility Principle** (**SRP**) states that each class should have only one responsibility, meaning it should do one thing and do that thing well. A responsibility is a reason to change, so each class should have only one reason to change. If we group together the functions that need to change for the same reason, and separate out the things that change for other reasons, we can create a class that follows this principle.

If a class has multiple responsibilities, there is a likelihood that it is used in a greater number of places. When one responsibility is changed, not only do we run a higher risk of introducing defects into other responsibilities in the same class, but there is a greater number of other classes that might be impacted.

By following the single responsibility principle, if we need to change a particular responsibility, that change would be located in a single class. This is the way to create an orthogonal software system.

Applying this principle does not necessarily mean, as some posit, that each class should only have a single public method. Although it does reduce the size of classes, the goal is to have each class have a single responsibility. Fulfilling a single responsibility may require multiple public methods.

This principle is related to the SoC principle because, as concerns are separated from each other, it facilitates the creation of classes that have a single responsibility. Following the DRY principle also helps us to abide by the SRP. By removing duplicate code and placing it in a single location so that it can be reused, the classes that need the logic do not have to repeat it and therefore do not need to be responsible for it.

Let's take a look at an example of the SRP. It is written in C#, although you will get the idea even if you do not use that particular programming language. We have an email service that is responsible for sending out emails. There is a requirement to log information to a log file, so it also contains logic to open, write to, and close a log file on a file system:

```csharp
public class EmailService : IEmailService
{
    public SendEmailResponse SendEmail(SendEmailRequest request)
    {
        if (request == null)
            throw new ArgumentNullException(nameof(request));

        SendEmailResponse response = null;

        try
        {
            // Logic to send email

            // Log info about sent email
            LogInfo("Some info message");
        }
        catch (Exception ex)
        {
            // Log details about error
            LogError("Some error message");
        }

        return response;
    }

    private void LogInfo(string message)
    {
        // Logic to write to file system for logging
    }

    private void LogError(string message)
    {
        // Logic to write to file system for logging
    }
}
```

As you can see in this simple example, this class has more than one responsibility: sending out emails as well as handling the logging. This means that it has more than one reason to change. If we wanted to change how emails were sent out, or allow for the logging to target cloud file storage instead of a file on a local file system, both would require changes to the same class.

This violates the SRP. Let's refactor this class so that it is only responsible for one thing:

```
public class EmailService : IEmailService
{
    private readonly ILogger _logger;

    public EmailService(ILogger logger)
    {
        if (_logger == null)
            throw new ArgumentNullException(nameof(logger));

        _logger = logger;
    }

    public SendEmailResponse SendEmail(SendEmailRequest request)
    {
        if (request == null)
            throw new ArgumentNullException(nameof(request));

        SendEmailResponse response = null;

        try
        {
            // Logic to send email

            // Log info about sent email
            _logger.LogInfo("Info message");
        }
        catch (Exception ex)
        {
            // Log details about error
            _logger.LogError($"Error message: {ex.Message}");
        }

        return response;
    }
}
```

Now, the `EmailService` class is only responsible for sending out emails. The logic for logging has been abstracted out to an interface. This dependency is injected in through the class's constructor, and the implementation will be responsible for how logging works.

This class is now only responsible for a single thing and therefore only has one reason to change. Only changes related to the sending of emails will require modifications to this class. It no longer violates the SRP.

Open/Closed Principle (OCP)

The **Open/Closed Principle (OCP)** states that software components, such as classes, should be open for extension but closed for modification. When requirements change, the design should minimize the amount of changes that need to occur on existing code. We should be able to extend a component by adding new code without having to modify existing code that already works.

When Dr. Bertrand Meyer first came up with the principle in his book *Object Oriented Software Construction*, it focused on using implementation inheritance as the solution. If new functionality is needed, a new subtype is created and the base class and any existing subtypes could remain unchanged.

Software engineer Robert C. Martin, popularly known as Uncle Bob, redefined the principle in his article *The Open-Closed Principle*, and later in his book *Agile Software Development, Principles, Patterns, and Practices*, by stressing the importance of abstraction and the use of interfaces. Using interfaces, we can change implementations as needed. In this way, we can change behavior without having to modify existing code that relies on the interfaces.

Let's take a look at an example. In this program, we have a Shape class with Rectangle and Circle classes that inherit from it. A Canvas class has methods that allow us to draw the shapes:

```
public class Canvas
{
    public void DrawShape(Shape shape)
    {
        if (shape is Rectangle)
            DrawRectangle((Rectangle)shape);

        if (shape is Circle)
            DrawCircle((Circle)shape);
    }

    public void DrawRectangle(Rectangle r)
    {
        // Logic to draw a rectangle
    }

    public void DrawCircle(Circle c)
```

```
    {
        // Logic to draw a circle
    }
}
```

If a new request comes in that requires us to be able to draw a new shape, such as a triangle, we will have to modify the `Canvas` class. This class has not been designed to be closed for modification and violates the OCP.

Developers will need to understand the `Canvas` class in order to add a new shape. Modifications to the `Canvas` class will require unit tests to be revisited and introduces the possibility that existing functionality could be broken.

Let's refactor this poor design so that it no longer violates the OCP:

```
public interface IShape
{
    void Draw();
}
public class Rectangle : IShape
{
    public void Draw()
    {
        // Logic to draw rectangle
    }
}

public class Circle : IShape
{
    public void Draw()
    {
        // Logic to draw circle
    }
}

public class Canvas
{
    public void DrawShape(IShape shape)
    {
        shape.Draw();
    }
}
```

The `Canvas` class is now much smaller, with each shape now having its own implementation of how to draw itself. If there was a requirement to add a new shape, we can create a new `Shape` class that implements the `IShape` interface without having to make any changes to the `Canvas` class or any of the other shapes. It is now open for extension but closed for modification.

Liskov Substitution Principle (LSP)

Inheritance is one of the four pillars of **object-oriented programming** (OOP). It allows subclasses to inherit from a base class (sometimes referred to as the parent class), which includes the properties and methods of the base class. When you first learned about inheritance, you may have been taught about "is a" relationships. For example, "Car is a Vehicle," if Car was a base class and Vehicle was a subtype of that base class.

The **Liskov Substitution Principle** (**LSP**) is an object-oriented principle that states that subtypes must be substitutable for their base types without having to alter the base type. If a subtype is inherited from a base class, we should be able to substitute the subclass for that base class without any issues. Subtypes extending a base class should do so without changing the behavior of the base class. When the LSP is violated, it makes for confusing code that is hard to understand.

For a given base class or an interface the base class implements, the subtypes of that base class should be usable through the base class or an interface the base class implements. The methods and properties of the base class should make sense and work as intended for all of the subtypes. If the classes work without an issue and behave as expected, the subtypes are substitutable for the base class. When the LSP is violated, this is not the case. Although the code may compile, unexpected behavior or runtime errors may be experienced.

A classic example to illustrate the LSP is that of a `Rectangle` class and a `Square` class. In geometry, a square is a type of rectangle, so every square is a rectangle. The only difference is that with a square all of the sides have the same length.

We can model this by creating a `Rectangle` class, which is a base class, and a `Square` class, which is a subtype that inherits from it:

```
public class Rectangle
{
    public virtual int Width { get; set; }
    public virtual int Height { get; set; }

    public int CalculateArea()
    {
```

```
            return Width * Height;
    }
}

public class Square : Rectangle
{
    private int _width;
    private int _height;

    public override int Width
    {
        get { return _width; }
        set
        {
            _width = value;
            _height = value;
        }
    }

    public override int Height {
        get { return _height; }
        set
        {
            _width = value;
            _height = value;
        }
    }
}
```

As you can see from this code sample, the `Square` class overrides how the width and height are set to ensure that they remain equal:

```
Rectangle rect = new Rectangle
{
    Width = 5,
    Height = 4
};
Console.WriteLine(rect.CalculateArea());

Square sqr = new Square
{
    Width = 4
};
Console.WriteLine(sqr.CalculateArea());

Rectangle sqrSubstitutedForRect = new Square
{
    Width = 3,
```

```
    Height = 2
};
Console.WriteLine(sqrSubstitutedForRect.CalculateArea());

Console.ReadLine();
```

The area of the `rect` object will calculate to 20 and the area of the `sqr` object will calculate to 16, as expected. However, the area of the `sqrSubstitutedForRect` object will calculate to 4 and not 6. As these classes are currently designed, the `Square` subtype is really not substitutable for the `Rectangle` base class.

This code will compile but it violates the SRP and leads to confusing results. This is a simplistic example, but you start to get the idea. With complex class hierarchies, violations of the SRP can lead to defects, some of which can be difficult to solve.

Interface Segregation Principle (ISP)

Interfaces define methods and properties, but do not provide any implementation. Classes that implement an interface provide the implementation. Interfaces define a contract, and clients can use them without concerning themselves with their implementation details. The implementation can change and as long as a breaking change is not made to the interface, the client does not need to change their logic.

The **Interface Segregation Principle (ISP)** states that clients should not be forced to depend on properties and methods that they do not use. When designing software, we prefer smaller, more cohesive interfaces. If an interface is too large, we can logically split it up into multiple interfaces so that clients can focus on only the properties and methods that are of interest to them.

When interfaces are too large and attempt to cover too many aspects of functionality, they are known as *fat* interfaces. The ISP is violated when classes are dependent on an interface with methods they do not need. Violation of the ISP increases coupling and makes maintenance more difficult.

Let's look at an example where we are creating a system for a business that sells books. We create the following interface and class for the products:

```
public interface IProduct
{
    int ProductId { get; set; }
    string Title { get; set; }
    int AuthorId { get; set; }
    decimal Price { get; set; }
```

```
    }

public class Book : IProduct
{
    public int ProductId { get; set; }
    public string Title { get; set; }
    public int AuthorId { get; set; }
    public decimal Price { get; set; }
}
```

Now, let's say that the business owners want to start selling physical disks of movies. The properties needed are very similar to IProduct, so an inexperienced developer might use the IProduct interface for their Movie class:

```
public class Movie : IProduct
{
    public int ProductId { get; set; }
    public string Title { get; set; }
    public int AuthorId {
        get => throw new NotSupportedException();
        set => throw new NotSupportedException();
    }
    public decimal Price { get; set; }
    public int RunningTime { get; set; }
}
```

AuthorId doesn't make sense for movies, but in this example, the developer decides to just mark the property as not supported. This is one of the *code smells* for violation of the ISP. If a developer of a class that is implementing an interface finds themselves having to mark properties or methods as not supported/not implemented, perhaps the interface needs to be segregated.

The Movie class also needs to represent the running time of the movie, which isn't a property needed by the Book class. If it is added to the IProduct interface, all classes that implement that interface will need to be modified. This is another code smell indicating that there may be an issue with the design of the interface.

If we were to refactor this code so that it no longer violates the ISP, we would separate the IProduct interface into more than one so that the single "fat" interface is separated into multiple smaller and more cohesive ones:

```
public interface IProduct
{
    int ProductId { get; set; }
    string Title { get; set; }
    decimal Price { get; set; }
```

```
    }

    public interface IBook : IProduct
    {
        int AuthorId { get; set; }
    }

    public interface IMovie : IProduct
    {
        int RunningTime { get; set; }
    }

    public class Book : IBook
    {
        public int ProductId { get; set; }
        public string Title { get; set; }
        public int AuthorId { get; set; }
        public decimal Price { get; set; }
    }

    public class Movie : IMovie
    {
        public int ProductId { get; set; }
        public string Title { get; set; }
        public decimal Price { get; set; }
        public int RunningTime { get; set; }
    }
```

We can see that the IProduct interface only contains the properties needed by all products. The IBook interface inherits from IProduct, so that any class implementing IBook will need to implement the AuthorId property in addition to everything in IProduct. Similarly, IMovie inherits from IProduct and contains the RunningTime property that is only needed for movie implementations.

We are no longer in violation of the ISP, and classes implementing these interfaces do not have to deal with properties and methods that are not of interest to them.

Dependency Inversion Principle (DIP)

The **Dependency Inversion Principle** (DIP) is a principle that describes how to handle dependencies and write loosely coupled software. In their book *Agile Principles, Patterns, and Practices in C#*, Robert C. Martin and Micah Martin state the principle as follows:

> *"The high-level modules should not depend on low-level modules. Both should depend on abstractions.*
>
> *Abstractions should not depend upon details. Details should depend upon abstractions."*

For example, let's say that **Class A** depends on **Class B** and **Class B** depends on **Class C**:

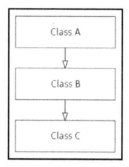

In a direct dependency graph, at compile time, **Class A** references **Class B** which references **Class C**. At runtime, the control flow will go from **Class A** to **Class B** to **Class C**. **Class A** and **Class B** will have to instantiate, or *new up*, their dependencies. This creates tightly coupled code that is difficult to maintain and test. Changes to one of the dependencies may require changes to the classes that use those dependencies.

Another disadvantage of this approach is that the code is not unit-testable because of its dependencies. We will not be able to create mock objects for dependencies because we are referencing concrete types rather than abstractions. There is no way to *inject* the mock objects so that we can create true unit tests that are not dependent on other classes.

Rather than high-level classes being dependent on lower-level classes, they should depend on abstractions through an interface. The interfaces do not depend on their implementations. Instead, the implementations depend on the interfaces:

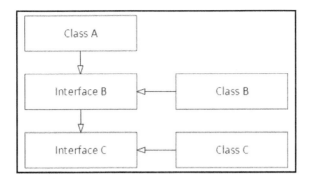

With an inverted dependency graph, at compile time, **Class A** depends on an abstraction (**Interface B**), which in turn depends on an abstraction (**Interface C**). **Class B** and **Class C** implement **Interface B** and **Interface C**, respectively:

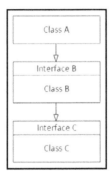

At run time, the flow of control goes through the interfaces, and each interface has an implementation.

The DIP is closely related to the inversion of control principle, with the inversion of control being applied to dependencies.

Inversion of Control (IoC)

Inversion of Control (**IoC**) is a design principle in which a software system receives the flow of control from reusable code, such as a framework. In traditional procedural programming, a software system would call into a reusable library. The IOC principle inverts this flow of control by allowing the reusable code to call into the software system.

Developers are now so familiar with using a variety of frameworks, and even multiple frameworks on a single project, that the principle of IoC is no longer a novel one. Although the principle of IoC can be applied to many more things than just dependencies, it has become closely related to dependencies for its IOC over them.

This is the reason why DI containers were originally, and sometimes still are, referred to as IoC containers. DI containers are frameworks that provide DI functionality, and we will discuss them shortly.

Dependency Injection (DI)

Dependency Injection (**DI**) is a technique that provides dependencies to a class, thereby achieving dependency inversion. Dependencies are passed (injected) to a client that needs it. There are a number of benefits to using DI in a software application.

Benefits of DI

DI removes hardcoded dependencies and allows them to be changed, at either runtime or compile-time. If the implementation of a dependency is determined at runtime rather than compile-time, this is known as late binding, or runtime binding. As long as we are programming to an interface, the implementation can be swapped out.

DI allows us to write loosely coupled code, making applications easier to maintain, extend, and test. As we know, when we need to make a change, loosely coupled code allows us to make a change in one part of our application without it affecting other areas of our application.

Testability increases in software applications that use DI. Loosely coupled code can be tested more easily. Code is written to depend on abstractions and not concrete implementations, so dependencies can be mocked with unit testing frameworks. Following the LSP, a class is not dependent on a concrete type; it is only dependent on the interface. As a result, we can inject mock objects for the dependencies by using the interface and writing unit tests.

Parallel development is made easier with DI. Developers can work on different pieces of functionality in parallel. Since the implementations are independent of each other, as long as the shared interfaces are agreed upon, development can occur at the same time. This is particularly beneficial on larger projects with multiple teams. Each team can work independently and share interfaces for the functionality that must be integrated.

DI patterns

The following are some of the patterns available that can be used for DI:

- Constructor injection
- Property injection
- Method injection
- Service Locator

The following section provides details on these various patterns.

Constructor injection

Constructor injection is a technique in which dependencies are passed through a class's constructor. This is an excellent way to inject dependencies because the dependencies are made explicit. The object cannot be instantiated without its dependencies.

If a class can be instantiated and its methods called, but the functionality does not work properly because one or more dependencies have not been provided, classes are being dishonest with their clients. It is a better practice to explicitly require dependencies.

The following example shows the constructor injection pattern:

```
public class Employee : Person
{
    private readonly ILogger _logger;
    private readonly ICache _cache;

    // Dependencies are injected via the constructor,
    // including the base class
    public Employee(ILogger logger, ICache cache,
        IOrgService orgService)
        : base(logger, orgService)
    {
        if (logger == null)
            throw new ArgumentNullException(nameof(logger));
        if (cache == null)
            throw new ArgumentNullException(nameof(cache));

        _logger = logger;
        _cache = cache;
    }
}

public class Person
{
    private readonly ILogger _logger;
```

```
    private readonly IOrgService _orgService;

    // Dependencies are injected via the constructor
    public Person(ILogger logger, IOrgService orgService)
    {
        if (logger == null)
            throw new ArgumentNullException(nameof(logger));
        if (orgService == null)
            throw new ArgumentNullException(nameof(orgService));

        _logger = logger;
        _orgService = orgService;
    }
}
```

In this example, you can see that the Employee class has three dependencies: instances of ILogger, ICache, and IOrgService. The Person class, which is the base class of Employee, has two dependencies: instances of ILogger and IOrgService.

Constructor injection is used to provide instances of all of the dependencies for both classes. In this example, notice that the Employee class passes the dependencies that the Person class needs to it. Both the Employee and the Person classes have a dependency to ILogger and only the Employee class has a dependency to ICache. The Employee class doesn't even use the orgService instance directly, which is why it is not assigned to a class-level variable, but since its base class needs it, it is a dependency that is injected in and then passed on to its base class (Person).

The dependencies that are injected in are assigned to readonly variables. In the C# language, the readonly keyword indicates that the field can only be assigned as part of its declaration or in the constructor. We will not be assigning an instance of the dependency anywhere else other than the constructor with constructor injection, so it can be marked as readonly.

There is a guard clause that ensures that the required dependencies are not null. If they are, an exception is thrown. If a valid instance is passed in, it is assigned to a private variable so that the instance can be used later in the logic of the class.

Property injection

Property injection allows clients to supply a dependency through a public property. If you need to provide callers with the ability to provide an instance of a dependency, such as to override the default behavior, you can use this injection pattern.

The first time the getter is called, if the dependency has not already been supplied, a default instance should be provided through lazy initialization:

```
public class Person
{
    private IOrgService _orgService;
    public IOrgService OrgService
    {
        get
        {
            if (_orgService == null)
            {
                // Lazy initialization of default
                _orgService = new OrgService();
            }
            return _orgService;
        }
        set
        {
            if (value == null)
            {
                throw new ArgumentNullException(nameof(value));
            }
            // Only allow dependency to be set once
            if (_orgService != null)
            {
                throw new InvalidOperationException();
            }
            _orgService = value;
        }
    }
}
```

If you want a dependency to only be supplied once through a setter, a check can be performed in the setter, as is done in the example.

For the lazy initialization, you will need a way to get the default instance. It is not ideal to instantiate, or *new up*, the dependency in the class. However, the default value could be provided by another means, such as constructor injection. The property would give you the flexibility to provide a different instance at runtime.

The property injection pattern provides dependencies in an implicit way. If a default instance is not provided in the getter when the dependency has not been previously set and the logic needs the dependency to work properly, an error or unexpected results could occur. If you are going to use this pattern over an explicit one, such as constructor injection, a default instance should be provided in some way.

Unlike the example for constructor injection, notice that the private class-level variable to hold the dependency (_orgService) does not have the readonly keyword. In order to use property injection, we need the ability to set the variable outside of the variable's declaration and the constructor.

Method injection

Method injection is similar to property injection, except a dependency is provided through a method rather than a property:

```
public class Person
{
    private IOrgService _orgService;

    public void Initialize(IOrgService orgService)
    {
        if (orgService == null)
            throw new ArgumentNullException(nameof(orgService));

        _orgService = orgService;
    }
}
```

Service Locator

The service locator pattern uses a locator object that encapsulates logic to determine and provide an instance of the dependencies that are needed. Although it will vary depending on your implementation, a sample call with a service locator might look something like the following, resulting in an instance being provided based on the specified interface:

```
var cache = ServiceLocator.GetInstance<ILogger>();
```

Using the service locator pattern to get dependencies is considered to be an anti-pattern by some people because it hides a class's dependencies. As opposed to constructor injection, where we can see the dependencies in the public constructor, we would have to look at the code to find dependencies being resolved through the service locator. Hiding dependencies in this way can lead to runtime or compile-time issues, and make it more difficult to reuse the code. This is particularly true if we do not have access to the source code, which might be the case if we are using code from a third party. It is preferable to use an explicit method to acquire an instance of a dependency.

DI containers

A **Dependency Injection** container, sometimes referred as **DI container** or **IoC container**, is a framework that helps with DI. It creates and injects dependencies for us automatically.

It is not necessary to use a DI container in order to take advantage of DI. However, using a DI container makes handling dependencies much easier. Unless your application is very small in size, leveraging a DI container will eliminate the repetitive grunt work of doing it manually. If you were to write some generic code to automate some of it, you are essentially creating your own container when you could use an existing framework built for that purpose. Dependencies go *n* levels deep and things can get complicated quickly.

If you do opt to use a DI container, there is a variety of containers available. While there are differences among them, they all come with some similar, basic functionality that will facilitate DI. Many of them will also come with other advanced features and your needs will dictate which features you use. Getting DI containers up and running to use the basic features is typically an easy and straightforward process.

Helping your team succeed

One of the many goals of a software architect is to help their team succeed and this can come in many forms. In this section, we will cover some of the practices that a software architect can put into place to help team members succeed. They include unit testing, ensuring that a development environment is easy to set up, pair programming, and code reviews.

Unit testing

Testing is one of those things that some developers do not enjoy doing, even though it is essential to develop high-quality software applications. Developers should test early and often, which is a practice of many agile software development methodologies.

If the practice of writing and executing unit tests is not already part of the organization, software architects should institute the practice. In this section, we will go over some of the essential details of unit testing.

What are unit tests?

Unit testing is the practice of testing the smallest testable units of a software system, such as methods, to ensure that they are working properly. It plays an important role in increasing the quality of your software. Functionality in a software system is decomposed into discrete, testable behaviors that are then tested as units.

Some of the principles we have discussed, such as creating loosely coupled code, following principles such as DRY, SoC, and single responsibility, and using techniques such as DI, create code that is independent and decoupled from dependencies. These qualities make our code testable and allow us to focus a unit test on a single unit.

Benefits of unit testing

There are important benefits to unit testing your software, such as improving the quality of the software. With good unit tests, defects can be found before code is checked in or before a build is attempted. By testing early and often, bugs can be fixed without affecting other code.

One way to make it easier to test early and often is to automate the unit testing. Unit testing is ideal for automation. While developers will want to manually execute unit tests as they change code or prior to check-ins, unit tests can be automatically executed as part of some process, such as a build process. We will discuss automation and build processes in more detail in `Chapter 13`, *DevOps and Software Architecture*.

Debugging is made easier with regular unit testing because the source of the bug can be narrowed down to recent changes. Unit tests also serve as a form of documentation. By looking at the unit tests, one can begin to understand what functionality a particular class provides and how it is supposed to work.

Properties of a good unit test

There are various properties that make for a good unit test. Keep them in mind when writing your unit tests. Unit tests should be atomic, deterministic, automated and repeatable, isolated and independent, easy to set up and implement, and fast.

Atomic

Unit tests should only test a single assumption about a small piece of functionality. This assumption should focus on a behavior of the unit being tested, with the unit typically being a single method. Therefore, multiple tests are necessary to check all of the assumptions for a given unit. If you are testing multiple assumptions in a single test or calling multiple methods in a single test, the scope of your unit test is probably too large.

Deterministic

Unit tests should be deterministic. If no code changes are made, unit tests should yield the same result every time they are executed.

Automated and repeatable

The benefits of unit testing are fully realized when the execution of unit tests are automated and repeatable. This will allow unit tests to be executed as part of a build process.

Isolated and independent

Each unit test should have the ability to be run independently of other tests and in any order. If tests are isolated and independent, it should be possible to execute any unit test at any time.

Unit tests should not depend on anything except the class we are testing. It should not rely on other classes, nor should it depend on things such as connecting to a database, using a hardware device, accessing files on a file system, or communicating across a network.

With a testing framework and a DI framework, we can mock dependencies for our unit tests. A mock object is a simulated object that is instantiated, perhaps with the help of a testing/mocking framework, that mimics the behaviors of the real object. By mocking objects for the dependencies of the class being tested, we keep the unit test independent of other classes. We can control the mock and specify what it will return based on some input.

Easy to set up and implement

Unit tests should be easy to set up and implement. If they are not, this is a *code smell*, which is a symptom in the system that may indicate a larger problem. The problem could be in the way that the unit being tested is designed or in the way that the test is being written.

Although we want a high amount of unit test coverage, we do not want developers to spend inordinate amounts of time writing a single unit test. Unit tests should be easy to write.

Fast

Unit tests should execute quickly. A complex software system that has adequate test coverage will have a large amount of unit tests. The execution of unit tests should not slow down development or build processes. Based on the other desirable properties of unit tests, such as being atomic, isolated, and independent, they should execute quickly.

The AAA pattern

The AAA pattern is a common unit testing pattern. It is a way to arrange and organize test code to make unit tests clear and understandable, and consists of separating each unit test method into three sections: *Arrange*, *Act*, and *Assert*.

Arrange

In this section of the unit test method, you *arrange* any preconditions and inputs for the test. This includes initializing values and setting up mock objects.

Depending on the unit test framework and programming language that you are using, some of them provide a way to specify methods that will execute prior to the execution of the unit tests for that test class. This allows you to centralize arrangement logic that you want to execute prior to the execution of all of your tests.

However, each unit test method should have an arrange section where you are performing initialization for that particular test.

Act

The Act section of a unit test method is where you *act* on the unit that is being tested, referred to as the **System Under Test** (**SUT**). Logic should invoke the method being tested, passing in values, such as mock objects, that were previously arranged.

Assert

The Assert part of a unit test method is where you *assert* that the results are what you expect. It verifies that the method executed and behaved as expected.

Naming conventions for unit tests

When naming your unit test classes and methods, you should follow a naming convention. This provides not just consistency, but allows your tests to be a form of documentation. Unit tests are intention-revealing in that they describe the expected behavior. If meaningful names are provided, everyone can know something about the purpose of the test class and its methods just by looking at the names.

Unit test class names

The naming of the test classes themselves and the namespaces they are in depend on the naming conventions that your project follows for classes. However, you should consider putting the name of the class being tested (the **System Under Test** (SUT) in the name of the class. For example, if you are testing a class named `OrderService`, consider naming the unit test class `OrderServiceTests`.

Unit test method names

The unit test methods should be given meaningful names that provide, at a glance, their purpose. Characteristics such as the method being tested, some indication as to the specific condition(s) and input(s) of the test, and the expected result of the test are all useful to provide.

For example, if we are testing the `CalculateShipping` method on the `OrderService` class, we might have test method names such as:

- `CalculateShipping_NullOrder_ThrowsArgumentNullException`
- `CalculateShipping_ValidOrder_CalculatesCorrectAmount`
- `CalculateShipping_ExpeditedShipping_CalculatesCorrectAmount`

The exact naming convention for unit test methods is up to you, but the important point is to come up with one and to use it consistently in order to provide meaningful information to those who will be looking at them.

Code coverage for unit tests

Code coverage is a measure of how much of the source code is being covered by tests. Many tools exist that will help you to calculate code coverage. Software architects should stress the importance of aiming for exhaustive test coverage to ensure that all code paths are tested.

Keep in mind that the code coverage percentage is just part of the consideration when deciding whether or not you have adequate coverage. The code coverage percentage will let you know what percentage of the paths are covered (as in paths that are executed at least once). However, this does not mean that all of the important scenarios concerning your functionality is covered. Code coverage calculations do not consider the range of values that are possible for the various inputs, and additional tests may be necessary to cover different situations.

Keeping unit tests up to date

Unit tests are a form of documentation for your system, describing its functionality and the expected behavior. Software architects should encourage their team to not only execute unit tests regularly but to keep them up to date. As requirements change or new functionality is added, unit tests need to be changed or added.

After changes are made, developers should modify any tests that need to be changed and then execute all of the unit tests to ensure there are no unintended consequences.

One thing that I have seen slip through the cracks before regarding keeping unit tests up to date are bug fixes. If a bug is found, the unit tests did not cover that particular scenario. One or more unit tests should be created that incorporate the situation into the tests to ensure it remains fixed. It is a concept expressed by the saying that *bugs should only be found once*.

Teams that are diligent about updating unit tests for changed requirements and new functionality sometimes miss this important point. As a software architect, you can remind your teams of it. The knowledge gained from discovering and resolving that bug should not be lost. Once it is documented in the tests, from that point forward, the tests will check for that type of bug to ensure that it never returns.

Setting up development environments

Software architects should review the process of setting up a new development environment in order to minimize the amount of time that it takes. Most teams do not want to add any extra time to a schedule that may already be tight. The process should not be more difficult than necessary.

New developers may join the team or existing team members may need to start working on a different machine. All too often, setting up a new development environment to the point where a developer can start coding takes an inordinate amount of time. There may be complexities involved with the setup, but it should be made as easy as possible.

Make sure that the process of granting access to new team members, installing the necessary software (for example, development tools), getting the latest code from version control, compiling the code, and running the application is a smooth process. There are tools available that can create and deploy images of environments for physical and virtual development machines.

Sometimes there are subtle things that need to be done, such as making certain changes to a configuration file, in order to get the application working on a development machine. This type of knowledge can sometimes become *tribal knowledge*, or information that is known by some individuals but is unwritten and not known by everyone.

The goal is to get the developer up and running as quickly as possible so that they can focus on the real complexities of their job. If something is making the process difficult, examine the reasons behind it so that action can be taken to improve it. There may be ways to improve the process from both organizational and technical perspectives.

Providing a README file

A good README file should be made available for all projects within an organization. It allows developers to review the steps required to set up an environment. The README file should include the following:

- A brief description of the software project
- Instructions indicating what other software, such as development tools, need to be installed; this includes the location of setup files for the software that needs to be installed and any license keys or other information required for the installation
- Any special configuration that is necessary, such as how to point the application to a particular database
- Information on how to connect to version control in order to perform operations such as getting the latest codebase and checking in changes
- A creation date for the README file and/or a version number of the software it is intended for so that readers can know whether they are looking at the correct version
- Any relevant licensing information
- Contact information for more help

Pair programming

Pair programming is an agile software development technique where two developers work together on the same deliverable, whether a technical design or coding. In the case of programming, the person who is coding is the *driver* while the other person, who is observing, is the *navigator*. The roles of *driver* and *navigator* can alternate at a prescribed interval (for example, every hour) or the roles can be switched at any time that the two people feel is appropriate. Regardless of the role, each person should be an active participant.

Benefits of pair programming

As a software architect, you may want to consider using this technique with your team as it yields a number of benefits.

Pair programming can improve code quality. Having an additional set of eyes looking at the work may allow the pair to notice a problem or an opportunity that would not have been apparent if each person was working alone. Also, the driver will have a tendency to be more careful when coding with someone else watching, which may lead to better code overall.

Working collaboratively during pair programming to accomplish a goal can be beneficial. If the two individuals have different skillsets, they can bring both to bear on the work, and some of these skills will be transferred. In addition to getting work done, sessions can act similar to a training session in this regard. Working together also helps to enforce and spread knowledge of things such as coding standards.

Pair programming allows developers to become more familiar with the codebase. It provides opportunities for more than one person to be knowledgeable about a particular part of the system. Eventually, if something has to be changed with the code, more than one person will be familiar with it. Pair programming tends to create a culture of collective ownership of the codebase.

To fully realize this benefit, it is a good practice to rotate pairs and not just have the same two people always pair up. More knowledge will be shared when the pairs are rotated.

Pair programming can serve as training for less experienced developers or those who may be new to the project. Using this technique provides an opportunity for a software architect or senior developer to teach someone.

Software architects are encouraged to participate in pair programming. Rather than become an *ivory tower architect*, isolated from the rest of the team, software architects should work closely with team members. By staying active in the codebase, software architects will stay immersed in the project. In addition, software architects can share their knowledge and experience while pair programming with the developers on the team.

Using pair programming when it is needed

The use of pair programming does not have to be an all-or-nothing proposition. Although some teams might choose to do all of their development work in pairs, it certainly does not have to be done that way.

Pair programming sessions can be conducted as often as you like. It may not be beneficial to pair program to accomplish an easy task. You may choose to do it when there is a particular reason to do so, such as bringing two resources together that complement each other due to different skillsets or pairing up a software architect with a junior developer so that the session can serve as a learning experience.

Reviewing deliverables

Software architects are responsible for following an organization's review process and may have a role in shaping the process. Completed deliverables should be reviewed to ensure that they are correct and to identify any potential problems.

It is important for management and software architects to establish a culture within the organization so that the review process is viewed in a positive manner. It is important for team members to understand that the focus of reviews is on helping each other find defects, to learn, and to foster communication among the team.

Some of the methods that can be used to review deliverables include code reviews, formal inspections, and walkthroughs.

Code reviews

Code reviews are evaluations of code, typically conducted by peers. Code reviews involve one or more people, other than the developer of the code being reviewed, who examine code changes to find any problems.

The main focus of code reviews is to find both technical and business logic defects. However, code is also reviewed for other things, such as ensuring coding standards are being followed and finding opportunities for improvement.

An organization should have a process in place for code reviews. Some IDEs, software repositories, and other tools provide functionally that facilitate collaborative code reviewing. The process typically involves the following:

- The author requests a code review from one or more people
- The requested reviewers either accept or decline the request for a review
- Communication takes place between reviewers and the author so that comments and feedback can be exchanged
- Any defects that are found are recorded, assigned (typically to the author), and corrected
- Fixes to defects are tested

Software architects should have some degree of involvement with code reviews. The extent of their involvement may vary depending on the project and the organization, but it is beneficial for the software architect to stay involved at this level.

Reviewers should try not to review too many **lines of code** (LOC) at any given time. There is only so much a typical person can process at a time, and once most people go beyond five hundred lines or so, their effectiveness drastically diminishes.

It may be helpful to use a checklist during code reviews. The checklist can serve as a reminder of issues to look out for that have been found to be problematic in the past. Defects that are found during a review need to be recorded so that the issues are not left unaddressed.

Formal inspections

Formal inspections, as you might imagine from the name, are a more structured way of reviewing deliverables. It is a group review method and has been found to be quite effective at finding defects. The main goal of formal inspections is to evaluate and improve the quality of the software system.

Formal inspections are meetings in which deliverables, such as a design or code, are reviewed in order to find defects. Formal inspections are scheduled in advance, and participants are invited to the meeting.

Roles for a formal inspection

In a formal inspection, invited participants are assigned a role that they will play. Roles include leader/moderator, author, reviewer, and recorder/scribe. The following is the description for all the roles:

Leader/moderator: A moderator facilitates the meeting and is responsible for obtaining a productive review. They ensure the meeting progresses at an appropriate pace. They should encourage participation when necessary and follow up on any action items after the meeting is over. They may be required to summarize or provide a report on the inspection.

Author: The author is the person who created the design or wrote the code that is being reviewed in the inspection. Their role can be rather limited during the meeting. They may be required to explain anything that is unclear or to provide reasons why something that appears to be a defect is actually not one.

Reviewer: One or more individuals, other than the author, serve as reviewers for the inspection. They can prepare for inspections by reviewing the deliverables before the meeting takes place. Any notes that were taken during preparation should be brought to the meeting so that those can be communicated at that time.

As is the case with other types of reviews, it may be helpful for reviewers to have a checklist of items that they want to focus on for the review. Reviewers should be technically competent and can give positive as well as negative feedback.

Recorder/scribe: The recorder, or scribe, is responsible for taking notes during the meeting. They should record any defects found as well as action items. Although a scribe could also be a reviewer, the moderator and the author should not play the role of scribe.

Inspection meeting and follow-up

During the actual inspection meeting, reviewers should focus on identifying defects and not on solutions. After the meeting, it is typical that an inspection report is produced, summarizing the results of the inspection.

Any defects that were found during the inspection should be placed in a backlog or otherwise assigned to someone for resolution, such as the author. Follow-up should take place, usually by the moderator, to ensure that any action items were completed.

Walkthroughs

A **walkthrough** is an informal method of review. In a walkthrough, the author of a design or code deliverable hosts a meeting in which they guide reviewers through the deliverable.

Unlike a formal inspection, participants are not assigned specific roles (other than the host/author). Walkthroughs are flexible and an organization can choose how they want to organize a walkthrough based on their needs.

Participants can prepare for a walkthrough by looking at the deliverable beforehand. The focus of the walkthrough is to identify potential defects. Although the focus is not to correct any defects found, unlike formal inspections, the group can decide to allow suggestions of changes that can be made to the deliverable. Similar to formal inspections, management should not attend a walkthrough so as not to influence the meeting in any way.

Walkthroughs have been found to not be as effective as other review methods for evaluating and improving deliverables. However, they do allow a larger number of reviewers to participate at once. This provides an opportunity to get feedback from a more diverse group.

Summary

Even though software engineering is a relatively new discipline compared to other types of engineering, a number of principles and practices have been established to create high-quality software systems.

We learned that to design orthogonal software systems that can be extended while minimizing the impact to existing functionality, we need to focus on loose coupling and high cohesion. To minimize complexity in our software applications, a number of principles can be applied, such as KISS, DRY, information hiding, YAGNI, and SoC.

The SOLID design principles, which include the SRP, OCP, LSP, ISP, and DIP, can be used to create code that is more understandable, maintainable, reusable, testable, and flexible. A number of practices, such as unit testing, pair programming, and reviewing deliverables can be used to identify defects and improve the quality of software systems.

Software architecture patterns are reusable solutions that can be used to solve recurring problems. In the next chapter, we will go over some of the common software architecture patterns so that you will be aware of them and can apply them appropriately to your software applications.

Software Architecture Patterns

7

Software architecture patterns are one of the most useful tools that can be leveraged for designing a software architecture. Some of the design issues we face as software architects already have proven solutions. Experienced software architects are knowledgeable about available architecture patterns and can recognize when one can be applied to a given design scenario.

This chapter begins by explaining what software architecture patterns are and how they can be used. It then goes into detail about some commonly used architecture patterns, including **layered architecture, event-driven architecture (EDA), Model-View-Controller (MVC), Model-View-Presenter (MVP), Model-View-ViewModel (MVVM), Command Query Responsibility Segregation (CQRS)**, and **service-oriented architecture (SOA)**.

In this chapter, we will cover the following topics:

- Software architecture patterns
- Layered architecture
- Event-driven architecture , including event notifications, event-carried state transfer, and event-sourcing
- Model-View-Controller pattern
- Model-View-Presenter pattern
- Model-View-ViewModel pattern
- Command Query Responsibility Segregation
- Service-oriented architecture

Software architecture patterns

A **software architecture pattern** is a solution to a recurring problem that is well understood, in a particular context. Each pattern consists of a context, a problem, and a solution. The problem may be to overcome some challenge, take advantage of some opportunity, or to satisfy one or more quality attributes. Patterns codify knowledge and experience into a solution that we can reuse.

Using patterns simplifies design and allows us to gain the benefits of using a solution that is proven to solve a particular design problem. When working with others who are familiar with patterns, referencing one of them provides a shorthand with which to reference a solution, without having to explain all its details. As a result, they are useful during discussions to communicate ideas.

Software architecture patterns are similar to design patterns, except that they are broader in scope and are applied at the architecture level. Architecture patterns tend to be more coarse-grained and focus on architectural problems, while design patterns are more fine-grained and solve problems that occur during implementation.

A software architecture pattern provides a high-level structure and behavior for software systems. It is a grouping of design decisions that have been repeated and used successfully for a given context. They address and satisfy architectural drivers and as a result, the ones that we decide to use can really shape the characteristics and behavior of the architecture. Each pattern has its own characteristics, strengths, and weaknesses.

Software architecture patterns provide the structure and main components of the software system being built. They introduce design constraints, which reduce complexity and help to prevent incorrect decisions. When a software architecture pattern is followed consistently during design, we can anticipate the properties that the software system will exhibit. This allows us to consider whether a design will satisfy the requirements and quality attributes of the system.

Using software architecture patterns

Much like design patterns, software architecture patterns come into being after they are successfully repeated in practice. As a software architect, you will discover and use an existing pattern when appropriate.

The majority of the time, you will not be inventing or creating a new pattern. It is possible that you may find yourself tackling challenges and problems in a novel domain, requiring you to create truly new solutions that do not currently exist. However, even in that case the solution will not be a pattern yet. Only after it is repeated in practice and becomes known as a solution for a particular context and problem does it become a pattern.

Software architecture patterns can be applied to the entire software system or to one of the subsystems. Consequently, more than one software architecture pattern can be used in a single software system. These patterns can be combined to solve problems.

Overusing architecture patterns

While leveraging architecture patterns is a valuable tool, don't force the use of a particular pattern. A common mistake with design and architecture patterns is to use one even if it is not appropriate to do so.

A developer or architect may become aware of a particular pattern and then become overzealous in their desire to use it. They may apply a pattern just due to their familiarity with it.

The key is to gain knowledge of the patterns that are available and an understanding as to the scenarios in which they should be applied. This knowledge allows a software architect to select and use the appropriate pattern. A software architecture pattern should only be used if it is the best solution for a given design issue and context.

Understanding the difference between architecture styles and architecture patterns

You may come across the term **architecture style** and compare its meaning with the term **architecture pattern**. For the most part, these two terms are used interchangeably.

However, some people make a distinction between the two, so let's take a moment to explain the difference. It is not completely clear-cut, as the definitions vary depending on who you ask. One of the ways an architecture style is defined is that it is a set of elements, and the vocabulary to be used for those elements, that is available to be used in an architecture. It constrains an architecture design by restricting the available design choices. When a software system adheres to a particular architecture style, it will be expected to exhibit certain properties.

For example, if we were to follow the microservice architecture style for an application, which comes with the constraint that each service should be independent of the others, we can expect such a system to have certain properties. A system that follows a microservice architecture style will be able to deploy services independently, isolate faults for a particular service, and use a technology of the team's choosing for a given service.

A software architecture pattern is a particular arrangement of the available elements into a solution for a recurring problem given a certain context. Given a particular architecture style, we can use the vocabulary of that style to express how we want to use the elements available in that style in a certain way. When this arrangement is a known solution to a common, recurring problem in a particular context, it is a software architecture pattern.

This book does not focus on making a distinction between these two terms and, for the most part, uses the term **software architecture pattern**, as evidenced by the title of this chapter.

Now that we know what software architecture patterns (and styles) are, let's explore some of the commonly used ones, beginning with the layered architecture.

Layered architecture

When partitioning a complicated software system, layering is one of the most common techniques. In a **layered architecture**, the software application is divided into various horizontal layers, with each layer located on top of a lower layer. Each layer is dependent on one or more layers below it (depending on whether the layers are open or closed), but is independent of the layers above it.

Open versus closed layers

Layered architectures can have layers that are designed to be open or closed. With a closed layer, requests that are flowing down the stack from the layer above must go through it and cannot bypass it. For example, in a three-layer architecture with presentation, business, and data layers, if the business layer is closed, the presentation layer must send all requests to the business layer and cannot bypass it to send a request directly to the data layer.

Closed layers provide layers of isolation, which makes code easier to change, write, and understand. This makes the layers independent of each other, such that changes made to one layer of the application will not affect components in the other layers. If the layers are open, this increases complexity. Maintainability is lowered because multiple layers can now call into another layer, increasing the number of dependencies and making changes more difficult.

However, there may be situations in which it is advantageous to have an open layer. One of them is to solve a common problem with the layered architecture, in which unnecessary traffic can result when each layer must be passed even if one or more of them is just passing requests on to the next layer.

In our example of a three-layer architecture with presentation, business, and data layers, let's say that we introduce a shared services layer between the business and data layers. This shared services layer may contain reusable components needed by multiple components in the business layer. We may choose to place it below the business layer so that only the business layer has access to it. However, now all requests from the business layer to the data layer must go through the shared services layer even though nothing is needed from that layer. If we make the shared services layer open, requests to the data layer can be made directly from the business layer.

The important point for software architects to understand when designing a layered architecture is that there are advantages to closed layers and achieving layers of isolation. However, experienced software architects understand when it might be appropriate to open a layer. It is not necessary to make all of the layers open or closed. You may selectively choose which layers, if any, are open.

Tiers versus layers

You may have heard the terms **tier** and **layer** in reference to layered architectures. Before we proceed with discussing layered architectures, these terms should be clarified.

Layers are logical separations of a software application and tiers are physical ones.

When partitioning application logic, layers are a way to organize functionality and components. For example, in a three-layered architecture, the logic may be separated into presentation, business, and data layers. When a software architecture is organized into more than one layer, it is known as a **multi-layer architecture**. Different layers do not necessarily have to be located on different physical machines. It is possible to have multiple layers on the same machine.

Tiers concern themselves with the physical location of the functionality and components. A three-tiered architecture with presentation, business, and data tiers implies that those three tiers have been physically deployed to three separate machines and are each running on those separate machines. When a software architecture is partitioned into multiple tiers, it is known as a **multi-tier architecture**.

Keep in mind that some people use the two terms interchangeably. When communicating with others, if the distinction is important, you may want to be precise in your language and you may need to confirm with the other person what they mean when they use one of the terms.

Advantages of layered architectures

There are some key benefits to using a layered architecture. This pattern reduces complexity by achieving a **Separation of Concerns (SoC)**. Each layer is independent and you can understand it on its own without the other layers. Complexity can be abstracted away in a layered application, allowing us to deal with more complex problems.

Dependencies between layers can be minimized in a layered architecture, which further reduces complexity. For example, the presentation layer does not need to depend directly on the data layer and the business layer does not depend on the presentation layer. Minimizing dependencies also allows you to substitute implementations for a particular layer without affecting the other layers.

Another advantage of layered architectures is the fact that they can make development easier. The pattern is pervasive and well known to many developers, which makes using it easy for the development team. Due to the way that the architecture separates the application logic, it matches up well with how many organizations hire their resources and allocate tasks during a project. Each layer requires a particular skill set and suitable resources can be assigned to work on each layer. For example, UI developers for the presentation layer, and backend developers for the business and data layers.

This architecture pattern increases the testability quality attribute of software applications. Partitioning the application into layers and using interfaces for the interaction between layers allows us to isolate a layer for testing and either mock or stub the other layers. For example, you can perform unit testing on classes in your business layer without the presentation and data layers. The business layer is not dependent on the presentation layer and the data layer can be mocked or stubbed.

Applications using a layered architecture may have higher levels of reusability if more than one application can reuse the same layer. For example, if multiple applications target the same business and/or data layers, those layers are reusable.

When an application using a layered architecture is deployed to different tiers, there are additional benefits:

- There is increased scalability as more hardware can be added to each tier, providing the ability to handle increased workloads.
- A multi-tier application can experience greater levels of availability when multiple machines are used per layer. Uptime is increased because, if a hardware failure takes place in a layer, other machines can take over.
- Having separate tiers enhances security as firewalls can be placed in between the various layers.
- If a layer can be reused for multiple applications, it means that the physical tier can be reused as well.

Disadvantages of layered architectures

Although layered architectures are commonly used, and for good reasons, there are disadvantages to using them. Although the layers can be designed to be independent, a requirement change may require changes in multiple layers. This type of coupling lowers the overall agility of the software application.

For example, adding a new field will require changes to multiple layers: the presentation layer so that it can be displayed, the business layer so that it can be validated/saved/processed, and the data layer because it will need to be added to the database. This can complicate deployment because, even for a change such as this, an application may require multiple parts (or even the entire application) to be deployed.

Another minor disadvantage is the fact that more code will be necessary for layered applications. This is to provide the interfaces and other logic that are necessary for the communication between the multiple layers.

Development teams have to be diligent about placing code in the correct layer so as not to leak logic to a layer that belongs in another layer. Examples of this include placing business logic in the presentation layer or putting data-access logic in the business layer.

Although applications with good performance can be designed with layered architectures, if you are designing a high-performance application, you should be aware that there can be inefficiencies in having a request go through multiple layers. In addition, moving from one layer to another sometimes requires data representations to be transformed. One way to mitigate this disadvantage is to allow some layers to be open but this should only be done if it is appropriate to open a layer.

There are some additional disadvantages to layered architectures when they are deployed to multiple tiers:

- The performance disadvantage of layered architectures has already been mentioned, but when those layers are deployed to separate physical tiers, as is common, there is an additional performance cost. With modern hardware, this cost may be small but it still won't be faster than an application that runs on a single machine.
- There is a greater monetary cost associated with having a multi-tier architecture. The more machines are used for the application, the greater the overall cost.
- Unless the hosting of the software application is handled by a cloud provider or has otherwise been outsourced, an internal team will be needed to manage the physical hardware of a multi-tier application.

Client-server architecture (two-tier architecture)

Layered architectures became very prevalent with the popularity of client-server software systems. In a distributed application that uses a **client-server architecture**, also known as a *two-tier architecture*, clients and servers communicate with each other directly. A client requests some resource or calls some service provided by a server and the server responds to the requests of clients. There can be multiple clients connected to a single server:

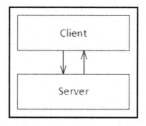

The **Client** part of the application contains the user interface code and the **Server** contains the database, which traditionally has been a **relational database management system (RDBMS)**. The majority of application logic in a client-server architecture is located on the server, but some of it could also be located in the client. The application logic located on the server might exist in software components, in the database, or both.

When the client contains a significant portion of the logic and is handling a large share of the workload, it is known as a thick, or fat, client. When the server is doing that instead, the client is known as a thin client.

In some client-server applications, the business logic is spread out between the client and the server. If consistency isn't applied, it can make it difficult to always know where a particular piece of logic is located.

If a team isn't diligent, business logic might be duplicated on the client and the server, violating the DRY principle.

There may be instances in which the same piece of logic is needed on both the client and the server. For example, there may be business logic needed by the user interface to validate a piece of data prior to submitting the data to the server. The server may need this same business logic because it also needs to perform this validation. While centralizing this logic may require additional communication between the client and the server, the alternative (duplication) lowers maintainability. If the business logic were to change, it would have to be modified in multiple places.

Using stored procedures for application logic

If application logic does exist in the database, it is commonly found in stored procedures. A stored procedure is a grouping of one or more **Structured Query Language (SQL)** statements that forms a logical unit to accomplish some task. It can be used to do a combination of retrieving, inserting, updating, and deleting data.

It used to be popular to use stored procedures with client-server applications because their use reduced the amount of network traffic between the client and the server. Stored procedures can contain any number of statements within them and can call other stored procedures. A single call from the client to the server is all that is needed to execute a stored procedure. If that logic was not encapsulated inside a stored procedure, multiple calls would need to be made over the network between the client and the server to execute the same logic.

Stored procedures are compiled the first time they are executed, at which time an execution plan is created that a database's query engine can use to optimize its use on subsequent calls. In addition to some performance benefits, there are security advantages to using stored procedures. Users and applications do not need to be granted permissions to the underlying database objects that a stored procedure uses, such as database tables. A user or application can execute a stored procedure but it is the stored procedure that has control over what logic is executed and which database objects are used. Stored procedures increase reusability in that once one is written and compiled, it can be reused in multiple places.

Although there are benefits to using stored procedures, there are drawbacks. There are limited coding constructs, as compared with high-level programming languages, that are available for use in application logic. Having some of your business logic located in stored procedures also means that your business logic isn't centralized.

In modern application development, application logic should not be placed in stored procedures. It belongs outside the data layer, independent and decoupled from the mechanism used to store the data. Based on that point, some have relegated stored procedures to simple CRUD operations. However, if that is the case, stored procedures are not providing much of a benefit.

Although application logic should not be placed in stored procedures, they can still be of use in some situations. For complex queries (for example, SQL queries with complex table joins and WHERE clauses) and queries requiring multiple statements and large amounts of data, the performance advantages of stored procedures can be useful.

N-tier architecture

With an **n-tier architecture**, also known as a **multitier architecture**, there are multiple tiers in the architecture. One of the most widely-used variations of this type of layered architecture is the three-tier architecture. The rise of the web coincided with a shift from two-tier (client-server) architectures to three-tier architectures. This change was not a coincidence. With web applications and the use of web browsers, rich client applications containing business logic were not ideal.

The three-tier architecture separates logic into presentation, business, and data layers:

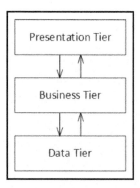

Presentation tier

The **presentation tier** provides functionality for the application's UI. It should provide an appealing visual design as it is the part of the application that users interact with and see. Data is presented to the user and input is received from users in this tier. Aspects of the usability quality attribute, which were discussed in `Chapter 4`, *Software Quality Attributes*, should be the concern of the presentation tier.

This tier should contain logic to render the user interface, including the placement of data in the appropriate UI components, formatting the data that is presented appropriately, and hiding/showing UI components as required.

It should also provide some basic validation to help users avoid or minimize mistakes, such as ensuring the correct type of data is being entered for a given control and that the data is in the correct format. Developers should be careful not to introduce business logic into the validation, which should be handled by the business tier.

The presentation tier should provide users with useful feedback, such as friendly and informative messages, tooltips, visual feedback, such as a progress bar for long-running processes, and notifications to inform users about the completion or failure of asynchronous operations.

Software architects should strive to design *thin clients* that minimize the amount of logic that exists in the presentation tier. The logic in the presentation tier should focus on user interface concerns. A presentation tier devoid of business logic will be easier to test.

Business tier

The **business tier**, which is sometimes referred to as the application tier, provides the implementation for the business logic of the application, including such things as business rules, validations, and calculation logic. Business entities for the application's domain are placed in this tier.

The business tier coordinates the application and executes logic. It can perform detailed processes and makes logical decisions. The business tier is the center of the application and serves as an intermediary between the presentation and data tiers. It provides the presentation tier with services, commands, and data that it can use, and it interacts with the data tier to retrieve and manipulate data.

Data tier

The **data tier** provides functionality to access and manage data. The data tier contains a data store for persistent storage, such as an RDBMS. It provides services and data for the business tier.

There are variations of n-tier architectures that go beyond just three tiers. For example, in some systems, there is a data access or persistence layer in addition to a data or database layer. The persistence layer contains components for data access, such as an **object-relational mapping (ORM)** tool, and the database layer contains the actual data store, such as an RDBMS. One reason to separate these into two distinct layers is if you wanted the ability to switch out your data access or database technology for a different one.

Event-driven architecture

An **event** is the occurrence of something deemed significant in a software application, such as a state change, that may be of interest to other applications or other components within the same application. An example of an event is the placement of a purchase order or the posting of a letter grade for a course that a student is taking.

An **event-driven architecture (EDA)** is a distributed, asynchronous software architecture pattern that integrates applications and components through the production and handling of events. By tracking events, we don't miss anything of significance related to the business domain.

EDAs are loosely coupled. The producer of an event does not have any knowledge regarding the event subscribers or what actions may take place as a result of the event.

SOA can complement EDA because service operations can be called based on events being triggered. The converse can also be designed, such that service operations raise events.

EDAs can be relatively complex given their inherent asynchronous, distributed processing. As with any distributed architecture, issues may occur due to a lack of responsiveness, performance issues, or failures with event mediators and event brokers (these components will be described shortly).

Event channels

Before we cover the two main event topologies for EDAs, let's go over the concept of event channels because both topologies make use of them.

Event messages contain data about an event and are created by event producers. These event messages use **event channels**, which are streams of event messages, to travel to an event processor.

Event channels are typically implemented as message queues, which use the point-to-point channel pattern, or message topics, which use the publish-subscribe pattern.

Message queues

Message queues ensure that there is one, and only one, receiver for a message. In the context of event channels, this means that only one event processor will receive an event from an event channel. The point-to-point channel pattern is utilized for message queue implementations.

The point-to-point channel pattern

The point-to-point channel pattern is a messaging pattern used when we want to ensure that there will be exactly one receiver for a given message. If a channel has multiple receivers so that more than one message can be consumed concurrently, and more than one receiver attempts to consume a message, the event channel will ensure that only one of them succeeds. Since the event channel is handling that, it removes any need for coordination between the event processors.

Message topics

Message topics allow multiple event consumers to receive an event message. The publish-subscribe pattern is used for the implementation of message topics.

The publish-subscribe pattern

The publish-subscribe pattern, which is sometimes referred to as pub/sub for short, is a messaging pattern that provides a way for a sender (publisher) to broadcast a message to interested parties (subscribers).

Rather than publishers sending messages directly to specific receivers as in the point-to-point channel pattern, the messages can be sent without any knowledge of the subscribers or even if there are no subscribers. Similarly, it allows subscribers to show interest in a particular message without any knowledge of the publishers or even if there are no publishers.

Event-driven architecture topologies

The two main topologies for EDAs are the mediator and broker topologies.

The mediator topology

A **mediator topology** for EDAs uses a single event queue and an event mediator to route events to the relevant event processors. This topology is commonly used when multiple steps are required to process an event.

With the mediator topology, event producers send events into an **event queue**. There can be many event queues in an EDA. Event queues are responsible for sending event messages on to the **event mediator**. All of these events, referred to as *initial events*, go through an event mediator. The event mediator then performs any necessary orchestration:

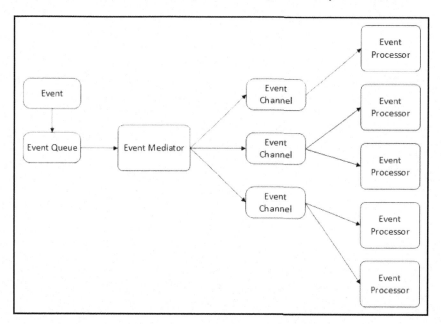

After the event mediator orchestrates each event from the event queue, it creates one or more asynchronous *processing events* based on the orchestration. These processing events get sent out to an **event channel**, which can either be a message queue or a message topic.

Message topics are more commonly used with the mediator topology due to the orchestration involved, which allows multiple event processors, which will perform different tasks, to receive an event message. This can be seen in the preceding diagram where some of the event channels are sending an event message to multiple event processors.

Event processors listen in on event channels to pick up events and process them in line with their design. In the *Event processing styles* section later in this chapter, we will cover the different processing styles typically used by event processors.

Event mediator implementations

An event mediator can be implemented in a number of different ways. For simple orchestrations, an integration hub can be used. These typically allow you to define mediation rules using a **domain-specific language** (**DSL**) for the routing of events. Domain-specific languages, unlike a general-purpose language, such as C#, Java, or UML, allow expressions to be written for a particular domain.

For a more complex orchestration of events, **Business Process Execution Language** (**BPEL**) can be used in conjunction with a BPEL engine. BPEL is an XML-based language that is used to define business processes and their behavior. It is frequently used with SOA and web services.

Large software applications with complex orchestration needs, which may even include human interactions, may opt to implement an event mediator that uses a **business process manager** (**BPM**). Business process management involves modeling, automating, and executing business workflows. Some business process managers use **Business Process Model and Notation** (**BPMN**) to define business processes. BPMN allows for business process modeling using a graphical notation. Business process diagrams created with BPMN are similar to activity diagrams in UML.

Software architects must understand the needs of the software application in order to select an appropriate event mediator implementation.

The broker topology

In a **broker topology**, the event messages created by event producers enter an event broker, sometimes referred to as an event bus. The event broker contains all of the event channels used for the event flow. The event channels may be message queues, message topics, or some combination of the two.

Unlike the mediator topology, there is no event queue with the broker topology. The event processors are responsible for picking up events from an event broker:

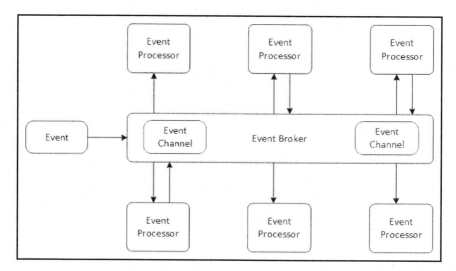

This topology is ideal when the processing flow is fairly simple and there is no need for centralized event orchestration. **Events** flow to the **event processor** from the **event broker** and, as part of the processing, new events may be created.

This can be seen in the preceding diagram, where in some cases, events are flowing from the event processors back to the event broker. A key to the broker topology is chaining events in order to execute a particular business task.

Event processing styles

Event processors are components that have a specific task and contain logic to analyze and take action on events. Each event processor should be independent and loosely coupled with other event processors.

Once event messages reach event processors, there are three prevalent styles for processing events: **simple event processing (SEP)**, **event stream processing (ESP)**, and **complex event processing (CEP)**. The type of event processing needed by a particular application depends on the processing complexity that is required. EDAs may utilize a combination of these three styles.

Simple event processing (SEP)

In SEP, notable events are immediately routed in order to initiate some type of downstream action. This type of processing can be used for real-time workflows to reduce the amount of time between the event taking place and the resulting action.

Simple event processing also includes functionality such as transforming event schemas from one form to another, generating multiple events based on the payload of a single event, and supplementing an event payload with additional data.

Event stream processing (ESP)

ESP involves analyzing streams of event data and then taking any necessary action based on that analysis. Events are screened based on various conditions and then either an action may be taken for the event or the event may be ignored. This type of processing is ideal for real-time flows in which decisions are also involved.

An example is a stock trading system in which an event takes place and enters an event stream when a stock ticker reports a change in price. Based on the price, an algorithm determines whether a buy or sell order should be created, and notifies the appropriate subscribers, if necessary.

Complex event processing (CEP)

In CEP, analysis is performed to find patterns in events to determine whether a more complex event has occurred. A complex event is an event that summarizes or represents a set of other events. Events may be correlated over multiple dimensions, such as causal, temporal, or spatial.

CEP can take place over a longer period of time as compared to the other types of event processing. This type of event processing might be used to detect business threats, opportunities, or other anomalies.

An example of functionality that uses CEP is a credit card fraud engine. Each transaction on a credit card is an event and the system will look at a grouping of those events for a particular credit card to try to find a pattern that might indicate fraud has taken place. If processing fraud is detected, downstream action is initiated.

Types of event-driven functionality

EDA can mean different things. There are three main types of functionality that can typically be found in systems that have an EDA: event notification, event-carried state transfer, and event sourcing. Event-driven software systems can provide a combination of the three.

Event notification

An architecture that provides **event notification** is one in which the software system sends a message when an event takes place. This functionality is the most common in software systems that have an EDA. The mediator and broker topologies allow us to implement event notifications.

There is a loose coupling between the event producer and any event consumers as well as between the logic that sends event messages and logic that responds to the events. This loose coupling allows us to change the logic in one without affecting the other. Event processor components are single-purpose and independent of other event processors, allowing them to be modified without affecting others.

The drawback to the loose coupling between event producers and event consumers is that it can be difficult to see the logical flow of event notifications. This added complexity also makes it more difficult to debug and maintain. There aren't specific statements you can look at to see what logic will be executed. A variety of event consumers, including ones in software systems other than the one that produced the event notification, may react to an event. Sometimes the only way to understand the logical flow is to monitor your systems to see the flow of event messages.

Event-carried state transfer

Event-carried state transfer is a variation on event notification. Its use is not as common as regular event notification. When an event consumer receives an event notification, it may need more information from the event producer in order to take the action that they want to take.

For example, a sales system may send a new order event notification and a shipping system may subscribe to this type of event messages. However, in order to take appropriate action, the shipping system now needs additional information about the order, such as the quantity and type of line items that are in the order. This requires the shipping system to query the sales system in some way, such as through an API, for this information.

While the event publisher may not need to know anything about their subscribers, the subscriber is coupled to the producer in the sense that it needs to be aware of the producer and have a way to get more information from the producer.

Callbacks to the system that produced an event notification for more data in order to handle an event increase network load and traffic. One way to resolve this is to add state information to the events so that they contain enough information to be useful for potential consumers. For example, an event notification for a new order could contain the line item details needed by the shipping system so that no callback is required. The shipping system can keep its own copy of only the order details that it needs.

Although more data is being passed around, we gain a greater level of availability and resilience. The shipping system can function, at least with orders it has already received, even if the order system is temporarily unavailable. The shipping system does not need to call back to the order system after the initial event notification is received, which can be particularly beneficial if contacting and receiving data from the order system is slow.

However, with greater availability comes lower consistency. The replication of some data between the order and shipping systems lowers the consistency of the data.

Event-sourcing

A system can use a data store to read and update the application's current state, but what if there are requirements to know the details of the state changes that got us to the current point? With **event-sourcing**, the events that take place in a system, such as state changes, are persisted in an event store. Having a complete record of all the events that took place allows it to serve as a source of truth. Replaying events from an event log can be used to recreate an application's state.

Event-sourcing works in a similar way to a transaction log in a database system. The transaction log records all of the modifications that have been made to a database. This allows for rollbacks of transactions and also allows us to recreate the system state up to a particular point, such as right before a failure occurred.

Events should be immutable as they represent something that has already taken place. Actions may take place downstream as the result of an event, so if an event could be changed after the fact, it could put your system in an inconsistent state. If an update or cancellation of an event is necessary, a compensating event should be created. Compensating logic can be executed based on such events and can apply the necessary business rules to apply counter-operations. This will ensure that the event store is still a source of truth and that we can replay all of the events to recreate an application's state.

The benefits of event-sourcing include the fact that it can aid in debugging a system. It provides the ability to take events and run them through the system to see how the system will behave. This can be used to determine the cause of a problem. Event-sourcing also provides detailed auditing. The complete record of events allows us to see what happened, how it happened, when it happened, and other details.

Although event-sourcing can be very useful, it does introduce some added complexity into a software system. Multiple instances of an application and multithreaded applications might be persisting events to an event store. The system must be designed to ensure that events are processed in the correct order.

The code that processes events and the event schema can change over time. Consideration must be given to ensure that older events, possibly with different event schemas, can still be replayed with the current logic.

If part of the sequence of events includes the use of an external system, consideration has to be given to storing the responses from the external system as events. This will ensure that we can replay events accurately to rebuild the application's state without having to call the external system again.

The Model-View-Controller pattern

The **Model-View-Controller** (**MVC**) pattern is a software architecture pattern that is widely used for the UI of an application. It is particularly well suited to web applications, although it can also be used for other types of applications, such as desktop applications.

The pattern provides a structure for building user interfaces and provides a separation of the different responsibilities involved. A number of popular web and application development frameworks make use of this pattern. A few examples include Ruby on Rails, ASP.NET MVC, and Spring MVC.

The MVC pattern consists of the **Model**, **View**, and **Controller**:

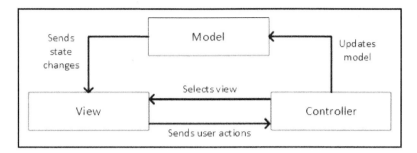

The model, view, and controller all have distinct responsibilities for the user interface. Let's take a look at each of them more closely.

Model

The model manages the application data and the state. Among its responsibilities is the processing of data to and from a data store, such as a database. A model is independent of the controllers and the views, allowing them to be reused with different user interfaces. This also allows them to be tested independently.

Models receive directives from controllers to retrieve and update data. Models also provide application state updates. In some variations of MVC, the model is *passive* and must receive a request to send out an application state update. In other variations, a view may be *active* and push notifications of model state changes to a view.

View

The view is responsible for the presentation of the application. It is the part of the application that is visible to the user. The view displays data to the user in an appropriate interface based on information received from the controller. If the model is providing application state updates directly to views, the views may also be updated based on these notifications.

As users manipulate a view, such as providing input or providing some user action, the view will send this information to a controller.

Controller

As users navigate a web application, requests are routed to the appropriate controller based on routing configuration. A controller acts as an intermediary between the model and the view.

A controller executes application logic to select the appropriate view and sends it the information that it needs to render the user interface. Views notify controllers of user actions so that the controller can respond to them. Controllers will update the model based on user actions.

Advantages of the MVC pattern

Using the MVC pattern allows for a separation of concerns. By separating the presentation from the data, it makes it easier to change one of them without affecting the other. It also makes each part easier to test. However, it is difficult to achieve a complete separation. For example, adding a new field to the application will require a change in both the data and the presentation.

The MVC pattern makes presentation objects more reusable. Separating the user interface from the data allows UI components to be reused. It also means that a model can be reused with more than one view.

The separation of the presentation from the business logic and data allows developers to specialize in either frontend or backend development. This can also speed up the development process as some tasks can take place in parallel. For example, one developer can work on the user interface while another works on the business logic.

Disadvantages of the MVC pattern

If your development team is not set up so that developers are focused on either frontend or backend development, this does require developers to be skilled in both areas (full-stack developers). This will require developers who are skilled in multiple technologies.

If a model is very active and is providing notifications directly to views, frequent changes to a model may result in excessive updates to views.

The Model-View-Presenter pattern

The **Model-View-Presenter** (**MVP**) pattern is a variation on the MVC pattern. Like the MVC pattern, it provides a separation between UI logic and business logic. However, the presenter takes the place of the controller in the MVP pattern.

Each view in the MVP pattern typically has a corresponding interface (view interface). Presenters are coupled with the view interfaces. As compared with the MVC pattern, the view is more loosely coupled to the model because the two do not interact with each other directly:

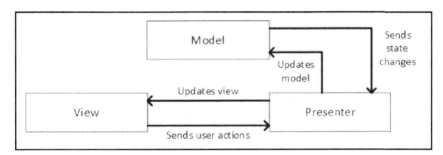

Both web and desktop applications can use the MVP pattern. The main components of this pattern are the **Model**, **View**, and **Presenter**.

Model

As was the case with the MVC pattern, the model represents the business model and the data. It interacts with the database to retrieve and update data. The model receives messages from the presenter for updates and reports state changes back to the presenter.

Models in the MVP pattern do not interact directly with views and only interact with the presenter.

View

The view is responsible for displaying the user interface and data. Each view in the MVP pattern implements an interface (view interface). As the user interacts with the view, the view will send messages to the presenter to act on the events and data.

Presenters are loosely coupled with views through the view interface. Views are more passive in the MVP model and rely on the presenter to provide information on what to display.

Presenter

The presenter is the intermediary between the model and the view. It interacts with both of them. Each view has a presenter and the view notifies the presenter of user actions. The presenter updates the model and receives state changes from the model.

A presenter will receive data from the model and format it for the view to display, taking an active role in presentation logic. Presenters encapsulate presentation logic and views play a more passive role.

Unlike the MVC pattern, where a controller can interact with multiple views, in the MVP pattern, each presenter typically handles one, and only one, view.

The Model-View-ViewModel pattern

The **Model-View-ViewModel (MVVM)** pattern is another software architecture pattern and it shares similarities with MVC and MVP in that they all provide a SoC. Partitioning the various responsibilities makes an application easier to maintain, extend, and test. The MVVM pattern separates the UI from the rest of the application:

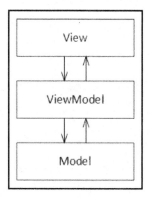

There is typically a significant amount of interaction between views and ViewModels, facilitated by data binding. The MVVM pattern works well for rich desktop applications, although it can be used for other types of application, such as web and mobile applications. An example of a framework that can be used to build MVVM applications is **Windows Presentation Foundation (WPF)**.

The main components of MVVM are the **Model**, **View**, and **ViewModel**. Let's take a look at each of these in more detail.

Model

The model in the MVVM pattern plays a similar role as in MVC and MVP. It represents the business domain object and the data. The model uses the database to retrieve and update data.

In MVVM applications, there may be direct binding with model properties. As a result, models commonly raise property changed notifications.

View

The view is responsible for the user interface. It is the part of the application that is visible to users. In the MVVM pattern, the view is active. Unlike a passive role where the view is completely manipulated by a controller or a presenter, and does not have knowledge of the model, in MVVM views are aware of the model and ViewModel.

While views handle their own events, they do not maintain state. They must relay user actions to the ViewModel, which can be done through a mechanism such as data binding or commands. A goal with the MVVM pattern is to minimize the amount of code in views.

ViewModel

The ViewModel in the MVVM pattern is similar to the controller and presenter objects that we covered with the MVC and MVP patterns in that they coordinate between the view and the model.

ViewModels provide data to views for display and manipulation, and also contain interaction logic to communicate with views and models. ViewModels must be capable of handling user actions and data input sent from views. It is the ViewModel that contains navigation logic to handle moving to a different view.

Views and ViewModels communicate through multiple methods, such as data binding, commands, method calls, properties, and events.

The Command Query Responsibility Segregation pattern

Command Query Responsibility Segregation (CQRS) is a pattern in which the model that is used to read information is separated from the model that is used to update information. In a more traditional architecture, a single object model is used for both reading and updating data:

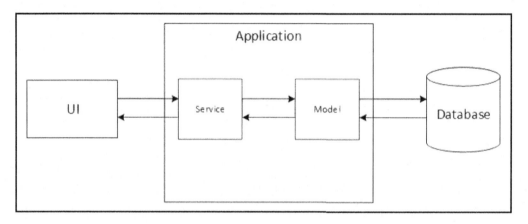

Compromises become necessary in order to use a single object model as domain classes are required to serve all purposes. The same representation of an entity must support all of the **create, read, update, and delete (CRUD)** operations, making them larger than they need to be in all circumstances.

They contain all of the properties the object will need for various scenarios. If the class is more than just a **data transfer object (DTO)**, it may also contain methods for behavior. With this approach, classes are not ideal for all of the situations in which they need to be used as there is often a mismatch between what is required by the read and write representations of the data. This can also make managing security and authorization more complex as each class is used for both read and write operations.

In a collaborative domain, multiple operations may be taking place in parallel on the same set of data. There is a risk of data contention if records are locked, or update conflicts due to concurrent updates. Workloads between read and write tasks differ, which means that they also have different performance and scalability requirements.

The query model and the command model

One way to overcome the challenges of using a single object model for both queries and commands is to separate the two. This pattern, known as CQRS, results in two separate models. The **query model** is responsible for reads and the **command model** is responsible for updates:

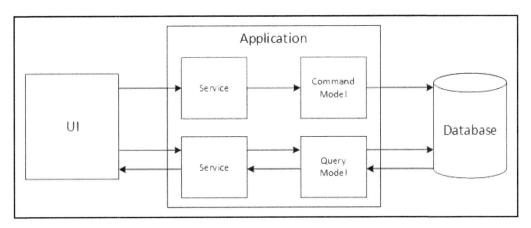

Query objects only return data and do not alter state, while command objects alter state and do not return data. Another way of looking at this concept is that asking a question (a query) should not alter the answer. In order to perform an action that will mutate state, a command is used.

When the system needs to read data, it goes through the query model, and when the system needs to update data, it goes through the command model. As part of processing a command, the system may need to read data, but beyond what is necessary for completing a command, the reading of data should go through the query model.

Although not required, if CQRS is taken to the next level, the query and command models can be made to utilize separate databases. This gives each of the two models its own schema, which can be optimized for its specific usage. If separate databases are used, the two databases must be kept in sync. One way to do that is through the use of events.

Using event-sourcing with CQRS

Although CQRS can be used without events, they do complement each other so it is common for systems that use CQRS to leverage the use of events. Events are one way to effectively communicate state changes so that the query model can stay up to date as the command model updates data.

As we saw in the *Event-sourcing* section earlier in this chapter, event-sourcing involves persisting events that take place in a system such that the event store can serve as the record of truth. When the command model alters the state of the system, events can be raised so that the query model can be kept in sync.

Keeping the query and command models in sync is necessary when the query and command models use separate data stores. In addition, a data store for the query model may contain denormalized data that has been optimized for particular queries. Having an event store allows us to replay past events to recreate the system's current state, which can be useful for updating the denormalized data in the query model's data store.

Advantages of CQRS

CQRS is well suited to complex domains and it provides a separation of concerns that helps to minimize and manage the complexity. Separating a system into query and command models makes it more maintainable, extensible, and flexible. Development teams can also be organized so that one team focuses on the query model while another focuses on the command model.

Segregating the responsibility between commands and queries can help to improve performance, scalability, and security. Performance can be improved by optimizing the schema specifically for each model. The schema for the query model can be optimized for queries, while the schema for the command model can be optimized for updates. Data in the query model's data store can be denormalized in order to increase the performance of queries that the application needs to execute.

Workloads between read and write operations will differ and using CQRS allows you to scale each of them independently of the others. Security is improved with CQRS because it makes it easier than with a single object model to ensure that only the right classes can update data.

Security can be easier to implement and test when using CQRS because each class is either used for reads or writes, but not both. This reduces the chance of inadvertently exposing data and operations that should not be available to a particular user in a certain context.

Disadvantages of CQRS

For systems that simply need basic CRUD operations, implementing a CQRS system may introduce unnecessary complexity. CQRS systems have a higher degree of complexity, especially when combined with event-sourcing. For this reason, it is important to understand that CQRS is not applicable to all situations. Software architects should be aware that CQRS does not have to be applied to the entirety of a software system. It can be applied to just some subsystems of a larger architecture where it will be of the greatest benefit.

While using different data stores for query and command models can improve performance and increase security, you do have to consider that when you perform read operations, you may be reading data that is stale.

If separate databases are used in a CQRS system, the database used for reads must be kept up to date with the database used for writes. The software system will follow an *eventual consistency* model where if no new updates are made to a given item, eventually all access to that item will acquire the latest data.

Whether the system is using event-sourcing or some other mechanism to keep the two in sync, there will be some time delay, even if it is a small one, before they are made consistent. This means that any data that is read could potentially be stale if the latest updates to it have not been applied yet. This is in contrast with a *strong consistency* model, in which all data changes are atomic and a transaction is not allowed to complete until all of the changes have been completed successfully or, in the case of a failure, everything has been undone.

Service-oriented architecture

Service-oriented architecture (SOA) is an architectural pattern for developing software systems by creating loosely coupled, interoperable services that work together to automate business processes. A service is a part of a software application that performs a specific task, providing functionality to other parts of the same software application or to other software applications. Some examples of service consumers include web applications, mobile applications, desktop applications, and other services.

SOA achieves a *SoC*, which is a design principle that separates a software system into parts, with each part addressing a distinct concern. We discussed *SoC* in `Chapter 6`, *Software Development Principles and Practices*. A key aspect of SOA is that it decomposes application logic into smaller units that can be reused and distributed. By decomposing a large problem into smaller, more manageable concerns satisfied by services, complexity is reduced and the quality of the software is improved.

Each service in a SOA encapsulates a certain piece of logic. This logic may be responsible for a very specific task, a business process, or a subprocess. Services can vary in size and one service can be composed of multiple other services to accomplish its task.

What makes SOA different from other distributed solutions?

Distributing application logic and separating it into smaller, more manageable units is not what makes SOA different from previous approaches to distributed computing. Naturally, you might think the biggest difference is the use of web services, but keep in mind that SOA does not require web services, although they happen to be a perfect technology to implement with SOA. What really sets SOA apart from a traditional distributed architecture is not the use of web services, but how its core components are designed.

Although SOA shares similarities with earlier distributed solutions, it is much more than just another attempt to create reusable software. The differences undoubtedly provide significant new value to organizations when implemented properly. Many benefits can be realized from a properly designed SOA.

Benefits of using a SOA

There are a number of benefits from using a SOA, including:

- Increases alignment between business and technology
- Promotes federation within an organization
- Allows for vendor diversity
- Increases intrinsic interoperability
- Works well with agile development methodologies

Increases alignment between business and technology

A SOA leads to increased alignment between business and technology. The fulfillment of business requirements needs business logic and business processes to be accurately represented in technology solutions. Business logic, in the form of business entities and business processes, exists in the form of physical services with an SOA.

This alignment of business and technology promotes organizational agility. Change is something that practically all organizations must face, and it exists due to a variety of factors, such as market forces, technology changes, new business opportunities, and corporate mergers. Regardless of the cause of change, SOA provides organizational agility through service abstraction and loose coupling between business and application logic. When changes are required, they can more easily be made so that the business remains in alignment with the technology.

Promotes federation within an organization

A SOA promotes federation. Federation in an organization is an environment in which the software applications and resources work together while simultaneously maintaining their autonomy. Federation gives organizations the freedom not to be required to replace all of their existing systems that must work together. As long as there is a common, open, and standardized framework, legacy and non-legacy applications can work together. Organizations have the flexibility to choose whether they want to replace certain systems, allowing them to use a phased approach to migration.

Allows for vendor diversity

Another advantage of SOA is vendor diversity. In addition to allowing organizations with potentially disparate vendors to work together, an organization can use different vendors internally to achieve best-of-breed solutions.

While it is not a goal of SOA to increase vendor diversity, it provides the option of vendor diversity when there is an advantage to introducing new technologies.

Increases intrinsic interoperability

SOA provides increased intrinsic interoperability for an organization. It allows for the sharing of data and the reuse of logic. Different services can be assembled together to help automate a variety of business processes. It can allow an existing software system to integrate with others through web services. Greater interoperability can lead to the realization of other strategic goals.

Works well with agile development methodologies

Another benefit of SOA is that it lends itself well to agile software development methodologies. The fact that complex software systems are broken down into services with small, manageable units of logic fits well with an iterative process and how tasks are allocated to resources.

You may also find that having developers take on tasks is easier with SOA because each task can be made to be manageable in size and more easily understood. Although this is beneficial for any developer, it is particularly helpful for junior developers or those who are new to a project and may not have as much experience with the functionality and business domain.

Cost-benefit analysis of SOA

As a software architect, if you are considering SOA for an application, you will need to explain the reasons why you are considering it. Adopting an SOA comes at some cost, but there are points you can make to justify the costs and ways that you can alleviate them.

The cost of implementing a SOA may outweigh the benefits for some organizations, so each case must be considered separately. While it may not be appropriate for some organizations to implement an SOA, for others a properly designed SOA will bring many benefits, including a positive return on investment.

Adopting SOA can be a gradual, evolutionary process. Because a contemporary SOA promotes federation, creating an SOA does not have to be an all-or-nothing process. An organization does not have to replace all existing systems at once. Legacy logic can be encapsulated and can work with new application logic. As a result, the adoption of SOA and its related costs can be spread out over time.

Adopting SOA leads to reduced integration expenses. A loosely coupled SOA should reduce complexity and therefore will reduce the cost to integrate and manage such systems. Loosely coupled services are more flexible and can be used in more situations.

SOA can increase asset reuse. It is common for each application to be built in isolation, leading to higher development costs and greater maintenance costs over time. However, by creating business processes by reusing existing services, costs and time to market can be reduced.

SOA increases business agility. Change is something that all organizations must face. Regardless of the cause of the change, by using loosely coupled services, organizational agility is increased and both the time and cost to adapt to change are reduced.

Adopting SOA reduces business risk and exposure. A properly designed SOA facilitates the control of business processes, allows for the implementation of security and privacy policies, and provides audit trails for data, which can all reduce risk. It can also help with regulatory compliance. The penalties for non-compliance can be significant, and SOA can provide organizations with increased business visibility that reduces the risk of changing regulations.

Challenges with SOA

Although adopting an SOA does provide many benefits, it also introduces some new complexities and challenges. SOA solutions may allow organizations to do more, including automating more of their business processes. This can cause enterprise architectures to grow larger in scope and functionality as compared to legacy systems. Taking on a larger scope of functionality will add complexity to a software system.

In an SOA, new layers may be added to software architectures, providing more areas where failure can occur and making it more difficult to pinpoint those failures. In addition, as increasing numbers of services are created, deploying new services and new versions of existing services must be managed carefully so that troubleshooting can be effective when an error occurs with a specific transaction.

Another challenge with successful SOA adoption is related to people and not technology. SOA is a mature architectural style that has been around a long time. The technology exists to allow organizations to automate a variety of complex business processes. However, people can be a challenge to SOA-adoption because there are still technical and business professionals who are not familiar with SOA and really do not know what it means. People can also be naturally resistant to change, and if your organization is not already using SOA, change will be necessary. In order for a SOA to be successful, there has to be buy-in from the people in the organization. They have to be committed and this comes down to the culture of the team and the people on it, including managers, software architects, developers, and business analysts.

Key principles for service orientation

Service-oriented solutions are designed so that they adhere to certain key principles. They are:

- Standardized service contract
- Service loose coupling
- Service abstraction
- Service reusability
- Service autonomy
- Service statelessness
- Service discoverability
- Service composability

These principles are detailed in Thomas Erl's book, *Service-Oriented Architecture, Second Edition*. Service-orientation principles are applied to the service-oriented analysis and design phases of the SOA delivery life cycle.

Standardized service contract

Each service should have a standardized service contract, consisting of a technical interface and service description. Even though we want services to be independent, they have to adhere to a common agreement so that units of logic can maintain a certain level of standardization.

In order to have standardized service contracts, all service contracts within a particular service inventory should follow a set of design standards. Standardization enables interoperability and allows the purpose of services to be more easily understood.

Service loose coupling

Services should be loosely coupled and independent of each other. Service contracts should be designed to have independence from service consumers and from their implementations.

Loosely coupled services can be modified faster and easier. Decoupling service contracts from their implementations allows service contracts to be modified with minimal impact to service consumers and service implementations. By minimizing the dependencies between services, each service can change and evolve independently while minimizing the effects of those changes on other services.

Service abstraction

Service contracts should only contain information that it is necessary to reveal, and service implementations should also hide their details. Any information that is not essential to effectively use the service can be abstracted out.

Design decisions, such as the technology used for a service, can be abstracted away. This follows the information hiding principle that was covered in Chapter 6, *Software Development Principles and Practices*. If a design decision needs to be changed later, the goal is that it can be made with minimal impact.

Service reusability

Services should be designed with reusability in mind, with their service logic being independent of a particular technology or business process. When services can be reused for different purposes, software development teams experience increased productivity, leading to savings in both costs and time.

Service reusability increases organizational agility because organizations can use existing services to respond to new business automation needs. Existing services can be composed together to create solutions for new problems or to take advantage of a new opportunity. Reusable services can accelerate development and may allow a feature or product to reach the market faster. In some cases, this can be critical for a project.

Decomposing tasks into more services for reusability requires more analysis and potentially introduces more complexity. However, when reusable services are designed correctly, there can be significant long-term cost savings. If a need arises that is satisfied by an existing service, resources do not have to be devoted to working on it.

Service reuse leads to higher quality software because existing services have already been tested. They may already be in production and, if there were any defects with the service, they may have already been exposed and corrected.

Service autonomy

Services should be designed to be autonomous, with more independence from their runtime environments. The design should seek to provide services with increased control over their runtime environments.

When services can operate with less dependence on resources in their runtime environments that they cannot control, this leads to better performance and increased reliability of those services at runtime.

Service statelessness

Service designs should strive to minimize the amount of state management that takes place, and separate state data from services.

Services can reduce their resource consumption if they do not manage state when it is unnecessary, which will allow them to handle more requests reliably. Having statelessness in services improves service scalability and improves the reusability of services.

Service discoverability

Services need to be discoverable. By including consistent and meaningful metadata with a service, the purpose of the service and the functionality it provides can be communicated. Service developers are required to provide this metadata.

Services should be discoverable by humans who are searching manually as well as software applications searching programmatically. Services must be aware of each other for them to interact.

Service composability

Services should be designed so that they are composable. This is the ability to use a service in any number of other services, and those services may themselves be composed of other services.

Some other service-orientation principles facilitate service composability. Service composition is heavily related to service reusability. The ability to create solutions by composing existing services provides organizations with one of the most important SOA benefits: organizational agility.

SOA delivery strategies

There are three main SOA delivery strategies: top-down, bottom-up, and agile. A delivery strategy is needed to coordinate the delivery of application, business, and process services.

The three SOA delivery strategies mirror the main approaches to software architecture design that were covered in Chapter 5, *Designing Software Architectures*.

The top-down strategy

The top-down strategy begins with analysis. It centers on the organization's business logic and requires that business processes become service-oriented. The top-down approach, when done properly, results in a high quality SOA. Each service is thoroughly analyzed, and as a result, reusability is maximized.

The downside is that this approach requires many resources, in terms of time and money. There is substantial pre-work that must take place with the top-down strategy. If an organization has the time and money to invest in a project, then this may be an effective approach.

It should be noted that, because analysis occurs at the beginning, it could be quite some time before any results are realized. This may or may not be acceptable for a given project. In order to meaningfully perform the service-oriented analysis and service-oriented design stages of the SOA life cycle, the top-down strategy has to be used at least to some extent.

The bottom-up strategy

The bottom-up approach, in contrast, begins with the web services themselves. They are created on an *as-needed* basis. Web services are designed and deployed based on immediate needs.

Integration with an existing system is a common motivation for using the bottom-up strategy. Organizations want to add web services to an existing application environment to allow for integration with a legacy system. A wrapper service is created to expose logic in an existing system.

Although this approach is common in the industry, it is not a valid approach to achieving SOA. In order to create a valid SOA later, a lot of effort and refactoring will probably be required. Web services created with this approach may not be *enterprise ready*. They are created to serve some need, so if you are not careful they will not take into consideration the enterprise as a whole.

The agile strategy

The third approach is an agile strategy, which is sometimes referred to as a meet-in-the-middle approach. It is a compromise between the top-down and bottom-up approaches. In this approach, analysis can occur concurrently with design and development. As soon as enough analysis has been completed, design and development can begin. While such efforts are underway, analysis continues with other functionality. This approach pairs well with an iterative, agile software development methodology.

This is sort of a *best-of-both-worlds* approach in that a proper design can be completed that will yield all of the service-oriented qualities. This approach can fulfill immediate needs while maintaining service-oriented qualities of the architecture.

However, as more analysis is finished, this approach may require completed services to be revisited. Services can become misaligned after ongoing analysis, requiring them to be refactored.

Service-oriented analysis

Service-oriented analysis is a stage in the SOA project life cycle and is used to decide what services should be built and what logic should be encapsulated by each service. The analysis is an iterative process that takes place once for each business process.

When a team is committed to building a SOA, it should perform some form of analysis specific to service-orientation and beyond standard analysis. One way that organizations can improve service modeling is how they go about incorporating service-oriented analysis and design into their software development process. Each organization has its own software development methodology and should determine how best to include service modeling into their own process.

Service-Oriented Architecture, Second Edition, by Thomas Erl, details three steps to service-oriented analysis: defining business automation requirements, identifying existing automation systems, and modeling candidate services.

Defining business automation requirements

The first step in service-oriented analysis is to define the business automation requirements for the business process being analyzed in the current iteration. Requirements can be gathered using the organization's normal method of eliciting and capturing requirements.

With those requirements, the business process we want to automate can be documented at a high level. The details of the business process are used when we model candidate services.

Identifying existing automation systems

Once the requirements have been established for the current iteration, the next step in service-oriented analysis involves identifying what parts, if any, of the business process logic are already automated.

Taking into consideration existing systems that may already automate all or part of any of the business processes allows us to determine what parts of the business processes still need to be automated. This information serves as an input when we model candidate services.

Modeling candidate services

The final step, modeling candidate services, consists of identifying service operation candidates and grouping them into candidate services. It is important to note that these candidate operations and services are abstract and a logical model. During design, other factors, such as constraints and limitations, will be considered. The final concrete design may differ from the service candidates.

Modeling candidate services should be a collaborative process between technical and business resources. Business analysts and domain experts can use their business knowledge to help the technical team define service candidates.

Service layers and service models

Enterprise logic consists of both business and application logic. Business logic is an implementation of the business requirements and includes an organization's business processes. These requirements include things such as constraints, dependencies, pre-conditions, and post-conditions.

Application logic is the implementation of business logic in a technology solution. Application logic might be implemented in a purchased solution, a custom developed solution, or some combination of the two. The development team works to design and develop the application logic. Topics such as performance requirements, security constraints, and vendor dependencies are considered in the technical solution.

Service-orientation is related to business and application logic because a SOA is a way to represent, execute, and share that logic. Service-orientation principles can be applied to both business and application logic.

The role of services is to realize the concepts and principles introduced by service-orientation. A service layer in a software architecture is typically placed between the business and application layers. This allows services to represent business logic and abstract application logic. Just as different applications within an organization's application layer can be implemented in different technologies, services within the service layers can also be implemented in different technologies.

Abstraction is one of the important characteristics of an SOA and it enables other key characteristics, such as organizational agility. Abstraction is critical because abstracting business and application logic allows for a service-oriented solution with loosely coupled services. Achieving the appropriate level of abstraction is not a trivial task, but it can be accomplished with a dedicated team. By creating layers of abstraction, or service layers, the team can figure out how services should represent application and business logic, and how to best promote agility.

During service modeling, it becomes apparent that there are some common types of services. These types are **service models**, which can be used to classify candidate services. Those candidate services can then be grouped together based on their service model into a *service layer*.

The three common service models (and layers) are task service, entity service, and utility service:

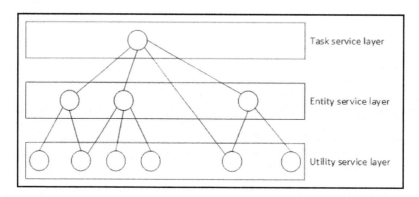

Task service

This type of service has a **non-agnostic functional context**, which means that it contains business process logic and was created for a specific business task or process. Task services do not have a great deal of reuse potential.

Task services typically compose multiple services in their logic and are sometimes referred to as *task-centric business services* or *business process services*.

If a task service has extensive orchestration logic or is hosted within an orchestration platform, it is sometimes referred to as an *orchestrated task service*. Orchestration logic automates the arrangement, coordination, and management of multiple services to accomplish a task.

Entity service

This service model has an **agnostic functional context**, meaning its logic is not bound to a single business process and is reusable. Entity services are business-centric services that are associated with one or more business entities. They are sometimes referred to as *entity-centric business services* or *business entity services*.

Business entities come from the business domain, and involving people on the team who thoroughly understand the business domain and business processes will be beneficial in performing the analysis needed to determine the appropriate entity services. Entity services may compose utility services in their logic.

Utility service

Utility services, like entity services, have an agnostic functional context. They contain multi-purpose logic and are highly reusable. The difference between entity services and utility services is that utility services are not associated with a business entity or business logic.

Utility services are concerned with technology-related functions, such as a software system's cross-cutting concerns. Examples include logging, caching, notifications, authentication, and authorization.

Service-oriented design

The service-oriented design phase begins once the analysis is complete. Having a thorough understanding of the requirements and using the service models from the analysis stage will allow for the creation of a proper service design.

The service-oriented design phase uses the logical candidate services that were derived during service-oriented analysis and creates the physical service designs. Before designing the implementation of the services, the first step is to design the physical service interfaces. We need to make decisions regarding the service interfaces based on the service candidates, the requirements that need to be met, as well as the organization and industry standards that will be required to have a standardized service contract. Once the service contracts have been established, the logic and implementation of the service can be designed.

Designing the service interfaces and implementing them are two distinct steps. We should fully focus on the service contracts first, independent of their implementations. Some teams design the two concurrently or skip to the development stage and just let the service interface *emerge* from the implemented service.

However, software architects should devote time to considering the service contracts before the implementations. Not only do we need to ensure that the service contracts satisfy the requirements, but they need to follow the key principles of service orientation, which include the fact that they should be loosely coupled from their implementations. Only after the service contracts have been established do we need to consider the design of the implementations.

Service interface design

One of the main goals of service-oriented design is to derive the physical service interface definitions based on the service candidates that were determined during service-oriented analysis. Service interface design is significant because the design phase is the first time that real technology is identified.

If you recall the key principles for service orientation, they need to be applied to the design of the service interfaces. Service contracts need to be standardized with each other and within a service inventory. They should be loosely coupled from their implementations, with design decisions abstracted out so that the interfaces only contain what is essential for service consumers.

Service interface design identifies internal and external exposure of the services. For example, an order posting service may need to be used externally as well as internally. This is an example of a service that may need more than one interface published for the same service. Each interface to the service may expose different operations and will require different levels of security and authentication. The differences must be determined and each interface must be designed prior to the design of the implementations.

In addition to developers, a service interface plays an important role in testing and quality assurance. Testers need the service interface to design their tests. Once the service interface is known, a test harness can be created that is capable of invoking the service that needs to be tested. Services need to be tested independently of other services as well as within the services that will be consuming it.

Service interface granularity

Making decisions about interface granularity can be very important in service-oriented design. Granularity can have a significant impact on performance and other concerns. Usually, a service interface contains more than one operation, and the operations of a service should be semantically related.

Fine-grained service operations offer greater flexibility to service consumers but lead to more network overhead, which could reduce performance. The more coarse-grained service operations we have, the less flexible they are, although they do reduce network overhead and could therefore improve performance.

Software architects should seek to find the right balance between the number of services and the number of operations in each service. You do not want to group too many operations into a single service, even if they are semantically related, because it makes the service too bulky and hard to understand. It may also increase the number of service versions that will need to be released going forward, as parts of the service need to be modified. However, if your service interface is too fine-grained, you may end up with an unnecessarily large number of service interfaces.

Service registries

A **service registry** contains information about the available services and is a key component of SOA governance. It helps to make systems interoperable and facilitates the discovery of web services. Although some organizations may find that a service registry is not needed, many SOA implementations can benefit from having a service registry. As an organization begins to publish and use more and more web services, some of which may be outside the organization, the need for a centralized registry becomes more apparent.

There are numerous benefits to using a service registry. By promoting the discovery of web services, organizations can facilitate reuse and avoid building multiple web services that perform similar tasks. Developers can programmatically query a service registry to discover web services that already exist that can satisfy their needs. Similar to the benefits that are derived from any type of reused code, quality is improved and there is an increased level of dependability from reusing web services. Reused web services have already been tested and are usually already being successfully used in another part of the system or in another system.

Service registries can either be private or public. As the name implies, public registries can include any organization. This even includes organizations that do not have any web services to offer. Private registries are restricted to those services that the organization develops itself or services that it has leased or purchased.

The benefits of public service registries include being able to find the right businesses and services for a particular need. It can also lead to new customers or allow more access to current customers. It could allow an organization to expand their offerings and extend their market reach. Service registries can be a useful and powerful tool for finding available web services since they can be searched manually by people or programmatically through a standardized API by an application. However, because of these capabilities, organizations should take the time to decide whether to use a public or private registry and what services they want to register into them.

One of the challenges of implementing a truly useful and reliable registry service is the administration of the registry. This includes keeping it up to date by adding new services, removing obsolete services, and updating versions, service descriptions, and web service locations.

Service descriptions

In order for services to interact with each other, they must be aware of each other. **Service descriptions** serve the important purpose of providing this awareness. They provide information about the available services so that potential consumers can decide whether a particular service will satisfy their needs.

Service descriptions help to foster loose coupling, an important principle of SOAs. Dependencies between services are minimized as services can work together simply through the awareness they have of each other through their service descriptions.

Any service that wants to act as an ultimate receiver must have service description documents. Service descriptions typically have both abstract and concrete information. The abstract part details the service interface without getting into the details of the specific technologies being used. The beauty of the abstraction is that the integrity of the service description is maintained even if the details of the technical implementation are changed in the future. The abstract description typically includes a high-level overview of the service interface, including what operations it can perform. Input and output messages of the operations are also detailed.

The concrete part of the service description provides details about the physical transport protocol that is connected to the web service interface. This specific transport and location information includes the binding (requirements for the service to establish a connection or for a connection to be established with a service), port (physical address of the web service), and service (a group of related endpoints) so that the web service can be used.

Possible challenges to developing service descriptions include the following:

- Decomposing web services properly based on business needs
- Determining the exact purpose and responsibilities of a particular service
- Deciding on the operations that a web service will need to provide
- Properly communicating a service's interface in the abstract part of the service description so that potential service consumers can make an informed decision based on their needs

Structuring namespaces

A **namespace** is a unique **Uniform Resource Locator (URI)**. Namespaces are used to group related services and elements together and to differentiate between different ones that share the same name. It is important for software architects to put thought into namespaces. By providing a unique namespace, even if your organization uses services from another one, your elements will be guaranteed to be unique. Even if two organizations have a service with the same name, they will be differentiated by their namespace.

In addition to providing unique names, namespaces are used to logically organize various services and elements. An appropriate namespace should provide meaning to the service or element so that someone who is looking at it can gain an understanding of the service. Namespaces make it easier to name new services as well as to find existing ones.

In order to select good namespaces, we have to consider how namespaces are structured. A company's domain name is an important part of a namespace and because domain names are unique, they are commonly part of a namespace. Typically, the role follows the domain name in a namespace. This will allow differentiation between schema (for example, message types) and interfaces (for example, web services).

A business area typically follows the role in the structure of a namespace. This is where domain experts and business analysts can assist software architects in coming up with a business structure that makes sense. Another part of a namespace that is common is some form of version or date. This allows differentiation between multiple versions of the same service or element. Versioning is another important use of namespaces.

Orchestration and choreography

Service orchestration and **service choreography** serve important roles in SOAs, as they are approaches to assembling multiple services so that they can work together.

Orchestration represents business process logic in a standardized way using services. It automates the execution of a workflow by coordinating and managing different services. In service orchestration, there is a centralized process containing fixed logic. An orchestrator controls the process by deciding which services to invoke and when to invoke them. Orchestration is analogous to the conductor of an orchestra, who unifies and directs individual performers to create an overall performance.

Interoperability for an organization is promoted in solutions using orchestration because of the integration endpoints that are introduced in processes. In a SOA, orchestrations themselves are services. This promotes federation because multiple business processes, potentially from different applications, can be merged together.

Choreography is another form of service composition. Choreographies define message exchanges and can involve multiple participants, each of which may assume multiple roles.

In contrast with orchestration, there is no centralized process, or orchestrator, that is controlling it. With choreography, there is an agreed upon set of coordinated interactions that specify the conditions in which data will be exchanged. Each service in a choreography acts autonomously to execute its part based on the conditions that were established and the actions of the other participants.

Both orchestration and choreography can be used for business-process logic owned by a single organization (intra-organization) and collaboration between multiple organizations (inter-organization). However, orchestration is less likely to be used when there are multiple organizations involved because you would need to own and operate the orchestration. Choreography allows for collaboration without having a single organization control the whole process.

Summary

Software architects should be familiar with software architecture patterns, as they are a powerful tool when designing a software architecture. Architecture patterns provide a proven solution to recurring problems for a given context.

Leveraging architecture patterns gives the software architect a high-level structure of the software system, and provides a grouping of design decisions that have been repeated and used successfully. Using them reduces complexity by placing constraints on the design and allows us to anticipate the qualities that the software system will exhibit once it is implemented.

In this chapter, you learned about some of the common software architecture patterns available, including layered architecture, EDA, MVC, MVP, MVVM, CQRS, and SOA.

The focus of the next chapter is on some of the relatively newer software architecture patterns and paradigms. These include microservice architecture, serverless architecture, and cloud-native applications. As cloud deployment of software applications becomes the dominant trend, these concepts become crucial for any software architect to understand.

8
Architecting Modern Applications

Modern applications deployed to the cloud have different expectations and requirements from applications designed in the past. New software architecture patterns and paradigms have been introduced to meet those expectations.

In this chapter, we will explore some of these patterns and approaches to software design and development. We will begin with a look at monolithic architecture, along with the reasons why it should or should not be used. We will then explore **microservice architecture (MSA)**, **serverless architecture**, and **cloud-native applications**.

In this chapter, we will cover the following topics:

- Monolithic architecture
- Microservice architecture
- Serverless architecture
- Cloud-native applications

Monolithic architecture

A **monolithic architecture** is one in which a software application is designed to work as a single, self-contained unit. Applications that have this type of architecture are common. The components within a monolithic architecture are interconnected and interdependent, resulting in tightly coupled code.

The following diagram shows an application with a monolithic architecture:

The different concerns of an application, such as user interface, business logic, authorization, logging, and database access, are not kept separate in a monolithic architecture. These different pieces of functionality are intertwined in a monolithic application.

Benefits of a monolithic architecture

Despite some obvious disadvantages to using a monolithic architecture, if an application is relatively small, then there are benefits to using one. Applications with a monolithic architecture typically have better performance. With the interaction between the machine running the application and other machines minimized, better levels of performance are realized.

Small applications that have this type of architecture are easier to deploy because of the simplicity of the high-level architecture. In spite of the tightly coupled logic, monolithic applications can be easier to test and debug because they are simpler, with fewer separate components to consider.

Monolithic applications are typically easy to scale because all it takes is to run multiple instances of the same application. However, different application components have different scaling needs and we cannot scale the components independently with a monolithic architecture. We are limited to adding more instances of the entire application in order to scale.

Drawbacks of a monolithic architecture

Although a monolithic architecture may work for some applications, as applications grow in size and complexity, there are serious drawbacks. Monolithic applications greatly inhibit the agility of the organization as it becomes difficult to make changes to the software. One aspect of this is the fact that continuous deployment is difficult to achieve. Even if a change is made to only one component of a monolithic application, the entire software system will need to be deployed. Organizations are required to devote more resources, such as time and testers, to deploy a new version of a monolithic application.

If the application is small, it can be easy to maintain due to the simplicity of the architecture. However, larger and more complex monolithic applications start to suffer in terms of maintainability. Tightly coupled components make it more difficult to make changes because a change in one part of the application is more likely to affect other parts of the application.

The large codebase of a monolithic application can make it difficult for team members to understand it. This is especially true for new team members as they attempt to become familiar with it and begin working with it.

Even loading a large, monolithic application into an **integrated development environment (IDE)** and working with it can be frustrating due to slower performance of the IDE. It also takes longer for such applications to start up, lowering the productivity of the team during development.

Monolithic applications require a commitment to a particular programming language and technology stack. Since the application is written as a single unit, it makes it more difficult to introduce different types of technology. In some cases, it can even make it difficult to move to a newer version of the same technology! If a migration to a different technology is needed, it requires the organization to commit to rewriting the entire application.

Larger and more complex applications benefit from dividing responsibilities up among multiple development teams, such as having each team focus on a particular functional area. However, this becomes difficult to do with a monolithic application as changes made by one development team may affect another development team.

Due to these drawbacks, software applications that are large and complex should move away from being a monolithic application. MSA and serverless architecture are alternatives to monolithic architectures. They address some of the concerns and limitations of monolithic applications.

Microservice architecture

The **microservice architecture (MSA)** pattern builds software applications using small, autonomous, independently versioned, self-contained services. These services use well-defined interfaces and communicate with each other over standard, lightweight protocols.

Interaction with a microservice takes place through a well-defined interface. A microservice should be a *black box* to the consumers of the service, hiding its implementation and complexity. Each microservice focuses on doing one thing well and they can work together with other microservices in order to accomplish tasks that are more complex.

A microservice architecture is particularly well-suited for large and/or complex software systems. In contrast with the monolithic architecture, applications built using a microservice architecture handle complexity by splitting the application into smaller services that are easier to manage. The following diagram illustrates a system that has a microservices architecture:

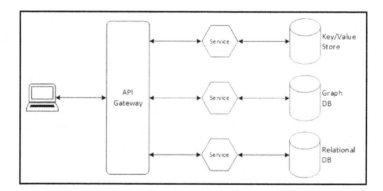

Incoming requests are commonly handled by an API gateway, which serves as the entry point to the system. It is an HTTP server that takes requests from clients and routes them to the appropriate microservice through its routing configuration. In the *Service discovery* section later in this chapter, we will take a closer look at service discovery to explain how API gateways can get the locations of available service instances.

SOA done right

Microservice architecture emerged, not as a solution looking for a problem, but as the result of the shortcomings and drawbacks of the traditional **service-oriented architecture (SOA)** and monolithic architecture.

SOA provides a number of benefits, which were covered in `Chapter 7`, *Software Architecture Patterns*, such as increasing the alignment between business and technology, promoting federation within an organization, allowing for vendor diversity, and increasing interoperability.

Although microservice architecture is a variation of the service-oriented architecture, there are key differences between the two. Some people even refer to the microservice architecture as *SOA done right*.

In addition to moving us away from monolithic architectures, microservice architecture improves on traditional SOA. Implementing SOA can be quite expensive, difficult to implement, and may be overkill for many applications. The microservice architecture pattern addresses some of these drawbacks. Rather than using an **enterprise service bus (ESB)**, as is common with SOA, microservice architecture favors implementing ESB-like functionality in the services themselves.

Characteristics of microservice architecture

There are a number of characteristics related to the microservice architecture. In this section, we will examine the following characteristics:

- Small, focused services
- Well-defined service interfaces
- Autonomous and independently deployable services
- Independent data storage
- Communicating with lightweight protocols
- Better fault isolation

Small, focused services

The functionality of a microservice should be small in scope. Each microservice should follow the tenet of the Unix philosophy that advocates for doing one thing and doing it well. Keeping the scope small for each service allows the complexity of the software to be better managed.

Applications with a microservice architecture are easier to understand and modify because every service has a focused responsibility. This allows the services to be developed faster. Smaller solutions are easier to load up and use in an IDE, which increases productivity. In addition, new team members are able to become productive in a shorter amount of time.

A microservice can be developed by a small team. This allows organizations to easily split up work among multiple development teams. Each microservice can be worked on by a single team, independent of other microservices. Tasks for different microservices can be worked on in parallel.

If a software system is also using **domain-driven design** (DDD), the concept of bounded contexts works well with microservices as it helps with the partitioning of services. In some systems, each microservice is implemented as its own bounded context.

Well-defined service interfaces

Microservices are treated like *black boxes*, hiding their complexity and implementation details from service consumers. This makes a well-defined interface, with clear entry and exit points, which is important to help facilitate microservices working together. Services interact with each other through their interfaces.

Autonomous and independently deployable services

An application using a microservice architecture consists of a system of autonomous services. The services should be loosely coupled, interacting through their well-defined interfaces and not dependent on the implementation of the service.

This allows the implementation of services to change and evolve independently of the other services. As long as the service interface is unchanged, modifying a microservice is less likely to require changes to other parts of the application.

Autonomous services are independently deployable, making it easier to deploy them to production. A microservice architecture enables continuous deployment because it is easier to release updates to the services. If a change is made to a microservice, it can be deployed independently of the other microservices.

The autonomy of the services increases organizational agility. It allows organizations to quickly adapt to changing business requirements and take advantage of new business opportunities.

Independent data storage

One of the characteristics that support service autonomy is that each microservice can have its own data store. This helps services to be independent and loosely coupled to other services. A service's data store can be altered without those changes affecting other services.

Designing each microservice to have its own data store may come in the form of a microservice having its own database, but that is not the only way to keep a microservice's data storage private. If the data storage technology is a **relational database management system (RDBMS)**, then in addition to the option of having a separate database server, data can be kept separate by designating certain tables to be owned by a particular service. Another option is to designate a schema that is to only be used by a single microservice.

In the *Polyglot persistence* section later in this chapter, you will learn about some additional benefits to using a separate database for each microservice.

Better fault isolation

A system built on a microservice architecture improves fault isolation. When one microservice goes down, other services can still operate normally, allowing other parts of the system to remain operational. This is in contrast to a monolithic application, where a fault can potentially bring down the entire system.

Communicating with lightweight message protocols

Microservices should communicate using well-known, lightweight message protocols. There is no rule dictating a particular protocol, and microservices can communicate synchronously or asynchronously. A common implementation for microservices is to have them expose HTTP endpoints that are invoked through REST API calls. For synchronous communication, REST is one of the preferred protocols. It is common for REST to be used with **JavaScript Object Notation (JSON)**. Service operations can accept and return data in the JSON format as it is a popular and lightweight data-interchange format.

Some applications may require asynchronous communication. A common messaging protocol used for asynchronous communication with microservices is **Advanced Message Queueing Protocol (AMQP)**. It is an open standard that can connect a variety of services, including those on different platforms and across organizations. It was designed for security, reliability, and interoperability.

AMQP can support the following types of message-delivery guarantees:

- **At least once**: A message is guaranteed to be delivered but it may be delivered multiple times
- **At most once**: A message is guaranteed to be delivered once or never
- **Exactly once**: A message is guaranteed to be delivered once and only once

Another protocol that is popular with microservices is **gRPC**. It was designed by Google as an alternative to REST and other protocols. It is an open source protocol that was designed to be faster and more compact than other protocols used for distributed systems.

gRPC is built on protocol buffers, also known as protobufs, which is a way of serializing data that is language and platform neutral. This allows gRPC to efficiently connect polyglot services because it supports a variety of programming languages. The increased prevalence of containerized applications and microservices has made gRPC popular. Given modern workloads, gRPC is an attractive choice because it is a high-performance and lightweight protocol. gRPC is inherently efficient, but it is also based on HTTP/2. This yields additional benefits such as decreased latency and higher data compression.

The communication protocol that you select for your microservice architecture really depends on your requirements. There is no *silver bullet* answer that will apply to all situations. The context of your design concerns will drive the selection, such as whether your communication needs are synchronous or asynchronous.

Designing polyglot microservices

One of the many advantages of using a microservice architecture is that it affords you the option of using multiple programming languages, runtimes, frameworks, and data storage technologies.

Monolithic applications focus on using a particular programming language and technology stack. Because that type of application is written as a single unit, it is more difficult to take advantage of different types of technology. However, complex applications need to solve a variety of problems. Being able to select different technologies for different problems can be useful rather than trying to solve all of the problems with a single technology.

A development team can select best-of-breed solutions depending on the task they need to complete. A microservice architecture allows teams to experiment and try out new technologies with, having to commit to them for the entire system.

Having polyglot microservices is certainly not required when using a microservice architecture. In many cases, an organization will focus on a limited number of technologies, and the skillsets of the development team will reflect that. However, software architects should be aware of the option and recognize opportunities where it can be used effectively.

Two of the concepts related to polyglot microservices are polyglot programming and polyglot persistence.

Polyglot programming

With **polyglot programming**, a single application uses multiple programming languages in its implementation. It can be useful to take advantage of the strengths of different programming languages to handle different tasks within an application.

A microservice architecture allows each microservice to be developed using the programming language that best fits the problem at hand. When a new technology becomes available, an existing application can take advantage of it for new microservices that are developed or for new versions of an existing microservice.

Polyglot persistence

Similar to polyglot programming, there is the concept of **polyglot persistence**, in which multiple persistence options are used within a single application. Different data storage technologies are better suited to different tasks, and microservices allows you to take advantage of that.

Each microservice is in charge of its own data storage, so it can choose the best data storage technology based on what it is trying to achieve. The following diagram depicts two microservices, each with its own database:

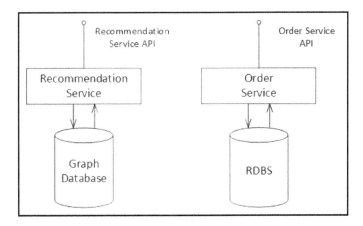

A microservice dedicated to providing product recommendations based on friends, ratings, and prior purchases would be ideal for a graph database. A product catalog with details about a company's products, requiring frequent reads and infrequent writes, could be implemented with a document database. When processing an order, the transactional capabilities of a relational database might be ideal.

A single microservice can even use more than one data storage technology, although that is fairly unusual in practice. It introduces extra complexity, and if you find yourself wanting to do that, you have to consider whether your microservice is too large in scope. In that case, perhaps the microservice needs to be divided into more than one.

Using too many technologies

As with many things, polyglot programming and polyglot persistence can be overdone. There is a cost to introducing too many disparate technologies within a single organization. Mastering a technology is difficult and you will need staff members who are well-versed in the technologies that you are using. The use of different technologies may create a need for more developer training, which costs the organization money as well as its employees' time.

Using different programming languages and data storage technologies introduces complexity into the build, deployment, and test processes. The software will need to be continually maintained after it is released to production, requiring a diverse development team capable of handling all of the different technologies.

Having the ability to take advantage of different technologies can be a valuable asset, but consideration must be made each time using a new one is being considered to ensure that it is the best decision for the project.

Considering service granularity

The granularity of a service refers to the scope of its business functionality, which varies for each service. With microservices, the goal is to have fine-grained services so that each one focuses on a single business capability.

It is important to get the granularity of microservices correct to ensure that the system consists of appropriately sized services. One of the goals of a microservice architecture is to decompose a domain into small, focused, and reusable services. Smaller services carry with them less context, increasing their level of reusability.

Nanoservices

Software architects and developers who are designing microservices should be careful not to make the granularity of their services too fine-grained, though. Services whose granularity is too fine-grained are referred to as **nanoservices** and this is considered an anti-pattern.

A system with very small services tends to have more services and, as the number of services in a system increases, so does the amount of communication that must take place. Services use up network resources that are not infinite, and services are bound by these limitations. Having too many services can lead to the reduced performance of your services and of your overall application.

When a system has many nanoservices, there is also an increase in the overall overhead for the services. Each service requires some management, including things such as configuration and entry into a service registry. Larger numbers of services lead to increasing amounts of overhead.

Nanoservices can lead to fragmented logic. If a single business task that fits well into a single, cohesive service is decomposed further into multiple, smaller services, the logic becomes separated. Making services unnecessarily small is part of the nanoservice, anti-pattern.

When the overhead of a service outweighs its utility, then it is a nanoservice and refactoring should be considered. Nanoservices can be refactored by either combining multiple nanoservices into a new, larger service or moving the functionality of each nanoservice into an appropriate existing service.

There may be exceptions in which a nanoservice is appropriately sized and does not require refactoring, so it is always prudent to use your best judgment. Although you do not want your system to consist of too many nanoservices, sometimes, the functionality of a particular nanoservice simply does not belong anywhere else.

Sharing dependencies between microservices

Development teams should avoid sharing dependencies, such as frameworks and third-party libraries, between microservices. You may have multiple microservices that share the same dependency, so it is natural to think about sharing them on the host to make them centrally available.

However, each microservice should remain independent of other microservices. If we want to update the dependencies, we don't want to affect any other services. Doing so would increase the risk of introducing defects and will broaden the scope of the testing that will need to be conducted related to the change.

Sharing dependencies also introduces host affinity, which we want to avoid. Microservices should function independently of the host they are deployed on because assumptions cannot be made regarding the host on which a service will execute.

Stateless versus stateful microservices

Each microservice can either be *stateless* or *stateful*. A system that uses microservices typically has a stateless web and/or mobile application that uses stateless and/or stateful services.

Stateless microservices do not maintain any state within the services across calls. They take in a request, process it, and send a response back without persisting any state information. A stateful microservice persists state in some form in order for it to function.

Rather than store this state internally, a microservice should store state information externally, in some type of data store. Examples of a data store to persist state include a **relational database management system (RDBMS)**, a NoSQL database, or some type of cloud storage. Persisting the state externally provides availability, reliability, scalability, and consistency for the state information.

Service discovery

The client of a service, whether it is an API gateway or another service, needs the ability to discover the location of a service instance. In a traditional distributed environment, service locations (IP address and port) are generally static, and a service instance can be found easily. For example, service locations could be read from a configuration file.

However, service discovery is more complex with a cloud-based application using microservices. The number and location of service instances changes dynamically in the cloud. A service registry can be used to keep track of service instances and their locations.

Using a service registry

A **service registry** plays a key role in service discovery. It is a database containing service instances and their locations. The service registry must be highly available and kept up to date. In order to be accurate, service instances must be registered and deregistered with the service registry. This can be accomplished through either self-registration or third-party registration.

Self-registration pattern

Using the self-registration pattern, service instances are responsible for registering with, and deregistering from, the service registry:

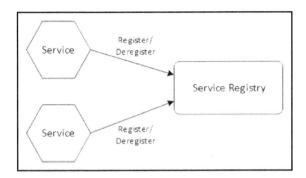

When a service instance starts up, it must register itself with the service registry. Similarly, when a service instance shuts down, it must unregister itself from the service registry.

This approach is relatively straightforward, although it does couple the service instances to the service registry. If you have a polyglot system in which different microservices are using different programming languages and/or frameworks, service registration logic must exist for each programming language and framework that is used for the development of your microservices.

It is a common requirement to have registered service instances periodically renew their registration or send a heartbeat request to indicate they are still alive and responsive. If a service instance does not do this, then they can be deregistered automatically. Doing this will handle situations in which a service instance is running but is unavailable for some reason. Such service instances may not be able to unregister themselves from the service registry.

For small applications, the self-registration pattern may be sufficient, but large applications will want to use the third-party registration pattern.

Third-party registration pattern

When using the third-party registration pattern, a dedicated component, sometimes referred to as the *service registrar*, handles registering, deregistering, and checking the health of service instances. Like the service registry itself, the service registrar is an important component and therefore must be highly available.

The following diagram illustrates the third-party registration pattern:

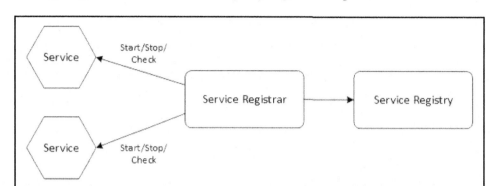

By either polling the available service instances or subscribing to relevant events, the service registrar can register new service instances and deregister service instances that no longer exist. It can perform health checks on service instances and take appropriate actions based on the result.

Unlike the self-registration pattern, the service instances are decoupled from the service registry. Services can focus on their single responsibility and not have to be concerned with service registration. If different microservices in your system are using different programming languages and/or frameworks, you do not need to implement service registration logic for each one that is used by the development team(s).

One drawback with this pattern is that unless the service registrar is a built-in component of your deployment environment, it is another component that must be set up and managed.

Types of service discovery

There are two main patterns for service discovery:

- Client-side discovery pattern
- Server-side discovery pattern

We will now look at both types in detail.

Client-side discovery pattern

With the client-side discovery pattern, the service client, whether it is an API gateway or another service, queries a service registry for the locations of available service instances:

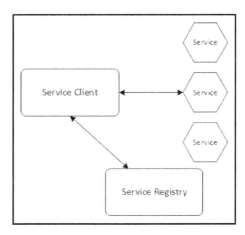

Once the locations of available service instances are obtained from the service registry, the service client uses a load balancing algorithm to select one of them. At that point, the service client can interact with a specific service instance.

This pattern is straightforward, although it does couple the service client with the service registry. For organizations that are taking advantage of using multiple programming languages and/or frameworks for their microservice development, service-discovery logic will need to be written for each programming language and framework that is used for the development of microservices.

Server-side discovery pattern

The other main pattern for service discovery is the server-side discovery pattern. The service client, such as an API gateway or another service, makes a request to a router. The router is typically a load balancer.

The following diagram illustrates the server-side discovery pattern:

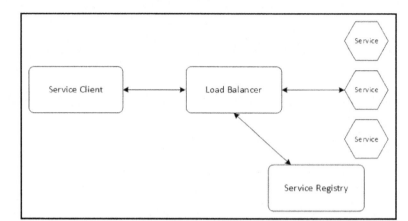

In this pattern, it is the load balancer that queries the service registry for the locations of available service instances. The service registry may be built into the load balancer or it may be a separate component. The load balancer is then responsible for forwarding the request to one of the available service instances.

Unlike the client-side discovery pattern, service clients are decoupled from the service registry. Service client code is simpler as it does not have to be concerned with interacting with the service registry or implementing a load balancing algorithm. Service clients can simply make a request to the load balancer. If different programming languages/frameworks are being used for microservice development, there is no need to implement service discovery logic for each one.

A drawback to this pattern is that unless the cloud provider is providing the load balancer and associated functionality (service registry), it is another component that must be installed and managed. Also, there are more network hops involved with this pattern due to the load balancer compared with the client-side discovery pattern.

Using microservices is not for everyone

As is the case with other types of architecture patterns, there are disadvantages to using a microservice architecture. The benefits of using a microservice architecture must outweigh the added complexity, so it is not the ideal solution for all types of applications.

As a distributed system, a microservice architecture introduces complexity simply not found in a monolithic application. When multiple services are working together in a distributed system and something goes wrong, there is added complexity in figuring out what and where something failed. A service may not respond downstream and the system must be able to handle the disruption.

Decomposing a complex system into the right set of microservices can be difficult. It requires a knowledge of the domain and can be somewhat of an art. You don't want a system with services that are too fine-grained, resulting in a large number of services. As the number of services increase, the management of those services becomes increasingly complex.

At the same time, you do not want the services of a system to be too coarse-grained, so that they are responsible for too much functionality. The last thing you want is a bunch of services that are tightly coupled, making it so that they have to be deployed together. If you are not careful, you will end up with a microservice architecture that is a monolith in disguise.

The use of multiple databases is another challenge when using a microservice architecture. It is common for a business transaction to update multiple entities, which will require the use of multiple microservices. With each one having its own database, this means that updates must take place in multiple databases. One way to handle this is through event-sourcing and having eventual consistency. Even if that is acceptable, implementation of event-sourcing is another added complexity.

Service clients, such as an API gateway and other services, will need a way to know the location of available service instances. Unless a cloud provider is providing a service registry and associated functionality, these additional components will need to be configured and managed.

Serverless architecture

Serverless architecture allows the rapid development of software applications that can handle various levels of traffic in production environments. The term *serverless* refers to the fact that compute services are provided without requiring you to manage or administer servers. Your code is executed on demand, as it is needed.

Utilizing compute services in this way is similar to how cloud storage is used. With cloud storage, you do not need to manage physical hardware and you do not need to know where the data is stored. You use as much or as little storage as you need.

Similarly, with serverless architecture, you do not need to deal with physical servers, and the complexity of how compute resources are provided is hidden from you. Software applications use as much or as little compute capacity as they need.

Serverless architecture is maturing and its use is increasingly common. It can be the ideal architectural choice for some software applications. A number of cloud vendors, including Amazon, Microsoft, Google, and IBM, provide compute services.

Serverless architecture can be used for many types of software applications and tasks. Some of the common types of applications that are suited to a serverless architecture include web applications, event-driven data processing, event workflows, scheduled tasks (CRON jobs), mobile applications, chatbots, and Internet of Things (IoT) applications. It is also good for data transformation tasks related to things such as images/video (for example, for the purposes of compression and/or optimization), voice packets, and PDF generation.

The following diagram shows an example of a system that has a serverless architecture:

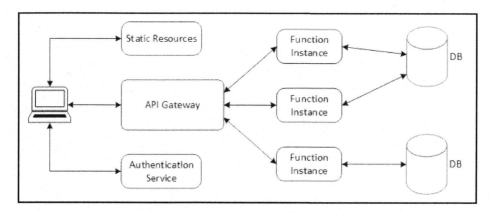

Serverless architectures use **function as a service (FaaS)** and **backend as a service (BaaS)** models to provide backend logic for software applications. The two are used together to provide the functionality of the application.

Function as a Service (FaaS)

In a serverless architecture, a small piece of code, like a function, can be executed using an ephemeral compute service to produce a result. This is known as **Function as a Service (FaaS)**. By ephemeral, we mean that it will only last for a limited amount of time. The code executes in a container that is spun up on invocation and then brought back down when it is complete.

Functions are typically invoked due to events or HTTP requests. When a function completes its processing, it can either return a value to the caller or pass the result to another function that will be invoked as part of a workflow. The output can either be structured, such as an HTTP response object, or unstructured, such as a string or an integer.

Each function should follow the **single responsibility principle** (SRP) and serve a single, well-defined purpose. Development teams can code functions to perform server-side logic and then upload the code to their service provider for on-demand execution. FaaS makes it easy to go from writing code on your laptop to having it execute in the cloud.

Functions should be designed to be idempotent, so that multiple executions of the same request yield the same result, and if the same request is processed more than once, there should not be any adverse effects.

Copies of messages may exist on multiple servers to provide redundancy and high availability. In order to ensure at-least-once delivery, it is possible that a function may be invoked more than once. For example, a server with a copy of a message may become unavailable when a message is received or deleted, leading to the same message being sent to a function again.

The functions in FaaS can be either synchronous or asynchronous, depending on the needs of the task. One of the ways that asynchronous functions work in FaaS is that the platform will return a unique identifier that can then be used to poll the status of the asynchronous operation.

An important part of a serverless architecture is its API gateway. An API gateway is the entry point to a system. It is an HTTP server that takes requests from clients and uses its routing configuration to route them to the relevant function container. The functions run in compute containers and should be stateless. The result of the FaaS function is then sent back to the API gateway and ultimately returned to the client as an HTTP response.

Implementations of FaaS that are available from providers include Amazon Web Services Lambda, Microsoft Azure Functions, Google Cloud Functions, and IBM Cloud Functions.

Backend as a Service (BaaS)

Backend as a Service (BaaS), which has its roots in **Mobile Backend as a Service (MBaaS)**, is a model that allows developers to take advantage of service applications provided by third parties. This reduces development time and costs, as teams do not have to write these services in-house. In contrast with FaaS, where development teams write their own code for the various functions, BaaS offers the use of existing services.

Examples of the functionality provided by service applications include a database, push notifications, file storage, and authentication services. In the serverless architecture diagram, the authentication service and the storage service for the static resources are examples of BaaS.

Advantages of serverless architectures

Using a serverless architecture provides many important benefits, which explains why it is becoming increasingly popular.

Cost savings

With a serverless architecture, your code is only executed when it is needed. You get utility billing, in that you are only charged for the actual compute resources that are used.

Organizations moving to a serverless architecture will reduce hardware costs, as there are no longer servers and network infrastructure to support. In addition, organizations do not have to hire staff to support all of that infrastructure. These cost savings are similar to what organizations might save from using **Infrastructure as a Service (IaaS)** or **Platform as a Service (PaaS)**, except that there are also reduced development costs (taking advantage of BaaS) and scaling costs (taking advantage of FaaS).

Scalable and flexible

You can't underprovision or overprovision your compute capacity with a serverless architecture. You avoid being in a situation where you do not have enough servers during periods of peak capacity or have too many servers sitting idly during off-peak periods.

The scalability and flexibility of serverless architectures allows for compute capacity to scale up and down as demand changes. You only use as much compute capacity as you need and you are charged for the amount that you use. Wasting compute capacity is kept to a minimum and organizations will experience lowered costs as a result.

Focus on building your core products

Another one of the main advantages of using a serverless architecture is that there are no servers to manage. This allows organizations to focus on creating solutions and shipping more features.

Not having to administer an infrastructure increases productivity and reduces the time to market. Even a small development team can start building an application and deploy it to production relatively quickly because they won't need to provision an infrastructure up front and they won't have as much to manage after deployment. A development team that wants to build an application quickly while worrying less about operational concerns will find serverless architecture attractive.

Polyglot development

A serverless architecture allows for polyglot development. Development teams are provided with the ability to select best-of-breed languages and runtimes based on the required functionality. It also gives teams a chance to easily try out and experiment with different technologies. Although there are limitations as to which languages are available to you, cloud providers are expanding their selection so that different languages can be used for the different functions being developed.

Disadvantages of serverless architectures

Although there are many benefits to using a serverless architecture, you should be aware that there are some drawbacks.

Difficulties with debugging and monitoring

There is complexity in debugging distributed systems using serverless architecture. When multiple functions integrate with each other to perform a task and something goes wrong, it can be difficult to understand when and why the problem occurred. Vendors provide tools for debugging and monitoring, but there is still a level of immaturity with the serverless architecture pattern. Serverless architecture applications will become more prevalent, but it is still relatively new compared to other types of software architecture.

Multitenancy issues

Multitenancy issues, while not unique to serverless systems, deserve consideration. Any time software for different customers are executed on the same machine, there is the possibility of one customer affecting a different customer. Examples of this include security issues, such as one customer being able to see another customer's data, or performance issues when one customer experiences a heavy load that affects performance for another customer.

Vendor lock-in

Vendor lock-in can be an issue with serverless architectures. You may think that moving from one serverless environment to another one would be easy, but it can be quite involved. In addition to your code being moved, each provider has specific formats and deployment methods. In addition, you may be taking advantage of technologies and tools specific to your vendor.

Some degree of refactoring will be required if you want to switch vendors. Ideally, your software application will not be reliant on a particular cloud provider. One way to mitigate this disadvantage is to use a framework that packages your application in a way that allows for deployment to any cloud provider. The Serverless Framework (`https://serverless.com`) is an example of such a framework.

Complexity of designing many functions

Software systems that have a serverless architecture tend to consist of numerous functions and there is inherent complexity in designing many functions. It will take time to make decisions on the granularity of functions provided in the serverless architecture. A good design provides a balance between having too many functions and having functions that are too large and difficult to maintain.

There is complexity in chaining multiple functions together in order to execute complex transactions. The design must consider how it needs to handle a situation in which one function in a chain fails. For example, in the event of a failure, the system may need to execute compensating logic to cancel a transaction.

Not as many runtime optimizations

Serverless architectures do not allow for much in terms of runtime optimizations. In a traditional environment, optimizations might be made regarding memory, processors, disks, and the network. However, cloud providers can assist with optimizations for you.

Still immature

Standards and best practices for serverless architectures have not been as thoroughly established as other types of software architecture. However, some organizations and development teams do not mind using cutting-edge technology if they can use it to their advantage. As time passes, this will become less and less of an issue.

Taking a hybrid approach to serverless

Using a serverless architecture for a software system does not have to be an all or nothing approach. In addition to new applications fully leveraging serverless architecture, you may choose to design a part of your system with a serverless architecture and use a different architecture pattern for the other parts of your system.

For example, an organization may elect to take a hybrid approach and build some new features for an existing application in a serverless environment and use them with other architecture environments.

Function deployment

When functions are deployed in a serverless system, they go through a deployment pipeline. While the steps in the pipeline can vary depending on the cloud provider, there are some fundamental steps that typically take place.

Developers must first upload the function definition, which contains specifications about the function as well as the code. The specifications and metadata include things such as a unique identifier, name, description, version identifier, runtime language, resource requirements, execution timeout (the maximum time a function call can execute until it is terminated), created date/time, and last modified date/time. When a function is invoked, it is invoked for a specific function version. The version identifier is used to select an appropriate function instance.

The following illustration shows a typical function deployment pipeline:

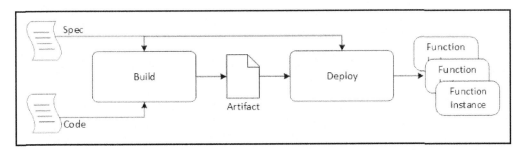

Along with the specification, the code itself and its dependencies must be provided (for example, as a ZIP file or a Dockerfile). If the code is stored in an external repository, the path of the code location along with the credentials required for access must be provided.

Once the functional definition has been uploaded to the cloud provider, the build process uses it for compilation to produce an artifact. The resultant artifact may be a binary file, a package, or a container image.

The starting of an instance function can be the result of **cold start** or **warm start**. With a warm start, one or more function instances have already been deployed and are ready to be executed when needed. A cold start takes longer since the function starts from an undeployed state. The function must be deployed and then executed when it is needed.

Function invocation

When functions are invoked, there are four main invocation methods that can be used to invoke a function:

- Synchronous request
- Asynchronous request
- Message stream
- Batch job

Synchronous request

When a client makes a synchronous request, it waits for a response. A request-reply pattern is used to handle synchronous requests. Examples of requests include an HTTP request or a gRPC call. The following diagram shows the flow of a synchronous request, which first goes through an API gateway:

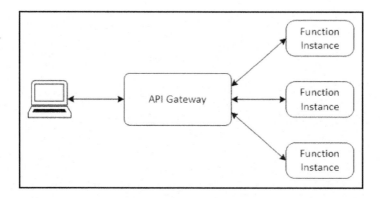

In order to locate a function instance, the API gateway will either use client-side service discovery or pass it on to a router (load balancer) for server-side service discovery. Once a service instance is located, the request is passed to it for processing. Once execution of the function is complete, the response is sent back to the client.

Asynchronous request (message queue)

When you want to process requests asynchronously, the publish-subscribe pattern can be used. Incoming requests are published to an *exchange*. Exchanges then distribute messages to one or more *queues* using rules called bindings. From there, function instances are invoked to process published messages:

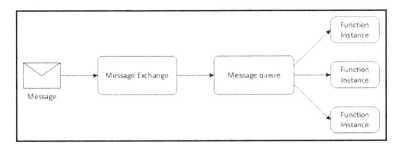

Examples of message queues include RabbitMQ, AWS Simple Notification Service, Message Queuing Telemetry Transport, and scheduled CRON jobs.

Message stream

When there is a need for real-time processing of messages, a message stream can be used. Message streams can ingest, buffer, and process large amounts of streaming data. When a new stream is created, it is typically partitioned into shards, with each shard going to a single worker (function instance) for processing:

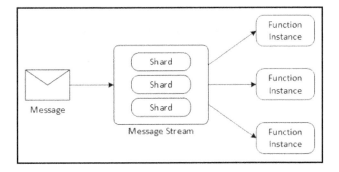

Examples of technologies for serverless message streams include AWS Kinesis, AWS DynamoDB Streams, and Apache Kafka.

Batch job

Batch jobs are placed in a job queue, either on-demand or based on a schedule. For the purpose of speeding up the execution of the jobs, the master/worker pattern can be used with jobs. The master/worker pattern, which is sometimes referred to as the master/slave pattern, speeds up jobs by splitting them up into smaller tasks so that the tasks can be processed in parallel.

The following diagram shows the processing of a job:

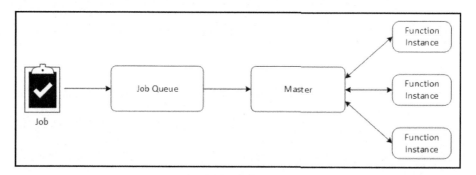

A component playing the role of **Master** splits the job (working set) up into tasks and launches workers. In this case, the workers are function instances and they can process tasks in parallel. Workers continue to pull from the working set until there are no more tasks to complete. The master gathers the results once the workers have all finished.

Cloud-native applications

Deploying a software application to the cloud does not make it cloud-native. It is about how the software is designed and implemented, not just where it is run. **Cloud-native applications** have been designed and developed from the ground up to be deployed in the cloud. In doing so, applications can take full advantage of their deployment environment.

In modern application development, the development team needs to have more knowledge about, and a vested interest in, how their application runs in production. Similarly, the operations team must be able to work with the development team to improve upon, over time, how the application is deployed and executes in a production environment.

Reasons to move to the cloud

In the early years of cloud computing, enterprises were hesitant to adopt cloud technologies within their IT organization. They had concerns such as losing control over their infrastructure, security, data risks, and reliability.

Since then, enterprises have increasingly relocated their IT workloads to the cloud. Many organizations have already done so or have plans to move their applications to the cloud. Major cloud providers, such as Amazon, Microsoft, and Google, are experiencing explosive growth and the competition between them is intensifying as more applications are deployed to the cloud.

There are a number of reasons that enterprises are moving their applications and data to the cloud.

Reducing costs

Cloud-based hosting reduces capital expenditure by eliminating the need to spend money on fixed assets such as hardware and software. It also reduces operational expenditure by lowering costs for such things as IT support staff and round-the-clock electricity needs for power and cooling.

Greater flexibility and scalability

Taking advantage of the cloud offers enterprises greater levels of flexibility. Workloads can scale up and down based on demand very quickly, even when large amounts of computing resources are suddenly needed. Large cloud providers have global scale. In addition to being able to deliver the right amount of compute resources at the right time, they can do so from the right geographic location.

Cloud computing allows businesses to grow relatively easily without having to make major adjustments to things such as the amount of hardware.

Automatic updates

The task of keeping infrastructure software up to date with the latest software and security updates is moved to the provider.

Updates to hardware are also taken care of by the cloud provider, including upgrades to servers, memory, processing power, and disk storage. Data centers are regularly updated with the latest generation of hardware, ensuring greater efficiency and faster performance.

Disaster recovery

Backup, disaster recovery, and business continuity are important concerns for software applications. Cloud computing provides these services easily and with less expense than doing it on your own.

For smaller businesses, the additional expense for disaster recovery can be burdensome. The option of deploying applications to the cloud has made it easier for even small businesses to have full backup and recovery capabilities in the event of a disaster.

What are cloud-native applications?

Cloud-native applications are specifically designed for the cloud model. Applications designed for the cloud are able to take advantage of it as their target platform, providing organizations with a competitive advantage, greater agility, easier deployment, on-demand scalability, reduced costs, increased resilience, and other benefits.

The expectations of today's modern applications are different from those of the past. Cloud-native applications have some distinct characteristics that allow us to meet those expectations and requirements. The **Cloud Native Computing Foundation (CNCF)** currently defines cloud-native as using an open source software stack to make applications that are containerized, dynamically orchestrated, and microservices-oriented.

Containerized

Containers are a way of packaging a software application. They are lightweight, stand-alone packages of software. The application, along with all of its libraries and dependencies, is bundled together in an immutable package.

The concept of containers for software is similar to the concept of using physical containers in the shipping industry. Prior to standardizing shipping containers, shipping could be an inefficient and complicated process. A wide variety of things in all shapes and sizes can be transported on the same cargo ship. Now that there are standardized shipping container sizes, we know what and how much will fit on a container ship, no matter what we are shipping.

Similarly, packaging your software with its dependencies in a container based on open standards allows us to know that it can be run anywhere that supports containers. It provides us with predictability in that we know the software will work as expected because the container is the same, no matter where it is executed. It eliminates the experience of having an application not execute properly on one machine only to have someone else on a different machine claim that *it runs on my machine*. Unexpected errors because of differences between machines and environments can be drastically reduced or even eliminated.

In a cloud-native application, each part of the system is packaged in its own container. This allows each part to be reproducible and allows resources to be isolated for each container.

Dynamically orchestrated

Making your application containerized is not enough. A cloud-native application will need the ability to run multiple containers across multiple machines. That is what will allow you to use microservices and to provide the fault tolerance capabilities.

Once you have multiple containers running on different machines, you will need to dynamically orchestrate them. The system must start the correct container at the right time, be able to scale containers by adding and removing them based on demand, and launch containers on different machines in the event of a failure.

There are a number of container clustering and orchestration tools available. Currently, the most popular is Kubernetes, which is sometimes referred to as K8S because there are eight letters in between the *K* and the *S*. It is an open source orchestrator that was originally developed by Google. Other container orchestration tools besides Kubernetes include Docker Swarm and Apache Mesos.

Cloud providers also have cloud-based container services. There is **Amazon Elastic Container Service** (**Amazon ECS**), which is Amazon's own container-orchestration service for **Amazon Web Services** (**AWS**). In addition to ECS, Amazon offers **Amazon Elastic Container Service for Kubernetes** (**Amazon EKS**), which is a managed service for Kubernetes on AWS. Amazon also offers AWS Fargate, which is a technology that can be used for Amazon ECS and EKS that lets you run containers without having to manage servers or clusters.

Microsoft's **Azure Container Service** (**AKS**) allows you to use a fully managed Kubernetes container orchestration service or select an alternative orchestrator such as unmanaged Kubernetes, Docker, or Mesosphere DC/OS. Google offers Google Kubernetes Engine, which is a managed environment for Kubernetes.

Microservices-oriented

A cloud-native application should be partitioned into microservices. Dividing an application into small, autonomous, independently versioned, and self-contained services increases organizational agility and the maintainability of the application.

No downtime

Applications today are expected to be available at all times, with no downtime. It has always been a goal to minimize downtime, but the days when it was acceptable to have a small maintenance window in which an application was not available are over.

Complex software systems will have failures and should be designed to expect failures to occur. Cloud-native applications are *designed for failure* and keep fault tolerance in mind so that they can recover rapidly and minimize downtime. If a physical server fails unexpectedly or is taken down as part of planned maintenance, a failover system will redirect traffic to a different server. Software components should be designed so that they are loosely coupled, such that if one fails, a redundant component can take over.

A single failure should not have the effect of bringing down the entire software system. For example, if an instance of a microservice fails, other instances can take incoming requests. If all instances of a particular microservice are not operational, the fault is isolated to only a portion of the system, so that the entire system does not fail.

Continuous delivery

Increasing competition and user expectations mean modern applications have shorter release cycles. Rather than having major releases that are months (or even years) apart, the ability to have application updates on a more regular basis (think weeks or days rather than months) is a necessity.

Cloud-native applications should release software updates rapidly. Shorter release cycles provide an opportunity to get feedback from users more quickly. Rather than having to wait a long period of time to receive feedback, continuous delivery gives us a much tighter feedback loop. The development team can respond more rapidly to users by using the feedback received to make adjustments and improve the software.

Cloud-native applications increase organizational agility. By releasing the software and receiving feedback regularly, an organization can respond to the market, competitors, and the needs of their customers quickly. This can give an organization a competitive advantage.

Support for a variety of devices

Cloud-native applications must be able to support a variety of devices. Users of modern applications use mobile devices, desktop machines, tablets, and other devices. They expect a unified experience across devices as well as the ability to seamlessly switch between devices. In order to provide this type of support, cloud-native applications ensure that backend services are able to provide the functionality that a variety of frontend devices need.

With the IoT, many other devices are now connected, which means that some applications will be required to support them. To handle a potentially large number of devices and the volume of data that they produce, highly distributed systems designed with a cloud-native approach are required.

Twelve-factor apps

The **twelve-factor app methodology** is a set of principles that can be followed when developing applications to be deployed to the cloud. It was originally written by the creators of Heroku, which is a popular cloud platform.

The principles of the twelve-factor app methodology can be used to design and develop cloud-native applications. An application that follows this methodology adheres to certain constraints and conforms to a *contract*. This gives it a level of predictability that facilitates deployment to the cloud. These factors make scaling easier, maximize portability, and ensure that the application can be continuously deployed.

In his book *The Twelve-Factor App*, Adam Wiggins describes the twelve factors as follows:

- **Codebase**: One codebase tracked in revision control, many deployments
- **Dependencies**: Explicitly declare and isolate dependencies
- **Configuration**: Store configuration in the environment
- **Backing Services**: Treat backing services as attached resources
- **Build, release, run**: Strictly separate the build and run stages
- **Processes**: Execute the app as one or more stateless processes
- **Port binding**: Export services via port binding
- **Concurrency**: Scale out via the process model
- **Disposability**: Maximize robustness with fast startup and graceful shutdown
- **Development/production parity**: Keep development, staging, and production as similar as possible
- **Logs**: Treat logs as event streams

- **Administrative processes**: Run admin/management tasks as one-off processes

In this section, let's explore the twelve tenets of a twelve-factor app in further detail.

Codebase

A cloud-native application should have one, and only one, codebase. Larger software systems may need to be decomposed into multiple applications, each of which should be treated as a separate application with their own codebase.

Each codebase should be tracked in a version control system and can be used for multiple deployments of the application. For example, a single codebase could be deployed to the development, QA, staging, and production environments:

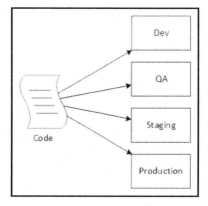

Dependencies

Dependencies for the application should be explicitly declared and isolated. A cloud-native application should not rely on the implicit existence of dependencies. No assumptions should be made as to what will be available in the execution environment, so applications should bring their dependencies with them and declare their dependencies both precisely and completely. The details of the dependencies should also include the specific version that is needed for each dependency.

Most modern programming languages and frameworks provide a way for an application to manage its dependencies. Sometimes these dependencies come in the form of a *package*, which is a distribution of software consisting of files typically bundled together in some type of archive file. A *package manager* is sometimes available, which is a tool that can help to install, upgrade, configure, and remove packages.

Configuration

An application's configuration consists of values that can vary across deployments, such as database connection information, URLs for web services, and SMTP server information for emails.

The configuration for a cloud-native application should be stored in the environment and not in the application code. The configuration will vary depending on the type of deployment (for example, whether the deployment is to development, staging, or production), while the code will not. There should be a strict separation between an application's code and its configuration.

Backing services

A *backing service* is any service that the application uses over the network that is separate from the application itself. Examples of a backing service include a data store, a distributed caching system, an SMTP server, an FTP server, and a messaging/queuing system.

The binding for each service should be stored in a configuration that is external to the application. The application should not care where the backing services are running and should not make any distinction between local and third-party services.

All backing services should be treated as attached resources, and the application should be able to attach and detach backing services without any code changes. For example, if a database goes down, it should be possible to detach it and attach a different database from a backup without making any code changes.

Build/Release/Run

Cloud-native applications should strictly separate the build, release, and run stages. The build stage is where the code is converted into an executable bundle. An application's declared dependencies are considered during this stage.

The result of the build stage is a *build*:

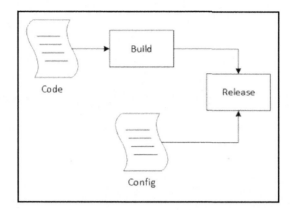

In the release stage, the build is combined with configuration information that is external to the application and it is deployed to a cloud environment. One build can be used for multiple deployments. The result of the release stage is an immutable artifact called a *release*. Each release should have a unique identifier, using a versioning scheme or a timestamp.

Once there is a release, in the run stage, also known as *runtime*, the application is executed in its environment. By the time the build and release tasks are complete, the run stage should be relatively uneventful and the application should simply work.

Processes

A cloud-native application should consist of one or more stateless processes, with any persisted data being stored using a backing service. The processes of an application following the twelve-factor app methodology are stateless and do not share anything. Adhering to this rule will allow your application to be more robust and to scale more easily.

For example, in order for a web application to be a cloud-native application, it should not rely on *sticky sessions*. Sticky sessions are where a router/load balancer can assign a single server to a particular user so that subsequent requests from the same user will be routed to the same server. Among other things, this could allow caching user session data in the memory of the application's process, with the expectation that subsequent requests from the same user will be routed to the same process and have access to the cached data. Instead of using sticky sessions, a cloud-native application should cache by some other means, such as using a distributed caching system like Redis or Memcached.

Port binding

Cloud-native applications are completely self-contained. Services should make themselves available to other services by specified ports. Similar to any backing services your application may be using, the API you expose may be the backing service for another application. This allows one app to be the backing service of another app.

Just as accessing a backing service should be achievable through a simple binding, such as a URL, other applications should be able to interface with your applications through a simple binding.

Concurrency

A software application consists of one or more processes and a cloud-native application treats processes as first-class citizens. Examples include a web process to handle HTTP requests and a worker process to handle an asynchronous background task.

The idea is that by running multiple processes for an application, it can run independently and concurrently. This allows a cloud-native application to scale out horizontally as needed.

Disposability

The processes of a cloud-native application should be disposable so that they can be started or stopped at any time. Processes should be designed so that they start up as quickly as possible and are able to shut down gracefully.

Cloud-native applications should be robust against crashing. In the event that an application does crash, it should have the ability to start back up without requiring extra effort. Applications with these qualities related to disposability allow for elastic scaling by the cloud provider as well as quick deployment of code and/or configuration changes. If the startup times for the processes of a cloud-native application are too slow, it can lead to lower levels of availability during periods of high-volume traffic.

Development/production parity

Cloud-native applications should minimize differences between development and production as much as possible. Gaps between different environments include differences in the tools and backing services used (including any differences in the versions), the time between when something is coded and when it is released, and the fact that different people may code the application versus deploy it.

Differences between development and production environments may cause issues to go undetected until the software is in production. One way to eliminate these differences and attain development/production parity is through the use of containers. Earlier in this chapter, we discussed containers and how they are used to bundle an application, along with all of its dependencies, into an immutable package. This container can then be executed anywhere, including development, staging, and production environments. Containers give us predictability because we know that the application will work in an identical way across the different environments.

Logs

Logs give development and operations staff visibility into the application, its behavior, and its exceptions. Logs are an important part of an application and will be discussed further in Chapter 9, *Cross-Cutting Concerns*.

Cloud-native applications should not be responsible for the routing and storage of its output stream. Rather than writing to or managing log files, each process should treat logs as event streams and simply write its event stream to **standard output (stdout)** and **standard error (stderr)**.

In a development environment, developers can view the stream to gain insight into the application's behavior. In a production environment, the stream should be captured by the execution environment and then routed to its final destination. For instance, the stream could be handled by a log management tool and persisted to a data store.

By following this guideline, cloud-native applications can dynamically scale to any number of machines and not be concerned with aggregating all of the log information. In addition, the method by which log information is stored and processed can be changed without any modification to the application itself.

Administrative processes

Periodically, there will be reasons that administrative tasks will need to be executed. Examples include a database migration, cleaning up bad data, or executing analytics for a report. When these needs arise, they should be executed as one-off processes in an identical environment as production. This means the scripts need to run against the same code and the same configuration as any other process executed using that release.

Administrative/management scripts for one-off tasks should be committed to the same code repository as the rest of the application and should ship with the rest of the code in order to maintain consistency and avoid synchronization issues between environments.

Summary

Software applications today have expectations and requirements that are different from the past. There are demands for greater availability, flexibility, fault tolerance, scalability, and reliability. Continuous delivery and ease of deployment may be requirements for organizations that want to increase their agility in order to keep their software applications closely aligned with their business goals and market opportunities. We examined how MSA, serverless architecture, and cloud-native applications can meet these types of demands and requirements.

In the next chapter, we will take a look at cross-cutting concerns. Most software applications have common functionality that is needed throughout the application, including in different layers of the application. This functionality is called **cross-cutting concerns**, and we will take a look at different types of crosscutting concerns and how to take them into consideration during design and development.

Cross-Cutting Concerns **9**

All software applications have various concerns, which are groupings of logic and functionality. Some of that functionality, known as cross-cutting concerns, is used in multiple areas of the application.

In this chapter, we will explore cross-cutting concerns and some general guidelines for handling them. We will take a look at different ways to implement them, including using **dependency injection (DI)**, the decorator pattern, and **aspect-oriented programming (AOP)**.

We'll go over some examples of cross-cutting concerns as well as some of the special considerations that should be made when dealing with cross-cutting concerns within microservices.

In this chapter, we will cover the following topics:

- Cross-cutting concerns
- General guidelines for cross-cutting concerns
- Implementing cross-cutting concerns with the use of DI and the decorator pattern
- Aspect-oriented programming
- Taking a look at various types of cross-cutting concerns
- Cross-cutting concerns for microservices, including the use of a microservice chassis and the sidecar pattern

Cross-cutting concerns

In a software system, a *concern* is a grouping of logic or functionality that the application is providing. The concerns of the system reflect the requirements. When designing a system, software architects should seek to follow the **Separation of Concerns (SoC)** principle, which was described in Chapter 6, *Software Development Principles and Practices*. It is a design principle that seeks to reduce complexity by dividing the software system so that concerns are kept separate.

There are two main types of concerns in a software system:

- **Core concern**: It represents functionality that is fundamental to the system and is a primary reason as to why the software is being written. For example, the logic related to the calculation of employee salaries and bonuses would be core concerns of a human resource management system. The logic for each core concern is typically localized to particular components.
- **Cross-cutting concern**: It is an aspect of the application that relies on and affects other concerns. It is functionality that is used in multiple areas, possibly spanning multiple layers of the application. Examples of cross-cutting concerns include security, logging, caching, and error handling. The logic for each cross-cutting concern is needed among multiple components.

In the following diagram, various core concerns are depicted, represented by **Module A**, **Module B**, and **Module C**. You can also see the cross-cutting concerns, which intersect the core concerns:

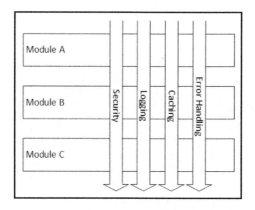

General guidelines for cross-cutting concerns

There are some general guidelines that we can follow when designing solutions for the cross-cutting concerns that we need in our applications.

Identifying cross-cutting concerns

As an initial step, software architects must be able to identify the cross-cutting concerns. By recognizing common functionality across modules and layers of the system, we can consider how concerns can be abstracted so that they are not duplicated. In some cases, the common functionality is identical among its different usages, while in others, refactoring may be involved to make the logic generic enough to be reusable.

Using open-source and third-party solutions

Once cross-cutting concerns have been identified, implementations must be provided for them. Software architects should consider solutions that have already been developed, such as open-source or third-party solutions, to satisfy the needs of cross-cutting concerns. Prior to spending resources developing an in-house solution, a capable solution may already exist. For example, for a logging cross-cutting concern, there is no reason to reinvent the wheel when frameworks exist that provide all of the functionality that you need.

Maintaining consistency

When satisfying the needs of cross-cutting concerns, software architects should ensure that each concern is implemented consistently. The cross-cutting concern should behave in a consistent way in each place that it is needed. This is one of the reasons why the implementation of a cross-cutting concern should not be duplicated in more than one place.

Avoiding scattered solutions

When implementing cross-cutting concerns, we want to avoid simply adding the functionality to each consuming class that needs it. This approach is called *scattering* since the implementation is scattered throughout the application. As a software architect, you will want to ensure that developers are not simply copying and pasting logic that they need in multiple places.

When an implementation for a cross-cutting concern is scattered because it is spread out among multiple modules, it violates the **Don't Repeat Yourself** (DRY) principle. Code must be duplicated in order to provide the functionality of the concern in multiple places. Code duplication is wasteful, makes it more difficult to maintain consistency, increases complexity, and needlessly makes the codebase larger. These qualities all make maintenance more difficult. If the logic that is duplicated needs to be modified, changes will need to be made in multiple places.

Avoiding tangled solutions

When logic for a cross-cutting concern is mixed with logic for a different concern (either a core concern or another cross-cutting concern), it is known as *tangling* because the logic for disparate concerns is tangled together.

An implementation that is tangled is likely in violation of the separation of concerns principle and tends to suffer from low cohesion. Mixing concerns increases the complexity of the software and reduces its quality. It lowers maintainability because changes to both core and cross-cutting concerns are made more difficult.

When designing the solution for a cross-cutting concern, we want to avoid tangling. Part of accomplishing that is to make the logic for the cross-cutting concern loosely coupled with the code that needs it. Cross-cutting concerns should not be tightly coupled with other concerns so that all concerns can be easily maintained and modified.

Another principle that we should follow in order to avoid a tangled solution is the **Single Responsibility Principle** (SRP). A class should be responsible for one thing and do that one thing well. If it is responsible for a core concern, such as some piece of business functionality, it should not also be responsible for implementing a cross-cutting concern. A responsibility is a reason to change and a class should have only one reason to change.

A class responsible for a core concern should not need to be modified if we want to change the implementation of a cross-cutting concern that it uses. Similarly, the implementation of a cross-cutting concern should not need to be modified if we need to change the implementation of a class that uses it.

Avoiding a tangled solution also allows us to adhere to the **Open/Closed Principle** (**OCP**), which states that software components should be open for extension but closed for modification. When we want to add cross-cutting concerns to business functionality, we should have the ability to do so by extending the component with new code without being required to modify the existing business logic.

Implementing cross-cutting concerns

Implementations should follow the design goals of cross-cutting concerns by maintaining consistency, not being scattered, and not being tangled. There are several different approaches that can be taken when implementing cross-cutting concerns. These include DI, the decorator pattern, and AOP.

Using dependency injection (DI)

One approach to handling cross-cutting concerns is to use the DI pattern, which we covered in Chapter 6, *Software Development Principles and Practices*. This pattern can be used to inject cross-cutting dependencies into classes that need them. This allows us to write loosely coupled code and avoid scattering. The logic for the cross-cutting concern will not be duplicated in multiple places.

For example, if we had an Order class that had logging and caching cross-cutting concerns, we could inject them like this:

```
public class Order
{
    private readonly ILogger _logger;
    private readonly ICache _cache;

    public Order(ILogger logger, ICache cache)
    {
        if (logger == null)
            throw new ArgumentNullException(nameof(logger));
        if (cache == null)
            throw new ArgumentNullException(nameof(cache));

        _logger = logger;
```

```
        _cache = cache;
    }
}
```

By eliminating hard-coded dependencies of cross-cutting concerns through the use of DI, it also provides us with the ability to change the implementation of a cross-cutting concern, either at runtime or compile-time. We may want to use a different implementation for a cross-cutting concern at runtime based on something such as a configuration setting. As long as we have a common interface that is used by each implementation, this approach would allow us to change the implementation without having to recompile and redeploy the application.

Using DI for cross-cutting concerns also increases the testability of the application. Any code that has a cross-cutting concern is dependent on the abstraction of that concern, not the concrete implementation, which allows us to mock the dependencies in our unit tests.

However, there are some disadvantages to this approach. It does require you to inject dependencies for cross-cutting concerns everywhere that you need them. While this makes it consistent with how you may be approaching other dependencies, some cross-cutting concerns are needed in many places (for example, logging), and it may become tedious to inject it in all of the places that need it.

Although this approach eliminates scattering, it does not eliminate tangling. If you take this approach, you will have cross-cutting logic mixed in with your other logic. In the preceding order class, code that uses the logging and cache objects that were injected in the constructor will be located throughout the Order class, mixed with logic for other concerns.

Using the decorator pattern

Another approach to implementing cross-cutting concerns is to use the **decorator pattern**. The decorator pattern can add behaviors dynamically to an object, including behaviors for cross-cutting concerns. It is essentially like creating a wrapper to handle a cross-cutting concern around some other object. The following diagram shows the decorator pattern:

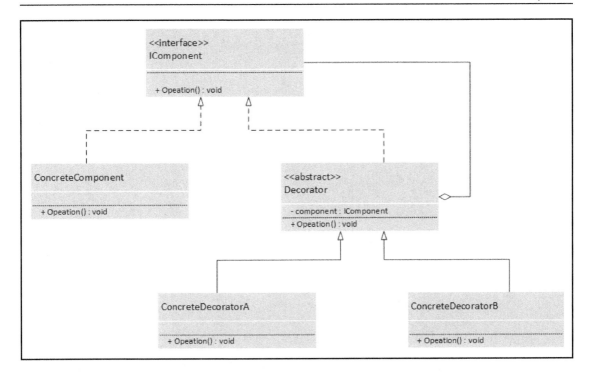

In the preceding diagram, the **ConcreteComponent** class implements the **IComponent** interface and is a class that can either be used on its own or wrapped in one or more decorators. The **Decorator** class is an abstract class that also implements the **IComponent** interface and wraps (has a reference to) the component. Each concrete decorator class inherits from the **Decorator** class and adds its behavior.

For example, let's say we have an `IAccountService` interface with a `Save` method and an `AccountService` concrete component that implements that interface:

```
public interface IAccountService
{
    void Save(IAccount account);
}

public class AccountService : IAccountService
{
    public void Save(IAccount account)
    {
        // Save logic
    }
}
```

The `Save` method in the `AccountService` class only contains logic related to the save (represented by the `Save logic` code comment) and does not contain logic for any cross-cutting concern.

An abstract decorator class can be created that also implements the `IAccountService` interface and will wrap the `AccountService` class. You may notice that we are also using DI in conjunction with the decorator pattern:

```
public abstract class AccountServiceDecorator : IAccountService
{
    protected readonly IAccountService _accountService;

    public AccountServiceDecorator(IAccountService accountService)
    {
        _accountService = accountService;
    }

    public virtual void Save(IAccount account)
    {
        _accountService.Save(account);
    }
}
```

We can now create concrete decorators for the account service. The following is one for logging:

```
public class LoggingAccountService : AccountServiceDecorator
{
    private readonly ILogger _logger;

    public LoggingAccountService(IAccountService accountService,
        ILogger logger)
        : base (accountService)
    {
        _logger = logger;
    }

    public override void Save(IAccount account)
    {
        _accountService.Save(account);
        _logger.LogInfo($"Saved account: {account.Number}");
    }
}
```

We can also make one for caching:

```
public class CachingAccountService : AccountServiceDecorator
{
    private readonly ICache _cache;

    public CachingAccountService(IAccountService accountService,
        ICache cache)
        : base(accountService)
    {
        _cache = cache;
    }

    public override void Save(IAccount account)
    {
        _accountService.Save(account);
        _cache.Put(account.Number.ToString(), account.Name);
    }
}
```

The concrete decorator classes, LoggingAccountService and CachingAccountService, contain logic for the cross-cutting concern for which they are responsible. This logic can occur either before or after the logic of the core concern. One challenge with this approach is the fact that you may want to execute cross-cutting logic, not just before or after core logic, but also in the middle of the core logic. One way around this is to make your methods smaller so that there are additional points where cross-cutting logic can be executed.

The fact that the concrete decorator classes all implement the IAccountService interface (through their decorator parent class), means that we can have an instance of the account service that contains logic for multiple cross-cutting concerns. For example:

```
IAccountService accountService = new AccountService();
IAccountService loggingAccountService =
    new LoggingAccountService(accountService, logger);
IAccountService cachingAndLoggingAccountService =
    new CachingAccountService(loggingAccountService, cache);
```

The instance of the account service being held by the `cachingAndLoggingAccountService` variable has been decorated with both logging and caching functionality. The account service has been wrapped by multiple decorators:

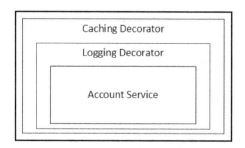

As with other types of dependencies, a DI container can handle dependency chains for you so that when you want a concrete instance of `IAccountService`, you will receive one that has been decorated with all of the cross-cutting concerns, without having to do the wiring up yourself.

Using the decorator pattern in conjunction with DI will allow you to write logic for the cross-cutting concerns that are neither scattered nor tangled with other logic. However, it does require you to create the decorator classes. For any cross-cutting concerns that are needed in many classes, large software systems will require a large number of decorators to be created. This work can be tedious and repetitive, although some of the code could be generated automatically through code generation.

In addition to DI and the decorator pattern, another approach to handling cross-cutting concerns that you can consider is to use AOP in your project.

Aspect-oriented programming

Aspect-oriented programming (AOP) is a paradigm that was created to handle the scattering and tangling of boilerplate code in **object-oriented programming (OOP)**, such as the code necessary for cross-cutting concerns. Gregor Kiczales and other researchers at Xerox PARC, which is now known as PARC, a Xerox company, did the original research on the topic. They eventually wrote a paper, *AOP*, in which they described a solution for handling cross-cutting concerns.

In order to gain an understanding of AOP, let's take a look at some of its fundamental concepts, as follows:

- **Aspect**: The aspect is the modularization of a concern that cuts across multiple areas of the application. It is the logic for the cross-cutting concern itself, such as logging or caching.
- **Join point**: A join point is a location in between logical steps of your program, such as after your program starts, before/after creating an object, before/after calling a method, and before the program ends.
- **Pointcut**: A pointcut is a set of join points. They can be fairly simple or rather complex. Examples of simple pointcuts include before/after any object is created or before/after any method is called within a class. An example of a complex pointcut is after any public method in a particular class except for the add, update, and delete methods. As you can imagine, there is quite a bit of flexibility in defining pointcuts.
- **Advice**: The advice is the code that actually performs the cross-cutting concern. In the case of logging, it would be the statements that perform actions, such as writing to the log.

Types of advice

There are different types of advice that are typically supported by AOP tools:

- **Before advice (on start)**: Before advice executes before a join point. It cannot prevent the flow of logic proceeding on to the join point.
- **After returning advice (on success)**: After-returning advice executes after a join point has completed successfully (no exception was thrown).
- **After throwing advice (on error)**: After-throwing advice executes if an exception occurred in the method.
- **After advice (finally)**: After advice executes after a join point exits, whether the method completed successfully or an exception occurred.
- **Around advice**: Around advice surrounds a join point so that it can execute logic before and after a method is invoked. It also has the ability to prevent a method from executing by either returning its own value or throwing an exception.

Weaving

Weaving is the process of applying the advice (logic for the cross-cutting concern) to the logic of the core concern. Code for each cross-cutting concern is placed in a single location, making it easy to maintain and modify the various aspects. If changes need to be made to the advice of a cross-cutting concern, they can be made in a single place. For example, if we need to change the logic for logging, it can be done in one place rather than in all of the core concerns that use logging.

Once the advice for a cross-cutting concern has been established, weaving combines it with the logic of various core concerns wherever it is needed. In the following diagram, the `Employee` class represents some logic for a core concern. The `LoggingAspect` class represents the advice. The logic is combined (weaved) together to form the result:

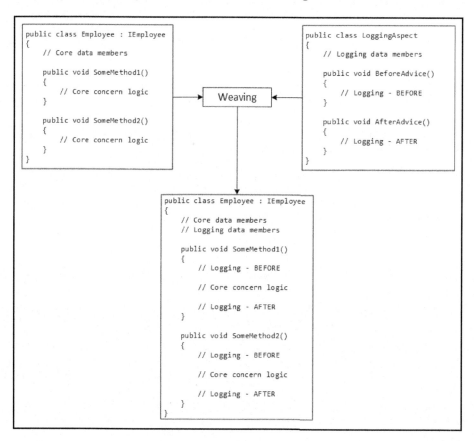

Before a class can be used, weaving must take place to combine its logic with the logic for all of the different cross-cutting concerns that the class uses. AOP tools either perform weaving at compile-time or at runtime.

Compile-time weaving

AOP tools that employ *compile-time weaving* perform an additional step to attach aspects after a program is compiled. A program is first compiled as it normally is, resulting in a DLL or EXE. Once the program has been compiled, it is run through a post-compilation process. This process is handled by a post-processor that is provided with an AOP tool.

The post-processor takes the DLL or EXE and adds the aspects to it. Using configuration, the post-processor knows where to apply the advice, such as before a method is executed or when an exception is thrown. The resulting **DLL/EXE** has both the logic for the core concern and all of the advice:

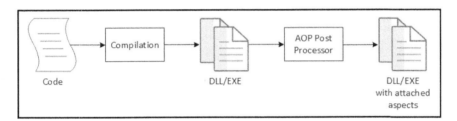

One of the benefits of compile-time weaving is that there is no overhead during runtime to perform the weaving. However, because the aspects are weaved at compile-time, you will not be able to change them at runtime through configuration.

Runtime weaving

Runtime weaving does not take place until after the application starts executing. The advice for an aspect and the code that it will be applied to are both instantiated at runtime. Unlike the compile-time weaving approach, no post-compilation changes are made to binaries.

The way that runtime weaving works is similar to the decorator pattern that was described in the *Using the decorator pattern* section that appeared earlier in this chapter. The main difference is the fact that an AOP tool can generate the decorator classes at runtime without requiring developers to manually create them beforehand. The AOP tool generates a proxy object dynamically, which implements the same interface as the target object and can delegate to the target object while weaving the advice with the core logic.

An advantage of runtime weaving is that there is no post-compilation process involved. The machine that is compiling the application, whether it is a development machine or a build server, will not require extra software (a post-processor from an AOP tool) to complete the compilation. Runtime weaving also affords you the flexibility of configuring aspects so that they can be changed at runtime. The disadvantage of runtime weaving is that, unlike compile-time weaving, there is some amount of overhead involved at runtime to perform the weaving.

Types of cross-cutting concerns

There are a variety of different types of cross-cutting concerns that may be part of a software application. This is by no means an exhaustive list, but some common examples of cross-cutting concerns include the following:

- Caching
- Configuration management
- Auditing
- Security
- Exception management
- Logging

Caching

Leveraging the use of caching in a software application is a common way to improve performance. It may be used in a variety of places where data is being read, making it a cross-cutting concern for the application.

A reusable caching service should provide the ability to perform operations, such as putting data in a cache, getting data out of a cache, and setting policies on how and when cached data will expire.

When designing a software system, software architects must make a decision on the type of caching that the system will use. The two main types of server-side caching are an in-process cache and a distributed cache. With an in-process cache, the cache is local to the application instance. Load balanced applications will have multiple instances of the application, each of which will have their own in-process cache. A distributed cache offers a single logical view of the cache even when there are application instances on multiple servers.

We will be examining the use of caching further in Chapter 10, *Performance Considerations*.

Configuration management

Configuration management involves deciding what options for a software application should be made configurable and how that configuration will be stored, protected, and modified. In order to provide flexibility in how your application behaves and give it the ability to run in a variety of environments, configuration options should be made available. These options should be made external to the application so that they can be modified without requiring recompilation of the application.

A software application needs to be deployed and used in multiple environments, such as development, testing, staging, and production. In addition, it may use a number of different infrastructures and third-party services. Examples include a database, a service registry, a message broker, an email (SMTP) server, a payment processing service, and a message broker. Different environments may require different configuration values for these various services.

Externalizing the configuration settings allows us to use our application in different ways and in different environments without having to change application code and recompile the application.

It also makes deploying the application to a cloud environment easier. If you recall from Chapter 8, *Architecting Modern Applications*, one of the factors in the twelve-factor app methodology is to ensure that there is a strict separation between an application's code and its configuration.

As a software architect, you should consider which settings need to be configurable in your application. Only the settings that need to be configurable should be made available for modification. Including unnecessary configuration options can lead to an application having an excessive amount of settings, which will only make it more difficult to use and understand. Software applications with overly complex configuration increase the likelihood of incorrect configuration, which can lead to the application not working properly or can make the application vulnerable to security breaches.

A release of a software application is an immutable package, whether that software is being deployed on its own server, on a **virtual machine (VM)**, or on a container image. However, that immutable package needs to have the ability to be deployed in different environments. Externalizing the configuration will give you that ability.

Auditing

A cross-cutting concern of many software applications is the auditing of data changing operations. There may be requirements to maintain an audit trail that includes information about a data change, such as the date/time that it occurred and the identity of the individual who made the change.

There may be a requirement to record information about the nature of a particular data change, such as the old and new values. In event-driven systems, persisting events and their details can serve as the audit trail.

Security

Security is a significant cross-cutting concern. It includes the authentication of users and the authorization of the operations the user can perform with the software application. Once a user is authenticated and their identity is known, their authorization must be checked in order to determine which operations they are capable of executing within the application.

We will be examining security-related topics, including authentication and authorization, in Chapter 11, *Security Considerations*.

Exception management

An exception is a type of error that occurs during program execution that we expect may happen. They are issues that are known to occur and an application can be designed to recognize and handle them.

Exceptions can occur for a variety of reasons. Some examples include attempting to use a null object reference, attempting to access an array using an index that is out of range, exceeding a specified timeout, being unable to write to a file, or the inability to connect to a database. Many programming languages provide ways to handle exceptions and transfer the flow of execution to a different part of the logic. For example, in the C# language, we can use try/catch/finally statements to handle exceptions.

Ineffective exception management makes it more difficult to diagnose and resolve issues with the application. A failure to handle exceptions properly can also lead to security issues. Exception management should be treated as a cross-cutting concern and a centralized exception management approach should be designed for the application. A software application should have consistency in terms of how exceptions and errors are handled.

Common boilerplate code to perform operations such as the logging of exceptions (logging is its own cross-cutting concern) and communicating the fact that an exception occurred back to the user can be handled in a centralized and consistent way. When logging and communicating exception details, sensitive information should not be revealed. All exceptions should be logged as the information may be helpful in resolving an issue. When exceptions are logged, any additional details, such as contextual information, should be added to make the information more useful.

A good exception management strategy should also take into consideration unhandled exceptions and design a way to deal with them. Failures in the application should not leave it in an unstable state or corrupt data.

Logging

Logging is an important part of software applications, allowing you to know what your code did when it was executed. It provides you with the ability to see when things execute as expected and, perhaps more importantly, assists you in diagnosing problems when they do not. The availability of logs can really help you to troubleshoot application issues.

Common characteristics of log entries include the following:

- **Date/time**: It is imperative to know when the event took place
- **Source**: We want to know the source/location of the event
- **Log Level/Severity**: It is helpful to know the level/severity of the log entry
- **Message**: Log entries should have some sort of description or detail explaining the log entry

Understanding log levels

Most logging frameworks support the ability to specify a log level or the severity of each log entry that is created. Although the log levels vary depending on the framework used, some common log levels include the following:

- **TRACE**: Use this level for *tracing* the code, such as being able to see when execution flow enters and exits specific methods.
- **DEBUG**: This level records diagnostic details that can be helpful during debugging. It can be used to make note of when certain aspects of the logic are completed successfully. It can also provide details such as executed queries and session information, which can be used in determining the cause of an issue.

- **INFO**: This level is for logging details about normal operations during the execution of logic. It is common for INFO to be a default log level. It is for useful information that you want to have but typically won't spend much time examining under normal circumstances.
- **WARN**: When you have a situation in which incorrect behavior takes place, but the application can continue, it can be logged at the Warn level.
- **ERROR**: Use this level for exceptions and problems that caused an operation to fail.
- **FATAL**: This level is reserved for the most severe errors, such as those that may cause the shutdown of the system or data corruption.

Logging frameworks typically allow you to configure the level at which logging will take place, such as being able to specify a minimum log level. For example, if the minimum log level is configured as Info, then logging will take place for the log levels of INFO, WARN, ERROR, and FATAL.

A detailed log level, such as TRACE, is not typically used for sustained periods, particularly for a production environment. This is due to the high volume of detailed entries that will be produced, which can degrade performance and excessively use up disk and bandwidth resources. However, when diagnosing an issue, being able to change the log level to DEBUG or TRACE temporarily can provide valuable information.

Routing log entries

Many logging frameworks provide functionality that allows you to configure routing rules for log entries. These may be based on the log level, the source, or some combination of criteria. Log entries can then be set up to target different destinations. Some examples of destinations for log entries include the console, text files, databases, email, and the Windows Event Log.

Writing logs to text files on local disks has been a common practice, but when your application is running on many different servers, it becomes difficult to search through all of the files without the use of tools. This issue is further exacerbated when your application is running in the cloud. Given the elasticity provided by hosting your application in the cloud, the number of servers running your application at any given time and their location are dynamic.

As was mentioned in Chapter 8, *Architecting Modern Applications*, cloud-native applications should simply treat their log as event streams and should not be responsible for the routing and storage of those streams. Instead of writing to a log file, it should write event streams to **standard output (stdout)** and **standard error (stderr)**. Your application may scale out to any number of machines, and no assumptions should be made as to where your application will run or where log information will be stored. You can either leverage services that your cloud provider makes available to aggregate and store log information, or you can provide your own implementation.

Using Elastic Stack

One of the solutions to centralizing your logging functionality so that log information can be consolidated and managed is the Elastic Stack. The Elastic Stack is an integrated solution of open-source products that offer a highly scalable end-to-end solution for aggregating, searching, analyzing, and visualizing logging data.

It was formerly known as (and you may still hear it referred to as) the ELK stack, an acronym that represents the solution's use of the **Elasticsearch**, **Logstash**, and **Kibana** products. A data shipper product named **Beats**, which is part of Elastic Stack, was not part of the original ELK stack. One type of data shipper within Beats is **Filebeat**, which can be used for text log files.

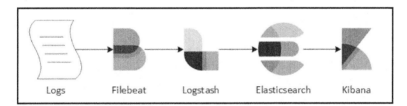

Logs → Filebeat → Logstash → Elasticsearch → Kibana

Elasticsearch

Elasticsearch is an open-source, distributed search engine and document database that can store, search, and analyze data. Among its many uses, it can store all of the log data that your application produces.

Elasticsearch allows you to quickly search through data, and its capabilities include full-text querying. As your system grows, it can horizontally scale to handle large amounts of data, even if there are billions of log lines. It is easily extendable by adding nodes and resilient to failing nodes.

Elasticsearch can be configured so that it will send notifications based on certain conditions. Log data is continually monitored and, if the conditions are met, notifications can be sent to targets such as email or other incident management tools.

Elasticsearch makes use of RESTful APIs and **JavaScript Object Notation (JSON)**. It supplies clients in a number of programming languages, including Java, C#, Python, JavaScript, PHP, Curl, Perl, and Ruby. In addition, the Elasticsearch community has contributed support for a number of other languages. There is a large community behind Elasticsearch and it provides good support and an extensive knowledgebase for questions and issues.

Logstash

Logstash is an open-source log-parsing engine that provides functionality to parse, transform, and transport data. It aggregates, filters, and supplements data from a variety of sources. One of the many uses to which it is particularly suited is the ingestion and processing of log data.

Logstash can perform tasks such as transforming unstructured data into structured data, filtering out certain types of data, and adding to the data. Once Logstash is done processing data, it can forward it to a destination. For example, altered log data can be transported to Elasticsearch. If a Logstash node fails, it can guarantee at-least-once delivery through the use of its persistent queue.

Kibana

Kibana is a free tool that allows you to explore and visualize your Elasticsearch data. It is written in Node.js and has a web-based frontend. It provides a visualization of Elasticsearch data, allowing you to create useful dashboards that includes charts, graphs, histograms, and other visualizations. It is extensible and gives you the ability to create your own visualizations.

Visualizations created by Kibana can be easily distributed and shared with others. Kibana dashboards can be integrated with your application or you can simply share a URL to a dashboard with others. Reports can be exported to various formats, such as Portable Document Format (PDF) and comma-separated values (CSV).

Beats

Beats is a platform for small, lightweight data shippers. These data shippers gather data from potentially large numbers of different sources and send it to Logstash or Elasticsearch. Beats has shippers for all kinds of data:

- **Filebeat**: Text log files
- **Metricbeat**: Metrics for systems and services
- **Packetbeat**: Network monitoring
- **Winlogbeat**: Windows event logs
- **Auditbeat**: Audit data
- **Heartbeat**: Uptime monitoring

The open-source community has created beats for many other sources. Libbeat is the common library for forwarding data, which can be leveraged to create custom beats.

For logging, Filebeat can be used to aggregate log data. It is also container-ready and can be deployed in its own container on the same host. Once deployed, it can collect logs from all of the containers running on that host.

Filebeat works seamlessly with Logstash. During periods where there is a higher volume of log data being processed, Logstash can let Filebeat know to slow down the reading of the log data until the volume lowers so that processing can return to the regular pace.

Cross-cutting concerns for microservices

Providing cross-cutting concerns for microservices requires some additional consideration. In this section, we will take a look at using a microservice chassis and the sidecar pattern to handle some of the difficulties with implementing cross-cutting concerns for microservices.

Leveraging a microservice chassis

In a monolithic application, cross-cutting concerns can be designed and developed once. After their development is complete and they are available for use, they can be leveraged throughout the application.

Microservices are independently deployable, self-contained services. As a result, implementing a cross-cutting concern has to be done repeatedly for each microservice. This can make it prohibitively expensive for an organization to develop microservices when considering the development resources that would be needed. A system may consist of hundreds of microservices, and your team may be creating new ones throughout the life of the application. The process of creating a new microservice should be made as fast and easy as possible, and you are not going to want to implement cross-cutting concerns for each one.

To overcome this challenge, a **microservice chassis** can be used. A microservice chassis is a framework that can take care of many of the cross-cutting concerns for microservices and do so in a way that allows all of your microservices to utilize the functionality.

Some examples of a microservice chassis include Spring Cloud, Microdot, Gizmo, Go kit, and Dropwizard. Each microservice framework is different, but some of the cross-cutting concerns that they handle include the following:

- Logging
- Externalized configuration
- Metric reporting and instrumentation
- Service registration and discovery
- Health checks
- Tracing

It should be noted that it is not required that you use an open-source or third-party microservice chassis. It could be a framework that you develop within your organization, specifically tailored to your needs and using the technologies that you choose. The important point is to have a microservice framework that you can reuse so that you are not implementing the same cross-cutting concerns multiple times. Once a microservice framework is in place to handle cross-cutting concerns, the development team can focus on the core concerns of the microservices themselves.

Using the sidecar pattern

One of the options available to you when developing microservices is polyglot development. You have the flexibility to use multiple programming languages, runtimes, frameworks, and data storage technologies. Microservices are independently developed and deployed, allowing you to select best-of-breed technologies to accomplish the given task.

If your software system is taking advantage of polyglot microservices, it can make it difficult to maintain libraries for cross-cutting concerns. You would need one for each programming language that you are using, resulting in duplication of effort and a lower level of maintainability.

One solution to this problem is to use the **sidecar pattern**. The logic for cross-cutting concerns are placed in their own process or container (known as a sidecar container or a sidekick container) and then attached to the **primary application**. Similar to how a motorcycle sidecar is attached to a motorcycle, the **sidecar application** is attached to the primary application and runs alongside it:

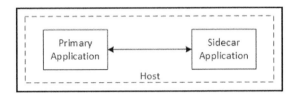

Use of the sidecar pattern allows the programming language and framework of the primary application to be different from that of the sidecar application. When used for cross-cutting concerns in a heterogeneous environment, it means that you will not need to develop logic for a cross-cutting concern in each programming language that is being used.

Primary and sidecar applications have access to the same resources. This makes it easy, for example, for a sidecar application that has the purpose of monitoring the health of the primary application to monitor its system resources.

This pattern is also useful when the sidecar application is owned by a different organization or a different team. Even if you do not have control over the implementation of the sidecar application, you will be able to use it with your primary application.

For **inter-process communication (IPC)** between the primary application and the sidecar application, it is a best practice is to use a communication mechanism that is language and framework agnostic. Although IPC between the primary and sidecar applications is generally fast because they are located on the same host, there will be some overhead involved due to the communication as compared with in-process communication. If the interface is chatty (more fine-grained operations requiring an increased amount of communication between the two processes) and performance needs to be optimized, use of the sidecar pattern may not be ideal.

Summary

Cross-cutting concerns are an important part of a software application. In this chapter, you learned what cross-cutting concerns are and how to avoid scattering and tangling the solutions for cross-cutting concerns.

In this chapter, we learned how we can use DI, the decorator pattern, and AOP to implement cross-cutting concerns. This chapter provided some examples of common cross-cutting concerns, such as caching, configuration management, auditing, security, exception management, and logging. We also explored using a microservice chassis and/or the sidecar pattern when implementing cross-cutting concerns for microservices.

In the next chapter, we will take a look at the performance considerations that software architects make. We will explore the importance and fundamentals of performance in a software application. Various performance improvement techniques will be detailed. The chapter will also cover the topic of concurrency and how parallel execution can speed up the performance of multi-processor or multi-core systems.

Performance Considerations **10**

Users have high expectations when it comes to the performance of the applications they use. Performance needs are requirements that must be met and their importance should be reflected in the fact that the entire team must take ownership of performance. Performance is a quality attribute and should be considered throughout the development of an application.

After taking a look at the importance of performance and some of the common terminology related to it, this chapter will describe a systematic approach to improving performance. We will also cover server-side caching, web application performance, and techniques to improve database performance.

In this chapter, we will cover the following topics:

- The importance of performance
- Performance terminology
- Taking a systematic approach to performance improvement
- Server-side caching, including different caching strategies and usage patterns
- Improving web application performance, including HTTP caching, compression, minifying resources, bundling resources, using HTTP/2, using content delivery networks, and optimizing web fonts
- Database performance, including designing an efficient database schema, using database indexes, scaling up/out, and concurrency

The importance of performance

The performance of a software application indicates the responsiveness of the operations that it can perform. Users have greater expectations today in terms of the responsiveness of the applications that they use. They demand fast response times regardless of their location or the device that they are using.

Most importantly, software must serve its functional purpose, be reliable in its operation, and provides its functionality in a usable way. If it does not, then the speed of the application will not matter. However, once those needs are met, performance is of high importance.

Performance affects user experience

The speed of your application plays a major role in the overall **user experience** (UX). A user's satisfaction with the application is influenced by the speed of the application. The performance of your application affects the organization's bottom line, whether it is because customers are being gained/lost for a customer-facing site or because productivity is being gained/lost for an enterprise application.

For web and mobile applications, the loading time for a page is a major factor in page abandonment. If a page takes too long to load, many users will simply leave. This is evident when we look at things such as a site's bounce and conversion rates.

Bounce rate

A *bounce* occurs when a user has just a single-page session on a site and leaves without visiting any of the other pages. The **bounce rate**, which is sometimes referred to as the exit rate, is the percentage of users who bounce:

$$Bounce\ rate = \frac{Total\ number\ of\ bounces}{Total\ entries\ to\ a\ page}$$

As you would expect, as page load times increase, so too does the bounce rate. Examples of actions that result in a bounce include the user closing the browser window/tab, clicking on a link to visit a different site, clicking the back button to leave the site, navigating to a different site by typing in a new URL or using a voice command, or having a session timeout occur.

Conversion rate

The **conversion rate** is the percentage of site visitors who ultimately take the desired conversion action. The desired conversion action depends on the purpose of the site, but a few examples of common ones include placing an order, registering for membership, downloading a software product, or subscribing to a newsletter.

The conversion rate is represented by the following formula:

$$Conversion\ rate = \frac{Number\ of\ Goal\ Achievements}{Visitors}$$

Websites that have poor performance will have a lower conversion rate. If a site is slow, users will simply leave the site and go somewhere else.

Performance is a requirement

Speed is a feature of your application and if it is not fast enough, then it is not good enough. Performance is a quality attribute of software systems and cannot be considered as just an afterthought. It should play an integral part throughout the life cycle of a software application. It is a requirement of the system and, like other requirements, it must be unambiguous, measurable, and testable.

When we discussed requirements in Chapter 3, *Understanding the Domain*, it was stated that requirements must be specified clearly, measurable with specific values/limits when appropriate, and testable so that it can be determined whether the requirement has been satisfied. For example, it is not sufficient to simply state that the *web page must load in a timely manner*. In order to make it unambiguous, measurable, and testable, it would have to be written to state that the *web page must load within two seconds*.

Treating performance as a requirement also means that we should have tests for it. We can measure how long it takes to execute tests and assert that they can be completed within a time limit. While performance tests are not executed as often as unit tests, it should be easy to execute performance tests regularly.

Page speed affects search rankings

Page speed is a consideration in a site's mobile search ranking in Google search results. Currently, this criterion only affects pages with the slowest performance, but it shows the importance Google places on web page performance. For customer-facing websites, you do not want performance to negatively affect your site's search ranking.

Defining performance terminology

Before we explore the topic of performance further, let's define some of the common terms related to performance.

Latency

Latency is the amount of time (or delay) it takes to send information from a source to a destination. A phrase you may hear regarding latency is that it is the time spent *on the wire*, since it represents the amount of time a message spends traveling on a network. Something is *latent* if it is dormant and we must wait to perform any further processing while a message is traveling across a network.

Latency is usually measured in milliseconds. Factors such as the type of network hardware being utilized, the connection type, the distance that must be traveled, and the amount of congestion on the network all affect latency.

In many instances, a significant portion of the total latency takes place between your office or home and the **internet service provider (ISP)**. This is known as **last-mile latency** because even if data travels across the country or even the world, it can be the first or last few hops that contribute most to the total latency.

Throughput

Throughput is a measure of a number of work items per a particular time unit. In the context of a network, it is the amount of data that can be transferred from one location to another in a given amount of time. It is typically measured in **bits per second (bps)**, **megabits per second (Mbps)**, or **gigabits per second (Gbps)**.

In the context of application logic, throughput is how much processing can be done in a given amount of time. An example of throughput in this context would be the number of transactions that can be processed per second.

Bandwidth

Bandwidth is the maximum possible throughput for a particular logical or physical communication path. Like throughput, it is typically measured in terms of a bit rate, or the maximum number of bits that could be transferred in a given unit of time.

Processing time

Processing time is the length of time that it takes for a software system to process a particular request, without including any time where messages are traveling across the network (latency). Sometimes a distinction is made between server processing time and client processing time.

A variety of things can affect processing time, such as how the application code is written, the external software that works in conjunction with the application, and the characteristics of the hardware that is performing the processing.

Response time

Response time is the total amount of time between the user making a particular request and the user receiving a response to that request. Although some people use the terms latency and response time interchangeably, they are not synonymous. For a given request, response time is a combination of both the network latency and the processing time.

Workload

Workload represents the amount of computational processing a machine has been given to do at a particular time. A workload uses up processor capacity, leaving less of it available for other tasks. Some common types of workload that may be evaluated are CPU, memory, I/O, and database workloads.

Taking regular measurements of workload levels will allow you to predict when peak loads for your application take place and also allow you to compare the performance of your application at different load levels.

Utilization

Utilization is the percentage of time that a resource is used when compared with the total time that the resource is available for use. For example, if a CPU is busy processing transactions for 45 seconds out of a one-minute timespan, the utilization for that interval is 75%. Resources such as CPU, memory, and disk should be measured for utilization in order to obtain a complete picture of an application's performance. As utilization approaches the maximum throughput, response times will rise.

Taking a systematic approach to performance improvement

When looking to improve the performance of an application, the entire development team should be involved. Teams will have greater success at optimizing performance when the entire team, and not just certain individuals, take ownership of the performance of the software application.

When engaging in an effort to improve performance, it can be helpful to follow a systematic approach. An iterative process that consists of the following steps can be used for performance improvement:

- Profiling the application
- Analyzing the results
- Implementing changes
- Monitoring changes

The following diagram illustrates this process:

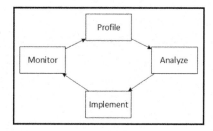

Let's now take a closer look at each of the steps in the process.

Profiling an application

The first step is to *profile* the application. Profiling is an analysis of a software system that results in measurements of the system's execution. Development teams should not be guessing where performance issues exist, as they will not always be where you expect. Rather than guessing, development teams should be acquiring precise measurements. These measurements can then be used to make decisions. Examples include how much time a particular method takes to execute, how often a method is called, the time spent in communication, the amount of I/O that is taking place, and how much of the CPU and memory is being used.

There are profiling tools, called *profilers*, available that can be leveraged to profile an application. Two broad categories of how profilers collect information are through instrumentation and by sampling. An effective profiling strategy might use both types of profilers to understand where performance issues may exist in a software system.

Instrumentation

When **instrumentation** is used, code is added to the software system being profiled in order to collect information. For example, to collect data on the time spent in a method and to get a count of how many times the method is used, instrumentation code is executed at the beginning and end of the method.

Instrumentation code can be manually added by the development team. However, profilers can add instrumentation automatically. Some profilers that use instrumentation modify source code, while others work at runtime. Either way, instrumentation can provide a great level of detail. However, a disadvantage of instrumentation is that the instrumentation code can affect the measurements. The degree of the effect really depends on what data is being collected and the extent of the instrumentation.

For example, the instrumentation code itself takes some time to execute. Profilers can take this into consideration by calculating the overhead they incur and subtracting that amount from their measurements. However, adding code to a method can change CPU optimizations and change the way that it executes the method. Consequently, very short methods can sometimes yield inaccurate results.

Statistical profilers

Profilers that work by **sampling,** which are sometimes known as **statistical profilers**, let applications execute without any runtime modifications. This type of profiling is conducted outside of the application's process and overcomes some of the disadvantages of instrumentation.

An **operating system (OS)** interrupts the CPU at regular intervals, giving it an opportunity for process switching. Sampling works by collecting information during these interruptions. Sampling is less intrusive than instrumentation, as it allows the software system to execute close to its normal speed. The downside is the fact that the data collected are is often an approximation and is not as numerically accurate as data that can be collected through instrumentation.

Analyzing the results

Once performance data is collected through profiling, it can be used to identify performance issues and areas of the application that are bottlenecks. **Bottlenecks** are parts of the software system that limit performance. These parts in the software are unable to keep pace given their capacity and a particular amount of work, which in turn slows down the overall performance of the application.

The focus of the performance improvement effort should be on optimizing the bottlenecks of the application. Software architects should not focus their attention on optimizing non-bottlenecks unless all of the identified bottlenecks have been addressed and there is time to optimize non-bottlenecks.

Some common bottlenecks include CPU, memory, network, database, and disk utilization. Different problems will lead you to different solutions. For example, if the network is too slow, you can look into ways to send less data across, such as compressing or caching data. If the database is too slow, you can work with the **database administrator** (DBA) to add indexes, optimize queries, make use of stored procedures, and possibly denormalize some of the data. If the CPU is the bottleneck, you can look into getting a faster processor, adding processors, storing/caching data so that it doesn't need to be calculated, or making improvements to the algorithms being used.

Some bottlenecks will lead you to conclude that you need to either scale horizontally or scale vertically. Vertical scaling involves increasing the capacity of existing servers by adding resources, such as adding memory and processors, replacing existing processors with faster ones, and increasing the size of available disk space. Horizontal scaling involves adding servers to your pool of resources in order to scale wider and handle more traffic.

Implementing changes

Profiling the application and analyzing the results are necessary steps prior to implementing any changes to improve performance because we do not want to make changes unless we know that it will be worth it. Once those steps are complete, though, we are ready for the development team to actually implement the changes based on the results of the previous steps.

The analysis may identify multiple areas that need improvement. Software architects should consider implementing one set of changes at a time, so as not to mix results and make it more difficult to recognize new performance issues that may have been introduced. When selecting which set of changes to implement for a particular iteration, the most important bottleneck and the one that is expected to provide the biggest payoff should be prioritized.

Monitoring results

Even once changes have been implemented to improve performance, the process is not complete. We must monitor the results to determine whether the changes that were implemented resolved the performance issues that were identified.

When changes are implemented to fix a bottleneck, either the performance issue will remain unresolved, it will be fixed, or the bottleneck will be transferred to another part of the system. If the issue is not fixed, one should consider whether it is appropriate to undo the changes that were made. Software architects need to be aware that eliminating one bottleneck may reveal another one. We must monitor the results because we may need to conduct additional iterations of the performance improvement process.

Even if our application is now performing in a satisfactory way, it must be monitored because things can change over time. As the source code changes with the introduction of new features and bug fixes, new performance issues and bottlenecks may be created. Other changes may also occur over time, such as a change in how many users the application has and how much traffic the application is generating.

Server-side caching

Software architects should take advantage of caching in order to improve performance and scalability. Caching involves copying data that may be needed again to fast storage so that it can be accessed quicker in subsequent uses. We will discuss HTTP caching and the use of content delivery networks in the *Improving web application performance* section later in this chapter. In this section, we will focus on **server-side caching** strategies.

Server-side caches can be used to avoid making expensive data retrievals from the original data store (for example, a relational database) repeatedly. The server-side cache should be placed as close to the application as possible to minimize latency and improve response times.

The type of storage used for a server-side cache is designed to be fast, such as an in-memory database. The more data and users that an application has to handle, the greater the benefits of caching.

Caching data in distributed applications

In distributed applications, there are two main types of data caching strategies that you can use. One is the use of a private cache and the other is a shared cache. Keep in mind that you can use both strategies in a single application. Some data can be stored in a private cache, while other data can be stored in a shared cache.

Using a private caching strategy

A *private cache* is held on the machine that is running the application that is using it. If multiple instances of an application are running on the same machine, then each application instance can have its own cache.

One of the ways that data is stored in a private cache is in-memory, which makes it extremely fast. If there is a need to cache more data than can fit in the amount of memory available on the machine, then cached data can be stored on the local file system.

In a distributed system using the private caching strategy, each application instance will have its own cache. This means that it is possible for the same query to yield different results depending on the application instance.

Using a shared caching strategy

A *shared cache* is located in a separate location, possibly accessible through a cache service, and all application instances use the shared cache. This resolves the issue of different application instances potentially having different views of cached data. It also improves scalability because a cluster of servers can be used for the cache. Application instances simply interact with the cache service, which is responsible for locating the cached data in the cluster.

A shared cache is slower than a private cache because rather than being available on the same machine as the application instance, it is located somewhere else; there will be some latency involved in interacting with the cache. However, if a greater level of consistency with data is important, the extra latency may be worth it.

Priming the cache

Software architects should consider *priming the cache*. This means that an application pre-populates the cache at application startup with data that will either be needed at startup, or is widely used enough that it makes sense to make the data available in the cache right from the start. This can help to improve performance as soon as initial requests are received by the server.

Invalidating cached data

Phil Karlton, while working at Netscape, once said:

> *"There are only two hard things in Computer Science: cache invalidation and naming things."*

The joke is funny because there is truth to it. Data in a cache may become stale if it is changed after it was placed in the cache. *Cache invalidation* is the process of replacing or removing cached items. We must ensure that we are handling cached data properly so that stale data is replaced or removed. It may also be necessary to remove cached items if the cache becomes full.

Expiring data

When data is cached, we can configure the data to expire from the cache after a specified amount of time. Some caching systems allow you to configure a system-wide expiration policy in addition to an expiration policy for an individual cached item. The expiration is typically specified as an absolute value (for example, 1 day).

Evicting data

A cache may become full, in which case the caching system must know which items it can discard in order to make room for new data. The following are some of the policies that can be used to evict data:

- **Least recently used (LRU):** Based on the assumption that cached items that have recently been used are the most likely to be used again soon, this discards items that were least recently used first.
- **Most recently used (MRU):** Based on the assumption that cached items that have been recently used will not be needed again, this discards items that were most recently used first.

- **First-in, first-out (FIFO):** Like a FIFO queue, this discards the item that was placed in the cache first (oldest data). It does not take into consideration when the cached data was last used.
- **Last-in, first-out (LIFO):** This approach is the opposite of FIFO in that it discards the item that was placed in the cache most recently (newest data). It does not take into consideration when the cached data was last used.
- **Explicitly evicting data:** There are times when we want to explicitly evict data from a cache, such as after existing data is deleted or updated.

Cache usage patterns

There are two main ways that an application works with a cache. The application can either maintain the cache data itself (known as a cache-aside pattern), including reading/writing to the database, or it can treat the cache as the system of record and the cache system can handle reading/writing to the database (including read-through, write-through, and write-behind patterns).

Cache-aside pattern

In the cache-aside pattern, the application is responsible for maintaining the data in the cache. The cache is kept *aside* and it doesn't interact with the database directly. When values from the cache are requested by the application, the cache is checked first. If it exists in the cache, it is returned from there and the system-of-record is bypassed. If it does not exist in the cache, the data is retrieved from the system-of-record, stored in the cache, and returned.

When data is written to the database, the application must handle potentially invalidated cached data and ensure that the cache is consistent with the system-of-record.

Read-through pattern

With the read-through pattern, the cache is treated as the system-of-record and has a component that is able to load data from the actual system-of-record (the database). When an application requests data, the cache system attempts to get it from the cache. If it does not exist in the cache, it retrieves the data from the system-of-record, stores it in the cache, and returns it.

Write-through pattern

A caching system that uses the write-through pattern has a component that has the ability to write data to the system-of-record. The application treats the cache as the system-of-record and when it asks the caching system to write data, it writes the data to the system-of-record (the database) and updates the cache.

Write-behind pattern

The write-behind pattern is sometimes used instead of the write-through pattern. They both treat the cache as the system-of-record but the timing of the write to the system-of-record is slightly different. Unlike the write-through pattern, in which the thread waits for the write to the database to complete, the write-behind pattern queues the writing of the data to the system-of-record. The advantage of this approach is that the thread can move on quicker, but it does mean that there is a short time when the data between the cache and the system-of-record will be inconsistent.

Improving web application performance

In this section, we will look at techniques that can be used to improve the performance of web applications. These techniques include, but are not limited, to:

- HTTP caching
- Compression
- Minification
- Bundling
- HTML optimization
- HTTP/2
- Content delivery networks (CDNs)
- Web font optimization

Leveraging HTTP caching

Many roundtrips between a client and a server may be necessary to load a page, and retrieving resources for that page from the server can take up significant amounts of time. The ability to cache resources that might be needed again so that they do not need to be transferred over the network on subsequent trips is an important part of improving web application performance.

Browsers are capable of caching data so that it doesn't need to be fetched from a server again. Resources such as CSS or JavaScript files might be shared across multiple pages of your web application. As a user navigates to various pages, they will need these resources multiple times. In addition, users may return to your web application at some point in the future. In both cases, taking advantage of **HTTP caching** will improve performance and benefit the user.

To take advantage of HTTP caching, each response from your web server must include the appropriate HTTP header directives. The cache policy you decide to implement is ultimately dependent on the application's requirements and the type of data being served. Each resource may have different requirements related to caching that should be considered. Using the various header directives available to you will provide you with the flexibility to meet your requirements. Let's look at some of the header directives you can use to control HTTP caching.

Using a validation token

A common scenario with HTTP caching occurs when a response has expired from the cache but has not changed in any way. The client would be required to download the response again, which is wasteful since the resource has not changed.

A validation token in the `ETag` header of a response can be used to check whether an expired resource has changed. Clients can send the validation token along with a request. If a response has expired from the cache but the resource has not changed, there is no reason to download it again. The server will return a 304 Not Modified response and the browser will then know that it can renew the response in the cache and use it.

Specifying cache-control directives

Cache-control directives in a response can control whether the response should be cached, under what conditions it can be cached, and for how long it should be cached. If a response contains sensitive information that you do not want cached, a *no-store* cache-control directive can be used, which will prevent browsers as well as any intermediate caches (for example, a content delivery network), from caching the response. Alternatively, a response can be marked as *private*, which will allow caching in a user's browser but not in any intermediate caches.

A cache-control directive that is slightly different than *no-store* is the *no-cache* directive. It is used to specify that a response should not be used from the cache until a check is performed with the server first to see whether the response has changed. The validation token must be used to make this determination, and only if the resource has not changed can the cache be used.

The *max-age* directive is used to specify the maximum amount of time, in seconds, that a response can be reused from the cache. The value is relative to the time of the request.

You may find yourself in a situation where you want to invalidate a cached response even though it has not expired yet. Once a response is cached, it will continue to be used unless it expires or the browser's cache has been cleared in some way. However, there may be times when you want to change a response before it has expired. This can be accomplished by changing the URL of the resource, which will force it to be downloaded. A version number, or some other identifier such as a fingerprint of the file, can be included as part of the filename. Using this technique provides differentiation between different versions of the same resource.

Taking advantage of compression

Compression is an important technique for improving performance. It is the use of an algorithm to remove redundancy in a file in order to make it smaller. This improves transfer speed and bandwidth utilization.

Software developers do not need to programmatically compress data that is to be transmitted. Servers and browsers have compression implemented already. As long as both the server and the browser understand the compression algorithm, it can be used. It is just a matter of ensuring that the server is configured properly.

The two main types of compression that are used to improve web performance are file compression and content-encoding (end-to-end) compression.

File compression

Files that you transmit, such as images, video, or audio, can have high rates of redundancy. When a web page is downloaded, images might account for the majority of the bytes being downloaded. These types of files should be compressed to save storage space and increase transfer speed.

There are various tools and algorithms that can be used to compress different file formats. Among the choices you can make, depending on your needs, is whether to use a lossless or a lossy compression algorithm.

Lossless compression

With lossless compression, all of the bytes from the original file can be recovered when the file is decompressed. This type of compression algorithm may be necessary if the file you are compressing cannot afford to lose any information.

For example, if you are compressing a text file of data, source code for a program, or an executable file, you cannot afford to lose any of the contents and would want to use a lossless compression algorithm. For image, video, and audio files, you may or may not require lossless compression, depending on your needs for file size and quality.

Graphics Interchange File (GIF) and **Portable Network Graphics (PNG)** are examples of image file formats that provide lossless compression. If animation is required, you will want to use the GIF format. If you want to preserve high-quality images and not lose any fine detail, the PNG image format should be used.

Lossy compression

If a lossy compression algorithm is used, some of the bytes from the original file will be lost when the file is decompressed. For a file in which you can afford to lose some bytes, you can achieve a smaller file size as compared to using a lossless compression algorithm.

This type of compression works well with images, video, and audio because the loss of redundant information may be acceptable. There are different degrees of lossy compression, and how aggressive you are with the optimization depends on the trade-off you are willing to make between file size and quality. In some cases, you can use lossy compression and there will be no perceptible difference to the user.

Joint Photographic Experts Group (JPEG) is an example of an image file format that provides lossy compression. If you do not need the highest quality image and can afford to lose some fine detail in the image, JPEG can be used.

Content-encoding (end-to-end) compression

Significant performance improvements can be made when using content-encoding. The server compresses the body of an HTTP message prior to sending it to the client. It will remain compressed (end-to-end compression) until it reaches the client. Any intermediate nodes that it may pass through while traveling to the client do not decompress the message. Once the message reaches the client, the client decompresses the body of the HTTP message.

In order to use content-encoding, the browser and server must agree on the compression algorithm to use via *content negotiation*. Content negotiation is the process of selecting the best representation of particular content.

There are a number of different types of compression, but **gzip** is the most common. It is a lossless type of compression. Although it can be used for any stream of bytes, it works particularly well on text. Brotli (content-encoding type of **br**) is an open source, lossless data compression library. It is newer than gzip, but it is gaining support and popularity.

You should take advantage of content-encoding as much as possible, except when transferring files that have already been compressed with the aforementioned file compression, such as image, video, and audio files. This is because you will typically not gain anything by compressing something twice, and it could even lead to a file size that is slightly larger than if it is just compressed once.

Minifying resources

Minification is the process of removing all unnecessary or redundant data from a resource. It can be used to remove characters from source code that are not needed without changing any of the functionality.

Files such as JavaScript, HTML, and CSS are great candidates for minification. Although the minified files that result from the process are not as human-readable as their original counterparts, the file size will be smaller, resulting in faster load times.

For example, let's take the following JavaScript code:

```javascript
// Class representing a rectangle
class Rectangle {
    constructor(height, width) {
        this.height = height;
        this.width = width;
    }
```

```
    // Method to calculate area
    calculateArea() {
        return this.width * this.height;
    }
}
```

After minifying it, it appears as follows:

```
class
Rectangle{constructor(t,h){this.height=t;this.width=h}calculateArea(){retur
n this.width*this.height}}
```

You can see that unnecessary characters for formatting and code comments have been removed and the names of the constructor parameters have been shortened. There are a number of tools available to you that can minify files. Some of the tools focus on a particular type of file (for example, JavaScript, HTML, or CSS). It is best to minify files prior to using the compression technique discussed in the *Taking advantage of compression* section.

It is a good practice to keep two versions of code files that are minified: a version that has not been minified for debugging purposes and a minified version for deployment. They can be given different filenames so that it is clear which one is the minified version. For example, invoice.min.js could be used as the name for the minified version of invoice.js.

Bundling resources

The first step in reducing the number of HTTP requests that need to be made in order to load a page is to remove all unnecessary resources. Once that is done, most web pages will still require multiple files of the same type, such as JavaScript or CSS files, in order to load. During development, it makes sense to separate this type of code into multiple files. However, the use of more individual files translates into more HTTP requests.

Bundling is the process of combining multiple files of the same type into a single file, which can then be transferred in a single request. The technique of bundling files is sometimes referred to as concatenating files. Fewer HTTP requests lead to faster page load performance. Bundling is a technique that is complementary with minifying files and the two are often used in conjunction with each other.

Bundling is an effective technique when we are using HTTP/1.1. In order to understand the reasons behind that, let's examine how assets are sent. In order to load a web page, the browser has to load each of the files that it needs, one at a time, over a connection, as shown in the following diagram:

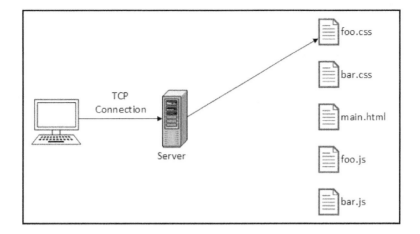

This process is too slow, so in order to get around this issue, browsers open up multiple connections per host, shown as follows:

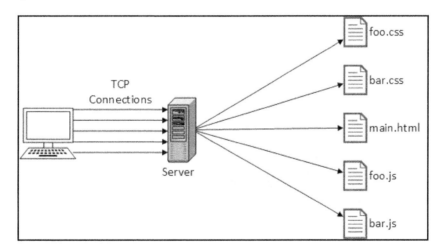

The maximum number of simultaneous connections that can be made per host varies by browser but a common number is six. The browser will handle these connections so application developers do not need to make any modifications to their application to take advantage of that feature. There is some overhead involved with setting up each connection but it is worth it in order to have multiple connections available for communication.

We can improve this approach by bundling the files so that fewer HTTP requests, and possibly fewer connections, will be necessary to get all of the required assets. In the following diagram, all of the CSS files are bundled together in **styles.css**, and all of the JavaScript files are bundled together in **scripts.js**:

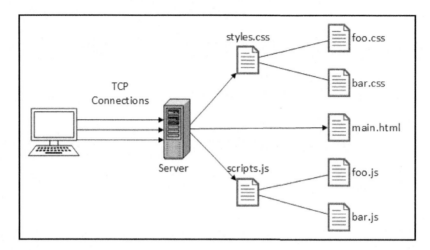

A downside of caching is that it can cause the cache to be invalidated more frequently. Without bundling, we can control the caching of each individual file. Once we start bundling, if any of the files within the bundle have changed, the entire bundle will need to be downloaded to clients again. If a file that is changed is contained within more than one bundle, it could cause multiple bundles to be downloaded again.

Even with the use of bundling, the number of assets that a web page needs may be higher than the maximum number of connections. This means that additional requests for assets from the same host are queued by the browser and will have to wait until a connection becomes available. To work around this limitation, the technique of **domain sharding** was introduced.

If there is a limit to the number of connections per domain, a workaround is to introduce additional domains. Domain sharding is a technique in which resources are split among multiple domains, allowing more to be downloaded in parallel. Instead of using the same domain (for example, www.example.com), we can use multiple subdomains (**shard1.example.com**, **shard2.example.com**, and so on). Each shard is allowed the maximum number of connections, increasing overall parallelism and allowing more assets to be transferred at the same time. In the following diagram, we are only returning three assets, which doesn't exceed the maximum number of connections per host. However, if we did need more assets, we could retrieve more before queuing by the browser would become necessary:

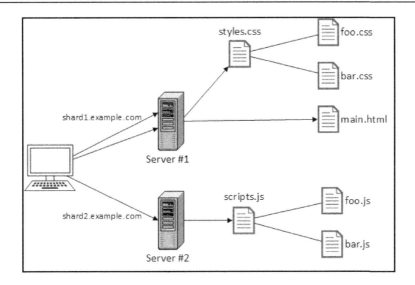

There is overhead involved with adding shards, though, such as additional DNS lookups, the additional resources required on both ends, and the fact that application developers will need to manage how to split up their resources.

Let's take a look at HTTP/2 now and learn how it can improve performance. Differences between HTTP/1.x and HTTP/2 affect how we want to approach techniques such as bundling and domain sharding.

Using HTTP/2

HTTP/2 is the latest version of the application layer protocol for data communication. It is not a complete rewrite of the protocol. The HTTP status codes, verbs, methods, and most of the headers that you are already familiar with from using HTTP/1.1 will continue to be the same.

One difference between HTTP/2 and HTTP/1.1 is the fact that HTTP/2 is binary, whereas HTTP/1.1 is textual. HTTP/2 communication consists of binary-encoded messages and frames, making it more compact, efficient to parse, and less error-prone. The fact that HTTP/2 is binary is what enables some of the other HTTP/2 features that improve performance.

Multiplexing

One of the most important features of HTTP/2 is *multiplexing*. Multiplexing is the ability to send multiple HTTP requests and receive multiple HTTP responses asynchronously through a single TCP connection, as shown in the following diagram:

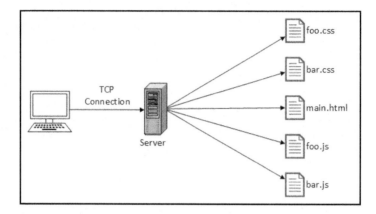

HTTP/1.1 does not support multiplexing, which is what led to the various workarounds to improve performance. With HTTP/2, we should no longer be concatenating files into a small number of large bundles. The expensive cache invalidation of a bundle that is necessary when any of the files in the bundle are changed can now be avoided or minimized. We can now transfer more granular assets, either by not bundling at all or having an increased number of bundles, where each one contains a small number of related files rather than just a few bundles containing many. A more granular approach allows us to provide an optimal cache policy for each individual file or bundle, maximizing the amount of content that is coming from our cache.

Another technique that is no longer necessary with HTTP/2 is domain sharding. Through the use of multiplexing, we can download multiple assets at the same time using a single connection. The overhead for each shard, which may have been worth it with HTTP/1.1, is no longer necessary.

Server push

HTTP/2 provides a feature in which the server can *push* responses that it thinks a client will need. When a resource is requested from a client, it may contain references to other resources that are needed. Rather than wait for the client to send additional requests for these required resources, the server already knows what resources will be needed and can proactively send them.

This feature is similar to *inlining* a resource, which is a technique that is sometimes used to improve performance by reducing the number of requests necessary. Inlining is accomplished by embedding a resource, such as JavaScript, CSS, or images, into an HTML page. With server push, there is no longer a need to inline resources. We get the same advantages of inlining but with the added benefit of keeping the assets in separate files, each with their own caching policies.

There are a few caveats with the server push feature. You should be careful not to push too many assets at once; you do not want to delay rendering of the page and negatively affect perceived performance. You should put thought into what assets you are pushing and be selective about it.

If server push is not used properly, resources that a client already has could be transferred to it unnecessarily, which would actually hurt performance. As of today, use of the server push feature may require some experimentation in order for it to be used in an optimal way. Some web servers have the functionality to mitigate the problem of pushing assets that the client does not need, and some browsers may introduce a *cache digest* so that a client can let the server know what assets it already has in its local cache.

Header compression

HTTP/2 performs header compression to improve performance. With HTTP/1.x, headers are always sent as plain text, but HTTP/2 uses the HPACK compression format to reduce the size. HPACK is used for compression with HTTP/2 because it is resilient to some of the security attacks that target compression, such as Compression Ratio Info-leak Made Easy (CRIME).

HPACK uses Huffman coding, a lossless data compression algorithm that can significantly reduce the size of the headers, reducing latency and improving performance.

Implementing HTTP/2

In order for a client to use HTTP/2, all that is needed is that the browser must support it. The latest versions of most browsers support HTTP/2. On the server side, the steps required to configure HTTP/2 support varies. A number of web servers provide support for HTTP/2 and the list continues to increase. In most cases, servers will need to support both HTTP/1.1 and HTTP/2, so typically a server needs to be configured to fall back to HTTP/1.1 if a client does not support HTTP/2.

Using content delivery networks (CDNs)

Users visiting a website may potentially be located anywhere in the world. Round trips between clients and servers will take longer if the distance between them is greater. The additional latency may be just milliseconds but it all contributes to the overall time it takes to receive a response.

Content delivery networks (CDNs) are a geographically distributed group of servers that can deliver content to users quickly. The nodes of a CDN are deployed in multiple locations so that they are distributed spatially. This provides us with the ability to reduce network latency and serve up content closer to the end users, which improves load times.

CDNs are great for transferring website content, such as JavaScript, HTML, CSS, image, video, and audio files. In addition to reducing the physical distance between users and content, CDNs improve load times through efficient load balancing, caching, minification, and file compression.

The reliability and redundancy of web applications are increased when a CDN is used because when traffic increases, it can be load balanced among multiple servers. If a server, or even an entire data center, is having technical issues, traffic can be routed to servers that are operational. CDNs can also help to improve security by mitigating **distributed denial-of-service (DDoS)** attacks and maintaining up-to-date TLS/SSL certificates.

Optimizing web fonts

Good typography is an important part of designing a good user interface, readability, accessibility, and branding. There was a time when web designers were limited in the fonts they could use because there were only so many fonts that were guaranteed to be available on all systems. These were known as *web safe fonts*.

It is possible to use fonts other than just the *web safe fonts*. For instance, in CSS, you can use the `font-family` property to specify a list of fonts that can be used for an element, as follows:

```
p {
    font-family: Helvetica, Arial, Verdana, sans-serif;
}
```

With this approach, the browser will use the first one that it finds available on the system. A disadvantage of using this approach is that during testing you have to ensure that all of the fonts will work properly with your application.

A CSS feature called **web fonts** was introduced to overcome some of the challenges. It provides you with the ability to download font files so that any browser that supports web fonts can make the fonts that you want to use for your page available. Text using web fonts is selectable, searchable, zoomable, and will look good in a variety of screen sizes and resolutions.

However, the use of web fonts means that additional resources must be loaded. If a website or web application is using web fonts, it is important to consider them as part of your overall web performance strategy. Optimization of web fonts can reduce the overall size of a page and decrease rendering times. One thing that you should do is minimize the number of fonts (and their variants) that you use on your pages to minimize the number of resources that are needed.

To use web fonts, you must first select the one or more fonts that you want to use and consider the character sets that you need to support based on any localization requirements. The size of a font file is dependent on the complexity of the shapes in the various characters that make up the font.

Unfortunately, there is no standard on font formats, which means that different browsers support different font formats. This lack of a standard means that as of right now, you will need to support four different font formats for each font, and they are as follows:

- **Web Open Font Format version 2 (WOFF 2.0)**
- **Web Open Font Format version 1 (WOFF)**
- **TrueType font (TTF)**
- **Embedded Open Type (EOT)**

Once the web fonts have been selected, the `@font-face` CSS rule allows you to use a web font by allowing you to specify the font and the URL location where the font data can be found. Regardless of which web font you select and which of the four font formats is being used by a particular user, compression is effective in reducing the font size and should be used to improve performance. WOFF 2.0 and WOFF have built-in compression, but the TTF and EOT formats are not compressed by default, so servers should use compression when delivering these formats.

Web fonts can be large Unicode fonts with support for a variety of characters, not all of which will be needed at a given time. The `unicode-range` property in `@font-face` can be used to split up a font into multiple subsets so that only the characters that are actually needed will be downloaded.

One more note about optimizing fonts is to keep in mind the fact that font resources are not updated frequently. You should ensure that this type of resource is cached with a caching policy that will allow them to live in the cache for a long period of time, with a validation token so that even once it expires, it can be renewed in the cache and not downloaded again as long as it has not changed.

Optimizing the critical rendering path

An important step in reducing the amount of time that it takes for a page to render is to optimize the **critical rendering path** (CRP). The critical rendering path is the set of steps in between a browser receiving bytes from a server (for example, HTML, CSS, and JavaScript files) and the processing involved to render pixels on the device's screen.

Before a page can be rendered by a browser, it must construct both the **Document Object Model (DOM)** and the **CSS Object Model (CSSOM)**. The HTML and CSS markup for the page are needed for this process. The DOM and the CSSOM are then combined to form a render tree, which has both the content as well as the style information for what will be visible on the screen.

Once the render tree has been constructed, the browser moves to the layout stage where it calculates the size and position of the various visible elements. Finally, the paint stage is reached, where the browser uses the results of the layout to paint pixels to the screen.

Optimizing the critical rendering path is the process of minimizing the time it takes to perform these various steps. We are mostly concerned with the portion of the page that is *above the fold*, which refers to the part of the page that is visible without scrolling. The term is a reference to the upper half, or visible portion, of a folded newspaper. Until the user scrolls down a page, which may not even occur, they will not see what is *below the fold*.

We want to prevent render blocking by reducing, as much as possible, the resources that will prevent the content above the fold from rendering. The initial step in this process is to determine what resources are truly necessary for the initial rendering of a page. We want to get these critical resources to the client as quickly as possible to speed up the initial rendering. For example, the HTML and CSS that are necessary to create the DOM and the CSSOM are render-blocking resources, so we want to get them to the client quickly. Using some of the techniques described previously for web application performance, such as compression and caching, can help to load critical resources faster.

Resources that are not required for the above-the-fold content or are otherwise not critical for the initial rendering can either be eliminated, their download could be deferred, or they can be loaded asynchronously. For example, if there are image files that are not needed for initial rendering, they can be deferred, and in order to prevent DOM construction any blocking JavaScript files can be loaded asynchronously.

Understanding what is involved in rendering a page, taking the time to think about what the critical resources are for the initial rendering, and optimizing the critical rendering path will allow a page to be constructed faster. Making a web page almost immediately visible and usable greatly improves a user's overall experience, which reduces the bounce rate and increases the conversion rate.

Database performance

A key part of a software system is the database. So, when looking to improve the performance of a system, improving database performance must be part of that effort. In this section, we will take a look at some of the things that can be done to improve database performance.

Designing an efficient database schema

The foundation of achieving peak database performance is an efficient and properly designed database schema. As a software architect, you may be working with a DBA who will be responsible for database design. However, it is good to be familiar with the different aspects of achieving a good database design.

Normalizing a database

Normalization is the process of designing tables (relations) and columns (attributes) so that they not only meet data requirements, but minimize data redundancy and increase data integrity.

In order to meet these goals, a database should contain the minimal number of attributes necessary to meet the requirements. Attributes with a close logical relationship should be placed together in the same relation. Redundancy of attributes should be kept to a minimum, which makes it easier to maintain data consistency and will minimize the size of the database.

Denormalizing a database

For performance and scalability reasons, there may be cases where it makes sense to denormalize part of the database. It is important to differentiate between a database that has not been normalized, and one that has been normalized and then is denormalized later. A database should be normalized first and then if there are cases where it makes sense to denormalize, it should be done after careful consideration.

Denormalization is a strategy used to improve performance, typically by shortening the execution time of certain queries. This can be accomplished by storing redundant copies of some data or grouping data together in order to minimize joins and improve query performance.

While denormalization might improve read performance, it will negatively affect write performance. Some mechanisms, such as a compensating action, will be required to keep redundant data consistent. Using database constraints can help to enforce rules that will keep the data consistent even when it is denormalized. Redundant data will also make the database larger and therefore take up more disk space.

Another reason to introduce denormalization is to keep historical data. For example, let's say that we have an address table and an orders table, and that each order is associated with an address. An order is created, and then in the future, that address is updated. Now when you look at the old order, you see the new address and not the address given at the time the order was created. By storing the address field values with each order record, you can maintain this historical data. It should be noted, however, that there are ways to accomplish this without denormalization. For instance, you could treat an address like a value object (immutable), and simply create a new address record when one is modified, leaving the one associated with the old address intact. Also, in an event-driven system, or one in which a data audit is being kept that stores the modifications that have been made to a record, you could *reconstruct* what the address was at the time the order was created.

Identifying primary and foreign keys

All of the primary and foreign keys for all of the tables in the database should be identified. The *primary key* of a table is the column, or combination of columns, that uniquely identify a row in the table.

Sometimes a row in a table must reference a row from another table. A *foreign key* is a column or combination of columns that hold the primary key value for a row in another table so that it can be referenced.

Database constraints based on the primary and foreign keys should be created to enforce data integrity. A *primary key constraint* for a table consists of the one or more columns that make up the primary key and a *foreign key constraint* consists of the one or more columns that make up the foreign key.

Selecting the most appropriate data types

When designing a database table, we should select the most appropriate data type for each column. In addition to the data type, the size and nullability of the column should also be considered. We want to choose a data type that will sufficiently hold all possible values but also be the smallest data type that is necessary. This will maximize efficiency not just for performance but also for storage size.

Using database indexes

Database indexes can be used to improve performance and provide more efficient data access and storage. They are stored on disk and associated with a database table or view to speed up data retrieval. The two main types of indexes are the primary/clustered index and the secondary/non-clustered index.

Primary/clustered indexes

When designing a table, one approach is to keep the rows unordered and create as many secondary indexes as necessary. Such an unordered structure is known as a *heap*. Another approach is to create a *primary index*, also known as a *clustered index*, to order the rows by the primary key. It is common to have a clustered index on a table which is known as a *clustered table*. The only time you might not want one is if the table is very small (and one that you know will remain small over time), such that the overhead of storing and maintaining the index is not worth it when compared to simply searching the table.

The one or more columns that make up the primary key of a table are the columns that make up the index definition. A clustered index sorts the rows in a table based on their key values and physically stores them on disk based on that order. Each table can only have one clustered index because the rows in the table can only be sorted and stored in one order.

Secondary/non-clustered indexes

In addition to specifying a primary index, many database systems provide the ability to create *secondary indexes*, also known as *non-clustered indexes*. The performance of a database can benefit from having secondary keys available for data access.

Non-clustered indexes are defined by one or more columns that are ordered logically and serve as pointers to find the rest of the data for a given record. The order of a non-clustered index does not match the physical order of how the records are stored on disk.

Non-clustered indexes provide a way to specify an alternate key other than the primary key for accessing records in a table. The key could be a foreign key or any column that will be frequently used in joins, where clauses, ordering, or grouping. The advantage of using non-clustered indexes is to improve performance for the common ways that data might be accessed for a particular table beyond the primary key. Sometimes the primary key is not the only way, and might not even be the most widely-used way, that records are retrieved from a table.

For example, let's say we have an `Order` table and a `Customer` table, with `OrderId` and `CustomerId` being the primary keys of those two tables, respectively. The `Order` table also has a `CustomerId` column as a foreign key to the `Customer` table in order to associate orders with customers. In addition to retrieving orders by `OrderId`, the system may need to retrieve orders by `CustomerId` on a frequent basis. Adding a non-clustered index on the `CustomerId` column of the `Order` table allows for more efficient data retrieval when it is accessed with that column.

Although non-clustered indexes are an important part of performance tuning a database, each table should be analyzed carefully when deciding which non-clustered indexes, if any, to add to a table and which column or columns should make up the index. As we will learn in a moment, there is overhead related to adding indexes to a table, so we do not want to add any unnecessary ones.

Having too many indexes

There is a cost associated with adding an index to a table, so when it comes to indexes, you can have too much of a good thing. Every time that a record is added or updated in a table, an index record also has to be added or updated, incurring some additional overhead to those transactions. In terms of storage, indexes take up additional disk space, increasing the overall size of your database.

The more indexes you have on a table, the more the query optimizer of the **database management system (DBMS)** will have to take into consideration for a particular query. The query optimizer is a component of the DBMS that analyzes queries to determine the most efficient execution plans for them.

For example, the query optimizer decides whether a particular join in a query should do a full table scan versus using an index. It must take into account, among other things, all of the indexes on that table. As a result, an increased number of indexes on a table could adversely affect performance.

For these reasons, one should be selective when considering what indexes to add to a table. Properly selected indexes will speed up data access performance, but you do not want to create unnecessary ones as they can slow down data access and operations, such as inserts and updates.

Scaling up and out

Scaling your database server vertically (up) or horizontally (out) to improve performance is not something that should be done without an understanding that it is necessary. Prior to scaling up or scaling out, software architects and DBAs should ensure that the database schema has been designed properly and that indexes have been applied properly. In addition, the application using the database should be optimized to improve performance and remove bottlenecks.

Once those measures have been taken, if the database server is experiencing high levels of resource use, it's time to consider scaling the server up or scaling it out. For database servers, it is best to scale up first by performing actions such as replacing the server with a better machine or by adding processors and/or memory.

Scaling up should be done first because there are additional complications with scaling a database server out. When you have multiple servers, you may need to horizontally partition some of the tables and consider data replication. Plans for disaster recovery and failover are also more complex when there are multiple database servers. However, if database performance is still not at the level you need it to be after scaling up, scaling out may be necessary.

Database concurrency

A relational database system can handle many simultaneous connections. Having a database that performs well is only useful if it can handle multiple processes accessing and changing data at the same time. This is what **database concurrency** is all about.

Concurrency control ensures that database transactions that are performed concurrently maintain data integrity. We'll now begin looking at concurrency by learning about database transactions.

Database transactions

A database transaction is a sequence of operations that are performed as a single unit of work. They play an important role in maintaining data integrity and consistency even when data is being accessed and changed at the same time. They provide units of work that either complete in their entirety or will not be committed at all.

Transactions can recover from failures and keep the database in a consistent state. Transactions also provide isolation so that a record that is in the process of being modified by one transaction is not affected by a concurrent transaction that must update the same record. Transactions, once they are complete, are written to durable storage.

Optimistic versus pessimistic concurrency control

Concurrency control ensures that databases transactions that are performed concurrently maintain data integrity. Many databases offer two main types of concurrency control: optimistic and pessimistic.

Optimistic concurrency control (or optimistic locking) works under the assumption that resource conflicts between multiple users, while possible, are not common. Therefore, it allows transactions to execute without locking resources. If data is being changed, resources are checked for conflicts. If there is a conflict, only one transaction is successful while the others fail.

In contrast, pessimistic concurrency (or pessimistic locking) assumes the worst, such as assuming that more than one user will want to update the same record at the same time. In order to prevent that, it locks the appropriate resources as they are required for the duration of the transaction. Unless a deadlock takes place, pessimistic concurrency ensures that a transaction will be completed successfully. It should be noted that most database systems have different types of locks. For example, one type of lock might specify that a record that is locked can still be read by another user, while another type of lock might prevent that type of read.

CAP theorem

The **Consistency, Availability, and Partition tolerance (CAP)** theorem, also known as Brewer's Theorem after Eric Brewer who published it, states that a distributed system can only achieve two of the following three guarantees, but not all three:

- **Consistency**: Every read either returns the latest data or an error. Every transaction either completes successfully and is committed or is rolled back due to a failure.
- **Availability**: A system always provides a response to every request.
- **Partition tolerance**: In a distributed system (data is partitioned to different servers), if one of the nodes fails, the system should still be able to function.

Databases will stress some of these guarantees over others. A traditional relational database management system will focus on consistency and availability. They will favor strong consistency, which is also known as immediate consistency, so that any read of the data will reflect any changes that have been made to that data. These types of databases will follow an ACID consistency model.

Some databases, such as some NoSQL databases, will value availability and partition tolerance over consistency. For such databases, eventual consistency, rather than strong consistency, is acceptable. Eventually, the data will reflect all of the changes made to it, but at any given point in time it is possible to read data that may not reflect the latest changes. These types of databases follow a BASE consistency model.

ACID model

Databases that want to ensure consistency and availability will follow the **ACID consistency model**. Traditional relational databases follow the ACID model. Database transactions adhere to the ACID properties in that they must be atomic, consistent, isolated, and durable. These properties guarantee the validity of the data even when errors or failures occur. Strong consistency will place limits on performance and scalability.

Atomicity

A transaction must be an atomic unit of work, meaning that either all of its data modifications are performed or none at all. This provides reliability because if there is failure in the middle of a transaction, none of the changes in that transaction will be committed. For example, in a financial transaction, you may insert one record to represent the credit part of the transaction and another to represent the debit part of the transaction. You don't want one of those inserts to take place without the other, so you place them both as part of one transaction. Either they will both be committed or neither of them will be committed.

Consistency

After a transaction takes place, all of the data must be in a consistent state. This property ensures that all transactions maintain data integrity constraints, leaving the data consistent. If a transaction leaves data in an invalid state, the transaction is aborted and an error is reported. For example, if you had a column with a check constraint that states a column value must be greater than or equal to zero (so as not to allow negative numbers), the transaction would fail if it attempted to insert or update a record with a value less than zero for that particular column.

Isolation

Changes made by concurrent transactions must be isolated from changes made by any other concurrent transactions. Many DBMSs have different isolation levels that control the degree to which locking occurs on data being accessed. For example, a DBMS may place a lock on a record being updated so that another transaction cannot update that same record at the same time.

Durability

Once a transaction completes and is committed, its changes are persisted permanently in the database. For example, a DBMS may implement durability by writing all transactions to a transaction log. The transaction log can be used to recreate the system state at any point, such as right before failure.

BASE model

Some databases, such as some distributed NoSQL databases, focus on availability and partition tolerance. In some situations, it may be an acceptable tradeoff to have eventual consistency, rather than strong consistency, in order to focus on partition tolerance, performance, and scalability. This approach enables a higher degree of scalability and can yield faster performance. These databases use the **BASE consistency model** instead of the ACID model.

Basic availability

Most of the time, conflicts do not take place. The database is available most of the time and a response will be sent for every request. However, conflicts can occur and the response may indicate that a failure occurred when trying to access or change data.

Soft state

Rather than following consistency requirements such as those in the ACID model, the concept here is that the state of the system could change over time. Even if no additional transactions are being created, changes could take place due to eventual consistency.

Eventual consistency

A data change will eventually propagate to everywhere that it needs to go. If there are no further changes to a piece of data, eventually the data will be in a consistent state. This means it is possible to read stale data if the latest updates to it have not been applied yet.

Unlike a strong consistency model in which all data changes are atomic and the transaction is not allowed to complete until either the change finishes successfully or is rolled back due to a failure, the system will not check the consistency of every transaction.

Summary

It is more important to ensure that your code is correct than fast. Fast performance is not of any use if the application does not yield the correct results. Having said that, performance is an important part of designing and developing a successful software application. It plays a large part in the overall user experience for people who use the application. Regardless of the device they are using or their location, users expect a high level of responsiveness from their applications.

Performance is a quality attribute of the software system and performance requirements should be documented. Like all requirements, they need to be measurable and testable. The entire team should take ownership of performance. A systematic, iterative approach to performance improvement can help a development team reach their performance goals. Some problems will only be discovered later, so development teams should be prepared to analyze and optimize in an iterative way. In this chapter, you learned how to use server-side caching, about different techniques to improve web application performance, and how to improve database performance.

In the next chapter, we will explore the various security considerations that a software architect must make. We will examine the goals of security and the design principles and practices that will help us to achieve them. The chapter will cover techniques such as threat modeling, and topics such as cryptography, identity, and access management, and how to handle common web application security risks.

Correct Reliable Usable(UX)
Performant
Secured

11
Security Considerations

Designing and developing software systems that are secure is of vital importance. A software application that does not follow secure practices creates vulnerabilities that can be exploited by attackers. The result of an attack can lead to unauthorized access to confidential data, financial losses, and ruining an organization's reputation.

We will explore the three states that information can be in and the main goals of information security, represented by the **confidentiality**, **integrity**, and **availability (CIA) triad**. We will take a look at how threat modeling can help to identify and prioritize threats. We will learn principles and practices that will help create secure applications by design.

The chapter will cover tools such as encryption and hashing along with the best ways to implement identity and access management. The chapter concludes by taking a look at some of the most common web application security risks and ways to mitigate them.

In this chapter, we will cover the following topics:

- Three states of information
- The CIA triad
- Threat modeling
- Principles and practices of creating software that is secure by design
- Cryptography (encryption and hashing)
- Identity and access management, including authentication and authorization
- Most common web application security risks

Securing software systems

Security is the ability of a software application to prevent and protect against malicious attacks and the unauthorized use of the application and its data. It involves protecting one of the most important assets that an organization can possess, which is information. Information assets include not just data but also things such as logs and source code. It is the responsibility of software architects and developers to protect software applications and data. When we are designing and developing software systems, this is why we must focus the proper amount of attention on security considerations.

Security is a quality attribute and, as is the case with other quality attributes that we have covered in this book, we must think about and document the requirements for quality attributes. Requirements for security must be specified and they must be precise, measurable, and testable. We need to be able to determine if we are meeting security requirements.

Different software systems have different security requirements so it is important to understand the security needs of the system. A website for a blog has very different security needs than a payroll application. There is a variety of different ways that an attacker can compromise a system, so threats must be considered carefully. It is difficult to just *add on* security later. Security is architectural and must be considered during requirements, design, development, and testing.

The three states of information

The information that we strive to protect can be in one of three states. It can either be at rest, in use, or in transit. Information in all of these states is vulnerable to attack and needs to be considered in the context of security.

Information that is at rest is currently not being accessed. It is stored in some form of persistent storage, such as a database or a file. It can eventually be accessed either through an application or directly if someone had access to the persistent storage.

Information that is in use refers to information that is currently being used by some process or application. It is data that is currently in a non-persisted state. Data currently in memory or in a CPU cache are examples of information that is in use.

Information that is in transit is in the process of being moved, perhaps over a network. It is potentially accessible as it is being transferred. Secure transmission of the data, using a secure channel, is necessary to provide secure communication of information.

The CIA triad

The CIA triad represents some primary goals for information security and the protection of information assets. The CIA triad summarizes the attributes that we want our software systems to exhibit. CIA stands for confidentiality, integrity, and availability:

You may see the CIA triad referred to as the AIC triad in order to avoid confusion with the Central Intelligence Agency.

Software architects should strive for a balance between the confidentiality, integrity, and availability of information. Let's now take a closer look at the three fundamental objectives of the CIA triad.

Confidentiality

Software applications should protect confidentiality. The information that a software application manages has value to its users and to the organization that created the application. Confidentiality involves preventing unauthorized individuals from accessing information.

The application must protect its data, particularly when the data is private and personal. This includes when data is in any of the three states of information. Information can be vulnerable to eavesdropping while it is being transmitted between services or authorized parties.

Integrity

Software applications should ensure integrity. The goal is to prevent unauthorized individuals from modifying or destroying information. No matter which of the three states of information the data is currently in, the application has a responsibility to ensure that it has not been tampered with by an unauthorized party.

Availability

Software applications need to maintain availability. When implementing security, availability is among the desired qualities. If the security mechanisms employed are overly extensive given the requirements, then the usability and availability of the system will be lessened.

Software applications must allow authorized individuals access to information in a timely and reliable way. Securing data serves no purpose if authorized users cannot get to it. The information that a software application manages only has value when the right people can access it when they need it.

Chapter 4, *Software Quality Attributes*, covered quality attributes, including availability. Part of what this involves is being able to detect, recover from, and prevent faults to ensure that the application and its data are available to users when they want it.

Threat modeling

Threat modeling is a structured approach to analyzing security for an application. A *threat* is a possible danger to a software system and may cause serious harm to it. Threat modeling is a process that identifies and prioritizes potential security threats so that a development team can understand where their application is most vulnerable. Threat modeling evaluates threats with the goal of reducing an application's overall security risks. Once the analysis is complete, a plan can be formulated to mitigate identified security risks.

Traditional approaches to software security may have focused on security from the defender's point of view. However, modern approaches use threat modeling to focus on security from the attacker's viewpoint. A *threat agent* is any individual or group that may attack a software system and exploit its vulnerabilities.

While threat modeling can be applied to an existing software system, the inclusion of threat modeling while designing and developing a software system is an effective way to ensure that security is an integral part of the system.

At a high level, software architects should seek to decompose the software system, identify and categorize threats, prioritize threats, and create ways to mitigate them.

Decomposing an application

While a new software system is being designed, or during the analysis of an existing software system, we want to begin threat modeling with an understanding of the software system. Decomposing an application helps us to understand our software application better and uncover security vulnerabilities. Decomposing an application includes knowing the assets that an attacker may be interested in, the potential attackers of the system, the interactions with external entities, and the entry points into the system.

Organizations and their software systems have assets, which are the things of value to attackers. Assets might be physical, such as obtaining login credentials or a software system's data. They can also be abstract, such as an organization's reputation.

Part of considering the various threats to your software system includes gaining an understanding as to who may be potential attackers. Attackers may be external or internal to an organization. You must consider both types of attacker, and in doing so will realize there may be different entry points into your application and different ways of attacking it. Attackers will be motivated by the assets you have identified, so taking assets into consideration will help you to identify potential attackers.

You need to understand how the software system interacts with different external entities. External entities include users as well as external systems. These interactions will allow you to identify entry points into your system, which are locations where potential attackers can interact with the software system. Attackers will focus their efforts on entry points as they provide opportunities for them to carry out their attacks.

Identifying and categorizing potential threats

Once we have a good understanding of the software system, we need to identify and categorize potential threats. In order to categorize threats, we have to agree on a threat classification model. A threat classification model provides a set of threat categories with definitions so that each identified threat can be categorized in a systematic and repeatable way. STRIDE is one type of threat classification model.

STRIDE threat model

STRIDE is a security threat model that was originally created by Microsoft. The name is an acronym that represents six threat categories:

- Spoofing identity
- Tampering with data
- Repudiation
- Information disclosure
- Denial-of-service
- Elevation of Privilege

Spoofing identity

Spoofing identity is the act of representing yourself as someone else. For example, if an attacker gained access to someone's authentication information, such as their username and password, they could use it to spoof an identity. Other examples of spoofing identity are forging an email address or the modification of header information in a request with the purpose of gaining unauthorized access to a software system.

Tampering with data

Tampering with data involves an attacker who modifies data. Examples of tampering with data include modifying persisted data in a database, changing data as it travels over a network, and modifying data in files.

Repudiation

Repudiation threats can occur if a software system does not properly track and log actions that take place. This allows users, legitimate or otherwise, to be able to deny that they performed a particular action. For example, an attacker could manipulate data and then deny responsibility. Without the system being able to trace the operations properly, there would be no way to prove otherwise. Such an attack could involve sending inaccurate information to log files, making the entries in the log files misleading and unusable.

In software systems, we seek *non-repudiation*, which is the assurance that a person cannot deny an action that they performed. Strong authentication, accurate and thorough logging, and the use of digital certificates can be used to counter repudiation threats.

Information disclosure

Information disclosure is a category of threat that involves a software system failing to protect information from individuals who are not supposed to have access to the information, for example, allowing an attacker to read data from a database or while it is in transit over a network.

The information that an attacker obtains could potentially be used for other types of attack. For example, an attacker can obtain system information (server OS version, application framework version, and so on), source code details, information from error messages, account credentials, or API keys. The information taken by an attacker can then be used as the basis for further, more damaging attacks.

Denial-of-service

A **denial-of-service (DoS)** attack takes place whenever an attacker is able to deny service to valid users. An attacker can flood servers with packets to the point that the servers become unavailable or unusable. If a large number of bogus requests are sent to servers, they can be overloaded such that they cannot fulfill legitimate requests.

While a DoS attack may be conducted by a single computer, one type of DoS attack, known as a **distributed denial-of-service (DDoS)** attack, floods a victim from many different sources. This makes it much more difficult to block the source of the attack as well as to differentiate between legitimate traffic and traffic that is part of the attack.

Elevation of Privilege

Elevation of Privilege (EoP) takes places when an attacker is able to gain authorization for operations beyond what was originally granted. For example, an attacker obtains read and write privileges for an application when they were initially only granted read privileges.

The dangerous aspect of this threat is the fact that the attacker is part of the trusted system itself. Depending on the privileges the attacker is able to obtain, they may be able to inflict a high level of damage.

Prioritizing potential threats

Once threats have been identified and categorized, we can prioritize them based on their potential impact on the software system, the likelihood that they may occur, and the ease with which they can be exploited. These qualities can be used to give a qualitative ranking (for example, High, Medium, and Low) to prioritize threats.

Another approach to prioritizing threats is to utilize a threat-risk ranking model. The DREAD risk assessment model is one example of this type of ranking model.

DREAD risk assessment model

DREAD is a risk assessment model that can be used to prioritize security threats. Like the STRIDE model, it was created by Microsoft. DREAD is an acronym that represents the following risk factors:

- Damage potential
- Reproducibility
- Exploitability
- Affected users
- Discoverability

Each risk factor for a given threat can be given a score (for example, 1 to 10). The sum of all the factors divided by the number of factors represents the overall level of risk for the threat. A higher score signifies a higher level of risk and would typically be given a higher priority when determining which threats should be focused on first.

Damage potential

Damage potential represents the level of damage that could be done to users and the organization if an attack were to succeed. For example, damage to an individual user's data would be rated lower than an attack that could bring down the entire system. Depending on the type of attack and the asset(s) being targeted, damage could be something concrete, such as financial liability, or abstract, such as damage to an organization's reputation.

Reproducibility

Reproducibility is a measure of how easy it is to reproduce a particular attack. An attack that can be reproduced reliably would be rated higher than one that is statistically unlikely to be exploited or one that cannot be reproduced consistently.

Exploitability

The exploitability of a threat describes how difficult it is to exploit a vulnerability. While some exploits are easily understood and could be done by anyone (even perhaps unauthenticated users), some require advanced techniques, tools, or scripts. A threat with a very low level of exploitability would be difficult to execute even with knowledge of the vulnerability.

Affected users

The affected users risk factor represents percentage of users that will be affected by a particular threat. While some attacks may only affect a small number of users, some can affect almost all users. The greater the number of users who may potentially be affected, the higher this risk factor should be rated.

Discoverability

Discoverability signifies how easy it is to learn about the vulnerability. A threat that is very difficult to uncover would be rated lower than one that has already been disseminated in the public domain.

Many security professionals believe that discoverability should not be part of the model because the overall threat ranking should not be affected by this factor. Security by obscurity is a weak security control and it is not wise to consider a security risk less of a threat simply because it is difficult to discover.

Some practitioners use a DREAD-D (DREAD minus D) model and eliminate discoverability altogether. Alternatively, a development team can assign the maximum rating for discoverability for each threat, which effectively removes it as a factor.

Responses to threats

Once we have identified, categorized, and prioritized the threats to our software system, we can produce approaches that document how we want to respond to the threats. In the *Software risk management* section of `Chapter 2`, *Software Architecture in an Organization*, we discussed software risk management in the context of project management and delivering a software application. The different risk management options can also be applied to the context of security threats. As a response to a security risk, we can avoid the risk, transfer the risk to another party, accept the risk, or mitigate the risk.

Avoiding the risk

Risk avoidance requires us to make changes so that the risk no longer exists or is reduced. It should be noted that not all security risks can be avoided, and avoiding a security risk can lead to other risks.

Transferring the risk

Transferring the risk to another party can be a viable strategy for some security threats. Some common ways in which risk can be shifted to another party is through an insurance policy and through contracts.

If an insurance policy is purchased, an insurance company will assume the financial risks that might result from a security threat. Keep in mind though that it may not be possible for insurance to make up for the damage that a security attack can inflict on an organization. If an organization's reputation is ruined and the trust of customers is lost, the consequences to a business can be catastrophic.

We can also transfer a security risk to another party by contracting out the work. We will discuss the different types of security control shortly but whether it is physical or technical security, we can opt to have another organization handle it for us through a contract. The contract can contain provisions that protect the organization should requirements not be met.

An example of this approach is hosting your application with a cloud provider. Some aspects of security can be transferred to the cloud provider, such as the physical security of facilities and servers, environmental security (for example, patching the servers for security threats and providing anti-virus/malware protection), and handling the security of your data.

Accepting the risk

Another approach would be to simply accept the risk. If the prioritization of a security threat is low based on factors such as the potential damage, reproducibility, exploitability, the potential number of affected users, and the effort it would take to mitigate the risk, it is sometimes decided to accept the risk.

Mitigating the risk

Risk mitigation of a security threat involves implementing some type of security control to mitigate the risk. The goal is to reduce or eliminate the possibility of the threat occurring and/or reduce the amount of damage that can result from the threat. There are different types of security controls that can be put in place to mitigate security risks depending on the nature of the threat.

Types of security control

Security controls are countermeasures or safeguards that are used to handle security risks. When taking a holistic approach to the security of your software application, a software architect must look at the different types of security controls that can be used, including physical, administrative, and technical security.

In addition to categorizing security controls by the manner in which they work, we can categorize security controls by their overall goal and purpose. A security goal can be used for prevention, detection, or a response to a threat. A security control can be described by a combination of these two different types of categorization. For example, a security control can be both technical and for the purpose of detection.

Physical security controls

Physical security consists of security measures that are put in place to prevent unauthorized access to facilities, equipment (for example, servers), personnel, and other resources. Physical security is a combination of multiple systems working together and may include gates, locks, key cards, video surveillance, lighting, alarm systems, and security personnel.

When you think about securing a software application, you may tend to focus on other aspects of security, but physical security should not be overlooked. Some security threats are only made possible when an attacker gains physical access to one or more resources. Attackers may be internal or external to the organization, so the use of multiple techniques is the most effective way of enforcing physical security.

For some organizations, this is yet another advantage of hosting their software applications in the cloud. Major cloud providers have a tremendous amount of experience operating data centers and provide a high level of physical security. It can be cost-effective, particularly for smaller organizations, to use a cloud provider and leverage their security as opposed to operating their own data center.

Administrative controls

Administrative controls include organizational policies and procedures that are put in place for security. An organization must consider security concerns in their overall organizational policies and procedures. Some examples of this include:

- Security awareness training for employees
- Escalation plan in the event of a security attack
- Employees being required to carry and display a photo identification card
- Policies regarding acceptable use of company hardware and networks
- Policies related to what type of software can be installed on company hardware
- Rules on how company and customer data is handled
- Implementation of company password policies, including the required level of complexity and requiring employees to change them periodically
- Required use of anti-virus software
- Procedures regarding required software updates, including operating system patches
- Rules related to opening and sending emails, including their attachments
- Policies related to remote access of company hardware and networks
- Procedures regarding the monitoring of servers
- Wireless network communication procedures
- A service continuity plan that can be used to keep a software system operational after an event such as a security attack or natural disaster

An organization's hiring practices for all of their employees should also consider security. They must include steps to minimize the potential of hiring someone who is or can become a security concern.

A pre-employment screening should be conducted prior to hiring a new employee in order to investigate and confirm the backgrounds of candidates. Background checks can include identity and address verification, a criminal history check, speaking with references, and confirming academic accomplishments.

Pre-employment screenings also typically involve a credit check. These types of check do not reveal a candidate's credit score or account numbers. An excessive number of late payments and the mishandling of personal finances may indicate that a candidate is not organized or responsible. If a candidate has excessive debt, is using a high percentage of their available credit, or is having other financial difficulties, there may be an increased likelihood of theft. Employers need to notify the candidate and get their permission in order to conduct a credit check. Laws regarding credit checks vary by state so the **human resources (HR)** department of an organization should be aware of any laws that it must follow.

Screening employees should not be considered a one and done type of event but rather a continuous process. Many employees do not have any intention of attacking the organization when they are hired, but things can change over time that cause an employee to change their motivations later. Organizations should also have procedures for the termination of an employee. A set of steps should be taken each time an employee quits or is otherwise terminated so that the different types of access they have been granted (for example, physical access to a facility, access to their email account, and network access) are revoked in a timely manner.

Technical security controls

Technical security controls utilize technology to provide security for a software system. These controls are implemented through technical solutions such as software, firmware, or hardware. We will discuss some of the technical security controls available to us later in this chapter, but examples include the use of encryption, hashing, authentication, authorization, logging, monitoring, utilizing proper communication protocols, hardware/network protection, and database security.

Prevention

The purpose of a prevention security control is to avert a security threat before it occurs. Preventing a security threat requires analysis and planning. Some physical, administrative, and technical security controls are used for prevention.

For example, locks and key cards are physical control measures intended to prevent a security attack. Security awareness training and company password policies are administrative examples of preventive controls. Technical controls that are preventive include encryption, hashing, authentication, authorization, installing operating system security patches, using anti-virus and malware detection software, and the use of firewalls.

Detection

Security controls designed to detect a security threat are an important part of an overall security strategy. Regardless of the preventive measures that are put into place, you should expect that they will fail and assume that a security attack will eventually happen. This will put you in the proper mindset to earnestly consider how to detect attacks. It is critical for your software to have the ability to detect and properly notify individuals when an attack occurs.

Security cameras, motion detectors, system monitoring, logging, auditing, and the use of anti-virus and malware detection software are all examples of detection security controls.

Response

The detection of threats has value only if there are available responses. Plans for the responses to various attacks should be made in advance. You do not want to be making important decisions in the middle of an attack.

Examples of a physical security response include the sounding of an alarm and the locking of doors. An administrative security control with the purpose of responding to a security threat is an escalation plan that dictates the actions to be taken in the event of an attack. Another example is a service continuity plan that ensures the software application will continue to be operational even in the face of an unexpected event such as a security attack, a natural disaster, or some other event.

Technical security controls used in the response of a security attack include taking servers offline, using anti-virus software to remove and quarantine a virus, rolling back to a backup version of the application, restoring data from a backup, and revoking user permissions/disabling a user account.

Secure by design

Software architects should strive to create software systems that are *secure by design*. By following proven security principles and practices, we can make our software applications more secure.

Minimizing the attack surface

The *attack surface* consists of all of the points that an attacker can use to get into a system. The design of a software system should attempt to minimize the total attack surface area as much as possible. Using different types of security control and following security principles and practices that are known to improve security can reduce the attack surface. One should consider the attack surface when choosing from among multiple approaches that will satisfy a particular functional requirement.

Defense in depth

Security tends to be more effective when a variety of techniques is used together. No security control is perfect, and **defense in depth** is the concept of using multiple techniques in conjunction and the belief that in doing so a software system will be made more secure.

If one security control fails, a threat may be prevented by another security control. Layering defenses using several independent methods will make it much more difficult to exploit a vulnerability.

Principle of least privilege (PoLP)

One of the security principle that can be applied to software systems is the **principle of least privilege (PoLP)**. The principle of least privilege, which is sometimes referred to as the principle of least authority, informs us that the least amount of privileges that are necessary should be granted to a user or process in order to reduce security risks. Following this principle is one way to minimize the attack surface.

In addition to each user being granted as few privileges as necessary, each component of a system should only be granted the privileges that are necessary. Components that are complex should not have a large number of privileges. If necessary, complex components may need to be split up into simpler components.

It may take some effort to determine what the least amount of privileges actually is, but even though it may be easier to assign more privileges than are necessary, being as precise as possible with the level of privileges that are necessary will minimize the attacker surface.

Avoiding security by obscurity

Security by obscurity, also known as security through obscurity, is the belief that a software system is secure as long as internal details are kept hidden and vulnerabilities are not known or are difficult to detect.

Software architects should not promote or encourage security through obscurity because it is a practice we would like to avoid. While it can help to provide some level of security, it is a weak security control. If it is used, it should be used in conjunction with other, stronger security controls.

Keep software designs simple

Simplicity in the overall design of the system is important for security because a system that software architects and developers have a difficult time understanding is one that may not be secure. A more complex system makes it more difficult to reason about all of the different threat possibilities. There is a greater likelihood of a mistake being made during implementation, configuration, or the use of a software system when it is complex.

Software systems that are more complicated tend to have a larger attack surface. As long as requirements are being met, simple and elegant designs should be favored over complex ones for a variety of reasons, one of which is security. As was mentioned in discussing the principle of least privilege, complex components may need to be re-designed in such a way to minimize complexity.

Secure by default

Secure by default, also known as security by default, is the concept of delivering your software in a state that maximizes security *out of the box*, without requiring any changes. If the software is configurable in a way that allows security to be reduced, that should be up to the user to change rather than be the default behavior. For example, if a software application allows **two-factor authentication (2FA)** to be configured, it should be turned on by default.

Default deny

Authorization within the application should follow a **default deny** approach whereby permissions must be granted as opposed to being denied. In other words, access should be denied by default unless it has specifically been granted, as opposed to a user being provided all access except for operations that have been specifically denied. This concept is related to, and complementary with, the idea of being *secure by default*.

Validating input

A number of software vulnerabilities can be avoided by being diligent about validating input from any untrusted sources. Whether it is user input from a user interface, command-line arguments being passed into a program, environmental variables, or data from third parties, the software application should be wary of it and validate it accordingly.

In the case of data from a third party, that party may have security policies and standards that differ from your own, so a software application should check the data that it receives from an external entity to ensure that it is valid.

Secure the weakest link

As the old saying goes, *a chain is only as strong as its weakest link*. This concept can be applied to software systems as well. Security of a software system is only as secure as its weakest component. Attackers will focus on the weakest component, so be sure that the weakest point in the system is secure enough.

Security must be usable

Legitimate users who are using the software in the way that it was intended to be used should only be impacted to the point that is required to make the system secure. The security controls that are used for a software application cannot be so intrusive that they interfere greatly with the usability of the application. If the security controls that are used are too annoying, users will seek to circumvent them.

A software application must be as secure as it needs to be but it should not be overly secure to the point where usability is ruined. If usability is affected too much, users will not want to use the software.

When designing security controls, we should strive to do so in a user-friendly way. This includes ensuring that the security mechanisms are easy to understand. Without compromising security, the amount that users have to remember and the amount of effort (for example, the number of mouse clicks) that a user has to perform to abide by security controls should be minimized where it is possible to do so.

Fail securely

Failures are bound to happen and a software application that handles security properly will **fail securely**. Software architects should design solutions that consider what should happen when something fails and ensure that the software system and its data remain in a secure state after the failure. Application code should be written in such a way that there is proper exception handling and the default behavior is to deny access when a failure occurs.

Cryptography

Cryptography is the study and practice of keeping information secret. It is used in information security to maintain the confidentiality and integrity of data as well as to enable non-repudiation. It allows for secure communication of information from unauthorized parties. In our look at cryptography, we will be examining encryption and cryptographic hash functions, which are tools that can be used to secure data.

Encryption

Encryption is the process of transforming ordinary data, which is referred to as *plaintext*, into a format that is unreadable, which is referred to as *ciphertext*. This prevents unauthorized parties from accessing it. Data is encrypted using an encryption algorithm in conjunction with an encryption key. Larger key sizes result in greater encryption strength but make the process of encryption/decryption slower.

Data that is encrypted can be reverted to its original value. Encryption is used over hashing when there is a need to know the decrypted value. For example, the encryption is used to send a secure message to someone, it must be possible for the recipient to decrypt the message or it will be useless. Decryption is the process by which data is decrypted so that an authorized party can read it again. The pair of algorithms used for encryption/decryption is called a *cipher*. There are two types of encryption:

- Symmetric (secret key)
- Asymmetric (public key)

Symmetric (secret key) encryption

Symmetric encryption, also known as secret key encryption, uses a single key for both encryption and decryption. Although it is generally faster than asymmetric encryption/decryption, the main drawback is that both parties must have access to the secret key.

Asymmetric (public key) encryption

Asymmetric encryption, also known as public key encryption, uses two keys to encrypt and decrypt data. One of the keys, called the public key, can be shared with everyone, while the other key, called the private key, is kept secret.

Both keys can be used to encrypt a message and the opposite key from the one used to encrypt a message can be used to decrypt it. For example, a public key can be used for encryption and the private key can be used for decryption. It is generally slower than symmetric encryption/decryption.

Cryptographic hash functions

A **hash function** is a function that returns a fixed output for a given input. The input can be any size but the output is of fixed size. The output of a hash function is commonly called a *hash*, but it can also be referred to as a message digest, digest, hash value, or hash code. If there will be no need to know the original value prior to hashing, then hashing should be favored over encryption

Some examples of hash functions include MD5, SHA-256, and SHA-512. For example, the following is the **Secure Hashing Algorithm 256 (SHA-256)** hash of the string `This is a message`:

```
a826c7e389ec9f379cafdc544d7e9a4395ff7bfb58917bbebee51b3d0b1c996a
```

In the case of SHA-256, no matter how long the input is, the hash will be a 256-bit (32-byte) hash value. This is useful because even if the input is very long (for example, the contents of a file), we know that the hash will be a fixed length. Unlike encryption, where the original value can be determined through decryption, hash functions are not reversible.

Hashes can be used for purposes such as comparing two files for equality without having to read all of the contents of both files, as a checksum for detecting errors during transmission of data, finding similar records or substrings, and in data structures such as a hash table or a Bloom filter.

A **cryptographic hash function** is a type of hash function that guarantees certain properties, making it secure and suitable for cryptography. The combination of these properties makes a hash function useful for cryptography. We can use cryptographic hash functions for things such digital signatures, HTTPS certificates, and in protocols such as SSL/TLS and SSH. *Non-cryptographic hash functions* are faster but provide weaker guarantees. The following are the main properties of a cryptographic hash function:

- **Quick**: Cryptographic hash functions are quick to generate a hash value for a given message. If a hash function is not fast, the performance of the processes that use it may reach unacceptable levels for the given use cases.
- **Deterministic**: It is deterministic in that the same message will always produce the same hash. It is this property that allows us to compare two hashes in order to determine if they represent the same original value, without knowing the original value.
- **One-way function**: It is a one-way function in that it is infeasible to generate a message from a hash without trying out all possible messages (brute-force search). Please note that, by infeasible, we mean that although it is not impossible, it is impracticable.

- **Collision resistant**: It is collision resistant in that it is infeasible to find two different messages with the same hash value. A collision takes place when two different inputs result in the same hash. There should not be any collisions with a secure hash function. Some hash functions, like MD5 and SHA-1, can result in collisions and should not be used for cryptographic purposes.
- **Small changes result in vastly different hashes**: A small change to a message should yield a new hash that is significantly different from the old one, such that it is not possible to correlate the two hashes. For example, the first of the two hashes below is from the string `Hello World` while the second one is from the string `Hello Worlds`. As you can see, even though the original strings are almost identical, the hashes are very different:

```
a591a6d40bf420404a011733cfb7b190d62c65bf0bcda32b57b277d9ad9f146e
b0f3fe9cdc1beeb7944d90e9b2e77b416fd097b5cc2c58838f8741e8129a1a52
```

Identity and access management (IAM)

Identity and access management (**IAM**) comprises policies and tools for managing digital identities and controlling access to information and functionality. Two of the fundamental concepts of IAM are authentication and authorization.

Authentication

Authentication is the process of determining if someone (or something) is who (or what) they claim to be. It deals primarily with validating the identity of a subject. Examples of a subject that may need to be authenticated include a user, a service, a computer, or an application.

In the early days of software development, applications would commonly maintain their own user profiles for authentication, which would include some type of unique identifier (for example, a username or email address) and a password. Users provide their identifier and password and, if they match with the values the application has for a user profile, then the user is considered to be authenticated.

What is multi-factor authentication (MFA)?

Multi-factor authentication (**MFA**) adds an extra level of security. In multi-factor authentication, a person has to present two or more authentication factors. The variation of multi-factor authentication in which only two authentication factors must be presented is called **two-factor authentication** (**2FA**). The following are different types of authentication factor:

- **Knowledge factor**: Something the person knows, such as a password or PIN
- **Possession factor**: Something the person has, such as a cell phone that can receive a code or a company identification card that can be swiped
- **Inherence factor**: Something the person is, using such as using a fingerprint scanner, palm reader, retina scanner, or some other type of biometric authentication

For example, as part of authentication, a software system may require that a user not only supply a password (a knowledge factor) but also enter a numeric code that is sent to the user's cell phone. The cell phone has to be in the user's possession in order for them to receive the code (a possession factor). In order for a hacker to break into an account, they would need to steal not only a user's password but they must also get possession of that user's phone.

Authorization

Authorization is the process of determining what a subject is permitted to do and what resources that subject is allowed to access. It involves granting rights to allow users or programs to have access to a system or parts of a system. The user or program must first be authenticated in order to determine whether they are who they claim to be. Once they are authenticated, they can be authorized to access parts of a system.

Software architects should consider the granularity of privileges. If privileges are too coarse-grained, they may be too large and encompass too many rights. This may require privileges to be granted more frequently and give recipients more access than is necessary. In these types of cases, consider splitting up privileges into more fine-grained privileges to provide greater access control.

Storing plaintext passwords

Although rare today, some applications persist passwords in plaintext in a data store. Obviously, storing passwords in plaintext is an anti-pattern because either an internal or external attacker could gain access to the database and all of the passwords would be compromised.

Storing encrypted passwords

To provide protection of passwords, some software applications encrypt the passwords. During registration, the password is encrypted prior to being stored. In order to authenticate, the encrypted password is decrypted using the appropriate algorithm and a key. The plaintext password entered by the user is then compared with the decrypted password.

However, because an encrypted value can be decrypted back to its original value, if an attacker can either intercept a decrypted password or obtain the details necessary to decrypt a password, security will be compromised. If you need to store passwords, encryption is not the method that we want to use.

Storing hashed passwords

As we learned in the *Cryptographic hash functions* section earlier in this chapter, cryptographic hash functions are one-way functions with no practical way of reversing the hash back to the original value. This characteristic makes them useful for password storage. It is imperative though that you select a cryptographic hash function that is not broken (does not have any known collisions).

As part of user registration, the password is hashed. When a user logs on, they enter their password in plaintext, which is hashed and compared with the stored hash value. However, hashing alone is not sufficient for storing passwords. A *dictionary attack* can be executed to guess a password by comparing it with a pre-compiled list. A table of pre-calculated hashes and their original values, called a *rainbow table*, can be used for comparison with a hash to determine the password.

In order to slow down dictionary attacks and the use of rainbow tables to the point where they are impractical, software applications should hash a combination of the password with some piece of random data, known as a *salt*. A new salt should be randomly generated for each password and be of sufficient length (for example, a 64-bit salt). It is the combination of the salt and the password that is hashed. When a salted hash is used in conjunction with a hashing function such as Argon2, scrypt, brcrypt, or PBKDF2, it makes it necessary for a rainbow table to be large enough that it is prohibitively difficult for attackers.

When a new user is registered, the plaintext password is combined with the salt, hashed, and the hashed value is persisted. When a user logs in, the entered password is hashed with the salt and the value is then compared with the persisted hashed value. This approach to managing identity and storing passwords as salted hashes is still in common use today. However, many modern applications have taken the responsibility of authentication and the storage of passwords away from applications and given them to a central identity provider.

Using domain authentication

Once enterprises started developing applications that lived in their own local networks, it made sense to leverage domain authentication. Rather than have each application implement authentication independently, the functionality was centralized. On Windows servers, the **domain controller** (**DC**), along with a directory service such as **Active Directory** (**AD**), can manage resources and users for the entire domain. When users log on to a company network, they are authenticated in that domain and authorization can be accomplished using the attributes of the user profile. For intranet applications, this approach works well and is still popular.

Implementing a centralized identity provider (IdP)

Many modern applications have to interact with APIs that are not in the same domain and may not be under its control. A web application, mobile application, or API may need to communicate with other applications and APIs outside its domain, requiring them to be public. Domain authentication is not sufficient for this case. The ability to grant access to resources across applications without sharing login credentials is a common requirement and can be accomplished by implementing a **centralized identity provider** (**IdP**).

Another advantage of an identity provider is that the applications that we build do not have to be responsible for authentication. Instead, that task becomes the responsibility of the identity provider. Functionality such as user registration, password policies, password changes, and handling locked out accounts can be handled by an identity provider. Once implemented, all of this functionality can then be reused across multiple applications. In addition to reusability, maintainability is improved because, if a change is required in any part of this functionality, it can be modified in a single location. For instance, we have already seen how best practices for authentication and password storage have changed over time. These could continue to change, and by using a central identity provider we would only be required to make modifications in one place.

OAuth 2/OpenID Connect (OIDC)

OAuth 2 is an open standard for authorization. It allows an application to be granted access to resources from another application and share its own resources with other applications. **OpenID Connect (OICD)** is an identity layer that sits on top of OAuth 2. It can be used to verify the identity of an end-user. Let us take a look at how OAuth 2 and OpenID Connect work together to enable us to implement a centralized identity provider/authorization server for the purpose of handling authentication and authorization.

OAuth 2 roles

OAuth 2 defines four roles:

- **Resource owner**: Represents the person or application who owns the resource for which we need to control access
- **Resource server**: The server that hosts the resources; for example, a resource server may be an API that stores data that an application needs to access
- **Client**: The application that is requesting the resource
- **Authorization server**: Server that authorizes the client application to have access to a resource

It should be noted that the resource server and the authorization server can be the same server, but for larger applications they are commonly separate servers.

Authenticating with the identity provider

Authentication performed by an authorization server along with OpenID Connect allows clients to verify the identities of users. The client application, which is referred to as the *relying party* because it relies on the identity provider, requires a user's identity.

A flow determines how identity and access tokens are returned to the client. There are various flows depending on the types of application that are communicating and how we want that interaction to work. In one example, the client application (relying party) redirects to the authorization server, which serves as the identity provider. It sends an authentication request to the *authorization endpoint*, as it is this endpoint that the client application uses to obtain authentication and grant authorization to the client application.

If the user is authenticated, the identity provider redirects back to the client application using a *redirection endpoint* to return an authorization code and an identity token. The identity token can then be stored in either web storage (local storage) or a cookie. In line with the OpenID Connect specification, an identity token is a **JSON web token (JWT)**.

JSON web token (JWT)

A JWT is an open standard for representing claims between two parties. It is lightweight, making it efficient to transport. The following is an example of a JWT:

```
eyJhbGciOiJIUzI1NiIsInR5cCI6IkpXVCJ9.eyJpc3MiOiJleGFtcGxlLmNvbSIsImp0aSI6Im
MxZDA2YWQxLTRkMTUtNGY1Mi04YmMzLWMwZmVlODI1NDA5OSIsIm5hbWUiOiJKb2huIFNtaXRoI
iwiaWF0IjoxNTU1OTk4NjEwLCJleHAiOjE1NTg1OTA2MTB9.29WdHTGR5egA5_Q4N9WXtQHO-
hJydVJou-YiQYQpkq8
```

Each JWT has three parts:

- Header
- Payload
- Signature

The three parts are concatenated together with each part separated by a dot (period). If you look closely at the JWT above, you will find the three periods and therefore will be able to determine the three parts.

Header

The header of a JSON web token typically has two pieces of information: the type of token ("JWT"), and the hashing algorithm being used (for example, HMAC SHA256). A sample header looks like the following:

```
{
    "typ": "JWT",
    "alg": "HS256"
}
```

The header is Base64Url encoded prior to concatenating it with the other parts of the JWT.

Payload

The payload of a JSON web token contains the *claims*. Claims are statements about the entity being authenticated (for example, the entity may be a user). There are three types of claims:

- Registered
- Public
- Private

Registered claims are claims that have been predefined. They are not required but represent common claims that may be useful. Some examples of registered claims include:

- **Issuer** (iss): Issuer of the token
- **Subject** (sub): Subject of the token; claims are typically statements about the subject
- **Audience** (aud): Intended recipients of the token
- **JWT ID** (jti): Unique identifier for the token
- **Issued at** (iat): Timestamp representing when the token was issued; it can be used to determine the age of the token
- **Expiration time** (exp): Timestamp representing the time on or after which the token should no longer be accepted

Public claims are those that we can create ourselves. They should be defined as a URI with a namespace to avoid collisions. *Private claims* are custom claims that two parties agree to use in order to share information. Private claims are neither registered nor public.

The following is a sample payload:

```
{
    "iss": "example.com",
    "jti": "c1d06ad1-4d15-4f52-8bc3-c0fee8254099",
    "name": "John Smith",
    "iat": 1555998610,
    "exp": 1558590610
}
```

Like the header, the payload is Base64Url encoded.

Signature

The signature of a JSON web token ensures that the token was not altered at any point. If the token is signed with a secret key, then the signature also verifies the sender of the token. The signature is a hash that consists of the encoded header, the encoded payload, and the secret key using the hashing algorithm specified in the header. The following is an example:

```
HMACSHA256(
  base64UrlEncode(header) + "." +
  base64UrlEncode(payload),
  secretKey
)
```

Authorizing with the authorization server

Once a user is authenticated and the identity token and authorization code are returned, the client application can send a token request to the *token endpoint* in order to receive an access token. The token request should include the client ID, the client secret, and the authorization code.

An access token is then returned from the authorization server. Access tokens are not required to be JWTs but this standard is commonly used. Access tokens can be revoked, scoped, and time-limited, providing flexibility for authorization.

The application can then use the access token to request the resource from the resource server on behalf of the user. The resource server validates the access token and responds with the data.

Most common web application security risks

The **Open Web Application Security Project (OWASP)** is an online community focused on web application security. They offer useful information, including documentation, methodologies, and tools. I invite you to visit their website: https://www.owasp.org.

One of the things that they produce every year is a document listing the top web application security risks. In this section, we will take a look at some more recent risks.

Injection

This security risk occurs when untrusted data is sent to an interpreter and unintended commands are executed. This can cause unauthorized data to be accessed or manipulated. Anyone who can send untrusted data, including external and internal users, are possible threat agents.

A common form of injection is **SQL injection (SQLi)**, where SQL statements are included in data (such as user input) and are then unknowingly executed against the database. Among other things, a SQL injection attack could be used to retrieve, alter, or delete data. A **web application firewall (WAF)**, which sits between users and the web application, can protect software systems from some of the more common SQL injection attacks by using common signatures to identify SQL injection code. However, using a WAF is not sufficient, as it is impossible to identify all possible attacks. Validating untrusted data, using SQL parameters, and using the principle of least privilege are some techniques that can be used in conjunction with a WAF to prevent or lessen the effect of SQL injection attacks.

Broken authentication

A flaw in authentication and/or session management can compromise the security of a software system. Attackers can find a flaw in authentication or session management manually and then use automated tools to exploit it.

Some of the topics we have explored in this chapter, such as hashing passwords with a salt, using multi-factor authentication, and being secure by default by not deploying with default credentials, can help secure your system from authentication related attacks.

Password policies should be put in place to enforce minimum password length and complexity requirements, as well as to ensure passwords are rotated periodically.

Applications should always provide a logout feature and session timeouts should be short enough to prevent an attacker from gaining access simply by using a computer where the user did not previously log out. Session IDs should not be exposed in the URL (for example, URL rewriting), and session IDs should be rotated after a successful login. Information such as passwords, tokens, session IDs, and other credentials should be sent over secure connections.

Sensitive data exposure

This security risk involves not properly protecting sensitive data such as social security numbers, credit card numbers, credentials, and other important data. The first step is to identify what data elements (or combinations of data elements) are sensitive.

Only store sensitive data if it is necessary and discard it as soon as possible. Data that isn't retained in any way cannot be stolen. Earlier in this chapter, we discussed the different states of information. When sensitive data is at rest, it should be encrypted everywhere it is stored long-term, including backups of the data. When sensitive data is in transit, it should be encrypted with secure protocols. Strong and up-to-date encryption algorithms should be used along with proper key management.

Appropriate browser directives and headers should be set to protect sensitive data provided by or sent to the browser. You should consider disabling the caching of responses that contain sensitive data.

XML external entity (XXE) attack

An **XML external entity** (**XXE**) attack is one that can take place against an application that parses XML input. When XML input contains a reference to an external entity and is then processed by an XML parser that has not been configured appropriately, the application is vulnerable to this attack.

Denial of service (**DoS**), the disclosure of sensitive data, and **Server-Side Request Forgery** (**SSRF**) are all possible with an XXE attack. One type of DoS attack that is made possible with XXE is called a *billion laughs attack*. Sometimes this type of attack is referred to as an *XML bomb* or an *exponential entity expansion attack*.

Regardless of the name, it works by defining ten entities, the first of which is simply defined with a string. It is called a billion laughs attack because, in one common variation, the string "lol" is used. The following is an example of an XML document for this type of attack:

```
<?xml version="1.0"?>
<!DOCTYPE lolz [
 <!ENTITY lol "lol">
 <!ELEMENT lolz (#PCDATA)>
 <!ENTITY lol1 "&lol;&lol;&lol;&lol;&lol;&lol;&lol;&lol;&lol;&lol;">
 <!ENTITY lol2
"&lol1;&lol1;&lol1;&lol1;&lol1;&lol1;&lol1;&lol1;&lol1;&lol1;">
 <!ENTITY lol3
"&lol2;&lol2;&lol2;&lol2;&lol2;&lol2;&lol2;&lol2;&lol2;&lol2;">
 <!ENTITY lol4
"&lol3;&lol3;&lol3;&lol3;&lol3;&lol3;&lol3;&lol3;&lol3;&lol3;">
 <!ENTITY lol5
"&lol4;&lol4;&lol4;&lol4;&lol4;&lol4;&lol4;&lol4;&lol4;&lol4;">
 <!ENTITY lol6
"&lol5;&lol5;&lol5;&lol5;&lol5;&lol5;&lol5;&lol5;&lol5;&lol5;">
 <!ENTITY lol7
"&lol6;&lol6;&lol6;&lol6;&lol6;&lol6;&lol6;&lol6;&lol6;&lol6;">
 <!ENTITY lol8
"&lol7;&lol7;&lol7;&lol7;&lol7;&lol7;&lol7;&lol7;&lol7;&lol7;">
 <!ENTITY lol9
"&lol8;&lol8;&lol8;&lol8;&lol8;&lol8;&lol8;&lol8;&lol8;&lol8;">
 ]>
<lolz>&lol9;</lolz>
```

Each of the other entities is defined as consisting of ten of the previous entity. The XML document then consists of a single instance of the largest of these entities. When an XML parser loads the document, it expands that entity, which results in all of the other entities being expanded, to the point where there are a billion copies of the first entity. As you can see, the XML document is very small in size but the expansion takes up so much memory and time to parse that it causes a DoS.

One of the most effective ways of preventing this type of attack is to simply use a different data format, such as JSON. If XML must be used, disabling **document type definitions (DTDs)** completely is also effective. If that is not possible, then external entities or entity expansion must be disabled. Each parser is different so you will have to research how to go about making these configurations for the particular language/framework that you are using in your application. Make sure to upgrade all XML processors and libraries being used by the application so as to include the latest security fixes.

Broken access control

Exploitation of missing or broken access control is a common security threat. Lack of access control can be detected manually or, in some cases, by using automated tools. This can allow attackers to act with elevated privileges, which may allow them to retrieve, add, update, or delete data.

Applications must verify security rights not just on the UI side but also on the server side. Even if the functionality is hidden in the UI from users who do not have proper access rights, attackers may attempt to alter the URL, application state, identity tokens, or access tokens, or forge requests, to gain access to unauthorized functionality.

From the client side, development teams should ensure that the UI prevents the use of functionality by users who have not been granted access. On the server side, checks should be in place to prevent unauthorized access. Access tokens should be invalidated at the appropriate times, such as when a user logs out of the system.

The *deny by default* approach that was discussed earlier should be used to remove access control vulnerabilities or to minimize their effect. Access control failures should be logged and system administrators should be automatically notified when there are too many repeated failures. Software development testing must include the testing of access control.

Security misconfiguration

Misconfiguration of a software application is a major threat to security. Software applications that are more complex have a greater chance of being misconfigured. The application must be configured to be secure prior to deployment. This includes checking all settings before going into production, as many default values are not secure.

Everything that is unnecessary in a production environment should be disabled, removed, or simply not installed. Examples include accounts, privileges, ports, services, and accounts. Any default account passwords should be changed or the accounts should be disabled.

Some software applications use a number of tools and frameworks and they may not all be fully understood. It is critical that all components used within an application are configured properly. The software's error handling should not divulge too much information to users. For example, a detailed stack trace could be used by attackers for malicious purposes.

Development teams need to be aware of the vulnerabilities of the components they are using and keep up with the latest versions and patches to correct issues. A process must exist that will allow for keeping all software up to date, such as the operating system, the web/app server, database management system, and development frameworks. All too often, a vulnerability in a component has been corrected by a third party in a patch, but the patch is not installed.

Cross-site scripting (XSS)

Cross-site scripting (**XSS**) vulnerabilities allow attackers to execute scripts in the browser. The scripts might be designed to hijack a user's session, replace web site content, or redirect users. It is a highly prevalent security flaw. There are three major types of XSS attack:

- Reflected XSS
- Stored XSS
- DOM XSS

With *reflected XSS*, an application or API takes untrusted data and sends it to the browser without proper validation or escaping. *Stored XSS* is possible when an application or API stores user input data that has not been properly validated or escaped, which is viewed at a later time. *DOM XSS* is possible when data that is controlled by an attacker is included dynamically by a JavaScript framework, API, or other code.

Tests from the client side can ensure that there is validation to verify that all user-supplied input is safe and that all user supplied input sent back to the browser is properly escaped before it is included in the output page. The context-sensitive escaping of untrusted HTTP request data and client-side document manipulation can prevent various types of XSS attack.

Insecure deserialization

Deserialization exploits are possible when an attacker modifies an object that an application or API subsequently deserializes. If any classes can change their behavior either during or after deserialization, then remote code execution is possible, which can cause serious damage. Data structures that contain access control related data may also be tampered with, which could give an attacker unauthorized access or privileges.

To be completely safe from this vulnerability, an application could simply not accept any serialized objects from untrusted sources. When that is not possible, integrity checks should be made on serialized objects (for example, using a digital signature). Code that deserializes objects should be isolated and only be granted low-level privileges as much as possible. Deserialization exceptions should be logged.

Using components with known vulnerable components

Applications may consist of a variety of components, including third-party libraries and frameworks. A vulnerability in any of these components can compromise the overall security of the application.

Development teams must be aware of existing vulnerabilities in the components they are using, keep up with the latest announcements of new vulnerabilities, and apply patches and/or new versions that will fix vulnerabilities. If there are any unused dependencies or components, then they should be removed to reduce the possibility of exploits.

When obtaining components and libraries, be sure to get them from official sources and over secure links, or you will be inviting the possibility that such code has already been compromised. If your development team is using a component or library that is no longer being maintained, then any security flaws that exist are not being patched. You may need to consider moving to a different component or library. If that is not possible, then such components and libraries should be monitored for possible issues. If one is found and the source code is available, your development team may need to provide a patch.

Insufficient logging and monitoring

Insufficient logging and monitoring is an important security risk because it can help to enable so many other types of vulnerabilities. In order for attackers to be successful, they need to go undetected for as long as possible. When logging and monitoring are insufficient, then an attack can go unnoticed for a period of time.

A software system needs the ability to answer some fundamental who/what/when questions. Being able to associate user accounts with an event, reconstruct what happened before, during, and after an event, and know when different events occurred can all help you become aware of a security vulnerability.

Centralized log management is crucial because log data must be easy to consume. A system should be implemented that will send automatic alerts to the appropriate individuals based on logging and monitoring data. Do not neglect the fact that the logs themselves need to be secured. Unauthorized access to log data, wherever it is persisted, must be prevented in order to maintain the integrity of the log.

Unvalidated redirects and forwards

Web applications may redirect users to other pages and websites. Attackers can use redirects to send users to malicious sites or use forwards to access unauthorized pages. If possible, try to avoid redirects and forwards. If your application uses redirects and forwards, testing of them should include:

- A review of the code should be conducted for all uses of redirect or forward. For each use, identify if the target URL is included in any parameter values. If so, verify that the parameter(s) are validated to contain only an allowed destination or element of a destination.
- Someone on the team should spider the site to see if it generates any redirects (HTTP response codes 300-307, typically 302). Look at the parameters supplied prior to the redirect to see if they appear to be a target URL or a portion of such a URL. If so, change the URL target and observe whether the site redirects to the new target.
- All parameters in the code should be analyzed to see if they look like part of a redirect or forward URL so that those that are can be tested.

You should consider forcing all redirects to go through a page that notifies users that they are about to leave your site, with a link users can click on to confirm.

Summary

We learned about the CIA triad and its goals of providing confidentiality, integrity, and availability. Security is about tradeoffs, so you should try to maintain a balance between these goals. Software applications should be designed to be as secure as necessary, but requirements for quality attributes such as usability and availability must be met as well.

There are no silver bullets when it comes to implementing security. However, there are proven principles and practices we can use to secure our applications and data. This chapter examined threat modeling and different techniques to create applications that are *secure by design*.

We learned about cryptography, including encryption and hashing, and IAM. Software architects who work on web applications should keep up with the latest web application security risks so that they can be aware of them and learn how to mitigate them.

In the next chapter, we will learn about documenting and reviewing software architectures. Documentation of a software architecture is important so that the solution can be communicated to, and used by, others. The chapter will cover using the **Unified Modeling Language (UML)** to model the architecture and create architecture views. We will also explore the process of reviewing software architectures, including several proven review methods. Reviews of architectural decisions are important to ensure that the architecture will satisfy its requirements, including its quality attribute scenarios.

12
Documenting and Reviewing Software Architectures

An important aspect of being a successful software architect is the ability to record and communicate your architecture to others. We will begin by exploring the reasons why we document a software architecture. You will then become familiar with **architecture descriptions** (**ADs**) and the architecture views that are a part of them.

The chapter will provide an overview of the **Unified Modeling Language** (**UML**), which is one of the more popular and widely used modeling languages. You will learn about some of the most common UML diagram types.

As parts of a software architecture design are completed, the development team and relevant stakeholders need to review the architecture to determine whether it will satisfy the functional requirements and quality attribute scenarios. We will detail several different architecture review methods.

In this chapter, we will cover the following topics:

- Uses of software architecture documentation
- Creating architecture descriptions (ADs), including architecture views
- Overview of the UML
- Reviewing software architectures

Uses of software architecture documentation

Some software projects skip software architecture documentation altogether or do it merely as an afterthought. Some of the projects that complete architecture documentation only do so because it is required. For example, it may be required by an organization's process or there may be a contractual obligation to provide it to a client.

However, good software architects understand the value of documenting their software architecture. Good documentation serves to communicate the architecture to others, assist the development team, educate team members, facilitate architecture reviews, allow for the reuse of architectural knowledge, and help the software architect.

Communicating your architecture to others

A good software architecture is only useful if it can be communicated to others. If it cannot be communicated to others effectively, then those who need to build, use, and modify the architecture may not be able to do so, at least not in the way that the architect intended. During software architecture design, we identify all of the structures that make up the architecture and how they interact with each other. Documentation allows us to communicate those structures and interactions. The artifacts that are created when an architecture is documented focus on communicating the solution (architecture) to various audiences, which can be made up of both technical and non-technical people.

Software architects will need to communicate their architecture to the development team, management, and other stakeholders. Different stakeholders will have different reasons and priorities behind wanting to learn about the architecture, but a software architecture is abstract enough that a variety of people can use it to reason about a software system. Different types of architecture view can help to communicate the architecture to everyone who needs to understand it.

Assisting the development team

Documentation is useful to the team during the design and development of the software system. Learning about the structures and elements of the architecture and how they interact with each other will allow developers to understand how they should be implementing their functionality. By seeing the interfaces available, developers will gain an understanding as to what needs to be implemented and what is available to use in completed implementations. The documentation enables developers to complete their work in a way that abides by the design decisions that have been made for the architecture.

Software architecture also restricts some of the design choices available to developers and puts constraints on implementation, reducing the complexity of the software system. Architecture documentation communicates design decisions, which helps to prevent developers from making the wrong decisions about how a piece of functionality should be implemented.

Educates team members

Software architecture documentation is also beneficial in educating the developers on the team. Developers who are unfamiliar with the system, either because it is a new one that has just begun its design process or because they have joined an existing project, can use it as a guide to become familiar with the architecture. It is useful for software developers to understand the design decisions that shape the architecture they are using.

As a software architecture changes, the documentation should be updated as well. Good documentation will help to communicate any changes to the development team so that they can be aware of them.

Providing input for software architecture reviews

Software architectures are reviewed to ensure that they have the capability to meet requirements, including quality attribute scenarios. Architecture documentation is useful during this process because it contains details that will allow a review team to analyze an architecture and make these types of determination.

The documentation can also be used to evaluate and compare alternative software architectures. Architecture documentation helps those who are tasked with comparing architectures to accomplish their work by providing the necessary details to make informed and accurate evaluations.

Allowing for the reuse of architectural knowledge

Software architecture documentation allows architectural knowledge to be reused for other projects. The design decisions made, the design rationale that formed the decisions, and any lessons learned can be leveraged when other software systems need to be created or maintained.

Reuse allows organizations to be more efficient and productive with their software development. If an organization is developing a software product line, which consists of multiple products from the same company to address a particular market, the software products may have some similar functional and non-functional requirements and may share a similar look and feel in terms of the user interface. Parts of an architecture made for one software product may be useful for one or more of the other ones. Software architecture documentation can facilitate the reuse of an architecture.

Help the software architect

Documenting a software architecture helps the software architect. Software architects will be asked plenty of questions about the architecture by a variety of stakeholders and the documentation can help to answer them. It supports software architects to fulfill some of their responsibilities by providing artifacts with which to communicate the architecture to others, assist the development team, educate team members, review the software architecture, and pass on architectural knowledge for reuse.

Some projects are rather complex and it can be difficult to remember all of the structures that make up the architecture and how they interact with each other, even for the software architect who was directly involved. The documentation can help to remind a software architect of this information if it has to be revisited months or even years later.

A software architect may be trying to get a project off the ground or to gain funding for their project. Solid documentation can help the software architect achieve these goals by providing information to stakeholders. Software architects can use some of the completed documentation when they have presentations to give about the software.

If a software architect leaves the project or the organization, the documentation that is left behind can answer questions when the software architect is no longer available.

Creating architecture descriptions (ADs)

An **architecture description** (**AD**) is a work product used to express and communicate an architecture. The actual architecture of a software system is separate from the artifacts that describe and document it, such that we can create different artifacts for a given architecture.

ADs identify the stakeholders of the software system and their concerns. Stakeholders include people such as users, administrators, domain experts, business analysts, product owners, management, and the development team.

Each of these stakeholders has various concerns, which are either unique to them or shared with other stakeholders. Examples of system concerns related to architecture include the goals of the system, the suitability of the architecture to accomplish those goals, the ability of the architecture to meet quality attribute scenarios, the ease with which the software system can be developed and maintained with the architecture, and any risks to the stakeholders. ADs consist of one or more architecture views, with the views addressing the different concerns of the stakeholders.

Software architecture views

Many software systems are complex, making them difficult to understand. This is particularly true when one attempts to look at the whole system at once. **Architecture views** are used to ease understanding, as each one focuses on a specific structure or structures of the architecture. This allows a software architect to document and communicate only a small piece of the architecture at a time. Having multiple views represent an architecture allows the software architect to communicate it in a manageable way.

Deciding which views to create depends on the goals of the documentation and the audience. In the *Uses of software architecture documentation* section earlier in this chapter, we covered some of the reasons that documentation is useful. Different views will focus on different aspects of the architecture, so the intended usage of the architecture documentation will dictate the types of view that you create.

There is no definitive list of views that must be created. The same goes for deciding how many views to create. Each software project is different, so there is no set number of views that are required for all of them. The number of artifacts that need to be created for a software architecture is the amount necessary to effectively communicate your architecture to the different audiences that are interested.

There is a cost associated with creating and maintaining a view, so we only want to introduce a view if it is needed and will provide a benefit. We never want the documentation to be insufficient but we also do not want to spend inordinate amounts of time creating too much of it.

During software architecture design, informal documentation, in the form of sketches, should be made to record design decisions. These sketches may include items such as the structures, elements, relationships between elements, and architecture patterns used. These sketches are important to document the work that was done during design. While they are not complete enough to be released as the final documentation, they can be used as the basis for the architecture views once it comes time to formally document the architecture.

Software architecture notations

There are different types of notation that can be used with software architecture views. They help software architects to communicate their design and some of them can be used by tools for code generation.

Notations differ from each other predominately based on their level of formality. Notations that are more formal typically require more effort, not just in creating the artifacts but also in understanding them. However, they can provide more detail and reduce ambiguities that may exist with less formal notations.

There are many different notations. Each one is good for something but none of them are good for everything. When deciding which notation to use for all or some of your views, consider the purpose of the diagrams, the stakeholders that will be examining them, your familiarity with the notation, and the tools that are available to create them. The three main types of software architecture notation are:

- Informal
- Semiformal
- Formal

Informal software architecture notations

Informal notations are views of the architecture that are often created with general-purpose tools, using whatever conventions the team deems appropriate. Using this type of notation helps communicate the software architecture to customers and other stakeholders who may not be as technical or have the need for more formalized approaches. Software architects may consider using this notation for artifacts created for the project's management team. They can help project management to understand the scope of the project.

Natural language is used with the notation, so these types of artifacts cannot be formally analyzed and tools will not be able to automatically generate code from the artifacts.

Semiformal software architecture notations

A semiformal notation in views is a standardized notation that can be used in diagrams. However, fully-defined semantics are not part of a semiformal notation. Unlike informal notations, this type of notation allows for some level of analysis and can potentially be used to automatically generate code from the models.

UML is an example of a semiformal notation that is very popular for modeling. There are some notations that can be used with UML that extend it to provide more robust semantics, making UML more formalized.

Formal software architecture notations

Views of the architecture that use formal notations have precise semantics, usually mathematically based. This allows for formal analysis of both the syntax and the semantics. Tools can use artifacts created with a formal notation for automated code generation.

Some software projects choose to not use a formal notation because they require more effort to use, they require certain skills on the part of those creating the architecture views, and stakeholders may find them difficult to understand. Formal notations are not as useful for communication with non-technical stakeholders.

A number of formal notations exist, including various **architecture description languages (ADLs)**. An ADL is a formal type of expression that is used to represent and model a software architecture. **Architecture Analysis and Design Language (AADL)** and **Systems Modeling Language (SysML)** are two examples of ADLs. AADL was originally created to model both hardware and software. It can be used to describe a software architecture, create documentation, and generate code.

The book *Documenting Software Architectures – Views and Beyond* describes AADL as follows:

> *"The AADL standard defines a textual and graphical language to represent the runtime architecture of software systems as a component-based model in terms of tasks and their interactions, the hardware platform the system executes on, possibly in a distributed fashion, and the physical environment it interfaces with, such as a plane, car, medical device, robot, satellite, or collections of such systems. This core language includes properties concerning timing, resource consumption in terms of processors, memory, network, deployment alternatives of software on different hardware platforms, and traceability to the application source code."*

SysML is a general-purpose, graphical modeling language for systems. It is a standard that is maintained by the Object Management Group (OMG). It can be used for a number of activities, including specification, analysis, design, and verification.

SysML is a subset of UML and reuses some of the same diagram types. We will discuss UML in more detail shortly but here is a list of the SysML diagram types that are reused from UML without any modification:

- Use case diagrams
- Sequence diagrams
- State diagrams
- Package diagrams

The following diagrams have been modified in SysML from their UML counterparts:

- Activity diagrams
- Block definition diagrams
- Internal block diagrams

SysML also introduces some new diagram types that do not exist in UML:

- Requirement diagrams
- Parametric diagrams

Including design rationales

An architecture description should include the **design rationale** behind the design decisions being documented. In Chapter 5, *Designing Software Architectures*, we discussed the design rationale, which is an explanation that contains the reasons and justification for design decisions related to the architecture. Without documenting the design rationale, the reasons that a design decision was made will not be known. Recording the design rationale is beneficial even for those who are involved in a design decision, as the details of a decision can be forgotten over time.

It is not necessary (or practical) to record every design decision that is made but any decisions that are important to the architecture are candidates to be documented. When documenting a design rationale, keep in mind that in addition to including design decisions, it is sometimes useful to include details on why alternative approaches were not taken and why certain design decisions were not made at all.

Overview of the Unified Modeling Language (UML)

The **Unified Modeling Language** (**UML**) is a general-purpose, standardized modeling language. It is widely used and understood, making it a popular choice for modeling a software architecture. While this section is not intended as an exhaustive tutorial on UML, we will cover some of the most popular UML diagrams and their purpose. If you are already familiar with UML or prefer to use a different modeling language, feel free to skip this section.

Types of modeling

In UML, there are two main types of modeling: *structural modeling* and *behavioral modeling*. Structural modeling focuses on the static structure of the system, its parts, and how they are related to each other. They do not show details about the dynamic behavior of a system. Some of the structure diagrams in UML include:

- Class diagrams
- Component diagrams
- Package diagrams
- Deployment diagrams

Behavioral modeling shows the dynamic behavior of the components in a system. Unlike the static nature of structure diagrams, behavior diagrams describe changes to the system over time. Some of the behavior diagrams in UML include:

- Use case diagrams
- Sequence diagrams
- Activity diagrams

Class diagrams

Classes are templates (blueprints) for creating objects in a software system. They include attributes (member variables) that hold the state of an object and operations (methods) that represent behavior. **Class diagrams**, which are among the most popular of UML diagrams, show us the structure of a software system by allowing us to see the classes and their relationships. A number of team members may find class diagrams useful, including the software architect, developers, QA personnel, operations engineers, product owners, and business analysts.

A rectangle is used in a class diagram to graphically represent a class and each one can have up to three sections in it. The upper section shows the name of the class, the middle section contains the attributes of the class, and the bottom section details the operations.

Visibility

Visibility dictates the accessibility of a member (attribute or operation) and can be designated by placing a notation before the member's name. In general, you want to give only as much accessibility as is needed. The following table details the most common visibility notations:

Notation	Visibility	Description
+	Public	Member is accessible by other types.
#	Protected	Member is accessible within the same type as well as types that inherit from it.
~	Package	Member is accessible from any type within the same package. It is not accessible from outside the package, even if it is an inheriting class.
-	Private	Member is accessible only within the type that declares it.

For example, the following diagram shows the **Order** class, which has two private attributes, **OrderId** and **OrderDate**, as well as two public operations, **CalculateTax** and **CalculateTotal**:

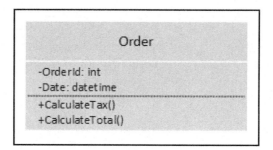

Association

An association is a broad term that refers to a semantic relationship between classes. If one class uses another class (unidirectional), or two classes use each other (bidirectional), they have a relationship. Relationships between classes are represented by an association, which is shown on a class diagram as a solid line:

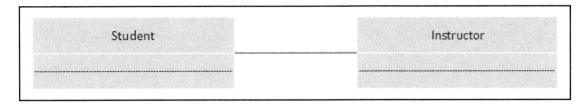

When there are no arrowheads at the end of the line, the navigability of the association is unspecified. However, in diagrams where arrows are used for one-way navigable associations, a line with no arrows is assumed to represent bidirectional navigability. In the preceding example, which would mean that both **Student** and **Instructor** are accessible from each other. Alternatively, a bidirectional association can be depicted by having an open arrowhead at the end of both lines.

If we want to model unidirectional navigability, an open arrowhead can be used. In the following diagram, class **B** is navigable from class **A**:

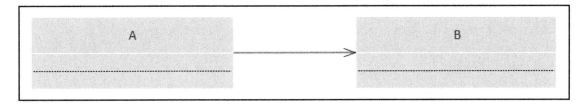

Aggregation and composition are subsets of association and are used to represent specific types of association.

Aggregation

Aggregation is a relationship in which a child object can exist independently of the parent. It is graphically represented by a hollow diamond shape. For example, in a domain with a **Tire** object, we can say that, even though a **Car** object has Tire objects, a **Tire** object can exist without a **Car** object:

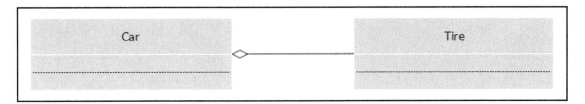

Composition

Composition is a relationship in which an object cannot exist independently of another object. It is graphically represented by a filled diamond shape. For example, in a domain with a **Room** object, we might say that a **Room** object cannot exist without a **Building** object:

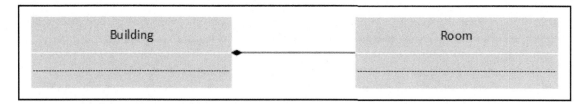

Multiplicity

Multiplicity allows you to define the cardinality of a relationship between classes. The multiplicity of a relationship describes the number of objects that can participate in it. The following table shows the different types of multiplicity that can be specified:

Notation	Multiplicity
0..1	Zero or one
1	One and only one
1..1	One and only one
0..*	Zero or more
*	Zero or more
1..*	One or more

For example, the following diagram depicts that each **Student** is taught by one or more instructors and that each **Instructor** teaches one or more students:

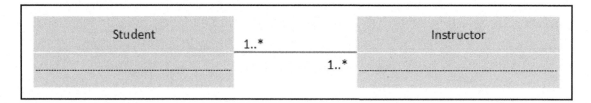

Dependency

A dependency is a type of relationship between UML elements, such as classes, in which one element requires, needs, or depends on another element. The dependency is sometimes referred to as a supplier/client relationship because the supplier provides something to the client. The client is either semantically or structurally dependent on the supplier. A dependency may mean that changes to a supplier may require changes to a client.

In an association, one class may have a reference to the other as a member variable. A dependency relationship is slightly weaker. For example, a dependency may exist because a return type or parameter for a method in one class references another class:

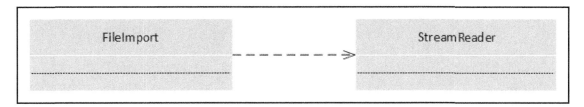

A dependency is graphically represented by a dashed line with an open arrowhead. In the preceding example, the **FileImport** class (client) depends on the **StreamReader** class (supplier). There can be many dependencies on a single diagram, so you may not want to show every dependency. However, you should show that are important to what you are trying to communicate in a particular diagram.

Generalization/specialization

Generalization is the process of abstracting common attributes and operations into a base class. The base class is sometimes referred to as the superclass, base type, or parent class. Generalization is also known as inheritance. The base class contains general attributes, operations, and associations that are shared with all of its subclasses. Generalization is graphically represented with a hollow triangle on the part of the connecting line that is closest to the base class.

Specialization is the converse of generalization in that it involves creating subclasses from an existing class. Subclasses are sometimes referred to as a derived class, derived type, inheriting class, inheriting type, or child class.

For example, our domain may have different types of account, such as a checking account and a savings account. These classes may share some of the same properties and behaviors. Rather than repeating what is shared in each of these account classes, our model may have an **Account** base class, which contains the generalized attributes and operations that are common to all account classes:

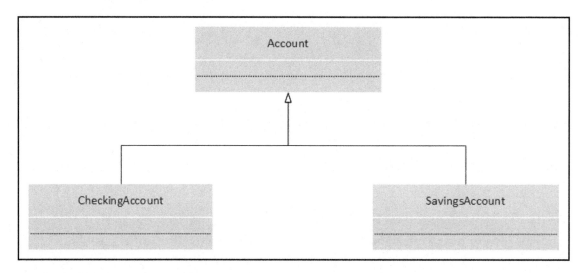

The **CheckingAccount** and **SavingsAccount** classes, which are subclasses, inherit from the **Account** class and demonstrate an *is a* relationship. **CheckingAccount** *is an* **Account**, just as **SavingsAccount** *is an* **Account**. **CheckingAccount** and **SavingsAccount** are specializations of **Account**.

Depending on the programming language used for implementation, it may be possible to allow some attributes or operations to be overridden in subclasses. Subclasses can also introduce their own specialized attributes, operations, and associations that are specific to their class.

Realization

Realization denotes a relationship in which one element *realizes* or implements the behavior that another element specifies. A common example of this is when a class implements an interface. Realization is graphically represented with a hollow triangle at the end of a dashed line, with the hollow triangle appearing closest to the element that is specifying the behavior.

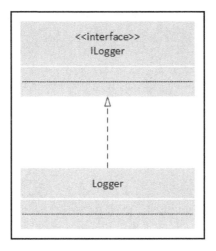

In the preceding diagram, you may have noticed that **ILogger** is designated as an interface. This designation is done through a *stereotype*. Stereotypes are one of the extensibility mechanisms available in UML, which allow you to extend vocabulary and introduce new elements. In this case, a stereotype has been used to indicate that **ILogger** is an interface.

Stereotypes are graphically represented by enclosing the name in guillemets (angle quotes). They are similar to the symbols for less than and greater than, which can be used if guillemets are unavailable.

Component diagrams

Component diagrams detail the structural relationship between components of a system. These diagrams are typically needed with complex software systems that consist of many components, as it is helpful to view the components and their relationships. They essentially depict how the components of a software system are wired together, which is why they are sometimes referred to as *wiring diagrams*.

Component diagrams help us to identify the interfaces between different components of our software system. Components communicate with each other through interfaces, and component diagrams allow us to see system behavior as it relates to an interface. Interfaces define a contract by defining the methods and properties that are required for implementations. Implementations can be changed as long as the classes that are dependent on them are coded for interfaces and not for specific implementations.

By identifying interfaces, we are able to identify the replaceable parts of our software system. Having this knowledge gives us the ability to know where we can potentially reuse a component that the organization has already created or where a third-party component could be used. Components that we create for a software system may also be leveraged in other software applications that the organization has in development or will develop in the future.

Knowing the components of a software system also makes it easier for project decision makers to divide up the work. Once the interface is agreed upon, one or more developers on the team, or even a separate team, can work independently of others in developing a component.

In a component diagram, components are graphically represented as a rectangle with a *component* symbol (a rectangular block with two smaller rectangles on the left side). For example, an **Order** component would look like the following:

Alternatively, the component stereotype can be used, either in addition to the component symbol or in place of it, to designate that an object on the diagram is a component.

Interfaces that a component provides are graphically represented by a *small circle* at the end of a line, which is also sometimes referred to as the *lollipop* symbol. Interfaces that a component requires are represented by a *half circle* at the end of a line, which is also referred to as a *socket*.

For example, let's say that our **Order** component implements the **IOrder** interface and requires an implementation of **ICustomer**. The **Customer** component implements the **ICustomer** interface:

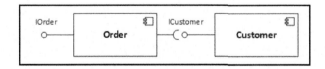

Keep in mind that components can contain other components. For example, we could model an **Order** system component that contains, within it, the **Order**, **Customer**, and other components, along with all of their relationships.

Package diagrams

In UML, packages logically group elements together and provide a namespace for the groups. Many UML elements, such as classes, use cases, and components, can be grouped together in packages. Packages can also contain other packages. **Package diagrams** are used to show the dependencies between packages in a software system.

The more complex a software system is, the more difficult it can be to understand all of the models. Package diagrams make it easier for people to reason about large, complex systems by grouping elements together and allowing us to see the dependencies.

In addition to modeling standard dependencies, we can model *package import* and *package merge* types of dependencies. A *package import* is a relationship between an importing namespace and an imported package. This can allow us to reference package members from other namespaces without fully qualifying them. A *package merge* is a relationship between two packages in which one package is extended by the contents of another package. The two packages are essentially combined.

A package is graphically represented in UML by a symbol that looks like a file folder with a name. The following is an example of a high-level package diagram for a layered application:

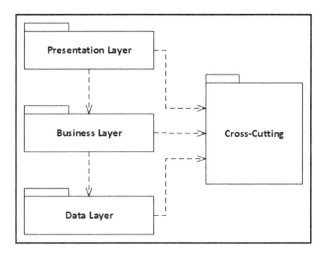

By looking at it, we can see that the **Presentation Layer** depends on the **Business Layer**, the **Business Layer** depends on the **Data Layer**, and all three layers depend on the **Cross-Cutting** package.

Deployment diagrams

Deployment diagrams represent the physical deployment of artifacts on nodes. An a*rtifact* is a physical piece of information, such as a source code file, binary file, script, table in a database, or document.

A *node* is a computational resource that artifacts are deployed on for execution. Nodes can contain other nodes. There are two types of node: device nodes and **execution environment nodes** (EENs).

- **Device**: A device represents a physical computational resource (hardware) that can execute a program. Examples include a server, laptop, tablet, or mobile phone. Devices may consist of other devices.
- **Execution environment**: An execution environment is a software container that resides in a device. It provides an execution environment for artifacts that are deployed on it. Examples include an operating system, a JVM, or a Docker container. Execution environments can be nested.

Deployment diagrams are used to show the software elements in an architecture and how they will be deployed to hardware elements. They provide a view of the hardware and the system's topology.

In a deployment diagram, nodes are graphically represented by a three-dimensional box. In the following example, there are three nodes. One represents the **Azure (App Service)**, one is **Desktop Device**, and one is **Mobile Device**. Notice that a <<device>> stereotype is used to indicate that a node is a device. The various nodes in the example contain components and the lines show associations between the nodes:

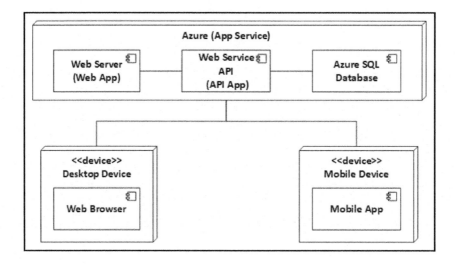

Use case diagrams

Use cases are text that describes a software system's behavior as it responds to requests from system users, known as *actors*. An actor is the role for someone or something that interacts with the system and can be a person, organization, or an external system.

Just like with classes in a class diagram, generalizations can be done on actors. *Actor generalization* is a relationship between actors in which one actor (descendant) inherits the role and properties from another actor (ancestor).

For example, if our domain had different types of managers, such as an **HR Manager** and a **Customer Service Manager**, they may both inherit from a **Manager** ancestor actor:

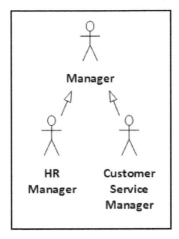

Actor generalization is graphically represented in the same way that generalization is with classes. It is done with a hollow triangle on the part of the connecting line that is closest to the *ancestor* actor.

Use cases are something that the system does or something that happens to the system. Use cases should be easy to read and are usually brief. Actors have goals and use cases describe ways to carry out those goals by using the software system.

A **use case diagram** is a graphic representation of a use case, the relevant actors, and their relationships. It details the actors and how they interact with the software system. Use case diagrams allow people to understand the scope of the software system and the functionality that will be provided to actors. They can be useful for traceability in that we can verify that a software system is meeting its functional requirements.

In a use case diagram, actors are typically represented by a stick figure with the name of the actor's role appearing underneath it. Use cases are graphically represented with a horizontally shaped oval. The name of the use case appears inside the oval:

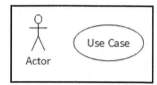

Lines are used to show associations between actors and use cases. Use case diagrams can describe context by showing the system's scope. A system boundary box can be used to present what is part of the system and what is external to it:

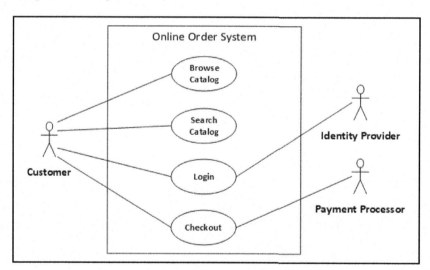

In the preceding diagram, there are three actors, all of which are external to the **Online Order System**. The **Customer** actor is a person but the **Identity Provider** and **Payment Processor** actors are external systems.

There are four use cases shown in this simplified example. The **Customer** is associated with all of them but the **Identity Provider** is only involved with the **Login** use case and the **Payment Processor** is only associated with the **Checkout** use case.

Sequence diagrams

Sequence diagrams model how components in a software system interact and communicate. They are one type of interaction diagram, which is a subset of behavior diagrams. Other interaction diagrams include the communication diagram, timing diagram, and interaction overview diagram.

Sequence diagrams describe a sequence of events from the software system. The following example shows the flow of logic within a system for price calculation:

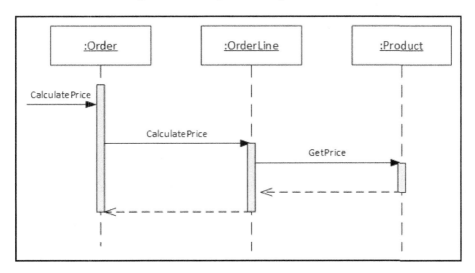

Sequence diagrams are sometimes referred to as event diagrams or event scenarios. They can be used to see how components interact with each other and in what order they do so. Some examples of what you might want to model using a sequence diagram include usage scenarios, service logic, and method logic.

Lifeline

In sequence diagrams, an object is graphically represented by a rectangle with its *lifeline* descending from the center of its bottom:

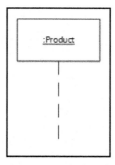

The lifeline shows the lifespan of the object and is represented by a vertical dashed line. The passage of time starts at the top of the line and goes downward. The rectangle can show both the name of the object and the class, separated by a colon, as follows:

```
objectname : classname
```

The object and class names are underlined. A lifeline can represent an object or a class. An object can be left unnamed if we are modeling a class or in cases where the object's name is unimportant. In that situation, you will simply see a colon followed by the class's name. Some people prefer to just see the class's name with no colon. If you are modeling objects and want to differentiate between different objects of the same class, you should specify an object name. When diagramming objects/classes, the attributes and operations of an object are not listed.

Activation boxes

Activation boxes on the lifelines show when an object is completing a task. For example, when a message is sent to an object, the time period from when the message is received until the response is returned can be represented with an activation box. Since activation boxes are on the lifelines, they also represent time. The longer the activation box, the longer the task will take to complete.

Messages

Arrows are used to graphically represent messages that are passed between objects. The type of arrow indicates the type of message that is being passed:

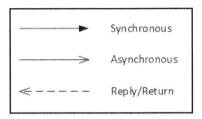

Synchronous messages are shown as a solid line with a solid arrowhead. A synchronous message is one in which the sender must wait for a response before it can continue. **Asynchronous** messages are represented by a solid line with a lined arrowhead. With an asynchronous message, the sender does not have to wait for a response before continuing. **Reply/Return** messages and asynchronous return messages are both represented by a dashed line with a lined arrowhead.

Loops

In order to model a loop in a sequence diagram, a box is placed over the part of the diagram that is iterating through a loop. An inverted tab at the top-left corner of the box is labeled with the word **loop** to signify that the structured control flow is a loop. The subject that is being iterated over is commonly labeled with a guard message that is placed below the inverted tab. In the following example, the logic is iterating over each line item in an order:

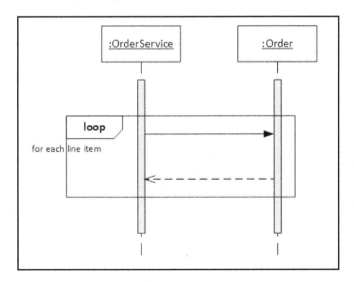

Optional flows

In a sequence diagram, you may need to model optional flows. These represent logic that will optionally be executed based on some condition. Similar to loops, an optional control flow is graphically represented with a box that is placed over the part of the diagram that is related to the optional flow. An inverted tab at the top-left corner of the box is labeled with **opt** to denote that it is an optional flow.

The condition for the optional flow can be labeled by using a guard message that is placed below the inverted tab. In the following diagram, an optional flow is executed only if a member is a platinum member:

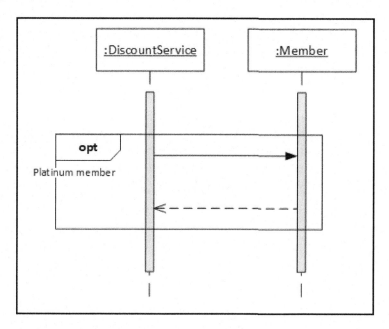

Alternative flows

When you want to model alternative (conditional) fragments in a sequence diagram, a box can be placed over the part of the diagram that captures the alternatives. An inverted tab at the top-left corner of the box is labeled with **alt** to denote that it is an alternative fragment.

Alternative flows are similar to optional ones so the two should not be confused with each other. While an optional flow checks a single condition and may or may not execute a fragment, alternative flows offer multiple possibilities. Only the alternative fragment whose condition is true will execute.

A guard message can be placed at the start of each alternative to describe the condition and a dotted line is used to separate each alternative. In the following diagram, there are two alternatives, one for platinum members and one for standard members:

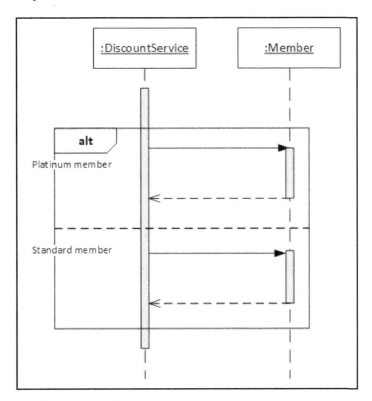

Activity diagrams

An **activity diagram** allows us to visually represent a series of actions in the form of a workflow. It shows a control flow and is similar to a flowchart. Activity diagrams can be used to model things such as a business process, flow within a use case, and procedural logic.

The following diagram shows the workflow for creating a new membership card:

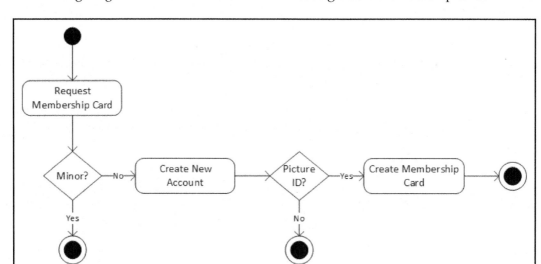

The activities in an activity diagram can either be sequential or concurrent. An activity is shown as a rectangle with rounded corners. The rectangle encloses all of the elements of an activity, such as its actions and control flows.

Start/end nodes

Some of the nodes that can appear in an activity diagram represent the different ways in which flows can begin and end:

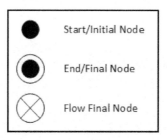

An activity diagram begins with an initial state, or start point, which is graphically represented by a small, solid circle (**Start/Initial Node**). The activity diagram ends with a final state that is graphically represented by a small, filled circle inside another circle (**End/Final Node**).

A **Flow Final Node**, which is a circle with an X inside, can be used to represent the end of a specific process flow. Unlike the end node, which denotes the end of all control flows within an activity, a flow final node represents the end of a single control flow.

Actions/Control flow

Actions are single steps within an activity. Like activities, they are also represented as a rectangle with rounded corners. A solid line with an open arrowhead is used to show control flow:

Decision/merge nodes

A decision occurs in a flow when there is some condition and there are at least two paths that branch from that decision. A label can be placed on each of the different branches to indicate the guard condition that would allow control to flow down the branch.

When you want to bring multiple alternate flows back to a single outgoing flow, a merge node is used. Both decision and merge nodes are graphically represented with a diamond symbol:

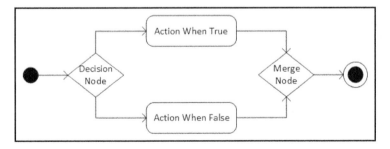

Fork/join nodes

When you want to model a single flow forking into two or more concurrent flows, you use a fork node. When you want to combine two or more concurrent flows back into a single outgoing flow, you use a join node. The following diagram illustrates a flow that has a fork and join node:

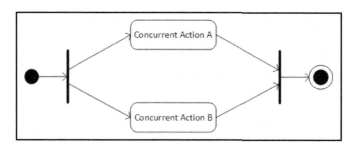

Both fork and join nodes are graphically represented with either a horizontal or vertical bar. The orientation of the bar is dependent on whether the flow is going from top to bottom or left to right. When fork and join nodes are used together, they are sometimes referred to as *synchronization*.

Reviewing software architectures

An important step in designing a high-quality software architecture is for it to go through a review process. Architecture reviews may also be conducted when an organization acquires software or to compare architectures. A review will determine whether the functional requirements and quality attribute scenarios can be satisfied with the software architecture. Reviewing the architecture helps the team find mistakes and correct them as early as possible. This can greatly reduce the amount of effort it takes to fix a defect and can help to avoid further rework.

In this section, we will be taking a look at the following software architecture evaluation methods:

- Software architecture analysis method (SAAM)
- Architecture tradeoff analysis method (ATAM)
- Active design review (ADR)
- Active reviews of intermediate designs (ARID)

Software architecture analysis method (SAAM)

The **software architecture analysis method (SAAM)** is one of the first documented methods for evaluating software architectures. The original purpose of SAAM was to assess the modifiability of a software system, although some have extended it to review a software architecture for a variety of quality attributes, including reliability, portability, extensibility, and performance.

Scenario-based analysis of software architecture

SAAM is a scenario-based review method, and can be an effective way to review a software architecture. A scenario is a description of the interaction between some source, such as a stakeholder, and a software system. It represents some use or expected quality of the software system and may consist of a sequence of steps detailing the use or modification of it.

Scenarios can be used to test software quality attributes, which is one of the purposes behind software quality attribute scenarios:

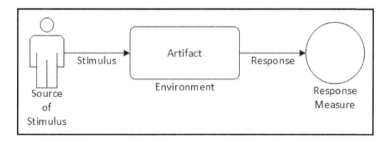

A software quality attribute scenario consists of the following parts:

- **Source of stimulus**: The source is some entity, such as a stakeholder or another software system, which generates a particular stimulus.
- **Stimulus**: The stimulus is some condition that requires a response from the software system.
- **Artifact**: The artifact is the software that is stimulated. It can be a part of the software system, the entire software system, or a collection of multiple systems.
- **Environment**: The environment is the set of conditions under which the stimulus occurs. For example, a particular configuration of the software or specific values in the data may be necessary for the stimulus to exist.

- **Response**: The response is the activity that takes place when the stimulus arrives at the artifact.
- **Response Measure**: When a response occurs, it should be measurable. This allows us to test the response to ensure that the software system meets the requirements.

SAAM steps

There are six main steps in the software-architecture analysis method: develop scenarios, describe the architecture, classify and prioritize scenarios, evaluate scenarios, assess scenario interactions, and create an overall evaluation.

Step 1 – Develop scenarios

Using requirements and quality attributes, we can identify the different types of functionality that the software system is supposed to support and the qualities it is expected to have. This knowledge forms the basis for developing scenarios. Quality attribute scenarios, with the source of the stimulus, stimulus, artifact, environment, response, and response measure defined for each one, provide the type of information that makes scenarios useful when reviewing an architecture.

A variety of stakeholders should participate in brainstorming for scenarios, as the different perspectives and needs of a diverse group of people with an interest in the system will help to ensure that no important scenarios are overlooked. It is often useful to take an iterative approach when developing scenarios because identifying scenarios can lead the software architect, development team, and other stakeholders to think of additional scenarios.

Step 2 – Describe the architecture

In this step, the software architect describes the architecture to the review team. Completed architecture documentation can be used as part of the presentation. Any notations used in the documentation should be well understood by all of the review participants.

Step 3 – Classify and prioritize scenarios

Each scenario that is created in *Step 1 – Develop scenarios*, is classified and prioritized in this step. Scenarios can either be *direct* or *indirect* scenarios. If the software system does not require any modifications to perform the scenario, it can be classified as a direct scenario. If the scenario is not directly supported, meaning that some change has to be made to the software system for the scenario, then it is an indirect scenario.

Once scenarios have been classified, they should be prioritized based on importance. This can be accomplished by using some type of voting procedure. The scenarios that are determined to be of highest priority to the review team as a whole can be used for the evaluation.

Step 4 – Evaluate scenarios

In this SAAM step, the scenarios are evaluated. For each of the direct scenarios, the software architect demonstrates how the architecture can execute it. For any indirect scenarios, the team should identify what has to be changed (for example, modification/addition/deletion of components) in order to execute each one. The team should estimate the level of effort necessary to change the system so that it can execute indirect scenarios.

Step 5 – Assess scenario interaction

In this step, the reviewers analyze the interaction of the scenarios. If multiple *related* scenarios interact with the same component, this may be acceptable. However, if multiple *unrelated* scenarios interact with the same component, it could be an indication of a poor design. Further analysis should be conducted to determine whether the component is lacking a clear separation of responsibilities.

Refactoring may be necessary to avoid different scenarios interacting with the same component. The component may have low cohesion, indicating that its elements are not closely related. It may also exhibit tight coupling, signifying that the component is highly dependent on another component. Low cohesion and tight coupling increase complexity and reduce the maintainability of the system. If such a situation exists, a component may need to be separated into multiple components.

Step 6 – Create an overall evaluation

With the prior steps completed, the review team should have a list of scenarios that have been classified, prioritized, and evaluated. The interaction of the scenarios may reveal potential issues with the design. Ultimately, the review team must make a decision as to whether the architecture is viable and can be accepted as is or if it has to be modified in some way.

Architecture tradeoff analysis method (ATAM)

The **architecture tradeoff analysis method (ATAM)** is another scenario-based architecture review method. ATAM is a successor to SAAM and improves upon it. ATAM has a focus on reviewing design decisions and quality attributes.

ATAM participant roles

The main participant roles during ATAM evaluation are the evaluation team, project decision makers, and stakeholders. The evaluation team, which should ideally be a group that is external to the software project, consists of a team leader, evaluation leader, scenario scribe, proceedings scribe, and questioner.

- **Team leader**: The team leader coordinates and sets up the review. They are responsible for creating the evaluation team as well as ensuring that the final report is produced.
- **Evaluation leader**: The evaluation leader runs the actual review. This includes facilitating sessions that create/prioritize/select/evaluate scenarios.
- **Scenario scribe**: The scenario scribe writes notes about the scenarios on a whiteboard or flipchart as the evaluation is taking place.
- **Proceedings scribe**: The proceedings scribe is responsible for capturing notes in electronic format. Details about scenarios are an important aspect of the evaluation that the proceedings scribe will capture.
- **Questioner**: The questioner focuses on raising issues and asking questions related to the architecture, with a particular focus on quality attributes.
- **Project decision makers**: The project decision makers are the individuals who have the authority to make changes to the software if necessary, including the power to assign/approve resources for work. Project sponsors, project managers, and software architects typically make up the project decision-maker group.
- **Stakeholders**: The stakeholders include anyone who has a vested interest in the software architecture and the system as a whole.

ATAM phases

There are four main phases involved with an ATAM evaluation of a software architecture:

- **Phase 0**: Partnership and preparation
- **Phase 1**: Evaluation

- **Phase 2**: Evaluation (continued)
- **Phase 3**: Follow-up

Phase 0 – Partnership and preparation

This initial phase is used to prepare for the evaluation. The leader of the evaluation team meets with the project decision makers to agree on details about the evaluation. An agreement should be reached on the logistics of the meeting as well as which stakeholders will be invited.

As part of the preparation, the evaluation team looks at the architecture documentation to become familiar with the software application and its architecture. Expectations are set by the evaluation team as to the information they expect to be presented during *Phase 1*.

Phase 1 – Evaluation

Phase 1 is the first of two phases dedicated to the evaluation of the architecture. In this phase, the evaluation team meets with the project decision makers. *Phase 1* consists of the following steps:

1. Present the ATAM
2. Present the business drivers
3. Present the architecture
4. Identify architectural approaches
5. Generate the quality attribute utility tree
6. Analyze architectural approaches

Step 1 – Present the ATAM

In this step, the evaluation leader explains the ATAM to the project decision makers. Any questions about the ATAM can be answered during this step.

If everyone in the meeting is already familiar with the ATAM, this step could potentially be skipped. For example, a development team may go through the ATAM phases and steps multiple times as it iteratively designs the architecture. If the team consists of the same members, it may not be necessary to go over the ATAM each time. However, if any participants in a given iteration are new to the method, either this step should not be skipped or there must be a suitable alternative for participants who are new to the method to learn it.

Step 2 – Present the business drivers

This step is used to present the software system from a business perspective to the various participants. The business goals, functionality, architectural drivers, and any constraints will help everyone to understand the overall context of the software system. This information is presented by one of the project decision makers.

Step 3 – Present the architecture

The software architect presents the architecture to the participants in this step. The software architect should provide sufficient detail about the architecture so that the participants can understand it.

The level of detail needed in the presentation can vary from project to project. It really depends on the quality attribute scenarios of the system, how much of the architecture design is complete/documented, and how much time is available for the presentation. In order to be clear what level of detail is expected, the software architect should use phase zero, when expectations are set, as an opportunity to ask for clarification.

Step 4 – Identify architectural approaches

By the time this step takes place, the participants should be familiar with the design concepts used in the architecture. This includes software architecture patterns, reference architectures, tactics, and any externally developed software. This information was available in *Phase 0* when the architecture documentation was reviewed, as well as in the prior step (*Step 3 – Present the architecture*) when the architecture was presented. This step is to simply record the design concepts used so that the list can be used in a subsequent step for analysis.

Step 5 – Generate the quality attribute utility tree

Quality attribute scenarios can be represented in a **utility tree**, which represents the usefulness (utility) of the system. Utility trees help participants understand the quality attribute scenarios.

The utility tree is a set of detailed statements about the quality attributes and scenarios that are important to the software system. Each entry in the tree begins with the quality attribute itself (for example, maintainability, usability, availability, performance, or security), followed by a subcategory that breaks it down with more detail, followed by a quality attribute scenario.

For example, under a software quality attribute such as Security, we may have multiple subcategories ("Authentication" and "Confidentiality"). Each subcategory will have one or more quality attribute scenarios:

Quality attribute	Subcategory	Scenario
Security		
	Authentication	
		User passwords will be hashed using the bcrypt hashing function.
	Confidentiality	
		A user playing the role of a customer-service representative will only be able to view the last four digits of a customer's social security number.
		A user playing the role of a customer-service manager will be able to view a customer's entire social security number.
Performance		
	Etc.	

In addition to identifying the quality attribute scenarios, the project decision makers should prioritize them. As with the SAAM, a voting scheme can be used to allow participants to prioritize the scenarios.

Step 6 – Analyze architectural approaches

The quality attributes that were determined to be of the highest priority in *Step 5 – Generate the quality attribute utility tree*, are analyzed, one by one, by the evaluation team in this step. The software architect should be able to explain how the architecture can satisfy each one.

The evaluation team looks to identify, document, and ask about the architectural decisions that were made to support the scenario. Any issues, risks, or tradeoffs with the architectural decisions are raised and documented. The goal of the team is to match architectural decisions with quality attribute scenarios and determine whether the architecture and those architectural decisions can support the scenarios.

By the completion of this step, the team should have a good understanding of the overall architecture, the design decisions that were made, the rationale behind the decisions, and how the architecture supports the main goals of the system. The team should also now be aware of any risks, issues, and tradeoffs that may exist. The completion of this step signifies the end of *Phase 1*.

Phase 2 – Evaluation (continued)

Phase 2 is a continuation of the architecture evaluation. It is normally scheduled to occur after a short hiatus (for example, one week) after the completion of *Phase 1*. Phase two involves a greater number of participants as compared with *Phase 1*. In addition to the evaluation team and the project decision makers, it is now time for the invited stakeholders to join the evaluation and participate.

This phase should begin with a repeat of *Step 1 – Present the ATAM*, if any of the new participants are unfamiliar with the approach. The evaluation team leader should also summarize what was accomplished in *Phase 1*.

Phase 2 consists of the following three steps:

> 7. Brainstorm and prioritize scenarios
> 8. Analyze architectural approaches
> 9. Present results

Step 7 – Brainstorm and prioritize scenarios

In this step, all of the stakeholders are asked to brainstorm scenarios. They should be encouraged to provide scenarios that are from their perspective and that are important to the success of their roles. Having a variety of stakeholders is helpful to get a diverse set of scenarios.

When there are enough scenarios, the group should look them over to see whether any of them can be removed or merged with others because of their similarities with other scenarios. The scenarios should then be prioritized by the stakeholders by voting in order to determine the most important scenarios.

Once a list of scenarios is determined, it should be compared with the scenarios that the project decision makers came up with for the utility tree in *Step 5 – Generate the quality attribute utility tree*. While the utility tree shows what the software architect and other project decision makers saw as the goals and architectural drivers of the system, this step allows the stakeholders to show what is important to them.

If the two prioritized lists of quality attribute scenarios are similar, it is an indication that the software architect and the stakeholders are in alignment. If any important quality attribute scenarios are uncovered that had not been considered previously, some additional work will be necessary. The level of risk is dependent on the nature and size of the needed changes.

Step 8 – Analyze architectural approaches

Similar to *Step 6 – Analyze architectural approaches*, the software architect describes to the group how the list of scenarios created by the stakeholders can be realized by the architectural approaches that have been taken with the system. The evaluation team can raise any issues, risks, and tradeoffs they see with the architectural approaches. The team should be able to determine whether the scenarios can be achieved by the architecture.

Step 9 – Present results

In the final step of the ATAM, any risks that were uncovered during the evaluation should be related to one or more of the business drivers identified in *Step 2 – Present the business drivers*. Project management will now be aware of the risks and how they relate to the goals of the system and will be in a position to manage those risks.

A presentation is given to the stakeholders that summarizes all of the findings from the evaluation. The output of the process includes the architectural approaches, the prioritized list of scenarios generated by the stakeholders, the utility tree, and documentation regarding the issues, risks, and tradeoffs identified. This output is presented and delivered by the evaluation team to the project decision makers and the stakeholders who participated.

Phase 3 – Follow-up

The evaluation team produces and delivers the final evaluation report in this phase. A common timeframe for this phase is one week, but it could be shorter or longer. The report may be given to various stakeholders for review, but once it is complete, the evaluation team delivers it to the individual who commissioned the review.

Active design review (ADR)

An **active design review** (**ADR**) is most suited for architecture designs that are in progress. This type of architecture review is more focused on reviewing individual sections of the architecture at a time, rather than performing a general review. The process involves identifying design issues and other faults with the architecture so that they may be corrected as quickly and early in the overall design process as possible.

One of the main premises of ADR is that there is too much information involved with reviewing an entire architecture at once and not enough time to do it properly. Many reviewers may not be familiar with the goals and details of every part of the design. As a result, no single part of the design ends up getting a complete evaluation. In addition, with more conventional review processes, there may not be enough one-on-one interaction between the reviewer and the designer.

ADR attempts to address these deficiencies by changing the focus from a more general review of the entire architecture to a series of more focused reviews. Questionnaires are used to provide more opportunities for interaction between reviewers and designers and to keep reviewers engaged.

ADR steps

There are five steps to the ADR process:

1. Prepare the documentation for review
2. Identify the specialized reviews
3. Identify the reviewers needed
4. Design the questionnaires
5. Conduct the review

We will now take a look at each of these steps in detail.

Step 1 – Prepare the documentation for review

In this step of ADR, preparation takes place for the review. This includes preparing the documentation for review and listing assumptions that are being made about the portion of the architecture being reviewed. The assumptions need to be made clear so that reviewers will be aware of them. These assumptions include any items that the software architect (or other designers) think will never change or are highly unlikely to change. In addition, any incorrect usage assumptions should also be provided. These are assumptions that the software architect (or other designers) deem to be an incorrect usage of the module and therefore should not take place.

Step 2 – Identify the specialized reviews

In this step, we identify the specific properties of the design that we want the focus to be placed on by the reviewers. Doing this gives reviewers a clear focus and responsibility for the specialized review that they will be conducting. For example, we may want an individual reviewer to be focused on one or more specific quality attributes.

Step 3 – Identify the reviewers needed

In this ADR step, the reviewers for the part of the design being reviewed are identified. We want reviewers to focus on the areas they are most suited to review. The goal is to get people with different perspectives and sets of knowledge to participate as reviewers.

Examples of reviewers include development team members who did not work on the part of the architecture being reviewed, technical staff from other projects, users of the system, non-technical reviewers who are specialists or have knowledge related to the software system, reviewers who are external to the organization, and anyone else who may be adept at identifying potential issues with a design.

Step 4 – Design the questionnaires

Questionnaires are designed in this step, which the reviewers will use while evaluating the architecture in the next step. Use of the questionnaires is intended to encourage reviewers to take on an active role and to get them to use the architecture documentation during the review. In addition to questions, questionnaires can contain exercises or other instructions for the reviewers to perform.

Questions/instructions should be phrased in an open, active way to encourage further thought and a more detailed response. For example, rather than asking if the part of the architecture being reviewed is sufficient, the instructions could guide the reviewer to provide an implementation in pseudocode that uses the portion of the architecture to accomplish some task.

Step 5 – Conduct the review

This step of the process is when the review takes place. Reviewers are assigned to the review and then a presentation of the module being reviewed is made. The reviewers then conduct their reviews, including the completion of the questionnaires. Sufficient time must be allotted so that the review can be completed properly.

Once the reviews are complete, a meeting is held between the reviewers and the designers. The designers can read the complete questionnaires and use the meeting as an opportunity to communicate with the reviewers and clarify any questions. The end result of the final step is to modify the architecture artifact, if necessary, based on any points made during the review.

Active reviews of intermediate designs (ARID)

Active reviews of intermediate designs (**ARID**) is an architecture review method that combines ADR with ATAM. This hybrid method takes from the ADR approach the focus of reviewing a software architecture while it is in progress and the emphasis on active reviewer participation. It combines this with the ATAM approach of focusing on quality attribute scenarios. The goal is to provide valuable feedback into the viability of the software architecture and uncover any errors and inadequacies with it.

ARID participant roles

The main participants in the ARID process are the ARID review team (facilitator, scribe, and questioners), the software architect/lead designer, and the reviewers:

- **Facilitator**: The facilitator works with the software architect to prepare for the review meeting and facilitates it when it takes place.
- **Scribe**: The scribe captures the issues and results of the review meeting.
- **Questioners**: One or more questioners raise issues, ask questions, and assist with creating scenarios during the review meeting.
- **Software architect/lead designer**: The software architect (or designer) is the person responsible for the design being reviewed. This person is responsible for preparing and presenting the design as well as participating in the other steps.
- **Reviewers**: The reviewers are the individuals who will be performing the review. They consist of stakeholders who have a vested interest in the architecture and the software application.

ARID phases

There are two phases involved in the ARID process, which consist of nine steps in all. The two phases are the *Step 1 – Pre-meeting* and *Step 2 – Review meeting* phases.

Phase 1 – Pre-meeting

The first phase is a meeting to prepare for the actual review. For a software architecture review, this meeting typically takes place between the software architect and the review facilitator. If someone other than the software architect is responsible for the design of the portion of the architecture being reviewed, this person should join the meeting with the review facilitator. The pre-meeting consists of the following steps:

1. Identify reviewers
2. Prepare the design presentation
3. Prepare the seed scenarios
4. Prepare for the review meeting

Step 1 – Identify reviewers

In this step in the ARID approach, the software architect and review facilitator meet to identify the group of people who will attend the review meeting. Management may also be involved with this step to help identify available resources.

Step 2 – Prepare the design presentation

During the actual review meeting, the software architect will present the design and any of the relevant documentation related to it. In this step, the software architect gives a preliminary version of the presentation to the review facilitator. This allows the software architect to practice the presentation and receive feedback from the review facilitator that may help to improve the presentation.

Step 3 – Prepare the seed scenarios

In this step of review preparation, the software architect and review facilitator work together to come up with *seed scenarios*, or a sample set of scenarios that the reviewers can use during the review.

Step 4 – Prepare for the review meeting

This step is used for any other tasks related to the preparation of the review meeting. It can be used to identify the materials that will be distributed to all of the reviewers, such as the architecture documentation, seed scenarios, questionnaires, and review agenda. A date, time, and location for the review meeting must be selected and invitations must be sent out.

Phase 2 – Review meeting

The second ARID phase is devoted to the review meeting. It consists of the following steps:

5. Present the ARID method
6. Present the design
7. Brainstorm and prioritize scenarios
8. Perform the review
9. Present conclusions

Step 5 – Present the ARID method

At the start of the review meeting, the review facilitator should present the ARID method to all of the participants. This step is similar to a step we covered in the ATAM in which the ATAM is presented to participants. As was the case in that step, if everyone who is participating is already familiar with the ARID method, this step could be skipped. However, if anyone is not familiar with ARID or needs a refresher, it should be presented.

Step 6 – Present the design

After the review facilitator has presented the ARID method, the software architect presents the architecture design. Questions regarding the design rationale or comments about alternative solutions should be avoided. The design facilitator can help to keep the meeting in line with its goals. The purpose of the review is to determine whether the designed architecture is usable, so factual questions for clarification and pointing out issues that should be addressed are the types of feedback that should be encouraged. A person playing the role of a scribe should take notes regarding any questions and issues that are raised.

Step 7 – Brainstorm and prioritize scenarios

During this step of the process, the participants brainstorm to come up with scenarios for the software system that will use the designed architecture. The seed scenarios that were created in phase one are included with the scenarios that are created in this step to form the available choices.

As with ATAM, participants should be encouraged to provide scenarios that are important to them. The process works best when there are a variety of stakeholders to ensure that different perspectives are considered.

The group can then analyze and prioritize the scenarios. It may make sense to combine some of the scenarios or identify some as being duplicates. The review group can vote on which scenarios are the most important. The scenarios that are prioritized as being the most important essentially define what makes the architecture usable.

Step 8 – Perform the review

The reviewers use the scenarios to determine whether the architecture solves the problem that is presented. Real code or pseudocode can be written to test the scenario. When the group feels that a conclusion can be reached (or time runs out), the review ends.

Step 9 – Present conclusions

With the review complete, the group should be able to draw conclusions as to whether or not the architecture is suitable for the key scenarios. Any issues with the architecture can be reviewed so that the architecture can be refactored to correct any problems.

Summary

Documenting a software architecture is an important step in delivering an architecture. The documentation communicates the architecture to others, assists the development team, educates team members, provides input for architecture reviews, and allows the reuse of architectural knowledge.

Architecture views, which are representations of an architecture, allow a software architect to communicate their architecture in a manageable and understandable way. There is a cost associated with creating and maintaining views though, so while we never want the documentation to be insufficient, we do not want to spend time working on views that are not needed. In this chapter, you were provided with an overview of the UML, one of the more widely used modeling languages. You learned about structural and behavioral modeling.

Reviewing a software architecture is important to determine whether the architecture will meet the needs of the system. This chapter provided details on several different architecture review methods.

In the next chapter, we will gain an understanding of what software architects need to know about DevOps, including its values and practices. We will learn how continuous integration, continuous delivery, and continuous deployment allow an organization to release software changes quickly and reliably.

13
DevOps and Software Architecture

DevOps is a combination of cultural values, practices, and tools that allow an organization to deliver software applications quickly. It is important for software architects to have an understanding of DevOps. An organization you work for may already be practicing it, or they may be interested in transitioning to DevOps. Either way, software architects within an organization play a role in helping and leading others to follow DevOps values and practices.

This chapter will explain the purpose behind DevOps, its values, and the reasons why organizations adopt them. It will cover the different types of tools used in DevOps as well as the important DevOps practices. You will gain an understanding as to how DevOps may affect architectural decisions, and about the different ways that the cloud can be utilized for deployment.

In this chapter, we will cover the following topics:

- DevOps
- DevOps toolchain
- DevOps practices
- Architecting for DevOps
- Deploying to the cloud

DevOps

DevOps is the set of tools, practices, and culture that enable both the development and operations terms to work together during the entire life cycle of building software applications. DevOps enables the continuous delivery of software, allowing organizations to respond quickly to changing market opportunities and allowing them to get customer feedback quickly.

DevOps involves collaboration between teams and the automation of processes to achieve a common goal of adding value to customers' experiences by delivering software changes quickly and with high quality. DevOps requires a cultural change within an organization, along with the use of new technologies.

Shift left is a common term associated with DevOps. The idea is to perform tasks earlier in the life cycle, or to shift them left in the timeline. This term became popular with testing (shift, left testing), meaning that the process of testing a software application should be moved to earlier in the overall development process.

DevOps has embraced this *shift left* mentality. In addition to testing earlier in the process (with automated tests), DevOps also considers what else can be moved to earlier in the process. Involvement of the operations team should *shift left* and begin working with the development team much earlier than has been done in the past. Rather than begin working together at deployment time, they should be working together throughout the software development life cycle.

Later in this chapter, in the *Continuous integration (CI)* section, we will take a look at how the practice of continuous integration *shifts left* the integration and building of software changes so that they take place sooner in the process. We'll also see how the practice of continuous delivery *shifts left* the deployment of software changes to production so that they reach users faster.

CALMS

CALMS is an acronym that represents the core values of DevOps. The original version was CAMS and the L was added later. CALMS stands for the following:

- Culture
- Automation
- Lean
- Measurement
- Sharing

Let's explore each of these core values in more detail, as they will give us a better understanding of what is involved with DevOps.

Culture

At its core, DevOps is a culture and a philosophy. It requires changing the culture of an organization by breaking down barriers between teams. To improve how work is done, sometimes organizations need to learn how to work differently. DevOps necessitates cross-functional teams and encourages teams with different skills and knowledge, such as development and IT, to work together. DevOps builds a culture of collaboration even between teams that, historically, may not have worked closely together.

Teamwork is an important value in DevOps. Teams such as development, operations, and quality assurance terms should be encouraged to communicate, work together, and get to know one another. Tighter integration between these teams can allow them to be more efficient, increase innovation, and deliver more value to customers.

Continuous improvement is also a part of the DevOps culture. DevOps culture values learning and using any knowledge gained for improvement. Different teams in an organization should learn from each other. If faults or other issues occur, team members should learn from those experiences so that they are not repeated. Everyone in the organization should participate in an ongoing effort to improve processes and products.

Accountability also needs to be part of the organizational culture. When mistakes are made, individuals and teams should take ownership of them. Rather than blaming other teams, everyone should be focused on fixing the issue and making improvements to prevent those issues from happening again.

Quality needs to be everyone's focus in a DevOps culture. For example, the development team should not rely on the quality assurance team to find defects. They need to be just as dedicated to finding defects and maintaining a high level of quality for the software systems they develop. As the rate of releasing changes to software is accelerated with DevOps, an effort has to be made by all teams in the organization to ensure that quality does not suffer.

Organizations should empower their employees as part of their culture. No matter what role an individual is playing on one of the teams, they should feel empowered to point out issues, stop a potential mistake that they see, or make a suggestion as to how to improve a product, service, or process.

Some organizational changes can be helpful when instituting a cultural change. Altering team structures, changing where teams sit in an office, and modifying processes are examples of organizational changes that may need to be made to help facilitate the desired cultural changes.

Automation

Automation involves taking manual processes and making them operate automatically so that they are repeatable. The first step in automating processes is to identify the current processes that are executed and understand how they work. We want to be able to identify bottlenecks and figure out where defects are most likely to be introduced. Once this understanding is in place, we can begin to select the appropriate tools to enable automation.

Automation is a great way for teams to improve the way that they work. An automatic process ensures better consistency and accuracy compared to a person executing the process manually. People make mistakes, and automation avoids that problem. An additional benefit of automating a process is that it does not tie up a team member because it can be executed on its own. Automatic processes can also be executed during off-peak hours to avoid conflicts with system resources. Automation is suited to a number of tasks, including unit testing and builds.

Automated processes can be executed quicker than manual ones, and are less prone to error. Instituting automated testing, build, and deployment processes is a key part of DevOps. Automated tests can be executed as part of an automated build process, ensuring that recently introduced changes do not unintentionally introduce a defect.

Automation also provides quick feedback when something goes wrong with a unit test, build, or deployment. This will give your organization the ability to quickly react to failures so that they can be corrected.

DevOps does not require automating everything, though. In some cases, an organization may have poor processes, and automating them just speeds them up. It is prudent to look for ways to improve a process before attempting to automate it. Each organization is different and has different needs, so finding the right balance of automation for your organization is important.

You may have a mix of different types of applications, including legacy applications. These applications may use different technologies and be deployed to different types of environments. Based on your organization's needs and bottlenecks, you should take into consideration the return on investment for automating a process. You may choose to start your focus on the processes that will most benefit the organization. Your organization may need different types of tools to automate different types of process.

Lean

Lean software development (**LSD**) took the best practices of lean manufacturing and applied them to software development. It aim to optimize processes and minimize waste during the software development process. Waste can be anything that increases time and effort, does not add business value for customers, and reduces the quality of the software system.

The ideas behind LSD not only complement agile software development methodologies, but they are also consistent with the core values of DevOps. There are seven lean development principles:

- **Eliminate waste**: Elimination of waste is important in lean processes. Unnecessary functionality, code, or effort is wasteful. Delaying the delivery of value to customers and inefficient processes are other examples of software development waste.
- **Build quality in**: Quality should be a focus for everyone. The writing of tests is one way to think about quality early in the process. The automation of tests helps to ensure that tests are automatically executed.
- **Create knowledge**: Team members should share knowledge within the team and across teams. Code reviews, documentation, pair programming, learning sessions, training, and collaboration tools can be used to teach and learn from others.
- **Defer commitment**: A decision should be made only after enough information has been collected to make a sound one.
- **Deliver fast**: Value should be delivered to customers quickly. This does not mean that the organization should do so recklessly, but rather that it should provide incremental changes reliably, quickly, and frequently.

- **Respect people**: As teams work together (and the individuals on those teams), they should do so in a respectful way. Communication and the handling of conflicts should be done in a respectful way.
- **Optimize the whole**: Processes should be optimized and bottlenecks should be eliminated when possible. Automation of tests, builds, and deployments are useful in optimization efforts.

Measurement

Teams must be able to measure improvement because if they cannot measure it, they cannot know whether process improvements, automation, and the introduction of other DevOps practices have actually worked. As a software architect, you need to be able to make decisions based on data that has been measured and not just your gut feeling. The data that is measured should be transparent and shared with the development team, operations, and other key decision makers within the organization.

Sharing

Sharing is another core value of DevOps. If DevOps is to succeed in your organization, information, tools, data, and the lessons that are learned need to be shared so that the organization can improve as a whole. Any feedback received, whether it is from external or internal sources, is more useful when it is shared with others.

Encountering failures in a software system may be inevitable but we need to be able to learn from those failures and make improvements based on them. Lessons learned should be shared between development and operations so that continuous improvement is possible. Part of changing the culture of an organization to follow a DevOps approach is fostering collaboration and communication among various departments. Sharing information is one of the ways that can change the culture.

Why DevOps?

As a software architect, you want to lead your organization so that it can deploy software faster, more frequently, and with fewer failures. Approaches other than DevOps do not focus on continuous delivery, so providing value to customers takes a longer period of time. An operations department can sometimes seem slow to react. Time can be wasted waiting for environments to be created and for applications to be moved from one environment to another. When these processes are manual, they can be wasteful and impede process rather than enable it.

When asking for resources, a development team may ask for more than they need (for example, asking for a larger than necessary physical server or VM), simply because the process is too troublesome and they do not want to go through the effort of upgrading it later. QA teams may be waiting for development teams to finish writing code so that they can test it.

All of this leads to the organization wasting both time and money. Software architects should be striving for greater efficiency in software development processes, with less manual work and automating more of the effort.

In today's competitive environment, organizations need the ability to deliver quickly. In order to gain an advantage, they need to add incremental value for their customers by delivering frequent changes that contain new features, bug fixes, and other improvements. DevOps allows the organization to deliver value faster. Through continuous delivery, new versions of the software can be deployed quickly and with high quality.

Customers have a lower tolerance for system outages now, so it is imperative to have processes in place that detect faults quickly and allow fixes to be deployed easily. The goal is to minimize the number of system outages and their duration. There is an increased chance of errors with manual processes. Automating processes reduces the chance for errors. When failures do occur, you will want to recover from them quickly. DevOps can help you to achieve these goals.

Software applications today tend to be more complex and have more complicated deployments. A DevOps approach will lead organizations to automate their builds, eliminating the possibility of errors caused by mistakes in a manual process.

Practicing DevOps properly will lead to a greater level of cooperation between development and operations teams, leading to a decrease in deployment time and an increase in reliability. Encouraging information within the organization to be shared will lead to less dependence on tribal knowledge. Collaboration across teams increases the amount of information that is shared.

DevOps toolchain

Toolchains are a set of programming tools that are used in combination to perform a task. A **DevOps toolchain** focuses on the development and delivery of software systems. Software architects responsible for selecting tools should aim to achieve consistency with the DevOps tools. For example, it is better to use the same deployment tool for all of our environments than use different ones for different environments.

In an organization that embraces DevOps, it is not just the development team that uses software tools to perform their jobs. Operations staff should use many of the same techniques as developers. For example, the assets related to operations should be checked into source control and have automated tests.

DevOps tools are generally categorized as supporting one or more of the following activities:

- **Plan**: The plan category of tools help you to define the requirements of the application and plan the work. The activities that take place around planning vary depending on the methodology being used, but generally involve product owners and business analysts evaluating requirements and other requests. The business value and effort are evaluated and work is planned for a release.
- **Create**: Create tools are software that help in some way with design, coding, and building activities. Examples of these tools include **integrated development environments** (**IDEs**), version control repositories, build automation tools, and configuration management tools.
- **Verify**: Verification tools consist of software that help to ensure the quality of a software release. Some verification activities occur during *create* activities, while others occur once some part of the software is complete. Functional and non-functional testing must take place, and DevOps tools can help to automate some of the testing. Verification tools can help with performance, acceptance, regression, and release testing. Static analysis tools can help to analyze the code, and security tools can help to identify vulnerabilities.
- **Package**: Packaging tools are used for the tasks associated with preparing a release once it has been verified and is ready for deployment. Packaging configuration and triggering releases are some of the activities involved in packaging.
- **Release**: The tools in the release category are used for release-related activities. They assist teams with the scheduling and coordination of deploying software systems into different environments, including production.
- **Configure**: Tools are available that assist with the configuration of software applications. The configure category includes tools that help with configuration management, application provisioning, and the configuration of infrastructure resources.

- **Monitor**: It is critical to monitor software applications to identify issues and gain an understanding as to their impact. Production metrics give an organization the insight necessary to understand what the problem areas are with a software application. Monitoring the performance of a software application will ensure that end users are not encountering bottlenecks when they use the software. When we covered CALMS, it was mentioned that measurement is one of the core values of DevOps. Monitoring tools can help teams measure their applications in order to determine whether, and how much, automation efforts have improved a process or product.

DevOps practices

There is variation depending on the organization and the software development methodology used, but in a DevOps release cycle, the following major activities generally take place:

- Development
- Integration
- Build and unit testing
- Delivery to staging
- Acceptance testing
- Deployment to production

The following diagram illustrates a typical DevOps release cycle:

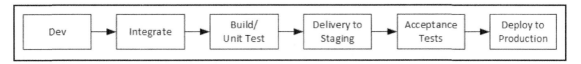

Three of the main DevOps practices are continuous integration, continuous delivery, and continuous deployment. These practices revolve around the key activities of a DevOps release cycle, so let's explore them in more detail.

Continuous integration (CI)

Continuous integration (CI) is the practice of developers merging their changes into a shared source control repository as often as possible. Using some type of version control system is a necessity. Developers should commit changes on a frequent and regular basis. This reduces the number of conflicting changes and makes it easier to resolve conflicts when any exist.

In the DevOps release cycle, the activities covered by continuous integration include development, integration (the checking in of changes into a version control system), and an automated build with automated unit testing:

Some may consider the delivery to staging phase that occurs after a build is complete as part of continuous integration, while others see that as the next step in overall continuous delivery.

Automated builds

Two of the key aspects of continuous integration is to build all commits and to have a build process that is automated. A build converts source code, files, and other assets into a software project that is in its final, usable form. This may include things such as the following:

- Dependency checking
- Compiling source files
- Packaging compiled files into a compressed format (for example, JAR or ZIP)
- Creating installers
- Creating/updating database schema
- Executing data change scripts to modify data in a database
- Running automated tests

As a software architect, you will want to establish an automated build process if one is not already in place. Some builds require many steps, and performing these manually creates many opportunities for mistakes to take place. Automated builds eliminate the variation that can take place with manual builds, ensuring consistency between builds.

Automated builds are what make it possible to execute builds at any time. In the practice of continuous integration, automated builds are essential, and should take place when changes have been checked in to a version control system. The duration of automated builds should not be too long (for example, less than 20 minutes) to allow continuous integration to be feasible.

Software versioning

As part of the build process for your software, you will need to think about how you want to version your software. *Software versioning* is the process of assigning a unique number or name to the software you are building.

It is beneficial to use a formal convention for software versioning. Once a formal convention has been established, it provides everyone who is interested in the software, both internally and externally, with knowledge about the state of the software. Without the use of a formal versioning convention, version numbers are meaningless to users and useless for dependency management. A meaningful version number communicates to interested parties information regarding the intention of the version and the extent of the changes in the version. One of the software versioning conventions that can be used is semantic versioning.

Semantic versioning, also referred to as **SemVer**, is a popular convention that can be used for software versioning. Semantic versioning uses a three-part version number that follows the *MAJOR.MINOR.PATCH* format. For example, a version number might be 1.5.2.

A new MAJOR version indicates that breaking changes are included with the version. A new MINOR version means that additions and changes have been made, but the software is backward-compatible. A new PATCH version indicates that bug fixes are included with the version and that the software remains backward-compatible. Following this versioning scheme makes, it easy to tell what type of changes are included in a new version, and provides the ability to anticipate breaking changes. When your software is in its initial development phase, the version number typically starts with 0.1.0. From there, the minor version can be incremented with each subsequent release.

As part of the version number, you can communicate the software's current stage of development. If you are using semantic versioning, the stage can be designated as part of the pre-release identifier. Following the *MAJOR.MINOR.PATCH* part of the version number, you can signify that it is a pre-release version of the software by following the number with a hyphen and any series of identifiers, separated by dots. Any version number that contains a hyphen and one or more identifiers denotes that it is a pre-release version, regardless of the value of the identifiers. Some valid examples of version numbers with pre-release identifiers include 1.5.2-beta, 1.6.3-alpha, 1.6.3.-alpha.1, 1.3.2-0.0.1, and 1.3.2-z.7.x.23. Pre-release versions of software may be unstable and have a lower precedence than normal versions.

Automated testing

Automated tests should be executed as part of the automated build to ensure that no defects have been introduced since the last successful build. Automated testing, along with automated builds, allows the development team to validate the merged changes quickly. With continuous integration, errors are detected sooner, making them easier to resolve. Changesets tend to be smaller in size, and there will be fewer of them to integrate at once. This makes it easier to identify and resolve any issues that exist for a particular build. By integrating work continuously, we avoid a situation in which a large number of changes are merged at once.

It is important to have automated tests when practicing continuous integration. Although it is technically possible to practice continuous integration without the use of automated tests, having automated tests will increase quality and lessen the amount of time that quality assurance must spend using manual testing techniques. Automated tests can quickly inform developers when new commits have caused an issue.

The results of a build should be made available to the team so that it is easy to see whether there is a build break. In such cases, the appropriate developer can easily be made aware so that the issue can be fixed. If there is a situation in which some changes are reverted because of an issue, the amount of changes that are lost is minimized due to the continuous integration of the team.

One thing to consider with continuous integration is that writing a complete set of automated tests does take effort. The quality of the tests must be high or defects may be introduced into the system that go undetected for a period of time.

Continuous delivery (CD)

Continuous delivery (CD) is the ability of an organization to release changes to users quickly and in a sustainable, repeatable way. The software is released in short cycles, which reduces the risk, cost, and effort of delivering changes to customers. Organizations that practice continuous delivery have automated their testing as well as their build process.

The aim of continuous delivery is to have your software application in a state where it can be deployed to production at any time. This is an important part of DevOps. Continuous delivery includes all of the major activities that take place in a DevOps release cycle. In addition to development, integration, and an automated build with automated unit testing, which are all part of continuous integration, continuous delivery also includes automated delivery to staging, automated acceptance testing, and deployment to production:

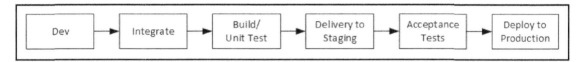

With continuous delivery, as opposed to continuous deployment, which we will cover next, deployment to production is a manual process. The organization can decide to release at whatever time interval they want (for example, daily, weekly, or monthly). However, the benefits of continuous delivery are increased if deployments take place as early as possible. Changes will be made available to users sooner and feedback can be received sooner. Each set of changes is smaller, making it easier to troubleshoot an issue if there is a problem.

After deployment to production, post-deployment tests are typically executed. The extent of the post-deployment testing varies, but at the very least it should consist of smoke testing. A *smoke test* ensures that all crucial functionality is working properly in the target environment. A smoke test is not as exhaustive as full software testing, but it can be performed quickly to determine whether the deployment in the target environment is stable.

Continuous deployment

Continuous deployment essentially takes continuous delivery one step further. Like continuous delivery, continuous deployment aims to enable organizations to release changes to software systems quickly and reliably. It differs from continuous delivery in that it automates the deployment to production.

Continuous delivery ensures that the software application can be delivered to staging, along with the execution of rigorous tests, using automation. When done properly, the software application should be in a state that it can be deployed to production at any time. Continuous deployment merely automates the final step so that all changes are automatically deployed to the production environment.

When the organization, the business, and the nature of the software application allow for it, continuous deployment is an ideal DevOps goal in that it automates the process from beginning to end, and is the quickest way to move application changes into production.

However, in some cases, continuous deployment is not practical. There may be business reasons that an organization does not want to automatically deploy all changes to production. Some organizations prefer that the final step, the deployment to production, be a manual process. Software architects, along with other key decision makers within the organization, will have to decide whether continuous deployment is appropriate for the organization.

Architecting for DevOps

As a software architect, you should consider DevOps when making architectural decisions. Some of the DevOps practices that we have discussed are independent of architecture and do not require specific architectural decisions to be made. However, certain architectural approaches may be required in order to realize the full benefit of some DevOps practices.

Important quality attributes for DevOps

Software systems that have been architected for DevOps should place importance on quality attributes, such as testability, deployability, and maintainability. Testability is a valued quality attribute because the ability to test the system is crucial, particularly since there will be automated tests. In order to architect a system to be testable, components need to be isolated from each other so that they can be tested independently. Each component must be controllable so that we can dictate input and how that input will exercise the capabilities of the component. It must be possible to observe the input and output of components so that it is possible to determine whether it is working properly.

In order to make and deploy changes quickly, the system must be highly maintainable. Minimizing complexity as much as possible aids us in achieving this goal. It makes it easier to understand how the system works and how to implement changes. Minimizing complexity enables shorter cycle times because small, incremental changes are easier to make. Reducing the size of components, increasing cohesion, and reducing coupling all help to make a system more maintainable. A system that is less complex and more maintainable is also easier to deploy and test.

Continuous delivery (and continuous deployment, if that is being practiced) requires a software system to be architected for deployability. Deployability is a measure of how easily and reliably a software system can be deployed from staging (or development) into production. Even if a system is testable, if changes cannot be pushed to production properly, then the utility of continuous delivery is lost. Increased deployability of a software system will shorten deployment time and decrease software system downtime.

Minimizing the difference between environments can go a long way in improving deployability. Staging and production should be as similar to each other as possible. When they are, successful delivery to a staging environment is a good predictor of a successful deployment to production.

Deployability is increased when an application and its configuration are kept separate. Configuration information that can vary from one environment to another (for example, database connection information) should be kept in external configuration and not be part of the application's code.

In order to enable DevOps, a software application needs to exhibit these types of quality attributes. Software projects that do not practice DevOps may not place an emphasis on these types of requirements. However, DevOps requires software architects and development teams to place more of a focus on them.

Operations should be considered when determining requirements. Requirements for robust monitoring and logging can help operations to detect faults quickly and record information that can be used to diagnose issues. Intrusive architectural changes are typically not necessary to add these types of capabilities, but they are important when changes to a software system are being made quickly and often. Software architects should *design for failure*. In other words, we should expect that failures will occur, but fault tolerance should be part of the system so that recovery can be completed quickly in order to minimize downtime.

Some architecture patterns complement DevOps

Some software architecture approaches, such as the microservice architecture pattern, lend themselves well to the types of requirements we have discussed for DevOps. It is not uncommon for an organization that is moving to either DevOps or microservices to then adopt the other. A microservice architecture works well with continuous delivery.

You may recall from `Chapter 8`, *Architecting Modern Applications*, that a microservice architecture consists of small, focused services with well-defined interfaces. The fact that each microservice focuses on a small piece of functionality makes it easier and less risky to make changes. Well-defined interfaces facilitate the swapping out of one microservice implementation for another one. As long as the interface remains the same, the implementation can change.

Each microservice should be autonomous and independently deployable. These qualities allow an organization to make changes to one microservice and deploy it without affecting other microservices. Each microservice can have their own independent data storage, further making them independent from other ones. The downtime to deploy a single microservice can be a quick and low-risk process.

Microservices provide better fault isolation than other architecture patterns, such as a monolithic architecture. If one microservice fails, it does not mean the entire software system will go down. Proper monitoring gives operations the ability to notice faults quickly, and if a recently deployed microservice is causing an issue, the team can revert back to the previous version.

DevOps does not require microservices, but the point is that certain architectural patterns work better than others with DevOps practices. Therefore, software architects must consider DevOps when making design decisions and creating architecturally significant requirements.

Deploying to the cloud

Transitioning to DevOps is commonly aligned with the use of the cloud. Many of the core values we have discussed, such as quick delivery and automated processes, are enhanced by deploying applications to the cloud.

In order to use the cloud in conjunction with DevOps, software architects should understand the different cloud types that are available, as well as the main cloud models. In this section, we will be exploring both of these topics in detail.

Cloud types

The three main types of deployment for cloud resources are a public, private, and hybrid cloud. Although they provide similar benefits, an organization must select the one that most matches its business needs.

Public cloud

A **public cloud** consists of cloud resources that are owned and operated by a third-party cloud provider. The resources and services are provided over the Internet and shared with other organizations. Public clouds are often multi-tenant, meaning that an organization's applications and data are hosted on the same hardware and networks with other organizations.

An organization will experience high reliability and practically unlimited scalability from the large number of resources that cloud providers own and manage. Organizations only have to pay for the services that are used and don't have to worry about the maintenance of the resources.

Although public clouds provide the best economies of scale among the different cloud types, it may not be the appropriate choice for some organizations. For data that is overly sensitive and/or subject to regulations, a public cloud may not meet all of a software application's requirements. With a public cloud, you lose some control over your data, which raises regulatory and compliance concerns regarding data storage and privacy. One example of this is the **Health Insurance Portability and Accountability Act (HIPAA)** of 1996, which protects patient information. You must be aware of regulations that may affect your software, and ensure that either your team or the cloud provider can meet those requirements.

Private cloud

A **private cloud** is made up of resources that are used exclusively by one organization. The physical resources can either be located at an organization's own data center or that of a third-party provider. Either way, all of the infrastructure is dedicated to a single organization. In contrast with a public cloud, it is a single tenant implementation.

Private clouds are costlier with more modest economies of scale. However, an organization will have greater flexibility in customizing the environment to meet its needs. One of the main reasons to opt for a private cloud is the greater level of control and the stronger security that is possible. Organizations can take advantage of cloud services while maintaining more control over their enterprise data, which is sometimes a requirement for security and privacy reasons.

However, a private cloud can be implemented by the organization or through a third-party cloud provider. When using a cloud provider, an organization can still benefit from high levels of reliability, efficiency, and scalability, just as they would with a public cloud. The main benefit of an on-premises approach is that an organization has complete control over the processes, data management policies, and physical resources.

A software architect should be mindful though, particularly if a private cloud is being chosen for security reasons, that a public cloud can be just as secure or even more secure than a private one if the private one is not implemented properly. A security hole turns a private cloud into a public vulnerability. If an organization implements their own private cloud, it is fully responsible for all aspects of it. Many of the steps required to implement a private cloud raise security issues that must be considered and addressed.

Cloud providers know that a secure cloud environment is essential to their business, so they devote resources to ensure that their environments are secure. Among the top priorities and core competencies of a cloud provider is security, which is typically not the case for organizations attempting to implement their own private cloud. For small and medium-sized businesses, it is difficult to achieve the same levels of reliability, efficiency, and scalability as a major cloud provider. Ultimately, though, deciding between a public cloud, on-premises infrastructure for a private cloud, and having a third party host a private cloud really depends on the needs and long-term strategy of your organization.

Hybrid cloud

A **hybrid cloud** is a combination of the public and private cloud types. For some organizations, it is a *best of both worlds* approach. With a hybrid cloud, an organization can have the benefits of a private cloud, but can still leverage the public cloud when it is needed.

Functionality that has higher volume and lower security needs could be hosted in a public cloud, while more mission-critical functionality and sensitive data can be served from a private cloud. Using a hybrid cloud can give an organization the control it needs from a private cloud with the flexibility to leverage the public cloud where it makes sense to do so.

For organizations with on-premises infrastructure, a hybrid approach allows it to transition to the cloud gradually. Legacy applications that have particular environment needs could be hosted on-premises while other applications are hosted in a public cloud.

A hybrid cloud approach allows for **cloud bursting**, also known as the **burst compute pattern**. The concept is that an application will run in a private cloud until it experiences a spike in demand that is large enough that it *bursts* into the public cloud.

The burst compute pattern is used when an application needs additional compute capability on an as-needed basis. Keeping hardware in-house to handle periodically increased needs can be costly, and the burst compute pattern is more cost-effective. It avoids having idle, over-provisioned resources. The public cloud handles the extra demand, and you are only charged for extra computing power when you need it.

A hybrid cloud can also come in handy for predictable outages, such as scheduled maintenance, rolling brown/blackouts, and natural disasters, such as hurricanes. Traffic can be handled by the public cloud during these periods.

Cloud models

The services that are provided for cloud computing can be categorized into different cloud models. They are as follows:

- Infrastructure as a Service (IaaS)
- Containers as a Service (CaaS)
- Platform as a Service (PaaS)
- Serverless/Function as a Service (FaaS)
- Software as a Service (SaaS)

The models differ in their level of abstraction and the amount of control and responsibility that you have:

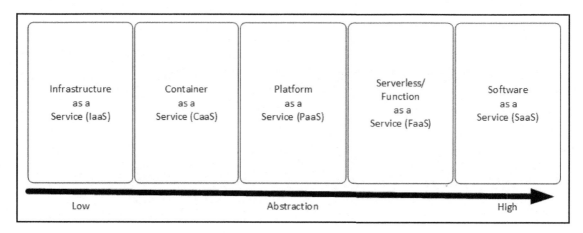

As you move to the right in the diagram, the level of abstraction is higher, and you have less control and fewer responsibilities in regards to the infrastructure. Having fewer responsibilities in terms of the infrastructure means that you can then devote more time to writing the actual application logic and adding more business value for your customers.

Infrastructure as a service (IaaS)

On the far left of the spectrum is **Infrastructure as a Service** (**IaaS**), in which you rent the hardware that you need. You are not responsible for maintaining the hardware that you use as it is taken care of for you by the provider. Things such as the storage drives, network components, and cooling systems are maintained for you.

However, you are responsible for just about everything else. In addition to your own application, you have to purchase, install, configure, and maintain things such as the **operating system** (**OS**), patches and security updates, anti-virus software, and middleware. You are also responsible for server and logical network configuration. Although you have quite a bit of control, you need to devote time to the management of these resources.

Common reasons to use IaaS include website hosting, web apps, test/development environments, storage/backup/recovery needs, and big data analysis. An important advantage of IaaS is that it eliminates the capital expenditure on hardware. The cost of ongoing maintenance for that hardware is also reduced. Not having to devote resources to the purchase and maintenance of hardware allows organizations to focus on their core business. It also increases organizational agility as teams can respond quickly to new market opportunities and release applications faster.

When organizations first adopt cloud technologies, IaaS is a common starting point as it makes a migration to the cloud fast and easy. IaaS is typically similar to how organizations already run their **information technology** (**IT**) departments, further easing the transition.

Containers as a Service (CaaS)

One of the application development and deployment models used for cloud-native applications is **Containers as a Service** (**CaaS**). It builds upon IaaS by adding a container orchestration platform, such as Kubernetes, Docker Swarm, or Apache Mesos. With CaaS, developers and IT staff work together to build, ship, and run applications.

Cloud-native applications are containerized and dynamically orchestrated. A CaaS approach gives development teams control over how their application and dependencies are packaged, making them fully portable. Containerization allows applications to *run anywhere*. Teams can deploy the application to different environments without needing to reconfigure them. Containers can run on **virtual machines** (**VMs**), on a developer's machine, in a private cloud with on-premises equipment, or in a public cloud.

Having the ability to dictate the dependencies of the application, along with their specific versions, and have them deployed along with their configuration provides a consistent environment in which your application will execute. It gives you predictability as to how the application will behave, and increases reusability. It's a great way for a development team to deploy their cloud-native, containerized application to the cloud.

While this model gives quite a bit of control to development teams, it does mean that there are greater responsibilities. In a similar way to IaaS, you are still responsible for the operating system, patches, and security updates for the OS, logging/monitoring, capacity management, and the scaling of the application.

The difference between CaaS and IaaS is the use of containers rather than virtual machines:

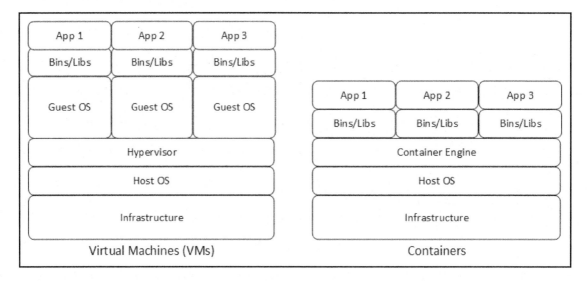

VMs are commonly used with IaaS as a way to run multiple applications on a single server and isolate them from each other. When using virtual machines under IaaS, a **hypervisor** runs the virtual machines as guests. Hypervisors are situated between the OS and the hardware, forming the virtualization layer. Pools of hypervisors have the ability to support and manage large numbers of virtual machines.

The machine (host) has a full copy of the operating system, but so does each virtual machine that is running an instance of your application. The application and operating system are bundled together, such that each application has a copy of the operating system for themselves. It allows a single physical machine to host multiple applications and have each one be isolated from the others. Utilization of server resources increase and costs decrease when sharing a physical machine, as compared to having a separate machine for each application.

While the first generation of cloud applications was made possible by VMs, the advent of containers improved upon some of the characteristics of VMs. With containers, the rough equivalent of a hypervisor is the **container engine**. Applications are still isolated from each other, but instead of virtualizing the hardware stack as is done with VMs, a container engine provides OS-level virtualization. Resources such as the CPU, memory, network resources, and storage are all virtualized at the OS level, allowing each container to have a view of the OS that is logically isolated from other containers.

Containerization is much more lightweight than using a VM because the OS kernel is shared. In contrast with VMs, which each have a copy of the OS, there is only one full copy of the operating system. As a result, containers have much lower overhead. They can start up very quickly, use less space on the disk, and use up far less memory. It is possible to put many more containers on a single server compared with virtual machines.

Virtual machines can be slow to start up and shut down since they come with a large overhead that includes a full copy of the operating system. This can lead to slow recovery should one fail. With a container engine and an orchestrator, the placement of containers can be dynamic and spread out, allowing for rapid recovery if there is a failure of the infrastructure or the application.

Platform as a Service (PaaS)

Platform as a Service (**PaaS**) provides development teams with a complete platform for developing and deploying applications in the cloud. This cloud computing model provides a higher level of abstraction than IaaS and CaaS. The hardware is provided and maintained as it is with IaaS, but there isn't as much interaction with the infrastructure. The platform abstracts away this interaction with everything that it provides.

Unlike IaaS, the operating system is provided and maintained for you, including the installation of patches and security updates. With PaaS, the development team does not have to manage the OS. In addition to the OS, providers make available a number of supporting software, tools, services, database management systems, and middleware.

The deployment and management of an application are easier, as an increased number of services are provided to assist with the common needs of application development and deployment. The availability of supporting services can greatly assist a DevOps organization. Having hardware, the OS, and other supporting software maintained for them saves organizations time and allows them to focus their resources on more important things, such as using their domain knowledge to build application code. It reduces development time and enables capabilities without adding any additional staff or time to the project.

One of the disadvantages with PaaS to be aware of is the fact that you lose control over the OS. There is also the potential for provider lock-in if an application relies on many of the specific tools and technologies that are made available by the provider.

In the early days of PaaS, the number of programming languages that a cloud provider supported might be limited. However, most cloud providers today support a variety of programming languages and runtimes.

Serverless/Function as a Service (FaaS)

Serverless architecture was covered in `Chapter 8`, *Architecting Modern Applications*, but let's differentiate it from PaaS. You may be thinking to yourself that serverless seems a lot like PaaS. Although there are similarities between PaaS and serverless solutions, serverless is not PaaS.

With PaaS, you need the ability to forecast your demand so that you can provide (and pay for) the capacity to meet your forecast. As a result, you still have to concern yourself with the amount of compute capacity you will need.

Unlike PaaS, with a serverless architecture, you will be charged based on a per-execution model and not for the time that the code is hosted. This is one of the main differences between PaaS and serverless. Serverless architectures are also designed to be capable of bringing an entire application up and down based on a request. You cannot under or overprovision your compute capacity with serverless. You will no longer find yourself in a situation where you do not have enough capacity during peak times, and during off-peak times your servers sit idle while you get charged.

Software as a Service (SaaS)

On the far right of the spectrum, we have **Software as a Service (SaaS)**, which is sometimes referred to as **on-demand software**. SaaS makes cloud-based software available to users over the Internet. With SaaS, everything is provided for you, including the software itself. The only thing you are responsible for is the configuration of the software. Unlike other software pricing models, customers don't have to pay for licenses to use the software. SaaS software is commonly charged using a subscription model based on a timeframe and the number of users.

Examples of SaaS are Salesforce, a **customer relationship management (CRM)** product, Google's Gmail, Microsoft's Office 365 productivity suite (Word, Excel, PowerPoint, Outlook, OneDrive), and storage solutions such as Dropbox. These are all hosted in the cloud and made available to users without them being responsible for anything other than their configuration.

The software is not installed on the user's own machine, which simplifies both maintenance and support. Technical staff is not required to install, manage, or upgrade the software.

Summary

Organizations can gain a competitive advantage by delivering software applications at high velocity, adding incremental value for their customers frequently and quickly. Having the ability to reliably deliver new improvements of software products to customers on a regular basis can differentiate an organization from its competitors.

The culture, practices, and technologies of DevOps can enable organizations to achieve these goals. Continuous integration, with automated builds and testing, allows changes to be validated quickly. Frequent check-ins make it easier to detect and resolve any problems. The practice of continuous delivery keeps software systems in a state where they can be deployed to production at any time. This type of organizational agility provides the option of releasing changes to users quickly and in a repeatable way.

Some DevOps practices do not require any architectural changes, but the needs of DevOps should be considered during requirements, as well as when making architectural design decisions. Consideration must be given to quality attributes, such as testability, deployability, and maintainability, when architecting a solution.

In the next chapter, we will learn what it takes to work on and with legacy applications. Refactoring and integrating legacy applications bring unique challenges that a software architect must be prepared to face.

14
Architecting Legacy Applications

The prevalent use of legacy software applications means that many software architects will end up working on one at some point in their career. As part of learning how to become a complete software architect, time needs to be invested in learning how to properly handle legacy software systems.

We will learn what a legacy application is and how to refactor it. In addition to a legacy application's code, we will examine other aspects of a legacy application that can be modernized, including the software development methodology, the build process, and the deployment process. The chapter will conclude by looking at topics related to integrating with a legacy application.

In this chapter, we will cover the following topics:

- Legacy applications
- Refactoring legacy applications
- Moving to an agile approach
- Modernizing build and deployment processes
- Integrating with legacy applications

Legacy applications

Many of us enjoy working on greenfield software systems, which are completely new systems that we can design from the ground up. Such systems do not have constraints based on prior work and do not need to integrate with existing systems. However, the new applications of today eventually become the legacy systems of tomorrow.

Software architects will often find themselves working on existing software systems and being able to do so well is a valuable skill. A **legacy application** is an existing application that is still in use but is difficult to maintain. There are a number of challenges with maintaining and using a legacy application.

Issues with legacy applications

Working with a legacy application usually brings with it various problems that need to be overcome. This is a part of the challenge when working with a legacy system. Perhaps most importantly, a legacy application tends to be difficult to maintain and extend. It may use older, possibly outdated, technologies and it may not follow best practices for software development.

A legacy application tends to be older, and over the life of the project many different developers may make modifications to it. **Software entropy**, or disorder in a software system, increases over time. This concept comes from the Second Law of Thermodynamics, which states that the level of entropy either stays the same or increases but it does not decrease. As modifications continue to be made on a codebase, the code can become brittle and messy, resulting in *spaghetti code*. If you have ever needed to make a modification to a legacy application but were afraid of breaking something, you know firsthand the difficulties of dealing with a legacy application.

A legacy system will almost certainly bear some amount of **technical debt**. Any design decisions that have been made for an application, in which an easier, quicker solution was selected over one that was a cleaner solution but would have taken longer to implement, incurs technical debt. Similar to a financial debt, technical debt is the cost of these decisions, such as the cost of any rework necessary to improve the system. Technical debt increases software entropy.

Deciding to incur technical debt is not necessarily a bad thing. Sometimes it makes sense to take the easier approach. For example, you may want to complete a feature faster to take advantage of a market opportunity. Whatever the reasons are, though, a software architect should realize that a legacy system will come with technical debt.

Some legacy applications rely on older versions of operating systems, other software, and/or hardware. These environments can become increasingly difficult to maintain over time. It also increases the possibility of vulnerabilities if security patches are either not available or not applied.

A legacy application may be one that has been inherited from another development team, who may no longer be available to answer questions about it. This may lead to a general lack of knowledge about the system. Documentation and unit tests for a legacy application may be lacking, making it more difficult to gain an understanding of the application and to make changes to it.

Why are legacy applications used?

While there may be challenges to using legacy applications, enterprises continue to use them for a variety of reasons. If they remain useful and still work as intended, an organization may see no reason to stop using them. In addition, the cost of replacing a legacy system may not outweigh the benefits. For example, the difficulties and cost of replacing a system that requires almost constant availability may be prohibitively high. Replacement of a large and complicated system can be a long and difficult process.

Rewriting a legacy system may be desirable for a development team, as it allows them to work on a greenfield system, but it may not be a good decision from a business perspective. Replacing a legacy system with a new system that performs the same functionality will cost an organization money while potentially not adding much new business value. A development team can certainly point out that a rewritten application will have increased maintainability and alleviate the other types of issue with legacy applications that we just covered. These benefits can result in cost savings over time, depending on how long the system will be in use. However, rewriting a legacy application, particularly a complex one that currently works, can be a tough sell to Management when it may not make financial sense. Modernization of a legacy application, during which it is refactored with the purpose of improving it, can be a less expensive alternative that poses fewer risks.

Another reason why a legacy application might continue to be used is if it is not well understood. If the original development team is no longer with the organization, the system is complex, or there is a lack of documentation, it will take more effort to replace the system. This type of barrier can be yet another reason why rewriting an application is put off.

More than just code

Software architects should understand that a legacy application does not just consist of the code. A legacy software system includes requirements related to the environment needed for it to run, such as any dependencies with particular versions of an operating system. It may require particular tools or certain versions of a tool, such as source code editing, build, version control, code coverage, code review, debugging, integration, documentation, static code analysis, and unit testing tools. Some of the tools required by a legacy application may not be supported any longer.

A legacy software system is also made up of its dependencies, such as those for other systems, third-party software, frameworks, and packages. Similar to tools, these dependencies can become outdated or may no longer be supported. Finally, a legacy system also includes its internal and external documentation. The documentation for some legacy systems is either sorely lacking or outdated. A combination of all of these factors makes up a legacy system and its overall level of quality. Each one, to some degree, affects quality attributes such as the maintainability of the overall system.

Where legacy systems exist, software architects overseeing them may need to be involved with refactoring, replacing, or integrating with them.

Refactoring legacy applications

When you begin working on a legacy application, you will want to refactor it in order to make it more maintainable. You may need to implement new features, fix defects, improve the design, increase quality, or optimize the application. In order to perform these types of task, the legacy system must be in a state where changes can easily be made and without much risk.

In the classic book *Refactoring: Improving the Design of Existing Code*, author Martin Fowler defines refactoring as ...*the process of changing a software system in such a way that it does not alter the external behavior of the code yet improves its internal structure.* Any refactoring that is performed should safely improve the code in some way, without affecting the business logic and expected functionality.

Before making any changes, it is helpful to have the right attitude when approaching a legacy codebase. All too often, a software architect or developer will be highly critical of a legacy application before even fully understanding the codebase. You should have respect for the original development team because there may be reasons why things were done a certain way and you may not always be aware of all of the decisions that took place and the rationale behind them.

As a software architect, you want to modernize and improve the legacy application that you have been tasked with overseeing. You do not want to focus on making unnecessary modifications, particularly if you do not yet fully understand the impact of the changes. For example, rather than making changes because you do not like how something was coded stylistically, you should focus your attention on making substantive changes that will have a positive impact on the codebase.

Refactoring a legacy application with the purpose of modernizing and improving it includes performing the following tasks:

- Making legacy code testable
- Removing redundant code
- Use tools to refactor the code
- Making small, incremental changes
- Transforming monoliths to microservices

Making legacy code testable

Many legacy software systems lack automated unit tests and only some of them have adequate code coverage. What may be even more problematic is that some legacy systems have not been developed with unit testing in mind, making it difficult to add tests later.

Adding unit tests to a legacy system that does not have them should be given a high priority. There are a number of benefits to making legacy systems (and all software systems, for that matter) unit-testable.

Benefits of unit testing

One of the biggest benefits of using unit tests on a legacy system is that it facilitates making modifications to the system, particularly for individuals who may not be familiar with the system. As you make changes to a legacy application, unit tests will ensure that the changes did not introduce new defects and that the functionality still works properly.

Regularly executing unit tests, such as after a change is made or as part of the build process, will make debugging any issues that are found easier. A developer will be able to narrow down the source of the problem to one of the recent changes.

The documentation for legacy applications may not be suitable but if the system has a good suite of unit tests, the tests can serve as a source of documentation. They help team members understand the system and allow them to learn what a particular unit of code was developed to do. When unit tests are lacking, just the act of writing the unit tests will help the team become more familiar with the codebase.

Refactoring for unit tests

The application may not have been designed to be unit-testable. Ideally, unit tests would be in place prior to performing any refactoring work. However, as a software architect, you may be faced with a dilemma if you need to refactor an application just so you can write unit tests.

When faced with a situation in which automated unit tests do not already exist, some initial refactoring may be necessary, just to allow for the creation of the initial set of tests. From that point, further refactoring and the addition of more unit tests will be possible.

Another approach for this situation is to write integration tests. Integration tests can then be executed before any refactoring changes to confirm that the original functionality works as intended. As refactoring work takes place, the integration tests can be executed often to ensure that nothing was broken. Integration tests do not use mocks or stubs but rather execute logic in dependencies. For this reason, they do require some more setup to ensure all of the components work. One added benefit of this approach is that once you are done, you will already have integration tests to go along with your unit tests.

Once unit tests have been written, they must be maintained going forward. As code is added or modified (for example, to implement a new feature or fix a bug), unit tests should be added or modified, as necessary, to keep the test suite up to date.

Where to start writing tests?

It can be difficult to know where to start when introducing unit testing in a legacy application. One approach is to start with the logic that is related to the most critical business functionality. With this approach, you will have unit test coverage for the most important components first.

Another approach is to consider the level of complexity of the components. Some people prefer to get the most complicated work out of the way first. An experienced development team may prefer this approach. Others would prefer to begin with less complex components and build up to the ones that will require more work. This approach may be more suited to a less experienced team.

When using the complexity level as a factor when deciding where to start, it doesn't have to be one way or the other. Some members of the team could begin with highly complex components while others start with less complex ones.

Removing redundant code

Any software application may contain redundant code, but legacy applications, which are older and are more likely to have been maintained by a variety of people, tend to have increased instances of code that is either duplicated or no longer needed.

When taking over a legacy application, a software architect should look to remove redundant code. Reducing the total lines of code minimizes complexity and makes the software system easier to understand. Code analysis tools can help to identify some types of code that are unnecessary. Refactoring unreachable, dead, commented-out, and duplicate code will improve the maintainability of the system. Let's look at each of these types of code in more detail.

Unreachable code

Unreachable code is code that can never be executed, regardless of the conditions at runtime. There is simply no control flow path that will lead to the code being executed. Code can become unreachable for a variety of reasons. Some examples include developers forgetting to delete obsolete code, code that was intentionally made unreachable so that it could potentially be used later, code strictly for debugging/test purposes that was not removed, modifications to other code that unknowingly made code unreachable, business logic/data changes that made code unreachable, and a programming error.

Static analysis tools can help you to find this type of code. If the unreachable code is the result of a bug and it is determined after analysis that the code is actually needed, then the defect should be corrected so that the code is no longer unreachable. However, if after analysis it is confirmed that the code is unnecessary, then it should be removed. The removal of unreachable code increases the overall maintainability of the software system. If unreachable logic was being kept in the code in case it would eventually be needed, version control software can be used to obtain it again rather than leaving it in the code.

Dead code

Some people use the terms unreachable code and **dead code** interchangeably but there is a subtle difference. While unreachable code can never be executed, dead code can be executed. However, when dead code is executed it has no effect on the output. For example, dead code might perform some logic that produces a result but then the result is not used anywhere.

Commented-out code

Commented-out code is code that is currently not in use and has been commented out by a developer rather than deleted. Code that is commented out is among the easiest types of code to remove. Sometimes a developer may comment out code with the intention of it only being temporary but then does not follow up later to either remove or uncomment the code.

Lines of code are sometimes commented out to serve as a record of previous logic. However, having a change history is one of the purposes of a version control system. Leaving code in the codebase that has been commented out only increases the size of the code and makes it less readable.

Duplicate code

Duplicate code is identical (or very similar) code that exists in multiple places. The parts of your codebase that are duplicated violate the **Don't Repeat Yourself** (**DRY**) principle. As we learned in Chapter 6, *Software Development Principles and Practices,* following the DRY principle means eliminating duplication in our codebase. Duplication of code is wasteful and makes the code more difficult to maintain. Some of you may have had the experience of needing to make the same code change in multiple places because of duplicate code.

Any instances of duplicate code should be abstracted out and placed in a single location. All of the places in the codebase that need the logic can then be routed through the abstraction. Eliminating code duplication will increase maintainability and the quality of the software. When the logic must be modified, it can be done in one place, eliminating the risk of missing one of the locations or not making a consistent change when the code is duplicated.

Using tools to refactor

When possible, take advantage of development tools available to you that will assist with refactoring a legacy application. Your organization may already have licenses for an **integrated development environment** (**IDE**) or other tools that can identify areas of the codebase that can be refactored. Some of them will perform some types of refactoring for you and provide you with a preview of the changes before it actually makes them. If your organization doesn't have a particular tool, it may be possible to purchase licenses for it based on your recommendations. If such purchases are not going to be possible (or simply because there are better options which happen to be free), consider using an open-source tool.

Making small, incremental changes

When refactoring a legacy application, some of the changes that you want to make may be large ones. However, keep in mind that in order to improve a legacy application, the changes do not have to be large and they do not have to be made all at once. Refactoring a legacy application can take time. Small, incremental changes can sometimes be the best approach to improving a legacy codebase. Write and execute unit tests to go along with your changes to ensure that your modifications do not have unintended consequences. With each refactoring, we want to leave the code better than it was before, without changing any of the functionality.

You and your development team may not even be granted time to make improvements. If one of you is tasked with some work, such as fixing a bug in the legacy application, take the opportunity to improve the area of the code that is being changed. Over time, more and more parts of the code will be improved.

Transforming monoliths to microservices

Your legacy application may have a monolithic architecture. In `Chapter 8`, *Architecting Modern Applications*, we learned that a monolithic application is designed to work as a single, self-contained unit. The code may have components that are tightly coupled and highly interdependent. If the application is large and complicated, it can be difficult to make changes to a monolithic application.

One approach to modernizing a legacy application is to begin introducing microservices. Microservices are small, focused, autonomous services that are independently deployable. Unlike a monolithic application, the microservice approach reduces the level of complexity by partitioning an application into small services that are easier to maintain and manage. In a legacy application, we can take pieces of logic and place them in microservices.

Places in the legacy application that need the functionality contained in a microservice can interact with it through its interface. Implementations of each service can be changed as long as the interface remains the same. It also provides the ability for a development team to modify a microservice independently of other services. In contrast with modifications made to a monolithic application, changes to individual microservices are less likely to require modifications in other places in the application.

There is better fault tolerance with microservices. If a legacy application has a monolithic architecture, a fault could bring down a large part of the application or even the entire application. When a single microservice fails, it will not cause the entire application to crash. Combined with proper monitoring, which will alert administrators to a fault quickly, a microservice can be restarted quickly. If there is an issue with the currently deployed version of a microservice, a new version that contains a fix can be deployed without having to deploy the entire application. It also provides the option of reverting to a prior version of the microservice if it does not contain the issue.

Migrating to the cloud

Migrating a legacy application to the cloud is another way that it can be modernized. Although not every legacy application will be compatible with every cloud service, there are migration paths that will allow you to take most legacy applications to the cloud. Certain cloud services will be more suited to a particular application.

There are a number of reasons why a legacy application will benefit from a move to the cloud. It can reduce costs while at the same time providing greater levels of availability and scalability. A cloud provider will be responsible for the hardware and infrastructure. Depending on the cloud model (for example, IaaS, PaaS, or FaaS), it may also be responsible for the operating system and other services.

Some legacy applications have security vulnerabilities because they rely on older hardware and software. If they are migrated to the cloud, the cloud provider can potentially handle tasks such as operating system updates, including security patches.

The 6 R's

The migration path to the cloud will vary from organization to organization and among different applications. The concept of the **6 R's** is used to describe different approaches to cloud migration. The 6 R's are:

- Remove (or retire)
- Retain
- Replatform
- Rehost
- Repurchase
- Refactor (or re-architect)

We will now explore each of these concepts in further detail.

Remove (or retire)

When taking into consideration a particular application, one option is to simply remove it. Some applications that an organization is hosting might not even be needed anymore, but have been kept running. If your organization is undergoing an overall migration to the cloud for a number of applications and services, this is an ideal time to evaluate your current applications. You may be able to identify some that no longer need to be kept available.

Retain

Some applications either cannot be migrated to the cloud or an organization may make a decision to not migrate them. In these cases, you will simply be retaining the application in its current environment. There are a number of reasons why an application may simply be retained. There may not be a business justification for moving an application to the cloud. For example, the cost of migrating to the cloud might be too high given the expected benefits.

Organizations that want a hybrid cloud will retain some of their applications in their on-premises infrastructure. In a hybrid approach, some applications will be migrated while others will remain hosted on-premise.

Replatform

Some legacy applications cannot be migrated to a cloud platform but an organization does not want to simply retain them in their current environment. For this type of situation, the application can be run on cloud-based IaaS servers using emulators. The application is emulated through a virtual machine to make it compatible with cloud technologies. This approach allows you to migrate to a newer platform/operating system and take advantage of its features. There are a number of tools and services available to assist with replatforming.

Rehost

Lift and shift is a migration strategy that involves moving a software application from one environment to another without redesigning the application. *Rehosting* is a lift and shift approach in which an application and its data are copied from physical or virtual servers to an IaaS solution. The application does not need to be changed and the cloud provider hosts the infrastructure. This is a quick, low-risk, and easy way to migrate an application to the cloud.

Rehosting can be the first step in a cloud migration for an application. Once the legacy application is running in the cloud, it may be refactored later in order to optimize it for its new environment. The fact that it is already hosted in the cloud may make that process easier.

Repurchase

Rather than move a legacy application to the cloud, an organization might decide to purchase a newer product and start using that one instead. This option is commonly associated with a move to a SaaS cloud model. Everything is provided for you with SaaS, including the hosting and the software. The organization only has to configure the software for use.

Refactor (or re-architect)

When refactoring an application for a cloud migration, you are making modifications to the application, possibly including its architecture. You may be refactoring the application to take advantage of the cloud-native features available in its new environment.

Legacy applications that are refactored properly will have greater availability, improved scalability, and faster performance. In addition to these advantages, an organization can realize cost benefits after the application has been migrated. The refactoring/re-architecting approach can potentially be quite involved though. Depending on what needs to be done, the migration process itself may take longer and cost more to execute.

Moving to an agile approach

A legacy application does not just entail the technology that comes with it. It was developed using a particular software development methodology. In some cases, that methodology might still be in use. If the methodology used is not a modern one, such as the use of a Waterfall methodology, part of modernizing a legacy application might include changing the development approach.

The agile methodology overcomes some of the limitations of older methodologies. While traditional software development methodologies focus on a lot of up-front planning and design, an agile methodology expects and embraces change. Agile methodologies are adaptive rather than predictive. Rather than focusing on predicting the outcome, it places emphasis on adapting. It is more responsive to change, which is important in today's competitive landscape.

An agile methodology will enable your team to accomplish some of the things we have discussed to improve a legacy application, such as refactoring it by making small, incremental changes. Each sprint can be focused on particular goals to improve the legacy application.

If you are introducing microservices, an agile methodology complements that approach well. An agile approach provides a structure that will allow a development team to work together effectively. It is also particularly suited to modern build and deployment processes.

Modernizing build and deployment processes

Another aspect of modernizing a legacy application is to update the build and deployment processes. If outdated, these processes cannot be completed as easily or quickly as modern processes. A legacy application might even need to be built and deployed manually, which can make it error-prone.

If the processes are complex and the documentation is poor, knowledge of the intricacies involved in the processes can be lost. There may be a reliance on certain individuals who know all of the details about the processes, which can be problematic when those people are away from work or decide to leave the organization entirely.

The initial step in updating these processes is to gain a detailed understanding of the current way that builds and deployments are done. You should also know about any differences that exist in the processes based on the environment (for example, development, staging, or production).

Automating the build and deployment processes

If the processes are not already automated, serious consideration should be given to automating them. Automation will allow builds and deployments to be completed quickly. If there are many steps, mistakes can be made when conducting the processes. Automation ensures consistency between builds and across different environments.

Without automation, there may be variation in the processes depending on who is doing them. Developers and operations engineers may also take it upon themselves to automate different aspects of the process and each may do so in a different way.

Automation provides quick feedback regarding any issues. It allows us to *fail fast*, which means we can also resolve any issue quicker. By combining automated builds with automated testing, we further improve the process. Executing automated unit tests during the build process will help to improve quality and allow us to become aware of any problems in a timely manner.

In `Chapter 13`, *DevOps and Software Architecture*, we learned about the DevOps practices of **continuous integration** (**CI**) and **continuous delivery** (**CD**). These practices are possible with automation, as will be explained in the following sections.

Practicing continuous integration (CI)

If they are not already doing so, developers working on legacy systems should begin practicing CI. As we learned in the last chapter, continuous integration involves committing code changes on a frequent basis.

Continuous integration will inform a developer of any issues with their code check-in earlier in the process. It will reduce the potential for conflicting changes. It will be easier to identify and resolve any issues when the set of changes are smaller and they are merged more frequently.

Practicing continuous delivery (CD)

A legacy application may not have been designed for CD. In `Chapter 13`, *DevOps and Software Architecture*, we learned that continuous delivery is the ability to release software changes to users quickly and in a reliable way. The build and deployment processes of a legacy application can be slow and tedious, particularly if they are performed manually.

If it is feasible to do so, a goal should be made to practice continuous delivery, so that the legacy application will be in such a state that it can be deployed to production at any time. Automating the build process and executing automated unit tests as part of that process is an important step in enabling continuous delivery.

A continuous delivery process for a legacy application should build and deploy the application to staging automatically. If the organization desires to do so, continuous delivery of the software system can be taken a step further by practicing continuous deployment. If continuous deployment is enabled, then the last step of the process is automated: deployment to production.

Updating the build tools

A legacy application may be using older build tools. Similar to other development tools, build tools are constantly evolving. If the legacy application you are working on is using an outdated build tool, there are probably better options available to you (or possibly newer versions of the tools already being used).

Software architects should look to update outdated build tools to improve the build and deployment processes. Good build and deployment tools can help you achieve your goals of practicing continuous integration and continuous delivery.

Integrating with legacy applications

Software architects may need to integrate a legacy application with another software application. If you are responsible for the legacy application, refactoring it may be necessary in order to modernize it to the point that it can be integrated with newer applications.

When integrating a legacy application with another application, some considerations should be made by the software architect.

Confirming the need for integration

Prior to expending the effort to integrate with a legacy application, thought should be given to ensure that the integration is necessary. Depending on the situation, it may be easier to migrate the functionality that is needed from the legacy application rather than move forward with integration.

When deciding to migrate or integrate, consider the amount of functionality that is needed from the legacy system and the complexity of that functionality. If there is a large amount of functionality and/or the functionality is highly complex, then more effort will be necessary to migrate it. It may be more cost-effective to integrate with the legacy system and to keep using it.

Another factor to consider is the long-term goals of the organization and the expected remaining lifetime of the legacy system. If there is a goal to retire the legacy system in the near future, then perhaps it makes sense to begin the process sooner, rather than using resources to perform an integration.

Determining the type of integration

There are different types of integration possible and there should be an understanding of what type is needed based on the business drivers and requirements. Some integrations may be required to take place in real time, where an action in one system triggers an action in an other system that must take place immediately. These types of integration can be more complex and expensive to implement.

In some cases, near real-time integration is sufficient. Near real-time integration is still quick but processing may be measured in minutes rather than seconds. If there is no requirement for such a quick action, batch integration may make the most sense. In contrast with real-time or near real-time integration, batch integration may take hours, or even days, to complete. Batch processing can be scheduled and processing can be executed during off-peak hours.

Some types of integration will be easier to implement and less disruptive to existing environments, so in addition to understanding business needs, having knowledge about the current environments is important.

Sharing functionality between systems

When a newer software application is integrated with a legacy one, some of the functionality may be duplicated across the two systems. Software architects should be aware of any overlaps because decisions will need to be made as to which system will be responsible for functionality that is shared. Any differences in shared business logic between the two systems should be identified, as those differences may play a factor in such a decision.

Any logic that is redundant between the two systems is a candidate to be exposed and shared so that it is no longer duplicated. This will ensure consistency of the logic. Quality and maintainability will be increased as the logic will only need to be maintained and tested in one location.

Performing data integration

When integrating and sharing data between two systems, we have to ensure that data can be combined from disparate sources in a meaningful way. There should be an understanding of the data in both systems and what they represent. We need the ability to identify whether or not a piece of data represents the same thing in both systems.

Data mapping between systems may be required to transform data from one system to another. When possible, redundancy in data should be removed and decisions need to be made as to which system will be responsible for certain pieces of data.

Summary

Despite the challenges of maintaining a legacy application, enterprises continue to use them for a variety of reasons. Working on a legacy application is a common task for a software development professional. Most of us have worked on a legacy application, and if you have not already, it is likely that you will at some point in your career. Software architects should be knowledgeable about how to effectively oversee one.

There is typically a need to make modifications to a legacy application to fix bugs and add new features. To make it easier for a development team to make these types of change, software architects may seek to refactor legacy applications to make them more maintainable. Software architects may also lead efforts to improve a legacy application by migrating it to the cloud and modernizing its build and deployment processes.

Up to this point, we have mainly focused our attention on technical topics. In the next chapter, we will learn the soft skills that software architects should possess. As you move from being a developer to a software architect, you will find that specific soft skills are useful.

15
The Soft Skills of Software Architects

When thinking about the software architect role, many people focus on technical skills. However, possessing soft skills is essential to being a successful software architect. Soft skills can be the difference between an adequate software architect and an exceptional one.

In this chapter, we will gain an understanding of what soft skills are and explore some of the soft skills that are useful to have for the software architecture role. These include communication, listening, leadership, and negotiation skills. We will also cover how to effectively work with remote team members.

In this chapter, we will cover the following topics:

- Soft skills
- Communication
- Leadership
- Negotiation
- Working with remote resources

Soft skills

Hard skills are concrete skills that can be defined and measured. They are typically job-specific and you can obtain them through education, training (both internal and external to the organization), and certifications. For a software development professional, these would include technical skills such as knowing a particular programming language or the use of a specific framework.

In contrast, *soft skills* are not as tangible and are much more difficult to define and measure. Soft skills are more related to interpersonal skills, such as leadership, communication, listening skills, empathy, negotiation, and patience. While you can improve soft skills through training, they are more innate than hard skills.

It is useful for software development professionals to have certain soft skills and to spend time improving them. As you move from a developer role to that of a software architect, the importance of soft skills increases. Being a software architect involves more than just technical knowledge. You must also have soft skills in order to be effective. The focus of this chapter is on the soft skills that are important for software architects.

Communication

Communication may well be one of the most important soft skills that a software architect can possess. While it is a useful skill for any software development professional, software architects, in particular, are required to communicate with a variety of team members and stakeholders.

When you need to communicate something, it is imperative to understand the message that you want to convey and to know your audience. This will allow you to choose an appropriate style with which to communicate your thoughts. It is not just about what you want to say but, rather, how you say it.

The chances that a project will be successful are increased when there is plenty of communication between everyone involved with it. This includes communication with developers, testers, business analysts, customers, management, and other stakeholders. Some of the people that you will need to communicate with will be technical while others will not. A software architect must be able to tailor their communications based on the audience.

Communicating the architecture

One of the more significant responsibilities of a software architect is to communicate details about the software system and its architecture to others. An architecture must be communicated to the development team so that developers can learn about the different structures and elements that make up the architecture and how they interact with each other. It is through this understanding that they will be able to implement the functionality.

A software architecture imposes some constraints on implementations and prevents developers from making incorrect design decisions. The details of a software architecture must be communicated to developers so that they can complete their tasks and understand the constraints, to avoid developing components that do not conform to the architecture.

Communicating about quality attributes

A software architecture can both enable and inhibit software quality attributes. We learned about quality attributes in `Chapter 4`, *Software Quality Attributes*. Examples of software quality attributes include maintainability, availability, performance, and security. A software architect has to communicate details of how design decisions will affect the quality attributes of a software system. Communication with product owners, business analysts, and other stakeholders might be necessary to make design decisions based on quality attribute tradeoffs.

Communicating expectations

Software architects will need to communicate with project management to assist with project scheduling and resource planning. A software architect's input from a technical perspective is necessary for effective project planning.

Once the project begins, a software architect will need to continue to communicate with management on the status of the project. In some cases, a software architect may be involved with communicating expectations to one or more customers. If a project does not meet the expectations of the client, it cannot be considered a success. An organization must ensure that it is on the same page as its clients, and one way to do this is to keep them in the loop regarding the current state of the project. The goal is to eliminate surprises to ensure that customers are satisfied.

The 7 Cs of communication

A set of tips regarding effective communication is known as the **7 Cs of communication**. There is some variation among these tips, both in the number (for example, some list only five *Cs*) as well as the terms used. The following section details some of the most common tips.

Clarity

Clarity is important to have in your communications. If your audience is not clear about what you are trying to say, your communication cannot be effective. The term *clear* is occasionally used in place of clarity. The message you are communicating should be understandable and clear to the people who are receiving it.

Consider your audience as well as your purpose when communicating with others. For example, if your audience is not very technical but you are discussing a technical topic, think about the language that you choose to use and how you elect to communicate your message. If you are going to use terms that a recipient may not understand, clarify their meaning.

Conciseness

When communicating, be concise without sacrificing any of the other Cs. Less is sometimes more. Use as many words as is necessary but do not be overly verbose. Being excessive with your wording has the potential to reduce clarity as others will struggle to understand the meaning of what you are communicating. Your audience will have a tendency to *tune you out* when you are not concise.

Conciseness emphasizes the important parts of your message by eliminating any unnecessary words. When you are concise, you avoid being repetitive. Conciseness will save time, which also means that there are cost savings. The people you are communicating with will probably prefer a concise message. When someone is known to be overly verbose, there may be others who try to avoid that person entirely.

If you want to be concise, think about what is really essential to the message you want to communicate. If it helps, put yourself in the place of the people you are communicating with and consider what they need to know in order to understand your message. If any material is irrelevant, you can exclude it.

If you are planning your remarks ahead of time, such as for a presentation, it may take some extra time to organize your thoughts and choose precise language that will allow you to be concise. However, this extra effort is worth it and your audience will appreciate it.

Concreteness

Concreteness involves being specific about what you say or write, as opposed to being vague and general. Concreteness helps to bring clarity to your message as it is less likely to be misinterpreted. Misunderstandings can create problems for both the sender and the recipient of a message, so it is best to be concrete when possible.

Use specific facts and figures rather than imprecise descriptions. Doing so will enhance your message and make it more interesting. Perhaps most importantly, being concrete makes it easier to communicate the full meaning of your message. However, do not give specific details if you do not have that level of information or if the exact figures are irrelevant to your message.

Use vivid language that will help the recipient build an image of what you are trying to communicate. Putting action in your verbs can also add to concreteness. When possible, use an active voice rather than a passive one. In the active voice, the subject of the sentence performs the action, as opposed to the passive voice, in which the subject receives the action. An active voice tends to be more concrete than vague.

Courteousness

When communicating with others, be courteous. Courtesy in your communications is being respectful of others. Politeness and fairness in all of your communications will make those who are listening to you more willing to embrace and absorb your message. Courteous communication fosters a positive work environment and will strengthen work relationships.

Be thoughtful, tactful, and respectful of the recipients of your communication. Be aware of any cultural differences that may exist between you and the recipients of your message to ensure that you do not offend anyone. Use nondiscriminatory words and expressions to ensure everyone is treated equally in terms of gender, race, religion, and ethnicity.

Consideration

Consideration focuses on keeping the recipients of your message in mind when you communicate something. Place an emphasis on *you* instead of *I* and *we*. Think about your recipients and take into consideration their viewpoints. Be aware of, and empathetic to, their views, emotions, and attitudes. As the sender of a message, put yourself in the shoes of your recipients to see whether there is a better way to communicate your message.

Consideration in your communications goes hand in hand with courteousness. Giving consideration to others, by giving careful thought to your message and your audience, is part of being courteous to others.

Correctness

You want to have correctness in your communications. Whatever information you are conveying should be accurate. Even if you follow the other best practices, if your message is incorrect, the purpose of your communication will not be fulfilled. If any facts and data are provided in your communication, ensure that they are accurate.

In addition to ensuring the correctness of your message, the grammar and vocabulary that you use in your communications, written or verbal, should be correct as well. In any written communication, be sure to use proper spelling and punctuation. Correctness will increase the audience's confidence level in you as the speaker (or writer) and it will help to convey your message.

Completeness

Your message should be complete. Completeness entails ensuring that your communication includes all of the information needed to understand and use it. To ensure completeness, ask yourself the five *W* questions (who, what, where, when, and why) and ensure that your message includes answers to any of the questions that are relevant.

If action needs to be taken or decisions need to be made related to the message you are communicating, providing a complete message will help to ensure that the right action and/or decision is made. Completeness saves time and reduces costs because extra effort is not needed to provide missing information or to correct decisions that have already been made based on incomplete information.

If someone asks a question about something you are trying to communicate, answer the question to the best of your ability. If you do not know the answer, say so honestly and clearly.

Listening skills

Listening skills are a crucial part of having communication skills. Listening is the ability to receive and understand what someone is saying to you. It allows you to receive a message from someone and be able to comprehend it. To be an effective communicator, you must also have an ability and willingness to listen. Communication does not just go in one direction but rather flows in both.

Software architects need to listen so that they can learn, understand, and obtain information. If you do not have adequate listening skills, having effective communication is difficult. A message can be lost or misunderstood by a recipient who is not listening.

Hearing is not listening

Keep in mind that listening and hearing are two different things. While the ability to hear is a physical process that happens automatically as long as someone does not have any hearing problems, listening requires effort. When someone is speaking to you, you must pay attention and put forth a concentrated effort to understand what the person is saying to you.

Showing empathy

To take listening skills to the next level, we need to be able to exhibit empathy towards others. Empathy involves understanding another person's point of view. Try to put yourself in the other person's position to feel what someone else is going through and what they may be thinking.

One way to develop empathy is to listen more and talk less. Ask questions that will help you to gain better insight into what someone is feeling, thinking, or needing. Having empathy will allow you to better understand the needs and challenges of your developers, customers, management, and others. Empathy can help to motivate your team and build better products for your customers.

Tips for effective listening

When you are listening to someone speak to you, face them and maintain eye contact. This will tell the speaker that you are engaged and it will help you to maintain focus. Be present and attentive to the speaker.

A common issue that prevents effective listening is when someone gets distracted and starts thinking about something else. A person might even start thinking about what they want to say next, which will make them miss part of the message. Try not to get distracted by other things, such as the speaker's appearance or another conversation that is going on near you.

Do not interrupt someone while they are speaking to you. Try to defer any judgment on what is being said and do not interrupt to impose your opinion or solutions on what is being said. Wait until there is a natural pause in the conversation to respond or ask questions. Once you can ask questions, you can inquire not just about anything that you did not understand, but also to confirm your understanding of what the speaker is saying.

Give a speaker physical and verbal feedback, such as nodding, making a facial expression, or saying something. Feedback will allow the speaker to know that you are listening. Show that you understand a speaker's perspective by reflecting on their feelings and providing feedback that you understand.

If you are not engaged with what is being said, the speaker may pick up on that. If you are not making eye contact, seem distracted, or are not giving any verbal and physical feedback, the speaker may notice that you are not paying attention. This can cause them to stop speaking and they may even become offended.

Giving presentations

Giving presentations is one form of business communication. Software architects will need to give presentations to different types of audience, so it is useful to work on this skill. A software architect may need to give technical presentations to development teams, sales presentations to potential customers, executive updates to management, and proof-of-concept demos to domain experts.

Becoming a good speaker does take practice. Public speaking does not come naturally to everyone but, like many other things, you will improve as you do it more. Practice it as much as possible because it will make you better at it.

The 4 Ps of presentations

The **4 Ps of presentations** represent a series of steps you can follow to give an effective presentation. The steps in this approach are:

1. Plan
2. Prepare
3. Practice
4. Present

Let's take a look at each of these steps in more detail.

Plan

The plan step is the initial step. You begin by determining the subject and purpose of your presentation. Are you looking to inform, persuade, or motivate the audience? As part of your planning, you should have an idea about who will be attending your presentation and what they expect to get out of it. What information do they want to know? Is the presentation a formal or informal one? Tailoring your speech to your audience will allow you to better connect with them and will help to ensure that it will be successful.

If it is not determined for you, you may have to determine the logistics of your presentation, including the date/time and the location. If your presentation will be done in person and not just online, become familiar with the venue if at all possible. Doing so is particularly helpful if you will be speaking to many people at a large venue, such as at a technical conference.

Many of your presentations may simply be conducted in your organization's office, which you will already be familiar with, but some of them will take place in other locations. You may not have access ahead of time to the location, but if you can arrive even just a little bit early, you can become somewhat familiar with the venue to minimize the chance of surprises. For example, it might be helpful to see what the stage, seating, lighting, and audio/visual equipment will be like ahead of time.

Prepare

Once the basics of the speech have been determined, it is time to begin preparing your presentation. It may be helpful to break down the content into an introduction, body, and a conclusion. The introduction should be kept fairly short and establish the overall topic and direction of your presentation. Audiences like to be entertained, so include some humor, if appropriate, in any part of your speech.

The body of the speech has the main content of your presentation. It should flow smoothly from the introduction and into the conclusion. It is useful to begin by making note of the major points you want to make.

If you are preparing any visuals for your presentation, such as slides, images, or code, be sure that the font size, resolution, and zoom level will be such that everything will be clearly visible to the audience. You should also spend time thinking about background and font colors to ensure optimal viewing. All too often, text or other visual items are too small to be clearly seen. You should avoid having to make adjustments, such as altering the font size or the zoom level, during the presentation.

When preparing slides, try not to place too much text on a single slide. This might not only be visually unappealing but your audience may end up spending too much time just reading your slide instead of listening to you. Slides should summarize what you are saying but you do not want to just be reading from your slides.

If your presentation involves a live demo, prepare the software you will need and perform any necessary setup in advance. As part of your preparation, consider things that could potentially go wrong and how you might handle those situations. For example, if your demo requires the use of a database server, consider what would happen if you were unable to connect to it for some reason. Perhaps you could use a local copy of the database to eliminate that risk altogether.

If you are going to be accessing certain files or executing software, prepare by creating shortcuts to those items so that everything that you will need can be accessed easily and quickly. You do not want to be struggling to find something as the audience just sits there and waits.

Practice

Once you have prepared your presentation, practice it until you are intimately familiar with it. Practice it as many times as you can because it will increase your confidence and reduce your nerves. You do not have to memorize it but you should know it well enough that you are very comfortable with the material.

You should consider practicing in front of other people if possible, such as family, friends, or colleagues. If your presentation has a time limit, practicing will help you to determine whether it is the appropriate length. If you will be performing a live demo, such as showing off functionality with the software being developed, or a technical one that involves coding, practice it many times so that you know what you will be clicking on, executing, and coding.

Present

Prior to actually presenting, you should have already planned, prepared, and practiced your presentation. When it actually comes time to present, your audience deserves a speaker who is prepared, punctual, and keeps to the allotted time (if any). Dress appropriately based on the type of presentation and the audience.

Start your presentation off right by making a good first impression. Establish eye contact, be as relaxed as you can, and try to be enthusiastic. If you do not have a microphone, be sure to speak loudly enough so that you will be easily heard. During your presentation, use the tips previously given for the *7 Cs of communication*, such as being clear, concise, concrete, courteous, considerate, correct, and complete.

If something goes wrong during the presentation, do not panic. Do your best to recover and move forward. Try to conclude your presentation on a positive note so that the audience can leave with an upbeat impression.

Leadership

Leadership is a key skill for software architects. There is no single approach to leadership that will fit every leader. You will have to discover for yourself the type of leadership style that goes with your personality and skills.

Similarly, no single leadership style works for everyone or every situation. The qualities people look for in a leader will vary from person to person. A single approach to leadership may not work for everyone you are leading. Try to be aware of the differences among the people you are working with and tailor your leadership accordingly. Attempt to provide what each person needs in a leader while at the same time remaining yourself. Let's take a deeper look at what it means to be a leader.

Getting others to follow you

A major component of being a good leader is how well you influence others in a positive way. Your actions, words, and overall attitude will influence others and it is your job as a leader to inspire your team to take positive and productive action.

How do you get others to follow you? Leaders have certain qualities that inspire others to follow them. You should work to earn respect and gain credibility among your colleagues. If you consistently deliver high-quality work, can be depended on, and are always there to help others, you will begin to earn respect and credibility. Conducting yourself with integrity will, over time, help to build trust between you and your fellow employees.

Dealing with challenges

Software projects can be difficult and involve many challenges. A leader stays fully committed through any setbacks. When a development team faces a barrier during the course of a project, a leader should provide motivation to the team and help them move forward. A software architect should be prepared to recognize and acknowledge setbacks and, when one inevitably arises, they should meet it with enthusiasm and help to resolve it Those around you will sense your positive attitude and that can be contagious.

Being a technical leader

Another crucial part of leadership for software architects is being a technical leader. If you are a senior software developer or engineer, you probably already exhibit some technical leadership skills and have put them to use. Software architects use these skills even more as one of their primary responsibilities is to provide technical leadership.

Software architects are ultimately the ones who are responsible for the software architecture and the technical direction of the system. Technical leaders provide the team with technical guidance and support.

They should demonstrate technical excellence in their work and guide others to produce work that is of similar quality. Technical leaders are *innovators*. They provide innovative solutions to complex problems and come up with innovative ideas for new features and products.

Technical leaders have a *vision*, which consists of ideas, a purpose, and a direction that they see a software project or an entire organization moving toward. Leaders should be able to clearly articulate their vision. A vision is important for a team or organization because it keeps them focused on the goals for the future, provides motivation, and challenges individuals to reach beyond what they may have aspired to without it. Employees want to feel that they are a part of something bigger than themselves.

Taking responsibility

Leaders take responsibility. If things go wrong, a leader clearly takes responsibility rather than seeking to blame others. Placing blame is looking back to the past while taking responsibility is forward-looking. The focus should not be on whose *fault* something is but on helping to fix the problem.

If something could have been done better, rather than focusing on the negative software architects should seek to understand what lessons can be learned from the situation. Improvements can then be suggested so that a similar mistake does not happen again. Once the issue is resolved, move forward and do not dwell on it.

Focusing on others

Another key difference between being a software developer and a software architect is a shift in focus regarding your priorities. As a software developer, your focus is more on yourself and improving your skills. When you are a leader, it is not about you but about the people who are following you. As you move from being a junior developer to a senior developer to a software architect, the focus increasingly shifts to others and helping them improve.

A leader should focus on everyone they can affect in a positive way, so your attention should go beyond just your developers. You can assist and enable others, such as customers, management, business analysts, product managers, and quality assurance professionals.

Delegating tasks

Unlike a developer role, a software architect may be involved in delegating tasks to others. You may now be delegating coding tasks to someone else rather than completing them yourself. Depending on how your team is organized, assigning tasks may be more the project manager's responsibility, but a software architect may be involved with management to some degree.

The responsibility for delegating tasks may be a departure from what you are accustomed to as a developer. However, delegation provides you with an opportunity to build trust with your team. A developer will realize that you trust them to perform a task and this responsibility will motivate them to perform at a high level.

Driving change

As a software architect, you may need to drive change within a project or organization. Leaders look ahead to take advantage of opportunities and notice what is currently not working around them. Leaders see these as catalysts to making changes. As was mentioned earlier in the chapter, being a leader means having a vision and being able to communicate that vision to others. However, we need to do more than just have a vision. We need to initiate the change that is necessary to fulfill our vision.

Rather than fearing change, initiating it to depart from how things are currently being done is how improvements for the future are made and allows an organization to grow. Whether it is the use of a new technology, moving to a better software development methodology, or improvements in an organizational process, software architects should be champions of change.

Sometimes a change may take place that is not initiated by you and is beyond your control, but leaders should expect and be able to handle such changes. In general, people are resistant to change, but leaders embrace it and motivate others to do so as well.

Experimentation is one way that change can happen. Don't be afraid to experiment and try something new. It is through experimentation that we can create new opportunities and make improvements. Experimentation does take effort and sometimes it does not result in a fruitful outcome. At the very least, you will have learned something from the process. Spending some time prototyping new ideas and exploring new ways to solve a problem can lead to positive change and growth.

Communication and leadership

One of the most important aspects of leadership is effective communication. It is because of this that communication was covered first in this chapter. Leadership and communication skills are highly interconnected. Whether or not you can be an effective leader is dependent on your communication skills. Communication skills help you to connect with others and this connection is necessary in order to lead. Whether you are sharing your vision, providing technical guidance, delegating tasks, mentoring others, or reporting status to management, you need to be able to communicate effectively.

Mentoring others

Serving as a mentor to others on the team is part of being an effective leader. Being a mentor can mean different things but it is essentially making yourself available to support, advise, and teach someone else. If you are open and available to help others, that is a component of being a great leader.

You should develop a relationship with anyone who you mentor because it will increase the chances that a mentorship will succeed. In addition to imparting professional advice about technical topics, do not forget to provide mentorship for soft skills, too!

When you are in the process of mentoring someone, put more weight on their importance than that of the organization. Encourage your mentee to discover and follow their goals and passions. Sometimes it might mean that an employee and job are not an ideal fit or that it might be time for the employee to go somewhere else to continue to grow. You should give the best advice you can to your mentee, without worrying about how it will affect the organization.

Mentorship does not just benefit the mentee. Most people enjoy the feeling they get from helping others. You may have been mentored by someone in the past and it's a good feeling to be in a position to pay it forward. Being a mentor can also help you become better at your own job, improve your leadership skills, and help you to gain credibility with your colleagues.

Leading by example

Leading by example is one way to lead others. If you say one thing but do another, you lose trust and credibility with those you are leading. As you go about your tasks, whether it is requirement gathering, architecture design, technical guidance, coding, or interacting with stakeholders, approach them in the right way and with a good attitude. Set an example as you perform your job, which will provide an opportunity for those around you to observe how you perform your tasks.

How you deal with different tasks, challenges, people, and situations will be observed by others. Your employees will learn from you and will ultimately follow your lead. Taking responsibility, delivering on your promises, and producing high-quality work will set an example that others will want to follow.

Depending on others

Good leaders are humble and are not afraid to admit when they don't know something. They should ask plenty of questions and shouldn't hesitate to lean on, and learn from, others. If you become a software architect, you may feel the pressure of people expecting you to have a wide range of technical knowledge. Don't avoid saying that you don't know about a particular topic or be reluctant to ask questions when you are unclear about something or need further information.

Sometimes people don't ask enough questions, either because they lack the time due to deadlines, are hesitant to reveal that they don't know something, don't want to bother others, or are simply lazy. Avoid being one of those people, because if you do not have a good enough understanding of the work at hand, you may make incorrect decisions that can be difficult to fix later.

Everyone has different strengths and weaknesses, and you will not be an expert on every topic. Your team will consist of a variety of individuals with their own strengths and weaknesses. Recognize the person who has more knowledge or experience on the topic in question and reach out to them. Collaboration with others will foster trust, which is a necessary component of leadership.

Listening to the suggestions of others may provide you with ideas you would not have thought of otherwise. It will give you different ways of looking at a problem and it will allow you to see things from another point of view. Keep an open mind and look forward to learning from those you lead.

Negotiation

As a software architect, you will be involved in obtaining buy-in and making decisions with your development team, customers, management, and other stakeholders. All of the individuals involved in making a decision may not be in agreement initially, so having negotiation skills is useful.

Negotiating is a way to settle differences, and a successful one ends with an agreement that is acceptable to all. In some cases, a compromise is reached to settle a negotiation. A successful negotiation is not just about achieving the best outcome from your point of view but also about seeking a result that is fair to everyone. You want to maintain relationships after a negotiation is over and there should be no surprises when the final outcome of the negotiation is reached.

A number of soft skills are interconnected, and improving one will help you with others. Having communication skills helps with negotiations and having strong negotiation skills is part of leadership. In order to be a good negotiator, you need to be a good listener, communicator, and collaborator. It also helps to have good interpersonal skills. No matter what your personal traits, improving your negotiation skills will come with more experience.

How negotiation skills may be used

As a software architect, you will utilize negotiation skills in a variety of situations. For example, you may be working with stakeholders to make decisions regarding quality attribute tradeoffs. These decisions will affect the software architecture. Further, enabling one quality attribute could hinder another one and there will be some negotiating as stakeholders come to this understanding.

A software architect may use negotiation skills when they need to obtain developer buy-in to take a particular approach or use a certain technology in a solution. There may be differing viewpoints among the multiple developers that make up a development team and it's the responsibility of a technical leader to persuade the team to take the approach or to help the team reach a consensus.

Another example is when a software architect is involved with negotiating with management regarding the usefulness/viability of a project, the number of resources that will be allocated to a project, the amount of time that will be given to complete a task, or the approval of different costs, such as licenses for a particular development tool.

Software architects may also be involved in negotiations with a customer. They may take part in sales pitches to potential new clients, participating in discussions regarding what features will be included, the technology stack that will be used, and the level of effort/cost required.

Informal/formal negotiations

In many cases, a software architect will use negotiation skills informally during discussions with others or in meetings. However, formal negotiations can take place as well. With a more formal negotiation, you may want to consider taking a more systematic approach to it.

Before a formal negotiation takes place, you should spend time preparing for it. Preparations should include devoting time to making logistical decisions, such as agreeing on a date, time, duration, and location for the negotiation.

More importantly, one of the first steps in a negotiation is to understand the interests of each party. A good place to start is to invest time in thinking about the varying viewpoints of the participants, possible compromises that can be made, and the possible alternatives that could be discussed.

Your team should know its **best alternative to a negotiated agreement (BATNA)**. The BATNA is the most preferred alternative if an agreement cannot be reached. Understanding your BATNA is valuable because it is difficult to make a wise decision without knowing all of the possible alternatives.

Once the negotiation begins, a discussion should take place where both parties explain their understanding of the situation and their viewpoint. Both parties should listen carefully to each other in a sincere effort to understand each other. Each party should describe their goals and what they hope to achieve as an end result. A software architect may need to provide clarification during this step, particularly on technical topics. Anything that is not clearly understood should be clarified. Anyone should feel free to ask questions or to seek clarification.

After everyone has a clear understanding of each other and their goals, the negotiation step can begin. The focus should be on achieving a *win-win* outcome so that both parties can walk away from the negotiation satisfied. A software architect can help during this stage by driving the parties to reach a consensus. Compromises may need to be made by one or both parties. Sometimes alternative approaches need to be explored in an attempt to reach a positive outcome.

The next step, agreement, takes place once the negotiation is complete. At this point, a successful negotiation will lead the parties to reach an agreement. If an agreement is not reached, further meetings may be necessary. If an agreement is reached, everyone should be clear on what has been decided. In the final step, the agreed course of action is implemented based on the group's decision.

Working with remote resources

Plenty of organizations use remote resources for a software project. A remote employee is anyone who performs work away from the office. It is sometimes referred to as telecommuting. Remote resources may be internal employees or those outsourced from another organization. A software architect should be aware of the benefits and challenges of having team members who are not co-located work together.

Benefits of using remote resources

Organizations may allow telecommuting because there are benefits for both the employee and the employer. Employees tend to like it and it can improve morale. Flexible work options may increase their productivity. Employers who allow employees to work remotely may find it easier to recruit and retain employees, which can lead to cost savings. In addition, an organization may not have to spend as much on office space.

If resources are outsourced, it is common for them to work remotely. Outsourcing can provide operational and recruitment cost savings as well, since an organization will not need to hire as much internal staff and provide them with benefits. You can scale teams up and down easier with outsourced resources than you can with in-house resources. Outsourcing also provides a partner to share risk, as some of the responsibilities are given to the outsourced vendor.

Challenges when using remote resources

Whatever the reasons are for an organization allowing employees to telecommute, a software architect may be required to work with remote resources. Despite the advantages of using remote resources, there are challenges and risks associated with it. It takes some additional skills to ensure that a project that uses remote resources will be successful.

Using remote resources effectively requires some planning, experience, and a good software development process. If you are not careful, using remote/outsourced resources can cause the project to take longer than expected and/or cause the quality of the software to suffer.

Communication

One challenge with remote resources is communication. With modern teleconferencing technology it is not as much of an issue, but sometimes face-to-face communication is simply better. Remote resources may be located in different time zones, which can make it challenging to have meetings. This is especially true if a resource is located far away, such as on the other side of the world. You have to be cognizant of everyone's time zones when scheduling meetings and be aware that it may mean that some of the resources will have to join a meeting very late or early in their day.

Cultural differences

If a remote employee, internal or outsourced, lives in a different country, you should be aware of any cultural differences when communicating with them. Individuals from both countries should make an attempt to learn the cultural norms of the other country to avoid misunderstandings or saying something that will offend someone. Different cultures may prefer to use different phrases or approaches. Taking the time to learn about each other's cultures will maximize the clarity of your communications.

Impromptu meetings

Impromptu meetings can sometimes be more difficult when everybody is not in the same location. With messaging tools, it can be just as easy to have a spontaneous meeting as being co-located, but if people are in different time zones, you are more likely to have to schedule things ahead of time. For example, if people are located many time zones away from each other, one person's work hours may be the middle of the night for someone else. Rather than have a spontaneous meeting, it might have to be scheduled for the next day. One advantage of this situation is that you may not be interrupted as much during your day for impromptu meetings. Remote employees are probably less likely to have interruptions in general, which reduces context switching and distractions. This can increase the productivity of a remote resource.

New employee onboarding

It can sometimes be more difficult for a software architect to incorporate a new team member when the person is remote. You have to transfer technical (and business) knowledge to a new team member as well as any other relevant information. This can certainly be accomplished with only online meetings but you have to make sure the new employee has all of the information they need to succeed. Pair programming can sometimes be an effective way of bringing a new technical resource up to speed.

Another method of transferring knowledge to a remote employee is to have them on-site for a small amount of time. It will give them an opportunity to learn from the team directly and they will be able to absorb some of the company's culture, norms, processes, and standards. Once acclimated, remote resources can then potentially train other employees. For example, if a trained employee is an outsourced one, they can return to their own company's office and train fellow employees who are working on the same project.

Work quality

One possible difficulty with outsourced resources is that the quality of work from these employees can vary. This can be true of any resource, but an organization may have less control over outsourced resources because they may not be directly involved in interviewing, hiring, training, and managing the resources.

A software architect should try to mitigate this risk. One way is to ensure that there are established code review and quality assurance processes. This can uncover defects, which can then be corrected, and provide an opportunity to give employees feedback. If a particular resource's work is not up to scratch, you can perhaps request that another resource replace that person.

Confidential company data

When you are working with outsourced resources, be careful about exposing confidential data to another company. One way that this risk can be mitigated is through legal agreements.

Another is to somehow mask, redact, or remove confidential data. Some data is sensitive and should be modified so that **personally identifiable information (PII)**, such as names, social security numbers, address/phone/email information, and other data elements, is somehow protected. Protecting sensitive data may even be applicable when the data will only be seen by internal resources, but more careful consideration should be given when any data will be seen and used outside the company.

Summary

While technical skills are important for a software architect, having soft skills is crucial to being effective in the role. Soft skills are not as easy to define and measure as hard skills and are more interpersonal in nature. Your personality traits play a role in how natural some soft skills come to you, but anyone can improve a soft skill by learning, practice, and experience.

This chapter looked at some of the soft skills that are particularly important for software architects, such as communication, leadership, and negotiation skills. Being an effective communicator is central to being a software architect. In addition to communicating your message, being a good communicator also involves being a good listener.

The ability to lead others is another soft skill that software architects should possess. Your responsibilities include providing technical leadership for your team, helping your team members succeed, and mentoring them. To get team members to follow you, you have to earn their respect and gain credibility. Communication skills are highly interconnected with leadership skills. Software architects also find negotiating skills valuable because they are involved in gaining buy-in and helping to reach consensus on a variety of issues and with different types of stakeholder.

In the next chapter, we will focus on evolutionary architecture. Change is inevitable, and modern software architectures are focused on being able to adapt. By making incremental changes and designing loosely coupled architectures, a software system is more likely to be successful in the marketplace and give its organization a competitive advantage.

16
Evolutionary Architecture

Many software applications are under constant pressure from both technical and business forces to change and must have the ability to adapt to change. Software architects must expect and embrace change by designing software architectures that have the ability to evolve.

Software development methodologies, in which large amounts of time were spent creating a **Big Design Up Front (BDUF)** and software architects tried to anticipate, plan for, and implement solutions for a wide variety of contingencies, are over. Rather than attempting to design an architecture that would almost never have to be changed, modern software development methodologies understand that changes will occur. By reading this chapter, you will learn how to create a software architecture that can adapt to change.

In this chapter, we will cover the following topics:

- Change is inevitable
- Lehman's laws of software evolution
- Designing evolutionary architectures

Change is inevitable

Change is one of the few things that you can count on and it is inevitable for software systems. It occurs during the course of the initial development as well as throughout its life during maintenance.

There was a time when we had a greater sense of control over real-world processes and what needed to take place as part of those processes. A big, up-front design would take place before any code was written. In an effort to exert control, software architects tried to predict and plan for every future contingency as we designed our systems. Software systems were viewed as being more static than we view them today, with behavior that would stay consistent over time.

As we know, software systems modeled after the real world are hardly static. Changes constantly take place and the software systems that are modeled after it must change as well. Although software does not wear out like a physical product can, it does undergo change over time.

Reasons for change

Changes might be initiated for technical or business reasons. From a technical perspective, some of the reasons that a software system may change include the use of new programming languages, frameworks, persistence technologies, and tools. New operating systems or versions of operating systems may need to be supported. There may be changes in the hardware that affect the software in some way. Your organization may decide to alter how an application is deployed, such as moving it to the cloud.

More so than in the early days of software development, a greater number of technology-related choices is available to us and it is now common to use an increased number of different technologies in a single project. This fact means that the technology stacks for our software systems are more complex and there are more opportunities for change to take place.

An organization's business is also a constant source of change. There may be changing functional requirements, a desire for new features, requests to improve quality attribute scenarios, a need to keep up with (or get ahead of) competitors, changes in the market, and regulatory changes. Organizations may also experience mergers, acquisitions, a change in their business/revenue models, and a need to introduce new products. More so than in the past, users have greater expectations of their software systems and what users want from them may change over time. An organization must be able to respond to changes in their market and with their users.

Expecting change

Whatever the reasons are that serve as the catalysts for change, most software systems will be affected by some of them over their lifetime. While we may not be able to predict what technical or business changes may take place, we do know that, with very rare exceptions, software systems will undergo change.

Software architects should expect change and design their software systems so that they are capable of withstanding and adapting to it. Designing a software system to have an evolutionary architecture is how we can handle inevitable change. In the *Designing evolutionary architectures* section later in the chapter, we will cover how to design software architectures that are capable of adapting to change, but first let's look at the origins of software evolution.

Lehman's laws of software evolution

Software evolution refers to the process of initially developing a software system and then iteratively making changes to it. Beginning in the 1970s, Manny Lehman and his colleagues studied the evolution of software systems. They identified a set of behaviors that became known as **Lehman's laws of software evolution**. Lehman's dedication to the study of continuous software modifications and their long-term effects earned him the nickname the *father of software evolution*.

Lehman's software categories

Lehman's laws take into consideration the fact that there are different types of software systems. In his paper *Programs, Life Cycles, and Laws of Software Evolution*, Lehman distinguished between three different types of system:

- S-type systems
- P-type systems
- E-type systems

In this section, let's look at these three types of system and learn which one is applicable to Lehman's laws of software evolution.

S-type systems

An *S-type* system is specifiable in that it has a well-known, exact specification and can be developed to that specification. It can be described formally and the solutions to such systems are well understood. It is not only possible to definitively determine whether the program is correct, it is also possible to provide a completely correct solution. The requirements of S-type systems are unlikely to change and they do not evolve.

An example of such a system is a calculator program or a program that performs very specific mathematical computations. These types of program have logic that will not change. Systems of this type are the simplest of the three types and are rare. As there is little chance of change with these systems, Lehman's laws do not apply to them.

P-type systems

A *P-type* system is one in which the problem may be precisely stated. The end result may be well known and it may even be possible to create an exact specification for the system. However, unlike an S-type system, either the solution is not well understood or it is simply impractical to implement a solution.

A common example of P-type systems is a program that can play chess by always making the best possible move with each turn. While it is theoretically possible to develop all of the sets of logic to determine what the program can do, in practice, it will not be feasible. The complexity of the logic is so high that the system will take too much time to calculate each move. If we were not allowed to apply heuristics to reduce the computational effort and take logical shortcuts, the solution would not be practical. Lehman's laws also do not apply to P-type systems.

E-type systems

An *E-type*, or embedded type, system is modeled after real-world processes and people. The majority of software systems are E-type systems. The term *embedded* does not mean the software is embedded in some device but rather that the system is embedded in the real world.

An E-type system affects the world it is in, which may create an evolutionary pressure for change. In addition, the world that is being modeled may undergo change. The needs of the business or its users may change, which will require the system to change. E-type systems must evolve in order to remain useful. For these reasons, Lehman's laws of software evolution apply to E-type systems.

The laws

Observations and behaviors related to the evolution of software that Lehman and his colleagues identified are known as *Lehman's laws of software evolution*. There are eight laws:

- **Law I**: Continuing change
- **Law II**: Increasing complexity

- **Law III**: Self-regulation
- **Law IV**: Conservation of organizational stability
- **Law V**: Conservation of familiarity
- **Law VI**: Continuing growth
- **Law VII**: Declining quality
- **Law VIII**: Feedback system

Let's look at each law in more detail.

Law I – Continuing change

Software systems must go through continuous change or they will progressively become less useful. If a software system does not adapt to the changing needs of the business and users, satisfaction with it will progressively decrease.

Law II – Increasing complexity

Over time, as a software system evolves and the number of changes performed on it increases, the complexity of the software system will increase as well unless effort is taken to reduce that complexity. The concept of software entropy was discussed in `Chapter 14`, *Architecting Legacy Applications*. Disorder in a software system, known as software entropy, increases as the number of modifications to the system increases.

Law III – Self-regulation

The evolution of a software system is self-regulating. Particularly with large systems, there are structural and organizational factors that affect and constrain changes to a software system. Structural factors include the size and complexity of the software system. As a software system grows, it becomes larger and more complex, making it increasingly more difficult to make more changes. For this reason, as a typical software system grows older, its growth will inevitably slow down.

Organizational factors such as gaining consensus on decisions and getting approvals to move forward with proposed changes influence the amount of change that can actually take place in a software system.

Law IV – Conservation of organizational stability

Over a software system's lifetime, its overall rate of development remains relatively constant and is independent of the resources assigned to its design and development. Some resources are more productive than others but regardless of the resources, the work output of a software project is fairly constant.

Law V – Conservation of familiarity

As a software system evolves, the group of individuals who are working on it must maintain the same level of familiarity with the system so that it can evolve without compromising the quality of the system. If we want the ability to handle whatever forces of change might affect the software system and make modifications in an efficient way, we have to maintain a deep understanding of the system.

Too much growth can decrease the level of familiarity as it becomes increasingly difficult to maintain the same level of knowledge over the technical and functional aspects of the system. For this reason, it is ideal if, during the lifetime of a software system, the amount of change in each release remains roughly the same.

Law VI – Continuing growth

This law states that, as a software system evolves so that it can continue to be useful and satisfy the needs of its users, it will continue to increase in size. The amount of functionality will increase, which means the technical implementation will grow larger as well. This law is related to Law II (increasing complexity) because, as a software system grows in size, the level of complexity will increase.

Law VII – Declining quality

As a software system evolves, its quality will decrease unless a concerted effort is made to maintain a high level of quality. Focus, discipline, and a rigorous effort must be sustained during the lifetime of the software system to minimize the number of defects that are introduced.

As more code is added to the system during its active life, there is the potential for an increase in the number of defects. Poorly designed enhancements may contain bugs or fail to satisfy some requirements. Maintaining the same level of quality is difficult as a software system increases in both size and complexity.

Law VIII – Feedback system

Software evolution is a complex process and requires feedback from a variety of stakeholders to ensure that the proper changes are being made and that the software evolves in a direction that yields noticeable and useful improvement.

Processes should be put into place so that feedback can be received and properly analyzed. Once that is done, appropriate action must be taken to incorporate the feedback into the system. To evolve the system properly, changes must be made to it based on feedback to ensure that the system continues to be useful.

Designing evolutionary architectures

We know that changes to the software systems that we work on are inevitable and that these software systems must adapt so that they can continue to be useful. As software architects, how do we create an architecture that can evolve to support change?

In Chapter 1, *The Meaning of Software Architecture*, we discussed what software architecture consists of. In part, it consists of design decisions for important aspects of the software system. They are among the earliest decisions that are made for a software system and are potentially the most difficult to change. Just as we strive to design other aspects of a software system to be highly maintainable and easy to change, at the heart of evolutionary architecture is the idea that we should be able to change software architecture easily as well. An evolutionary architecture should also be one that supports other types of modification to the system that do not involve changes to the architecture.

In the book, *Building Evolutionary Architectures*, authors Rebecca Parsons, Neal Ford, and Patrick Kua define evolutionary architecture in the following way:

> *"An evolutionary architecture supports guided incremental change across multiple dimensions."*

There are several important concepts in this definition, so let's examine them further.

Making guided architectural changes

Software architects should guide any changes to a software system's architecture so that the characteristics of the architecture remain intact. A software architecture is shaped by the design decisions that were made, which give it certain properties and enable particular quality attributes.

When an architecture must adapt to some technical or business change, it is not sufficient to simply make any change that will allow it to adapt. Software systems are dynamic and modifications to them can have unintended consequences. As an increasing number of changes are made to the software system and its architecture over time, a lack of oversight can allow the quality to erode. A software architecture's characteristics may change in unforeseen ways and it may no longer meet its intended purposes.

Software architects must guide the changes to ensure that the software system's requirements continue to be met and that the architecture continues to meet all of its goals. One way to guide architecture changes is through the use of fitness functions, which can help a software architect determine the impact of modifications.

Fitness functions

In evolutionary computing, a **fitness function** is a type of objective function that is used to determine how close a given solution is to achieving the desired result. They return the fitness of the solution. They are used in the design of genetic algorithms to generate an optimal solution for a given problem.

Fitness functions can be applied to a software architecture to determine how close the designed solution is to achieving the desired architectural characteristics. They are an objective way to assess a software architecture's characteristics. Fitness functions should be clearly defined and provide a quantitative measure of how fit a solution is for a particular problem. A quantitative result is what will allow us to compare the architecture before and after a change is introduced. They also allow us to compare different solutions to a problem and determine which one is optimal.

Categories of fitness functions

There are different categories of fitness function. They are not mutually exclusive. For example, a fitness function could be both atomic and temporal. The different fitness function categories include:

Atomic versus holistic

Atomic fitness functions focus on a single context and on one architectural characteristic. For example, a unit test that is designed to test one architectural characteristic is atomic. A holistic fitness function takes multiple architectural characteristics into consideration at the same time.

Having both atomic and holistic fitness functions is useful because a feature that works fine when tested atomically could fail when it is combined with other features. It isn't feasible to test every combination of all the architecture's characteristics, but a software architect can choose which important combination of characteristics should be tested.

Triggered versus continuous

Triggered fitness functions are executed based on some event. For example, they could be triggered as part of a build or unit test. A continuous fitness function runs constantly and its execution is not based on the occurrence of some event. An example of a continuous fitness function is a test, which monitoring tool may be executing constantly, that will produce an alert when a certain condition is met.

Static versus dynamic

A static fitness function is one in which the value for the condition that we are testing for is constant. A test may be looking to ensure that the result is less than some static numeric value or that a test that returns true or false returns the value that we expect. In contrast, the acceptable values of a dynamic fitness function may change based on a different context. For example, the desired result of a performance test might be different depending on the current level of scalability. At a much higher level of scalability, a lower level of performance might be acceptable.

Automated versus manual

Automated fitness functions are triggered automatically. They could be part of automated unit testing or an automated build process. When possible, automated fitness functions are ideal. However, there may be times when you may either need or want to execute a fitness function manually.

Temporal

Temporal fitness functions are based on a designated amount of time. While other fitness functions may focus on a change in the system, temporal ones are triggered based on time. For example, a fitness function may be created to ensure that, if a patch becomes available for a framework that is being used, it is applied within a certain number of days.

Intentional versus emergent

Many fitness functions can be defined early on in a project, once some of the characteristics of the architecture are known. These are known as intentional fitness functions. However, some characteristics of the architecture are not known right from the beginning, but emerge as the system continues its development. These fitness functions are known as emergent ones.

Domain-specific

Domain-specific fitness functions are based on specific concerns related to the business domain. Some examples include regulatory, security, and **personally identifiable information** (PII) requirements. A domain-specific fitness function can ensure that the architecture continues to conform to these requirements.

Examples of fitness functions

Fitness functions may come in the form of tests (automated or manual), monitoring, and the collection of metrics. Not all tests are fitness functions. Only those that actually assess a particular architectural characteristic are fitness functions.

For example, fitness functions can be created to calculate and use various software metrics to determine whether a software architecture continues to meet maintainability requirements. In `Chapter 4`, *Software Quality Attributes*, we discussed software metrics, such as **cyclomatic complexity, lines of code** (LOC), and the **depth of inheritance tree** (DIT) as measurements for maintainability. Fitness functions can allow you to know when a software system has exceeded its predefined acceptable levels for these metrics, providing you with an opportunity to analyze recent changes and determine whether refactoring is necessary.

Performance tests can be executed to ensure that the architecture continues to meet its requirements and that any recent changes to the software system have not negatively impacted its performance. Security tests can focus on the security dimension of a software system to ensure that changes have not introduced a security vulnerability.

Another example of a fitness function is the use of a **resilience engineering** (also known as **chaos engineering**) tool such as Chaos Monkey. Chaos Monkey is an example of a holistic, continuous fitness function that is used to reveal systemic weakness in your software application. This tool, created by Netflix, disables a computer in the system, on purpose, to determine whether it can properly tolerate a system failure. This particular fitness function is executed periodically and is always scheduled to run during business hours (and not on weekends and holidays) to ensure that, if the system does not behave as expected, engineers will be available to respond to the issue.

Using these various types of fitness function provides a software architect with information on how fit the overall architecture continues to be as changes are introduced and it continues to evolve. They provide a way to give a software architect confidence that the system continues to be capable and informs you if it is starting to decline in quality. Fitness functions facilitate the creation of an evolvable architecture.

Making incremental changes

One of the characteristics of an evolutionary architecture is that changes are made to the software system incrementally. Making incremental changes includes how we introduce changes to the system, how we build the system, and how the system is deployed.

In order to design an evolutionary architecture, we must make it easy to understand what is going on in the software system. The ease with which we can make a change is related to how much we understand the system. Making changes that are smaller in scope allows us to more easily understand what is being changed and reduces the risk of introducing a defect. It also makes it easier to code-review and test the changes that are being made to the system.

You may recall from the *Lehman's laws of software evolution* section earlier in this chapter that Law VIII stresses the importance of having a feedback system that allows important stakeholders to provide feedback on the system. Changes can then be made to the system based on the feedback. The iterative nature of agile software development methodologies and DevOps practices, such as **continuous integration** (**CI**) and **continuous delivery** (**CD**), facilitates giving of and allows that feedback to be received faster, which enables beneficial improvements to be delivered to customers faster.

In Chapter 13, *DevOps and Software Architecture*, we discussed CI and CD. An aspect of making incremental changes is having developers continuously integrate their changes into the system. By committing changes to a source control repository frequently, there is a reduced chance of merge conflicts, making it easier to resolve any that do occur. Automated builds that include automated testing give us feedback on our changes quickly. If there is a problem with a set of changes, they will be easier to fix because there will only have been so many changes committed since the last build.

CD is the practice of being able to release changes into production in a safe, repeatable, and sustainable way. A system that is highly adaptable has the ability to quickly react to change and release new versions quickly. Releasing incremental changes to users quickly makes your system highly evolvable. CD is about being able to produce low-risk, high-quality releases with a faster time-to-market.

Architectural changes across multiple dimensions

The final part of the definition for evolutionary architecture put forth by Rebecca Parsons, Neal Ford, and Patrick Kua is that an evolutionary architecture is one that can support change across multiple dimensions. A software system consists of different dimensions and a software architect must consider all of them to build a system that can evolve.

Software architects may naturally focus on the technical aspects of an architecture, such as its programming language, frameworks, and third-party libraries. However, software architects must also concern themselves with other aspects of the software system. The database (and its data), security, performance, and its deployment environment are all examples of different dimensions of the software system. To successfully maintain an evolvable architecture, the software architect must consider all of these dimensions as changes are made to it.

Loosely coupled architectures

When designing an evolutionary architecture, its components should be loosely coupled. In Chapter 6, *Software Development Principles and Practices*, we covered the importance of loosely coupled code. Coupling refers to the degree of dependency between components.

When modules are tightly coupled, it is more difficult to make changes. Changes to one component have a greater chance of affecting other components, increasing the total number of changes that have to be made. When you need to modify a tightly coupled system, more time and effort will be required for development and testing.

To ease the effort of making changes to the software system, dependencies between components should be minimized and all components should be designed so that they are as independent of each other as possible. Loosely coupled components reduce complexity (and typically increase cohesion), making your architecture more maintainable.

One example of loose coupling for an evolutionary architecture is to loosely couple the software system's cross-cutting concerns from the logic of the application's other concerns. By decoupling this type of logic, each cross-cutting concern can evolve separately from any logic that uses it. As we learned in `Chapter 9`, *Cross-Cutting Concerns*, logic for cross-cutting concerns may be needed throughout an application, so you want it to be loosely coupled to the other parts of your application. This will reduce code duplication and increase maintainability.

One way to do this is to make each cross-cutting concern its own service. Logic that needs one of those services will be dependent on its interface, allowing the implementation to change without affecting other parts of the application. This will allow cross-cutting concerns, such as caching and logging, to evolve over time.

Designing evolvable APIs

Another aspect of designing an evolutionary architecture is the proper design of the API. We cannot anticipate what changes may become necessary for an API. Message contracts that are used to communicate with an API may require modifications as a software system adapts to change. Some examples of the changes that can be made to an API include the amount of information that is sent or received, the names or data types of individual pieces of data, and the introduction of new representations of data to support different types of client.

Maintaining a system that can evolve requires that changes made to an API, particularly once it has been published, are given proper consideration. Your APIs should be designed to support evolution, allowing them to adapt to changes without breaking clients that already depend on them.

Applying Postel's Law to APIs

A helpful design guideline with regards to message contracts is the **Robustness Principle**, which is also known as **Postel's Law**. The idea behind Postel's Law is that you should be conservative in what you do and liberal in what you accept from others. This principle was originally proposed when designing the TCP protocol, but it is applicable to message contracts. We should be conservative in what we send but liberal in what we accept. In other words, the data that is sent out of our system should be kept to the minimum that is necessary. A message sender must conform to the message contract, and reducing the amount of data that an API exposes lessens the chances that a breaking change may be necessary for the contract.

In terms of being liberal in what is accepted, when an API is consumed by a software system, it should only extract what is needed from a message and ignore the parts that are not needed. Taking this approach minimizes what a software system depends on from a particular message and increases its resilience to change. If the parts that are not needed are changed in the future, the software system will not be affected.

Using standards in your software system

Using standards in your software system helps to create an evolutionary architecture. When making technology choices and design decisions, leveraging standards can make it easier to adapt the software system over time. Using a standard, such as a programming language, framework, third-party library, communication protocol, database, data interchange format, development tool, or some other design choice, can increase maintainability and allow your system to evolve more easily.

The use of standards generally makes integration with other systems easier to accomplish. In addition, finding resources to work on your software system who are familiar with the technologies that you have selected, not just during the initial development but during a potentially long maintenance life will be easier.

When faced with different alternatives, electing to use a standard approach may not always be the best choice. However, it is one factor that a software architect should consider given the possible benefits.

Last responsible moment (LRM)

The **last responsible moment** (**LRM**) is the strategy of delaying a decision until the moment when the cost of not making the decision is greater than the cost of making it. Design decisions made for a software architecture can be among the most important for a software system and they can be among the most difficult to change later.

With traditional software architectures, decisions were made very early in the project. In order to design an evolutionary architecture, it is beneficial to delay a decision until the LRM. This lessens the possibility that a premature decision will be made. Decisions that are made too early are very risky because they may end up being incorrect and then they will result in costly rework.

As long as the cost of delaying the decision is not greater than the cost of making one, waiting as late as you can to commit to a decision ensures that you will have the most information available to you. This will allow you to make an informed decision.

The challenge with the LRM strategy is that it can be difficult to determine when the LRM is going to take place. Costs and benefits are subject to change and it is not always clear when the optimal time is to make a decision until after that moment has passed. It is generally not as beneficial, if at all, to delay decisions that are not so important to the architecture. However, for important decisions, you will want to gather as much information as needed so that you can make a good decision when the appropriate time arrives.

Summary

Changes to a software system are inevitable as there is a variety of reasons why an application needs to be changed. Software architects should expect change and design their software architecture with that in mind.

To create an evolutionary architecture that is capable of adapting to change, software architects should guide architecture modifications to ensure that the characteristics of the architecture and its level of quality remain the same. Fitness functions can be used to help determine whether the architecture continues to achieve the required architectural characteristics.

When changes do need to be made to an application, following practices, such as making incremental changes and ensuring that architectural components are loosely coupled, will help to facilitate making modifications.

In the next chapter, we will take a close look at how to become a better software architect. Excelling as a software architect requires continuous improvement to maintain your skills and gain new ones. We will detail a number of different activities that you can do that will allow you to grow in the role.

17
Becoming a Better Software Architect

Once you advance in your career and become a software architect, the process of self-improvement and the advancement of your skills must continue. The role of software architect is a challenging one and the field of software development is constantly changing. Software architects must keep up with the latest trends and ensure that their skills remain relevant.

This chapter focuses on various ways that you can become a better software architect. From learning new things, participating in open source projects, writing your own blog, trying new technologies, and attending conferences, let's dive into how we can improve as software architects.

In this chapter, we will cover the following topics:

- Practicing continuous learning
- Participating in open source projects
- Writing your own blog
- Spending time teaching others
- Trying new technologies
- Continuing to write code
- Attending user groups and conferences
- Taking responsibility for your work
- Being proud of your work

Practicing continuous learning

Part of being a professional software architect involves continuously improving your knowledge portfolio. In the software development industry, technologies and development approaches are constantly changing. Just as software systems must adapt to a changing landscape, software architects must adapt as well. Existing skills can become obsolete and a vital part of maintaining your value is ensuring your skills remain relevant. Each software architect should remain humble and understand that there is so much that they do not know.

One of the things that can separate an average software architect or developer from a really good one is that individuals who set themselves apart are constantly trying to improve themselves. They are not satisfied with their current knowledge base and want to always learn something new. Great software architects understand that the field of software development is constantly changing and, in order to stay great in their profession, they have to keep up.

Even if you are strong in a particular language, tool, or framework, that skill can become stale as technologies evolve. For example, if you consider yourself an expert C#/.NET developer, but get away from practicing those skills for a while, you can lose some degree of that competence. In addition, that particular language and/or framework will have evolved over that time, and if you do not keep up with the changes, you may not maintain your expert level of knowledge.

Improving the breadth and depth of your knowledge

In Chapter 1, *The Meaning of Software Architecture*, we discussed having both *breadth* and *depth* of knowledge. Depth of knowledge refers to the extent of your expertise for a specific topic within a subject, while breadth of knowledge refers to the full scope of your expertise in a subject.

If you are playing the role of a software architect, you undoubtedly have some level of breadth and depth of knowledge. Continuous learning is not just about improving breadth or depth, it involves increasing both over time. There will be times when you want to focus on a particular topic to increase your depth of knowledge, while there will be other times when you will want to focus on increasing your depth of knowledge by expanding your body of knowledge and exploring new topics.

Software architects are expected to have breadth of knowledge because they need to be knowledgeable about a variety of topics related to software development. This book covers many of these topics. However, a single book cannot do justice to the amount of knowledge you may need for each topic. You may already have a lot of knowledge about particular topics, but for the ones you are less familiar with, you should invest time in learning more about them. Take a knowledge area that you perceive to be one of your weaknesses and turn it into a strength. It is that type of attitude that will lead to improvement and make you a better software architect.

Avoiding the law of the instrument

When considering what to focus on in your learning, it's not just about maintaining your current skill set but also about learning new things. Keeping up with current trends is an integral part of continuous learning.

Continuous learning is important for any software development professional, but this may be particularly true for software architects. If you are not aware of rising new technologies and software development approaches that you can leverage in your solutions, then when you are confronted with a design problem, you may only be able to recommend a technology that you have already been using. This idea is known as the **law of the instrument**, which is sometimes referred to as the law of the hammer or Maslow's hammer. The concept is summarized by the well-known saying: If the only tool you have is a hammer, everything begins to look like a nail.

However, solutions familiar to you may not be ideal for a given problem. Here is one area where having breadth of knowledge is useful. By expanding your knowledge, you will have more tools at your disposal. You may not be an expert in everything, but being aware of a variety of solutions to a problem and being able to understand the pros and cons of different technologies will allow you to select the most suitable approach for a situation.

Finding the time for learning

It can be challenging to find the time for learning and improvement. Between your work and personal life, devoting more time to your profession can be difficult. However, if you are passionate about software, you probably enjoy spending time learning new aspects of the field.

It is important to find a balance between your work and personal life so that you have sufficient time for both. A key to finding time for continuous learning is to make a commitment to it. Set realistic goals for yourself that reflect what you want to achieve. If you can dedicate some amount of time each week, it can really help your career. If you are very busy, try to find ways to multitask. You can listen to a podcast during your commute or watch educational videos while you use a treadmill.

Ways to keep your skills sharp

There are a number of ways to accomplish your learning goals. The very fact that you are reading this book shows that you are dedicated to learning and improving your skills. Books are a great way to learn new things. There are books on a wide variety of topics and new ones are constantly being published. E-books can be particularly convenient because they are portable, searchable, and instantly available. Since they do not take up physical space, you do not need a lot of space to store them, even if you have a lot of them.

Formal learning is what comes to mind for many of us when we think about learning. Even if you have already completed formal education, taking classes again, either individually or as part of a program, at a formal institution can be a good way to continue your learning. Many institutions now offer online classes, which can be more convenient for working professionals.

Classes do not have to be taken at formal institutions of learning. Many excellent classes are offered online by learning sites, such as Pluralsight, Lynda.com (LinkedIn Learning), Udemy, Coursea, and Microsoft Virtual Academy. Learning sites can be great for technical topics because sometimes formal institutions are slower to keep up with the latest trends.

Other ways of keeping up with technology news and the latest developments include reading articles on websites and blogs, listening to podcasts, and watching videos online. These activities do not necessarily require as much time as other ways of learning. You can read an article or blog post in a short amount of time and be selective about how many you read in a single sitting. You can listen to a podcast while doing something else, such as commuting to work.

While it can take time for books to be published and courses to be created, online posts, podcasts, and videos are published more frequently and can cover very current topics of interest.

One benefit of many of the other topics in this chapter, such as participating in open source projects, writing your own blog, and trying new technologies, is that they are additional ways you can maintain your skills and learn new ones.

Participating in open source projects

Working on an open source project or creating a new one can be a stimulating and rewarding way to become a better software architect. Unlike code you might write privately for learning or practice, the code that you write for an open source project is public. Many people have a tendency to write better code if it will be viewed by others. The transparency of an open source project may help make the code that you write better.

Another benefit from participating in open source projects is that it can improve your personal brand and/or your organization's brand. If people become familiar with your work or the work of your organization, it can advance your career and/or bring positive attention to your organization.

Organizations that become active in helping to maintain the open source software that they use become much more familiar with it as compared with just using it. The knowledge gained from having worked on it makes it easier for the organization to make additional changes later. The organization will also benefit from the knowledge of the other members of the community, who can answer questions and provide useful feedback.

Working on an increasingly higher number of open source projects can help you to get a job. This is not simply due to the fact that you are improving your skills, but also because some companies now look at a technical resource's open source portfolio and activity as part of the hiring process. While it may not play a large role in you obtaining a position somewhere, it can be beneficial even if it just helps you land an interview.

Creating your own open source project

You are not limited to working on existing open source projects. You can also create your own. If you are aware of some need or a problem that people are facing, you can create a solution to that problem and make it publicly available. It may be a problem that you have already faced and you may have already coded a solution.

Wrap up any solution that you want to make open source so that it can easily be used by others. Ensure that your code is understandable. Follow the principles and practices that we have covered in this book to make it maintainable as others will be using and modifying the code. When creating your own project, provide unit tests, documentation, and a README.md file for it.

You will also want to consider what open source license, if any, is appropriate for your project. An open source license defines the terms and conditions under which your software can be used, modified, and shared.

One set of open source licenses that is popular is a group of licenses that have been approved by the **Open Source Initiative** (**OSI**). Some of the OSI-approved licenses include (in alphabetical order):

- Apache License 2.0
- BSD 2-Clause "Simplified" or "FreeBSD" license
- BSD 3-Clause "New" or "Revised" license
- Common Development and Distribution License
- Eclipse Public License
- GNU General Public License (GPL)
- GNU Lesser General Public License (LGPL)
- MIT license
- Mozilla Public License 2.0

If you are contributing to an existing project, the easiest (and possibly required) approach would be to use the project's existing license. If you are creating a new project within a community that prefers to use a particular license, you will want to use that license for your project.

For some of your projects, you can choose to not use any license. By default, any creative work, which includes software, is copyrighted. Unless there is something specifying otherwise, no one is allowed to use, modify, distribute, or copy your work without the authorization of the author. There was a time in the past that the creator had to explicitly assert a copyright but that is no longer the case.

Writing your own blog

Maintaining your own blog is another activity that can make you a better software architect. Writing about technical topics can make you more familiar with them. Taking the opportunity to learn about something that you have been wanting to know more about and then writing about it can help to reinforce what you have learned. It provides a forum to demonstrate what you know.

It is beneficial to share your knowledge with other software development professionals. Informing others about a subject and knowing that it can potentially help them is a rewarding endeavor. Unlike a tweet or other type of social media post, a well-written article can remain visible and useful for a long time.

Increasing your visibility

A site that has well-written blog posts will increase your overall visibility and can earn you a positive reputation with others in the industry. A personal site with just your professional credentials and no blog may come across as stale and will not generate as much traffic. If you regularly create new posts, there will be a reason for visitors to come to the site more than once and you will be more likely to get new visitors.

Once visitors come to your site, they may see your online resume and credentials. Having a blog may lead to additional opportunities in your career. Just as with your public coding activity for open source projects, some employers will come across your personal site if you have one. It could be a factor in you getting an interview. Whether you are an independent consultant, run your own business, or work for an organization, your blog can also serve as a marketing tool in that it may attract new customers.

Starting your own blog

It is pretty easy to start your own blog as there is a low barrier to entry. Anyone can get one up and running in a relatively short amount of time. Even though you may have the skills to do so, rather than creating your site from scratch, you should consider taking advantage of the many blogging platforms that are available to you. It can take some time to write your blog's functionality, so instead of spending time coding that, you could be spending time writing content for your blog.

A blogging platform such as WordPress can provide all of the functionality that you need. Most platforms provide a number of ways that you can customize your site, including a variety of themes that let you select the look and feel of your site. After choosing a blogging platform, you will need to select and register a domain name, pick a host, and configure/customize your site. After that, it is all about writing and posting new content.

You will want to think about the overall theme and focus of your blog. Some blogs have a broad scope while others are much narrower in scope. If you are interested in blogging about a wide variety of topics, you will want your blog to cover a broad range. However, you may want your blog to be more focused. A broader focus will allow you to write about a lot more topics, but more visitors may subscribe to a more specialized blog that focuses on the topics that are of interest to them. Whatever you decide for the focus and scope of your blog, try to always honor it so that the expectations of your readers are met.

The most challenging part of maintaining your personal blog will be consistently writing new posts for it. However, there will be almost a limitless number of topics that you can use as a subject for a post. There will always be something that you are working on that might be beneficial to share or you will want to learn more about some new topic in a blog post.

Things to avoid

If your blog focuses on your professional life, you probably do not want to include too much content that is unrelated to your career. Some people like to include personal details on their site so that people can get to know them on that level. A moderate amount of that is fine if you want, but for the most part, you will want to focus on your career.

Another thing that you want to avoid is having a blog and then not posting to it for many months or even years. If your last posts are very old, visitors will assume the whole site is outdated and not being maintained. Contributing to your blog takes time, just like the other activities that are being suggested in this chapter. However, you should think of it as an investment in your overall career.

Spending time teaching others

A productive and rewarding way to become a better software architect is to devote time to teaching other developers and software architects. When you teach others a particular subject, it deepens your own level of understanding for that subject.

In your preparations for teaching, you will be reviewing material and consulting others. As part of that process, you may learn something new or be reminded of something when you had forgotten. There is also a good chance that you will learn something from the people you are teaching.

Teaching others may improve your organization and interpersonal skills. Preparing for a session in which you will be teaching requires you to organize it and the interaction with your students can improve your interpersonal skills. These types of skills are related to others, such as leadership, and may ultimately help to advance your career.

Finding opportunities to teach

Teaching can be done in a variety of ways. It is not as if it has to be conducted in a formal meeting or classroom setting. Perhaps one of the best and most frequent opportunities for you to guide others will be at your job. There will be teaching opportunities for you on any given workday.

As you work with your development team, you will undoubtedly encounter many situations in which you will want to explain something, provide guidance, or suggest an approach. If you conduct design or code reviews, those are excellent times that you can point things out to your team members. Remember to remain positive and encouraging when providing your feedback.

Sharing past experiences is a great way to teach others. As a software architect, you have plenty of experience from your previous work. Sharing real stories from your career can really benefit your colleagues.

One way to teach others is to simply set an example. As you go about your daily work, those around you will observe how you conduct yourself, solve problems, and complete tasks. If you do things the right way, others will learn from your example.

We have already discussed one way in which you can teach other people, which is to write and maintain a blog. It is an effective way of teaching others and you will be able to reach a larger audience. A blog allows you to easily engage with people who you do not even know and who may live far away from you. Presenting at a user group or conference provides another way to pass on your knowledge to others.

Learning new things can be challenging and it takes work to master a subject, so remember to be patient when teaching others. Patience is an important quality for both the teacher and the student. Some topics may be difficult for someone to comprehend at first. You do not want to get disheartened by this and you also want to prevent your students from getting too frustrated.

Being a mentor

Mentoring is one way to impart knowledge to others. In `Chapter 15`, *The Soft Skills of Software Architects*, when we covered soft skills, mentoring people was mentioned as part of leadership. Mentoring your development team is part of your role as a software architect.

Mentoring involves advising, supporting, and teaching someone else. While mentoring is beneficial to your mentees, it also provides advantages to you as the mentor. Not only will it make you feel good, but it improves your leadership skills and gives you more credibility with your colleagues.

Be sure to listen to your mentees so that you understand what they want to learn from you. Software architects can teach and mentor others not just by focusing on technical skills but also by giving advice about the organization, office politics, and soft skills. Using your own personal experiences, you can assist others by instructing them on topics such as their careers.

Raise the expectations of your mentees. The expectations that you have for them (and that they have for themselves) will have an impact on their performance. Raised expectations show that you have confidence in them and will encourage them to move outside their comfort zones, which is where true growth can happen.

Trying new technologies

Good software architects care about their craft and enjoy trying out new technologies and techniques. This does not necessarily mean that you need to be an early adopter of new technologies in your applications but it is important to have an understanding of trending technologies.

Software architects should learn a new technology, framework, language, tool, or other technology so that they understand the situations in which these should be applied. The more technologies you are familiar with, the greater the number of tools you have at your disposal. As you encounter different problems or want to take advantage of certain opportunities, having knowledge of a diverse array of tools will give you the power to select the most ideal one for a particular job. It will give you the ability to speak intelligently about different alternatives and allow you to articulate why one solution is better than another.

We have discussed ways in which you might go about learning new things, and these techniques can be applied to gaining an understanding of new technologies. We want to go beyond just being aware of these technologies. In order to understand them more deeply, a software architect should try them out.

Either as part of your job or in your own time, try out new technologies. Many of them will be free for you to try. A product that requires you to purchase it may have a free trial license available for the precise purpose of allowing people to give it a try.

Supplement your other types of learning by getting hands-on experience with the technology. Use a real or contrived problem and attempt to use the technology to solve it. You can create a **proof of concept (POC)**, which is a prototype of a solution to determine its feasibility for a real application.

As you get to know it better, you will form opinions about its applicability, ease of use, and other characteristics. You will begin to understand the advantages and disadvantages of the technology. When there comes an opportunity to use it, you will be able to give an informed opinion on whether or not it should be used.

Continuing to write code

In order for software architects to continuously improve, they should continue to write code. In Chapter 1, *The Meaning of Software Architecture*, we discussed ivory-tower software architects. They are architects who are isolated in some way from the rest of the team. Rather than having a hands-on approach, they design solutions at a high level but do not get involved with the actual coding of solutions.

If you do not exercise a particular skill, such as coding, over time you begin to lose it. You may also grow out of touch with what is involved in the implementation of different types of solution. You will lose your understanding of the challenges and issues that are facing your developers.

Assigning yourself coding tasks

One way to stay involved with coding is to have some of the development tasks on your project assigned to you. Having coding tasks assigned to you will allow you to stay close to the rest of the development team.

If there are no plans to have the software architect code, speak with your project manager to explain what you want to do. To accommodate your other responsibilities, you can agree to keep your coding assignments limited so that they do not take up all of your time.

Working on your own project

We have already discussed working on open source projects and trying out new technologies. Both of these activities will allow you to keep your programming skills sharp. In addition to those, working on your own side project is another way you can grow as a software architect.

The benefits of working on a side project are very similar to those of working on an open source project. In fact, your side project may be an open source project. However, you may not always find an existing open source project that you want to work on and you may not have any ideas for a new open source project. This should not prevent you from creating your own side project, as you can simply work on one privately. There may be times when you just want to work on something that will not be shared publicly.

Work on a project that challenges your current skills to facilitate your own personal growth. For example, if you are stronger working with backend code, focus on frontend code, and vice versa.

Reading code

Another way to keep your programming skills sharp when you may not be coding as much is to read other people's code. When performing the software architect role, you may find yourself coding less than when you played a developer role.

Performing code reviews for your project will keep you intimately familiar with the implementations created by the development team. Looking beyond your project, examine high-quality code that experienced professionals have written for other projects. Open source projects make it easy to analyze all types of code. Select a project that is of interest to you and examine the code.

Watching live-streamed programming sessions or online videos from well-known and respected programmers can inspire you and give you good ideas that you might be able to use in your own code. Pair programming with colleagues is another way to become familiar with code that you have not seen before.

Attending user groups and conferences

Attending and participating in user groups and conferences is a fun way to become a better software architect. There are many different conferences that take place each year and they cover a wide variety of topics.

Listening to the various presentations is a great learning experience. Some of the speakers are industry leaders and you can learn a lot from them. Some sessions reserve time for questions and you can take advantage of that to follow up on something that was presented. After the session is over, you may have an opportunity to talk with the presenter and ask questions.

The benefit of attending a user group or conference is that, after it is over, you can share what you learned with others who did not attend. You can take any new knowledge you gained and create a presentation of your own that you can then share with those in your organization.

Even if you cannot travel to some of the biggest and best conferences in the world, there may be some in your local area. Some conferences live-stream their sessions and/or make videos of their sessions available.

Presenting at a user group or conference

In addition to attending a user group or conference, you may be able to participate in some of them. Conferences and user groups need speakers and they may have openings at their next event.

While you may not have the opportunity to speak at any conference of your choosing, and some conferences may be prohibitively difficult for you to attend due to factors such as location and cost, you may be able to find one that you can attend. Search online and ask colleagues about user groups that meet up in your area, and about upcoming conferences that will be taking place nearby.

Many user groups and conferences have websites and other social media accounts that can provide you with more information. Come up with a clear idea for a topic that is of interest to you and is something you are excited to present. Once you have a topic, become familiar with the audience that will be attending. Keep the audience in mind when you create your presentation, including what you think they will want to get out of it.

Find out what it will take to allow you to participate and get on the schedule. You may need to submit a proposal that will need to get approved. Follow any guidelines that are provided by the user group or conference when submitting your proposal.

Once you find out that you have been granted the opportunity to give a presentation, you must start your preparations. In Chapter 15, *The Soft Skills of Software Architects*, we took a look at some of the things to consider when preparing to give a presentation, including the *4 Ps of presentations*. Those include what to do when planning, preparing, practicing, and presenting. Use those guidelines when developing your presentation.

Meeting new people

Meeting new people in your industry is another benefit of attending user groups and conferences. Discussing your profession with people outside your current professional and social circles exposes you to different viewpoints and ideas. If the only people you interact with regarding your craft are on your development team, this limits the range of insights that you can gain.

Networking before and after user groups and conference sessions will increase your personal network and can lead to additional opportunities. Discussing your experiences, including some of the challenges that you have faced, with other industry veterans can give you new ideas and insights.

Taking responsibility for your work

Software architects who excel in their role take responsibility for their work. As a leader of the team, it is important to take responsibility for your work and not make excuses. It is easy to take responsibility when things go well, but being a leader means accepting responsibility when things do not go well. When things go wrong, rather than making excuses or blaming others, it is more productive to use that time and energy to come up with options for how to alleviate the issue. I think that most people, including myself, really respect colleagues who take ownership and responsibility.

If everyone on the team takes responsibility, that type of collective attitude prevents *software rot* or disorder within a software system. Degradation of software can occur for a variety of reasons. One typical cause is the overall culture of the work environment. If a known issue is left unfixed, it becomes easier to leave other issues unresolved. Even if there is not sufficient time to resolve an issue immediately, take steps to protect the rest of the software from the offending code, such as commenting it out. As a software architect, you can create a culture that makes degradation unacceptable.

Sometimes problems are small and happen slowly over time. It can be easy not to notice them at first but, eventually, problems can get out of hand. The team should be continuously aware of the project's current state and of the big picture. Software architects should take the lead to ensure degradation does not take the team by surprise.

Attending to your well-being

A key aspect of being a better software architect has nothing to do with technical skills. We must not forget about your life outside software development and how it can have a positive or negative effect on your work.

A part of being great at your job is taking care of yourself both mentally and physically. In order to perform at your best, you need to do things such as get enough rest, and exercise, and eat healthy foods.

You must balance your life so that you are not overly focused on work. Remember to have fun and to enjoy your personal life. Take breaks and vacations from work to recharge and ensure that you are spending enough time doing other things.

Being proud of your work

Developing software is fun, rewarding, stressful, and full of challenges. It is not always easy, but it can be very enjoyable. As you strive to be the best software architect that you can be, do not forget to take pride in all of your accomplishments. There are only so many people in the world who get to do what we do: make software. Everyone can affect the world, even if it is only in some small way. One of the ways, and certainly not the only way, that you and I can make a positive difference is through the software that we create.

Perhaps we are making someone's job easier, helping someone complete a mundane task in a faster way, allowing someone to be more productive so that they have more spare time in their personal lives, or bringing additional joy into someone's life. You can derive great satisfaction from knowing that others are benefiting from your work and appreciate what you do. If you are not proud of your work, figure out what you can do to change that.

Summary

Becoming a software architect is a great accomplishment. However, you must seek to keep improving to excel in your role. You must continuously learn new things to increase both the breadth and depth of your knowledge. Reading books, taking classes, listening to podcasts, reading blog posts, and watching videos are all ways that you can learn new things.

Participating in open source projects, writing your own blog, teaching others, trying new technologies, writing code, and attending user groups and conferences are all ways you can continue to get better at what you do.

Stay curious, keep learning, and never stop asking questions. Have an open mind and continue to create new things. Always strive to make the things you put out in the world as good as they can be. Be a software architect.

Other Books You May Enjoy

If you enjoyed this book, you may be interested in these other books by Packt:

Beginning Java Data Structures and Algorithms
James Cutajar

ISBN: 978-1-78953-717-8

- Understand some of the fundamental concepts behind key algorithms
- Express space and time complexities using Big O notation.
- Correctly implement classic sorting algorithms such as merge and quicksort
- Correctly implement basic and complex data structures
- Learn about different algorithm design paradigms, such as greedy, divide and conquer, and dynamic programming
- Apply powerful string matching techniques and optimize your application logic
- Master graph representations and learn about different graph algorithms

Architectural Patterns

Pethuru Raj, Anupama Raman, Harihara Subramanian

ISBN: 978-1-78728-749-5

- Understand how several architectural and design patterns work to systematically develop multitier web, mobile, embedded, and cloud applications
- Learn object-oriented and component-based software engineering principles and patterns
- Explore the frameworks corresponding to various architectural patterns
- Implement domain-driven, test-driven, and behavior-driven methodologies
- Deploy key platforms and tools effectively to enable EA design and solutioning
- Implement various patterns designed for the cloud paradigm

Leave a review - let other readers know what you think

Please share your thoughts on this book with others by leaving a review on the site that you bought it from. If you purchased the book from Amazon, please leave us an honest review on this book's Amazon page. This is vital so that other potential readers can see and use your unbiased opinion to make purchasing decisions, we can understand what our customers think about our products, and our authors can see your feedback on the title that they have worked with Packt to create. It will only take a few minutes of your time, but is valuable to other potential customers, our authors, and Packt. Thank you!

Index

X

Y

Printed in Great Britain
by Amazon